WHAT THEY'RE SAYING ABOUT ROGER STONE

A *New York Times* Bestselling Author

"Roger Stone is one tough cookie... We appreciate him."
— President Donald J. Trump

"This book exposes the Bush Clinton connection and alliance."
— A. Gore Vidal.

"Stone exposed LBJ, now he rips the veil off the Bush crime syndicate."
— *East Orlando Post*

"Known for hard-ball politics and a cloak and dagger sensibility."
— *New York Times*

"Skilled in the dark arts of politics."
— *The Atlantic*

"The most dangerous man in America."
— *The Village Voice*

"Everything he's ever told me has been incredibly accurate."
— Alex Jones, *Infowars*

"Stone, the former Richard Nixon acolyte known for his media savvy."
— *CNN Politics*

"Stone is a real-life Ray Donovan — only his clients toil in state capitals and Washington, not Hollywood."
— *Go Up State*

"Roger Stone, a veteran political operative and unapologetic dirty trickster who is an ardent fan of the scandal-ridden but politically savvy Nixon."
— *Mother Jones*

"Roger Stone is the most elegant maître d' the American political sewer ever has had."
— *Esquire*

"He is capable of employing tactics other operatives wouldn't dream of, let alone try."
— *CNN*

"Stone is one of the best sources in Washington for 'inside dirt.'" — *Slate*

"Respected, hated, and always controversial." — *No Quarter USA*

"Politics is war, and he is one of its fiercest warriors, with the battle scars to prove it."
— *The Weekly Standard*

"Stone has honed his black-arts legend for 40 years. A notorious dandy in bespoke suits and two-tone suede spectator shoes." — *Newsweek*

THE BUSH CRIME FAMILY

THE BUSH CRIME FAMILY

The Inside Story of an American Dynasty

ROGER STONE
AND SAINT JOHN HUNT

Skyhorse Publishing

Skyhorse Publishing books may be purchased in bulk at special discounts for sales promotion, corporate gifts, fund-raising, or educational purposes. Special editions can also be created to specifications. For details, contact the Special Sales Department, Skyhorse Publishing, 307 West 36th Street, 11th Floor, New York, NY 10018 or info@skyhorsepublishing.com.

Skyhorse® and Skyhorse Publishing® are registered trademarks of Skyhorse Publishing, Inc.®, a Delaware corporation."

Visit our website at www.skyhorsepublishing.com.

10 9 8 7 6 5

Library of Congress Cataloging-in-Publication Data is available on file.

Previously published as *Jeb and the Bush Crime Family*.

Cover design by Brian Peterson
Cover photo credit © AP Images
ISBN: 978-1-5107-2140-1
Ebook ISBN: 978-1-5107-2144-9

Printed in the United States of America

This book is dedicated to Governor John Davis Lodge, my political mentor, who taught me that politics is the art of inclusion and who, under extreme pressure, refused to appoint Prescott Bush to fill a vacancy in the U.S. Senate, an act of courage.
    —Roger Stone

This book is also dedicated to my mother Dorothy Hunt, who White House Counsel John Dean said was "the savviest woman in the world," who had "the whole picture [of Watergate] put together." I miss you every day.
    —Saint John Hunt

This book is also dedicated to those brave journalists who have blazed the trail when it comes to exposing the crimes of the Bush family: Russ Baker, Nick Bryant, Kevin Phillips, James Moore, Craig Unger, Webster Griffin Tarpley, Anton Chaitkin, Peter Brewton, Bill Minutaglio, Terry Reed, and David Corn. While the authors disagree with them on some issues, we respect them all.
    —Robert Morrow

CONTENTS

FOREWORD BY CONGRESSMAN JOHN LEBOUTILLIER

"When Jeb was at Andover he ran an illegal drug and alcohol distributorship . . . selling pot and booze to his fellow students . . . but when the school authorities caught wind of it, Jeb sold out one of his partners and escaped by the skin of his teeth." This was told to me in the mid-1990s by my then-girlfriend, whose husband was one of Jeb's Andover partners in this scheme. But because Jeb Bush had recently lost his bid to be governor of Florida, I put it in the back of my mind; his older brother, George W.—known inside the Bush family as "Junior"—had won his election in Texas and was the focus of Bush World. Jeb retreated into the background—for a while.

It's funny how things come 'round in the world. Jeb, of course, went on to win two terms as Florida's chief executive and helped with the controversial recount in the 2000 Florida presidential election that made "Junior" our 43rd president. Today, even though Jeb suspended his campaign for the presidency, the events that occurred during our time at Andover are just as important for the American people to know.

In October 2006 I attended my 30th Harvard Reunion. During a cocktail party a classmate of mine who I didn't really know, Charles Hirschler, came up to me and began talking: "Did you know that while I was at Andover with Jeb Bush, he ran this drug dealership with two other guys . . . they were selling drugs and booze to students . . . but Jeb cut and ran and sold out someone to save himself?"

There it was again—more than a decade after I first heard it.

Then—again—in 2011, yet another Andover classmate of Jeb's said to me, "I never knew at the time why Jeb walked around the campus with his jaw hanging open . . . he was stoned all the time!"

Finally in the summer of 2015, a woman friend of mine who had been married to a guy in Jeb's Andover class told me over lunch, "Oh yeah . . . he told me all about Jeb's drug dealership."

So there we have it: four different guys who were either in Jeb's graduating class at Andover or a year ahead of him all confirming Jeb's role in this drug and booze dealership.

The American people needed to hear this before they voted. So I penned a 2013 column detailing the facts as I knew them and posted it on my website: johnlebout.com. I hoped someone in the media would someday use a search engine and find it and then do their own investigation.

In early 2015, just as the 2016 campaign heated up, David Margolick of *Vanity Fair* indeed found me because of my column and said, "I want to do an investigative piece about this." So I gave him the names and numbers of all the people mentioned above. And I then trusted that he would call them himself and hear the same things I had heard.

A few weeks later he called me back and said, "John, it never happened. There was no drug and booze ring at Andover at all."

I was flabbergasted.

When I asked him if he had talked to my sources, he told me that he had never talked to even one of the guys I mentioned who were at Andover with Jeb when it happened!

Who would know better than they would? Is it possible that four separate guys are all making up the same story over the course of three decades? Or, instead, is it possible—and in fact very likely—that the Bush Machine scrambled to debunk this story before it took hold?

To this day, I have to wonder why no legitimate journalist would do a proper investigation, talk to the primary sources—the guys who were there at Andover with Jeb Bush—and then tell it to the American people. That's why I am happy that Roger Stone and Saint John Hunt have written this book.

The people have a right to know the truth about the personal character of the candidates who asked for their votes. In the case of Jeb Bush, the American people needed to know that he did things at Andover that tell us a lot about his morals and his character. Indeed, the American people need to know more about the history of the Bush family.

—John LeBoutillier (R) served in the House of Representatives for New York's Sixth District from 1981 to 1983. He is a political commentator and author of several books, including the best-selling *Harvard Hates America*.

INTRODUCTION BY ROGER STONE

Forty-third president George W. Bush's biography of his father George Herbert Walker Bush is a whitewash of history and a warm-up act for the last contender from the House of Bush, Jeb.

Especially as he ages and cultivates his kindly, affable persona with the help of new biographies that ignore his dirty deeds, it's important to learn his true nature. As my colleague Russ Baker notes, the recently published *Destiny and Power: The American Odyssey of George Herbert Walker Bush* by Jon Meacham is the latest sycophantic whitewash of Bush's life as an "American success story," written with the full cooperation of the Bushes and serving entirely to cement the façade of H. W. as a mild-mannered public servant. Pulitzer Prize–winning and well connected, author Meacham is a former managing editor at *Newsweek*, a magazine with a history of CIA connections. That's why I had to write this book.

Missing is the entire Bush backstory: the family providing financing to the Nazis to buy arms; the support for eugenics; 41's involvement with the CIA in the Bay of Pigs; his evasions about November 22, 1963, and his name appearing in the address book of Lee Harvey Oswald's handler George de Mohrenschildt; his involvement in CIA drug running, and the murder of drug runner Barry Seal; the real reason Bush fell out with Ross Perot; and the real Bush connection to both the attempted assassination of Reagan and the attempt to set Reagan up in Iran-Contra . . . they have all been airbrushed out of *41: A Portrait of My Father*. All are missing from George W's book, which is a sanitized campaign biography.

I first encountered "Ambassador Bush" as he was then called in 1980 when working as a senior campaign aide for Governor Ronald Reagan. The Bush campaign was a curious collection of current spooks, "retired" spooks, and rich old WASPS from the right families. There was an endless stream of dirty tricks from the Bushites.

Bush would go to great lengths to become vice president in 1968, 1972, 1976, and 1980. The efforts to smear his rivals when he maneuvered for the nomination under Reagan in 1980 have never been revealed. Bush's role in making a deal with the Iranians to ensure the defeat of Jimmy Carter is something I have firsthand knowledge of.

Behind his rather goofy demeanor and colorful socks lies a vicious, ruthless, ambitious, power-hungry crony capitalist prepared to do and say anything to become president and pass it on to his sons.

As we know George H. W. Bush succeeded in reaching the throne, and there was a succession when his son George W. Bush attained the presidency. This would not pan out for the other Bush, Jeb. His was the weak link in the Bush family, and it was more than obvious. For Jeb's inability to "get hard" during the campaign, I am eternally grateful. Like a wild fire, those that seek to put them out must be extremely careful that they have not overlooked a tiny little spark that will reignite the raging inferno. The Bush fire is, in my opinion, much the same. Although Jeb has failed in his attempt, we must guard against the dying Bush ember reigniting in the future.

Whether Jeb decides to run again in 2020, or some other Bushwhacker runs, we just have to wait and see. Since the Bush family continues to morph and spread like a virus, we have to be on the lookout for new Bushes. Such is the case with George Prescott Bush. He just may be, in time, a presidential hopeful. As long as I'm here watching, writing, and reporting, you can be assured that I will continue my crusade to tell the American people the truth about the Bush Crime Syndicate.

Just because Fredo became president doesn't mean we now have to give it to Michael. We need another Bush like we need another Clinton.

—Roger Stone
Miami Beach
October 15, 2015

THE BUSH FAMILY CV

Samuel Prescott Bush
- Born October 4, 1863; Orange, NJ
- Died February 8, 1948; Columbus, OH
- Graduated from Stevens Institute of Technology, Hoboken, NJ, 1884
- Married Flora Sheldon 1894
- Married Martha Bell Carter after Sheldon killed in car crash in 1920
- General manager of Buckeye Steel Castings Company 1901
- President of Buckeye Steel Castings Company 1908–1927
- First president of Ohio Manufacturers Association
- Cofounder of Scioto Country Club and Columbus Academy
- Chief of the Ordnance, Small Arms, and Ammunition Section of War Industries Board 1918
- Member of Board of Federal Reserve Bank of Cleveland
- Appointed to Herbert Hoover's President's Committee for Unemployment Relief 1931

Prescott Sheldon Bush
- Born May 15, 1895; Columbus, OH
- Died October 8, 1972; New York, NY
- Graduated Yale University 1917
- Member of Skull and Bones

- Captain, U.S. Army 1917–1919
- Married Dorothy Walker, 1921
- Vice president investment bank A. Harriman & Co. 1924
- Partner Brown Brothers Harriman 1931
- Founding member and director in Union Banking Corporation
- Treasurer of first Planned Parenthood campaign 1947
- Chairman United Negro College Fund Connecticut branch 1951
- Republican candidate U.S. Senate 1950 (defeated)
- Republican candidate U.S. Senate 1952 to 1963—Connecticut
- Member U.S. Senate Banking Committee

George H. W. Bush
- Born June 12, 1924; Milton, MA
- U.S. Navy 1942–1945
- Married Barbara Pierce, 1945
- Yale University BA 1948
- Member Skull and Bones
- Member Brown Brothers Harriman
- Cofounder Zapata Petroleum Corporation 1953
- President of Zapata Offshore Company 1954
- Chairman Harris County (Houston) Republican Committee 1964
- Candidate U.S. Senate 1964 (defeated)
- Member U.S. House of Representatives 1966–1969
- Candidate U.S. Senate 1970 (defeated)
- UN Ambassador 1971–1973
- Chairman of the Republican National Committee 1973–1974
- US Envoy to China 1974–1975
- Director of CIA 1976–1977
- Ran for Vice President during the elections of 1968, 1972, 1976, and 1980
- U.S. Vice President 1981–1989
- 41st U.S. President 1989–1993

George W. Bush
- Born July 6, 1946; New Haven, CT
- Yale University BA 1968; Harvard Business School MBA 1975
- Member Skull and Bones
- Texas Air National Guard 1968
- Alabama Air National Guard 1972
- Married Laura Welch, 1977
- Candidate for U.S. House of Representatives 1978 (defeated)
- Founded Arbusto Energy (later changed to Bush Exploration)
- Co-owned the Texas Rangers 1989–1998
- 46th Governor of Texas 1995–2000
- Proclaimed June 10, 2000 to be Jesus Day
- 43rd US President 2001–2009

John Ellis "Jeb" Bush
- Born February 11, 1953; Midland, TX
- University of Texas at Austin (BA)
- Married Columba Garnica Gallo 1974
- Vice president Texas Commerce Bank, Caracas, Venezuela Branch 1977
- Chairman Dade County Republican Party 1984-1986
- Florida Secretary of Commerce 1987–1988
- Campaign manager for Ileana Ros-Lehtinen for Congress 1989
- Candidate for Governor of Florida 1994 (defeated)
- Joined the Board of Trustees of the Heritage Foundation 1995
- 43rd Governor of Florida 1999–2007
- Tenet Healthcare Board of Directors 2007
- Candidate for Republican Nominee for U.S. President 2015–2016

Neil Mallon Bush
- Born January 22, 1955; Midland, TX
- Tulane University BA 1977, MBA 1979
- Married Sharon Smith 1980–2003

- Married Maria Andrews 2004
- Chairman Points of Light
- Board of Directors Silverado Savings and Loan (Colorado) 1980s
- Failure of Silverado 1988
- Settled civil suit brought against him and Silverado
- Cofounded Ignite! Learning
- Consultant Kopin Corporation of Taunton, MA
- Founding director Foundation for Interreligious and Inter-cultural Research and Dialogue 1999
- Consultant Grace Semiconductor Manufacturing Corp. 2002
- Founding chairman of TX Oil 2010

Marvin Pierce Bush
- Born October 22, 1956; Midland, TX
- University of Virginia BA 1981
- Married Margaret Conway Molster 1981
- Director Securacom (now Stratesec) 1996–2000 (Securacom provided security for the World Trade Center)
- Director HCC Insurance Holdings
- Co-founded Winston Partners 1993
- President and director, Winston Capital Management LLC

George Prescott Bush
- Born April 24, 1976; Houston, TX
- Rice University BA 1988, University of Texas MA 2003
- Married Amanda L. Williams 2004
- Cofounded Pennybacker Capital, LCC
- Corporate and securities law with Akin, Gump, Strauss, Hauer & Feld
- Texas land commissioner 2014
- Deputy finance chairman of the Republican Party of Texas 2016

A DYNASTY OF DUPLICITY

I believe that banking institutions are more dangerous than standing armies.

—Thomas Jefferson

If the American people ever allow private banks to control the issue of their currency, first by inflation, then by deflation, the banks . . . will deprive the people of all property until their children wake-up homeless on the continent their fathers conquered. . . .

—Thomas Jefferson

These words were written by one of our country's most eloquent leaders over 200 years ago. If he, and others, have known all along, how could the rise of the banking powers have happened? The answer lies in the devious minds and calculated steps of a certain group of men whose ultimate ambition was to create a corporate banking cartel which owned all the people's money and ruled the masses with heartless indifference. This is that story.

From the late 19th century right up to the War on Terror, one family has ruled from the shadows as well as from the stage of international policy. In only four generations that family has seen two presidents, one senator, a director of the Central Intelligence Agency, and two governors. They have been involved in and enabled two world wars, countless other wars, the control of oil, the funding of Adolph Hitler and the Nazi movement, the building of America's railroads, drug smuggling on an international scale, and the gutting of America's savings and loans to the tune of billions of dollars. How could they have pulled this off? Why aren't they all in prison? This is their story. This is the story of the Bush family.

The names read like a who's who of an American political dynasty: Jeb Bush, George W. Bush, George H. W. Bush, and Prescott Bush. They also read like the names of one of America's top crime families like the Gambinos and the Bonannos of the American Cosa Nostra, better known as the Mafia. Few people equate the Bush family with the Gambino family, yet much has been revealed to show that both families are steeped in a tradition of criminal activity that can be traced along their family trees.

The most powerful members of the elite class often show little regard for law or morality, because they feel they can get away with it, because they often do. This is "elite deviance," a condition sociologists say exists in a society when the upper echelon of that society no longer believes that the rules apply to them. "It is not due primarily to psychopathological variables, but to the institutionalization of elite wrongdoing," said Professor David Simon in his landmark book *Elite Deviance*.[1] It is a phenomenon in which those with enough wealth, political influence, and personal connections can immunize themselves from the consequences for illegal acts that in the rest of the lowly world would bring severe, if not life-ending, repercussions.

They can commit crimes with impunity. The history of the Bush Crime Family is a century-long, multi-generational tradition of elite deviance.

The facts contained in this book are not presented merely to bash the Bushes, but as a public service. Two Bushes have already been elected president of the United States, and Jeb Bush is the latest contender. More Bushes will almost certainly rise to prominence in the future. Jeb's son is already on that path. The authors know that the American voters need to read the real history of the Bush family and their latest White House hopeful, before heading to the polls in a primary or a general election.

So who is the real Jeb Bush, and what is the real trail of privilege, elitism, ambition, and crime of the Bush Crime Family?

PART 1

JOHN ELLIS BUSH (AKA "JEB")

CHAPTER 1

JEB, THE LATEST CONTENDER

My dad is the greatest man alive. If anyone disagrees, we'll go outside.

—Jeb on his father, former president George H. W. Bush.[i]

Jeb Bush aimed to make the Bushes the first family ever to produce three presidents. Perhaps most alarming would be the proximity with which the three men would serve their terms. If Jeb Bush was elected in 2016, there would have been more Bush than non-Bush presidents (Clinton and Obama) since George H. W. Bush's election in 1988. Even more frightening is that some are already discussing the path to the White House for Jeb's son, George P. Bush, who was elected Texas land commissioner in January 2015.[2] It's a scary prospect that eerily resembles the political system that our country's founders were fighting to escape.

Of all the Bush gang, John Ellis (or just plain ol' "Jeb," as he preferred voters to think of him) is perhaps the worst, selling his family's influence the most and serving the public the least. He is the Bush who personifies the lust for power and wealth the most. No matter how much money and influence Jeb gets, it's never enough.

We all live with an understanding that the pampered elite will always have privileges, opportunities, and even exemption from punishment of misdeeds that most of us simply do not have. But most of these elite are not running for president of the United States. In the crowded field of Republican candidates for 2016, Jeb's family history and establishment connections in the party and throughout the nation made him unique.

Americans abhor a hypocrite more than anything else in politics. Republicans think of their party as standing for law and order, equality of opportunity, equal justice, and preserving American culture. Jeb has lived his life following exactly the opposite of these ideals. Republican primary voters, and all voters, needed to know about Jeb's history of arrogant hypocrisy.

Oddly, Jeb the Republican presidential hopeful has said that the president he most admires is Lyndon B. Johnson.[3] What does Jeb most admire about LBJ? Is it LBJ's contempt for the rule of law or his constant efforts to expand the reach of the federal government? Jeb said, "He went and he cajoled, he begged, he threatened, he loved, he hugged, he did what leaders do, which is they personally get engaged to make something happen." This vague description of LBJ's deal-making abilities is troubling, because LBJ's way of operating was famously unethical and led to a massive expansion of the U.S. as a welfare state, through the passage of the Great Society and War on Poverty legislation. Jeb admires LBJ for twisting enough arms to get massive government expansion through Congress. Republican primary voters should have been very disturbed by Jeb's admiration. But in the context of Jeb's life and record, his admiration for the bully and government-expander LBJ makes perfect sense.

Like LBJ, Jeb is a Big Government man. Although his Florida backers assure us he governed as a conservative, Jeb's actions and policies have actually warned us that, like his brother George W. Bush, he would have spent like crazy and expanded the government even further.

Jeb is a fan of higher taxes, too. His dad won over grass-roots conservatives in 1988 with his famous "Read my lips–no new taxes" pledge only to break that pledge at the urging of White House Chief of Staff John Sununu and Jim Baker aide Dick Darman (who hated to be described that way.) A former aide to Elliot Richardson, Darman worked against the conservative agenda in the Reagan and Bush White Houses. Conservative author M. Stanton Evans correctly called the day Bush signed the tax increase "The end of Reaganism." It planted the seeds of Bush's defeat in 1992. Yet Jeb defended the tax increase as, "the right thing to do." Together, Bush 41 and Bush 43 are responsible for 72 percent of our massive federal debt. Big Government man Jeb will continue the Bush spending spree if he gets to the Oval Office.

Jeb's own record tells us he's no fiscal conservative. During his eight years in the governor's mansion in Florida, spending skyrocketed. The Cato Institute noted that Florida general fund spending "increased from $18.0 billion to $28.2 billion during those eight years, or 57%" and that "total state spending increased from $45.6 billion to $66.1 billion, or 45%."[4] There is no reason to think his appetite for big spending would be any different in the White House.

Although Peter Baker of the *New York Times* reported in a breathless page one story that "Jeb isn't W,"[5] he'd spend at least as much. In terms of personality type, Baker was correct. Jeb is his mother's son—entitled, arrogant, and vindictive. As Michael Barbaro pointed out in the *Times*, Jeb masked his stridency and arrogance in his second bid for governor, but as S. V. Date showed in his classic book *Jeb–America's Next Bush*,[6] Jeb as governor was authoritarian, secretive, imperial, and skirted the law. But on policy, there is evidence that Jeb is W. Jeb never opposed expansion of the size and scope of government, wild spending, and mushrooming federal deficits. A hypocrite on social issues and a fiscal liberal, Jeb is gung-ho for the civil liberties–eroding Patriot Act and the failed War on Drugs.

The notion of Jeb as a successful, savvy businessman is absurd. Every dime he has was made by trading on family connections or the family name. He functioned as a de facto lobbyist for both the corrupt health care company IMC as well as housing builder Camilio Padrera, lobbying Cabinet members for administrative favors while carefully cloaking his compensation as "real estate fees."[7]

Virtually every one of Jeb's failed business enterprises is a carried interest in which he put up no cash but used his family name and connections to secure loans, financing, waivers, or other financially significant benefits. No less than five of Bush's former partners in these endeavors are in jail.

Bush served on the board of Innovita, a Ponzi scheme run by Claudio Osorio. Osorio got a $10 million loan from the Overseas Private Investment Corporation (OPIC) with the assistance of Bill and Hillary Clinton, whom he lavished with campaign contributions. At the same time, he paid Bush $460,000. When the entire phony enterprise collapsed, Bush grudgingly was forced to return $250,000.

Jeb Bush and his partner also got a $4 million federal bailout courtesy of the taxpayers when his father was vice president. When the S&L that loaned Bush $4.5 million failed, the office building that secured the loan was reappraised with a new value of $500,000, allowing Bush and his partner to walk out on a $4 million debt and keep the building.

Where Jeb has really made significant money is in "consulting" and big dollar honorariums for speeches. "Consulting" is a euphemism among political elites for "fixing."

Whether it's using drugs, connections to drug traffickers, or walking out on a $4.5 million loan, Jeb Bush pays no penalty and suffers no consequences. Jeb Bush says he is going to Washington to "fight the pampered elites."[8] The evidence shows *he* is the pampered elite.

Waiting for the Dough to Rise

In an interview on NBC's *Today* show in April of 2013, Barbara Bush was asked how she felt about Jeb seeking the presidency in 2016. She replied, "We've had enough Bushes."

She went on to say she thought there were many worthy candidates, telling anchor Matt Lauer, "There are people out there" who are qualified.[9] But by February of 2015, Barbara reversed her opinion, telling the press, "I changed my mind."[10] By then, Jeb claimed to be exploring a run but was actually well into a tremendous fundraising effort that worried many campaign finance watchdogs.

By the time he officially declared his candidacy, which was a foregone conclusion, he had already raised millions, including some major support from Wall Street.[11]

Jeb Bush waited quite a long time—until June 2015—to declare his candidacy so that he could raise unlimited funds for his Right to Rise Super PAC as a non-candidate for as long as possible. As an actual candidate, Bush's direct source of funds was limited to $2,700 per person per election.[12]

Everyone knew Jeb was going to run, despite his insistence that he was trying to decide from December 2014 until June. During those six months, he gave campaign-style speeches and visited Iowa, New Hampshire, and South Carolina, courting the wealthiest donors and best political talent in the country, and resigning from several corporate boards that posed potential conflicts of interest. He raised tens of millions of dollars, but still failed to gain any traction in the polls.

Watchdog groups were dismayed. Jeb's gaming of the system seemed to violate the spirit, if not the letter, of campaign finance law. "It's one of the great charades of American politics," said Fred Wertheimer of Washington-based Democracy 21. "It's simply thumbing your nose at the American people and saying, 'We're shrewd, we're going to circumvent these laws and you have to live by it.'"[13]

Paul S. Ryan of the Campaign Legal Center said: "The Supreme Court has recognized that a check above $2,700 directly to someone who admits they are a candidate could corrupt them and therefore can be limited. But we're to believe that the corruptive potential is miraculously washed from a $100,000 contribution handed to Jeb Bush for his Super PAC. It's absurd."

Jeb's advisers said he could have directly asked for money at the Super PAC events, but chose not to. That's a ridiculous claim. Why would Jeb need to ask people who have already donated thousands of dollars for tickets to attend his event to give him money?

The website for Bush's conventional Right to Rise PAC, ostensibly set up to help other Republican candidates and limited to $5,000 individual donations, featured Bush's picture and his political message. The website didn't mention Bush as a candidate at the time.[14]

Jeb's family connections were thought to have already given him a distinct advantage over the other GOP candidates and could yet win him the presidency. His skirting of campaign finance law is just another example of Bush dynasty entitlement. Despite criticism, there were no consequences.

Ana Navarro — Quintessential Bushie

The Bushies—blind followers of the Bush dynasty—are everywhere. They populate the radio and TV airwaves as supposedly unbiased pundits. They write opinion pieces across all the major newspapers and websites. But now they even inhabit daytime television—Ana Navarro was recently named a paid contributor on *The View*.

Navarro has been a longtime public supporter of Jeb Bush's presidential campaign. As a frequent pundit on the Sunday talk shows and CNN, Navarro has tried to rationalize Jeb's early disappointing poll numbers and sinking campaign. She was one of the early public backers in 2014 of a Jeb candidacy and tried to wash away the notion that after the failed presidency of his brother W., the American electorate would not welcome another Bush.

Like Jeb, Navarro is consumed by pro-Latin racial politics. Born in Nicaragua, Navarro ties her culture into her political affairs. She served as the national co-chair of John McCain's Hispanic Advisory Council where she was a national surrogate for the failed McCain 2008 campaign. She next worked as the national Hispanic co-chair for Gov. Jon Huntsman's 2012 campaign. (Incidentally, Jeb Bush Jr. endorsed Huntsman in 2012.[15])

Navarro is described as a "confidante" of Jeb Bush during her CNN appearances. The *New York Times* has explained that "her rollicking commentary and willingness to criticize

Republicans on same-sex marriage and immigration issues make her a favorite of TV bookers."[16] She does the Democratic Party's dirty work.

Navarro frequently spars with conservative pundits who support Ted Cruz, Ben Carson, and especially Donald Trump. Navarro scorns Trump so much that during the September 2015 CNN Reagan Library Debate, Navarro refused to attend a private dinner hosted by Wolf Blitzer because CNN contributor Jeffrey Lord, former Reagan political director and also a public supporter of Donald Trump's candidacy, was attending.

In a September 2015 CNN column, Navarro declared that she would only vote Republican in 2016 as long as the "Republicans do not end up nominating someone I consider borderline insane or a total jerk(.)" Navarro next proclaimed that she hopes "Joe Biden runs for President" because she "likes the guy."[17] Navarro the Bushie would rather have Joe Biden be president over a potential nominee of her own party.

Navarro's close affinity with Democrats also falls into her personal life. Navarro's longtime significant other, is Gene Prescott, a Democratic fundraiser who owns the grand Biltmore hotel in Coral Gables, Florida, "which hosts more Democratic and Republican political fundraisers than most any address in America."[18] Marco Rubio and Jeb Bush both work out at the Biltmore. Rubio even celebrated his 2010 surprise win for the Senate in one of the Biltmore's ballrooms.

In 2010, Navarro described the potential Rubio vs. Bush face-off as a "nightmare scenario." She even said that she would "get into the fetal position and lock myself in a room for nine months . . . That just cannot happen . . . If we have to all lock ourselves in the Biltmore until white smoke comes out and we pick one, that's what we will do."[19] Apparently the smoke picked Jeb. A Bushie will never betray her master.

Low Energy Stuff Happens

Rival GOP presidential candidate Donald Trump, who trounced Jeb in the polls, had repeatedly branded Jeb as a low-energy candidate, putting in little effort with no charisma. "I don't see how he's electable," Trump said in New Hampshire on August 19, 2015. "Jeb Bush is a low-energy person. For him to get things done is hard."[20] Jeb seemed to be sleepwalking through the primary season most of the time, waking up at times to say the wrong thing.

Despite spending his whole life in America's ruling class, with seemingly unlimited access to the advice and grooming that should make him a polished statesman, Jeb has often stumbled badly when speaking in public. His thoughtlessness recently showed itself in the wake of the Oregon mass shooting in October of 2015. Nine people were murdered in a killing spree on a college campus. When asked for his reaction, Bush said, "Stuff happens."[21] The uproar was, predictably, instantaneous, and seized-upon by opponents in both parties.

Politicians often say the wrong thing at the wrong time. Statements by politicians also are often taken out of context, distorted, or twisted and it isn't always fair. But with Jeb, gaffes like this are evidence of something much deeper and more disturbing. Was he too lazy to take the advice and coaching he surely had available to him? Was he not bright enough to do better? Maybe both, but the root problem is that he is so insulated from worrying about what common people think of him that he just doesn't care. His sheltered, privileged lifestyle has given him a lack of empathy that is apparent throughout his life.

Strangely, Jeb won't even admit to giving someone Cuban cigars. My friend Jesse Ventura, former Minnesota governor, told me this odd story.[22] Jesse is a staunch capitalist and has always believed that the trade embargo was a mistake—not solely because he used to like to smoke Cuban cigars. Jesse recently told me that he was visiting the Clinton White House and the topic of Cuba came up. Governor Ventura commented on his opinion of the embargo to President Clinton, but was immediately interrupted and advised not to talk about it by then-governor Jeb Bush. Jeb said he didn't want Cuba discussed and would gladly send Jesse all the Cuban cigars he wanted. Ventura later walked over to Bush and put an empty aluminum Romeo y Julieta cigar tube in the Florida governor's top pocket and said "there's my brand." Jesse said, 10 days later, "I got a box of Romeo y Julieta Cubans delivered to the Capitol in Minnesota." In 2015, Jesse recounted the story and Jeb denied that the cigars he sent Jesse were Cuban. This is just another obvious, yet bizarre lie by Jeb.

Republican voters are far more likely to take issue with Jeb over his stance on illegal immigration or medical marijuana than a box of Cuban cigars he sent to a fellow governor decades ago. So why lie? For Jeb and the rest of the Bush dynasty of deceit, it's a way of life. Imagine what he'll lie about if he gets to the White House.

The Millionaire Governor and the Quest for the White House

The Great Recession was especially great for Jeb. The *New York Post* reported in July 2015 that he had hauled in more than $29 million since leaving the Florida governor's mansion in 2007.[23]

He banked a $1.3 million salary from Lehman Brothers in 2007 and 2008 before the firm collapsed, and earned $2 million a year from Barclays Plc, his tax returns show.

"Thank God for term limits," Bush quipped, referring to joining Wall Street after serving two terms as Florida's governor.

Bush paid an average tax rate of 36 percent, the campaign said, as it released 33 years of tax returns in an effort to goad Hillary Rodham Clinton into more transparency.

Jeb earned $6 million in 2012 alone. He also profited from investments in Abbey Capital Fund, which according to SEC forms is headquartered in the Cayman Islands and Malta, locales often used to avoid taxation. According to the campaign, Bush lost money on the deal.

He earned $2.1 million giving speeches in 2013 alone. He has spoken to groups including the National Potato Council, the National Aluminum Association, and pharmaceutical giant Pfizer.

Since leaving office, Bush's earnings have been climbing. In 2007, his adjusted gross income was $2.2 million. By 2013—the latest tax year available—his income reached $7.3 million.

"I made less than Chelsea Clinton," Bush joked, referring to a report that Chelsea banked $65,000 for a speech. There it is again, the Bushes and Clintons gently ribbing each other as they carve up the country and rack up the big bucks.

The *New York Post* reported that Jeb, in fact, made nearly $10 million through speaking engagements alone in less than nine years.[24]

Jeb's favorite recurring speaking gig was Seoul-based metal company Poongsan Corporation, which he addressed nine times at the invitation of company chair Jin Roy Ryu. Ryu is listed as a trustee of the George H. W. Bush Presidential Library. The company does business with the U.S. Mint and the Pentagon.[25]

The Un-Conservative

Jeb Bush had the fundraising prowess and establishment connections to win the GOP 2016 nomination, but he still faced a tough, uphill battle to win the general election.

The GOP needed a "big tent" voting block if they were to win the White House in 2016. The conservative Republican voters who stayed home in 2008 and 2012 because they felt that McCain and Romney were not conservative enough and didn't represent them were faced with a conflict which presented them with serious reservations about voting in another Bush. As Trump entered the ring with fire and passion, Jeb cowered and shrank. As the potential candidates, one by one, fell by the wayside of public popularity, it became apparent that Trump might just be the face of a new GOP. Would Republican voters risk supporting the brash, untested Trump? The answer came quick enough.

After raising $155,142,617 million and spending $137,803,892 million, Jeb announced that he was suspending his campaign for the presidency. It was a short run lasting from June of 2015 to February 2016. In the last few weeks he even had Barbara Bush and brother George come out and support him. (He may have had decided earlier on that he would only bring ex-president George W. in as a final emergency measure). It was clear that either he had waited too long or, as I think, brother George was more of a negative than a plus. After all, George W. Bush left the White House with possibly the lowest approval rating in American presidential history. After losing the GOP primary in South Carolina, Jeb decided it was time to quit. As he announced his decision, he had this to say: "I'm proud of the campaign that we've run to unify our country, and to advocate conservative solutions . . . but the people of Iowa, New Hampshire, and South Carolina have spoken. Tonight I am suspending my campaign."

The devastating loss he suffered in South Carolina was the turning point. Both his father and brother had been victorious in the Palmetto State in their time and it should have been a win for Jeb as well. Marco Rubio, a one-time Bush protege, seemed to be a more capable candidate. For John Ellis Bush the end, at least in 2016, was certain. Just after Donald Trump's win, Jeb Bush, albeit through gritted teeth, tweeted Trump, offering his congratulations. "Congratulations on your victory." I don't think Bush's tweet was heartfelt. George H. W. and George W. both congratulated Trump by phone. Jeb's son George Prescott Bush campaigned for Trump as chairman of his state Republican Party's victory committee. There would have to be another time for perhaps Jeb himself, or another Bush. But this book is not about what could be, it's about what has been, it's about a family that for decades influenced foreign policy and subjected the American people to unjust wars and financial fraud.

CHAPTER 2

THE PREPPY DRUG DEALER

The first time I really got stoned was in Jeb's room.

—Peter Tibbetts, Jeb's classmate at
Phillips Academy in Andover[ii]

Jeb's lifelong desire for power and wealth and sense of entitlement were evident at an early age. Voters who have heard George H. W., George W., and Jeb speak of their support for the war on drugs may not know that Jeb was not only a heavy drug user, but also a drug dealer.[26] A spoiled rich kid, Jeb wanted to make money and gain popularity with the other pampered political progeny at the elite Phillips Academy in Andover, from which his father and brother had also graduated.

Former congressman John LeBoutillier has written that two classmates at his 30th Harvard reunion, both who were at Andover with Jeb Bush, said that Jeb not only ran a marijuana and alcohol ring in which he sold product to his schoolmates but also that he was a habitual marijuana smoker: "stoned all the time."[27]

Writing for *Vanity Fair*, reporter David Margolick noted that a Bush classmate said, "There was a kind of arrogance to him . . . I remember him smoking a lot of dope." The classmate remembered Jeb as a member of a "clique of wealthy kids." Another classmate told Margolick that Jeb was "slightly snarly and spoiled."[28]

Jeb's classmates at the elite Massachusetts school said that he sold drugs, including marijuana and hashish, and often bullied other students. Strangely, Jeb reportedly had no interest in the political issues of the day, including the war in Vietnam. Tennis and dope were his main interests, and he was nearly expelled for poor grades.

The *Boston Globe* reported that one of Jeb's classmates, Peter Tibbetts, said he smoked hashish in Jeb's dormitory room. "The first time I really got stoned was in Jeb's room," Tibbetts said. Not only did Tibbetts get high on pot and hash with Jeb, but he also said he participated with Jeb in bullying other students. Tibbetts was caught using drugs by the school administration. Not being a member of the Bush dynasty, Tibbetts was expelled for his drug use. As always, there were no consequences for Jeb.[29]

The narrative that Jeb pushes about his Andover prep school days is that he simply did some drinking and some pot smoking and struggled to find his way in such a competitive school, until a course-related trip to Mexico (on which he first met his future wife and began dating her) changed his life. That one trip suddenly, magically made him a serious, thoughtful man. That fictitious moment never took place. That epiphany never happened.

Jeb's arrogant, consistent pattern of breaking rules and laws without suffering any consequences because of his family name is perhaps first documented here. Jeb's elite deviance was solidified in those formative years. Young Jeb learned a very different lesson from most young people who dabbled in drugs or alcohol. He learned that he had immunity because of the Bush name and he would spend his whole life taking advantage of it.

Jeb's Cocaine Connection

That Jeb Bush was a pot dealer at Andover is beyond dispute, but there is also some evidence that Jeb dabbled in cocaine both as a dealer and user. Legendary CIA drug smuggler and pilot Barry Seal claimed to his Miami lawyer Richard Sharpstein that he had orchestrated an elaborate sting at the Opalocka airport in which the DEA got videotape of Jeb and his brother George W. Bush bringing a kilo into Florida for resale. Supposedly Seal, who was deeply involved in the trafficking of cocaine into the United States through rural airstrips in Louisiana, Texas, and Arkansas, threatened to expose the Bushes' role in the drug trafficking unless then-vice president George H. W. Bush got the IRS, who were pursuing Seal over his vast drug profits, off his back.

While I have been unable to prove this allegation, I did learn something even more incredible. The FAA ownership records of the turboprop King Air 200, which Seal used in the CIA effort to import drugs into the United States in order to sell them to raise cash to finance the Nicaraguan contras, show that the plane was subsequently purchased by the state of Texas, where it was used by Governor George W. Bush. Because the Barry Seal saga has more to do with George H. W. Bush than Jeb, we will explore it later.[30]

Legendary CIA operative Chip Tatum also claimed Jeb Bush was deeply involved with the CIA-led operation to traffic cocaine into the United States and sell it to raise money to fund the Nicaragua Contras after the US Congress cut off funding in the

Boland Amendment. Tatum claimed Arkansas governor Bill Clinton was in on the operation which Col. Oliver North ran.

Tatum wrote:

> Mr. North stated the following to the other passengers, "One more year of this and we'll all retire." He then made a remark concerning Barry Seal and Governor Clinton. "If we can keep those Arkansas hicks in line, that is," referring to the loss of monies as determined the week prior during their meeting in Costa Rica. I stood silently by the vat of leaves, listening to the conversation. General Alvarez had gone with the Contra leader to discuss logistics. The other three—North, Rodriguez, and Ami Nir—continued through the wooden building, inspecting the cocaine. North continued, ". . . but he (Vice President Bush) is very concerned about those missing monies. I think he's going to have Jeb (Bush) arrange something out of Colombia," he told his comrades, not thinking twice of my presence. What Mr. North was referring to ended up being the assassination of Barry Seal by members of the Medellin Cartel in early 1986.[31]

Seal thought he had blackmail info on the Bushes, until he ended up riddled with bullets on February 19, 1986 in Baton Rouge. In his book Terry Reed reports a conversation he had with Seal:[32]

"There ain't nuthin' in this world more powerful than good ol' fucking blackmail, Terry. And don't let anybody ever tell ya different. Jeeeeeesus Christ, I got some good shit on some big people," said Seal.

"What this blackmail, you're talking about?"

"Ever hear the old expression, it's not what ya know, it's who ya know? Well, whoever said that just hadn't caught the Vice President's kids in the dope business, 'cause I can tell ya for sure *what* ya know can definitely be more important than *who* you know."

"You gotta calm down and tell me what you're talking about, if you want me to know. What's this about the Vice President's kids and dope."

"I don't wannna tell ya too much, 'cause truthfully ya don't have a need to know. But Terry I been workin' with several federal agencies for the past couple of years as ya probably suspicioned. In the course of that business, a person can't help but run across some real *sensitive* information. It seems some major players in the Medellin Cartel, whom I personally know, ran across some knowledge that's very valuable to both the Republican and Democratic Party. Real national security stuff.

"It seems some of George Bush's kids just can't say no ta drugs, ha ha ha ha . . . Well, ya can imagine how valuable information like that would be, can't ya? That could get ya out of almost any kind of jam." Seal paused for a moment then asked, "Ya ever play Monopoly? The information I got is so good it's just like a get-out-of-jail-free card . . . ha, ha, ha, ha YEE-HAWWWW . . ."

"Barry, are you telling me George Bush's kids are in the drug business?"

"Yup, that's what I am tellin' ya. A guy in Florida who flipped for the DEA has the goods on the Bush boys. Now I heard this earlier from a reliable source in Colombia, but I just sat on it then, waitin' to use it as a trump card, if I ever needed it. Well, I need ta use it now. I got names, dates, places . . . even got some tape recordins'. Fuck, I even got surveillance videos catchin' the Bush boys red-handed. I consider this stuff my insurance policy. It makes me and my mole on the inside that's feedin' the stuff to me invincible. Now this is *real* sensitive shit inside of U.S. Customs and DEA and those guys are pretty much under control. It's damage control as usual."

In 1992, Jeb Bush decided to make a run for Florida governor. I was living in Hawaii when I heard about it. I had been online since late '91 and decided to cruise through CompuServe's political forums. I found one for Florida and logged on to a Republican forum. I contacted Dan Cobb, then-*Houston Chronicle* executive managing editor, to confirm whether or not he would stick by a story he had written. In 1979, Jeb and two friends had been arrested by the Houston Police and charged with cocaine possession. Cobb affirmed that he did indeed stand by the story. He also affirmed that chief reporter Zarko Franks would reiterate the same. I returned to the forum with a series of stinging accusations, and warned Florida Republicans of Jeb's background. I was met the next morning with an e-mail from Florida State Republicans threatening to sue me if I did not print a retraction. I printed what was NOT a retraction and reiterated that the *Chronicle* team would stand by the story. That was the last we heard of Jeb Bush that year. Had I not been so debilitated from a near-death injury, I would never have let this pass the last election cycle. I state uncategorically again, this incident happened, and George Herbert Walker Bush covered it up. The trips to Panama happened as well, of this I have no doubt. Kathy Farenthold had no bones to pick with anyone at the time she told me these things, and she indicated all the brothers were involved.

Lee Atwater, who was my partner in the political consulting form of Black, Manafort, Stone, and Atwater after leaving the Reagan White House as deputy political director, told me that he and Jeb had snorted lines of cocaine at the vice president's residence at the Naval Observatory on the night of Vice President George H. W. Bush's election to the presidency.

This was unusual because, although he was a habitual user of marijuana on the weekends, a pursuit in which I sometimes joined him, Atwater was generally disdainful of the use of cocaine. "It ain't natural," the wily South Carolinian said. "Marijuana is grown in the earth. Coke is too chemical-like," he said, seemingly oblivious to the fact that cocaine is refined from the coca leaf, which is also grown in the earth.

A prominent Tallahassee lobbyist told me that he also had snorted coke with Jeb Bush, which the governor said he did largely out of boredom with the slow pace of the state capital.

High Hypocrisy: Jeb Bush and the War on Drugs

Jeb's "conservative" stand on drugs is perhaps his most hypocritical position of all. As a heavy dope smoker and even a dealer in prep school and college, he started out early on a path that many young people do. But what makes him a phony is his tough stance against drugs as an elected official and a politician, particularly against marijuana.

Jeb even opposed the legalization of medical marijuana while he was governor of Florida. It was one of his campaign issues and he has continued to voice his opposition to it since leaving the governor's mansion. He was dead set against allowing those dying a slow, agonizing death to ease their suffering with any form of marijuana, but he's had as much pot as he's wanted his whole life without penalty. Jeb is not only without ideological consistency, but without empathy or compassion.

Rival GOP candidate Senator Rand Paul pointed out Jeb's hypocrisy on Fox News, stating, "When Jeb was a very wealthy kid at a very elite school, he used marijuana but didn't get caught, didn't have to go to prison." Paul again slammed Bush in the CNN debate, "I think it shows some hypocrisy that's going to be very difficult for young people to understand why we'd put a 65-year-old guy in jail for medical marijuana."[33]

Perhaps there is more to this story. In an incredible article in the *Daily Beast*, reporter Betsy Woodruff reports how George H. W. and Jeb Bush got campaign contributions from Leonel Martinez, a convicted trafficker of both marijuana and cocaine in Florida in the 1980s. Incredibly, Woodruff "excuses" Jeb for this shady association because he is a "drug warrior."

Again, this is classic "elite deviance" at play. "Elite deviance is not due primarily to psychopathological variables, but to the institutionalization of elite wrongdoing," said Professor David Simon in his landmark book *Elite Deviance*. Jeb is nothing if not an elitist. Even more than the pot and hash he's smoked, Jeb has been high on himself and his family's power.

The poster family for elite deviance, the Bushes play by different rules from most of us. Jeb has used and sold illicit drugs with no consequences at all, but he has supported stiff sentences for non-violent drug offenders and opposed the humane use of medical marijuana for the terminally ill. When it comes to a Jeb Bush White House, voters of all political stripes should *just say no*.

CHAPTER 3

JEB BUNGLES IMMIGRATION ISSUE

The 40 percent of the people that have come here illegally came with a legal visa and overstayed their bounds. We ought to be able to figure out where they are and politely ask them to leave.

—Jeb speaking to the National Automobile Dealers Association in San Francisco[iii]

Even moderate Republicans are fed up with the Republican Party's lack of conviction on key issues like immigration. Donald Trump's early lead in the polls proves that there is widespread support for enforcement of immigration laws. Jeb's policy positions tend to point in the opposite direction of both Republican primary voters and general election voters. He's a hardliner on issues that are increasingly unimportant to Republican and independent voters, like marijuana, and yet liberal on issues that have clearly struck a chord with voters of all affiliations in this cycle, namely immigration.

Trump gained a huge lead in the polls with Republicans by taking a hard-line stance on "anchor babies" and ending birthright citizenship. Jeb tried to attack Trump from both the left and the right. He used the term "anchor baby" himself and it blew up in his face. After facing criticism for using the term (which he had criticized Trump, who was trouncing Bush in the polls, for using) and being asked by a reporter about whether his use of the term would cost him the Hispanic vote, Jeb bungled his response terribly. He explained that he was really talking about Asians.

Jeb said, "Frankly, it's more related to Asian people."[34] He backpedaled, referred to birthright citizenship as a "noble idea" then pivoted back to attack Trump from the right, sniping that, "Mr. Trump's plans are not grounded in conservative principles."[35] Jeb stumbled and contorted so badly on the biggest issue of the season and may have alienated everyone on all sides of the issue.

Jeb Bush has repeatedly said that people who want our laws to be enforced are heartless and cruel. This is the same man who opposes allowing a terminally ill patient to ease their constant pain and discomfort with prescription medical marijuana.

Jeb said that people who illegally enter the United States do so "because they couldn't come legally, they come to our country because their families—the dad who loved their children—was worried that their children didn't have food on the table," Bush said. "And they wanted to make sure their family was intact, and they crossed the border because they had no other means to work to be able to provide for their family. Yes, they broke the law, but it's not a felony. It's an act of love. It's an act of commitment to your family. I honestly think that that is a different kind of crime that there should be a price paid, but it shouldn't rile people up that people are actually coming to this country to provide for their families."[36]

And he has picked the wrong issues to stand with the right on, like gay marriage.[37] He seems to have a knack for being on the wrong side of trending public opinion on many issues. While governor of Florida, he gave a group called the American Family Association a lucrative tax break. The AFA is the sort of group that tries to organize boycotts of movies, TV shows, and even theme parks that promote what they deem an anti–family values agenda. He defended giving the AFA a $600,000 tax subsidy around the same time he was vocally opposed to same sex marriage, which he called "legal protection" for "sodomy." The taxpayer money was supposed to go to developing a technology that would keep children safe from pornographic material on the Internet. Ironically, the AFA and other conservative groups criticized Jeb in 2005 for his investment of $1.3 million of state pension funds in a video rental chain that distributed pornography.[38]

The Liability of Jeb's Wife, Columba Bush

To many of the Beltway elite, Republican Party bosses and corporatist donors supporting Jeb Bush, one of Jeb's greatest assets is his connection to the Hispanic culture. In a February 2015 campaign conference call, Jeb claimed that "The fact that I'm bilingual, bicultural can't hurt" and will help as an asset for Hispanic outreach.[39] Jeb has frequently campaigned on the trail during this cycle in Spanish, even speaking Spanish during a large portion of his announcement speech.[40] Jeb even bragged during major TV interviews that he speaks "more Spanish than English at home."[41]

Jeb's infatuation with illegal immigrants and migrant workers has led him toward awkward and even dangerous policy proposals. In an April 2013 "Family Reunion" conference sponsored by the Hispanic Leadership Network, Jeb suggested that the mayor of Detroit should "repopulate" the city with immigrants to make it "one of the great American cities again." In the same interview, Jeb also said that he supports an accelerated path to citizenship for "Dreamers," children born in the United States to illegal immigrants.[42] This at the same time that millions of Americans under the age of 30 are suffering record unemployment, particularly in the African-American community.

Most disturbingly, in April 2014 during an event marking the 25th anniversary of the failed presidency of George H. W. Bush at the George Bush Presidential Library and Museum, Jeb told Fox News's Shannon Bream in a moderated interview that migrant workers crossing our border illegally is "an act of love" and those migrant workers who break the law should not be deported because "they could make a great contribution not only for their own families but also for us."[43]

Why would someone seeking to become the 45th president of the United States have such a public disregard for the rule of law and culture of the country he seeks to serve in the Oval Office? The answer is his wife Columba, a woman who could become the first Hispanic first lady and only the second born outside this country.

Columba Bush was born Columba Garnica Gallo in 1953 in León, Guanajuato, Mexico, 250 miles outside Mexico City. Primarily raised in León, Columba's father Jose Maria Garnica Rodriguez was a waiter. Even before Columba was born, Jose was sneaking into the United States illegally to work. From 1947 to 1949, he picked fruit illegally in Arizona.

Columba's childhood was difficult. Her parents lived under modest means. Unable to provide for his family, Jose presumably as an "act of love" crossed the border illegally once again in 1960. Columba visited her father frequently while he was a construction worker in California. The prospective first lady was in the United States as an illegal alien, not following the rule of law. Columba became estranged from her father after her parents divorced.[44]

Jeb met Columba by happenstance in 1971. On a two-month study abroad program during his senior year at Phillips Academy, Jeb "spotted" Columba on a Sunday afternoon at Leóns central plaza. On the stump, Jeb described the moment as "knock-down, knocked me out" love at first sight.[45] Two short years later, Jeb and Columba were married in the Catholic Center at the University of Texas where Jeb majored in Latin Studies. This must have been a shock to his patrician Episcopal parents.

This was a life-changing event for Jeb. He has said that his life can be divided into two parts: "b.c. and a.c.—before Columba and after Columba."[46] Jeb was subservient to Columba's cultural roots describing "appreciating the culture of (Columba as) the most powerful part of the relationship. Being able to share that culture and live in it has been one of the great joys of my life."[47] He even converted to Catholicism, further distancing himself from the roots of his family legacy.

Jeb has pursued his career despite Columba's dislike for the public life of a politician's wife. While Jeb may have drifted from the Mayflower Connecticut WASP elitist culture in his personal life because of Columba, the Kennebunkport, Maine hunt for power never left his blood. And this is the one pursuit Columba has begrudgingly accepted.

In 1979 while George H. W. Bush pursued the presidency and then was eventually nominated vice president by Ronald Reagan to unify the Republican Party, Columba remained a Mexican citizen. But in 1988, six weeks before the Florida GOP primary, Columba "surprised her in-laws with the announcement that she had become a U.S. citizen (.)"[48] She even gave a nominating speech to second H. W.'s nomination, in Spanish, from the convention floor in New Orleans.

In a 1991 *LA Times* interview, Columba admits she only became a U.S. citizen to vote for her father-in-law as president. She describes praying to the Virgin of San Juan "for strength." But Columba also includes disturbing details. Up until the 1988 election she never saw "any necessity to change my citizenship. **My husband wanted me to stay as a Mexican citizen**, [emphasis added] and the whole family has always respected my decision. I changed my citizenship to vote for my father-in-law."[49] How can the potential first lady only have loyalty to the United States because of her family's pursuit of power? And perhaps even worse, is it proper for the potential president to have wanted his wife to remain a Mexican citizen?

This is reminiscent of Michelle Obama's gaffe during the 2008 election when she stated, "For the first time in my adult lifetime, I'm really proud of my country . . . " because of Barack Obama's success in politics.[50] The American people have suffered enough through the questionable associations and frequent criticisms of the Obama administration. It is a precedent which should not be followed.

Columba has admitted that she is "not interested in politics."[51] She was frequently heard complaining to Jeb during his 1994 campaign "You've ruined my life."[52] Columba has said that "Jeb is a natural-born politician, but I'm not a political person."[53]

Columba was often nowhere to be seen during Jeb's gubernatorial tenure. Her most public charade in the public spotlight was the infamous 1999 incident where she was caught at Atlanta's Hartsfield International Airport lying to Customs officials about the $19,000 worth of clothing and jewelry she had bought during a five-day shopping spree in France. Jeb publicly admitted that "Columba meant to hide the shopping spree" from him and that she "intentionally misled" the Custom officials.[54] Ironically, the trip was Jeb's gift to Columba for "follow(ing) him around the campaign trail" during the 1998 election.[55]

Should Jeb be elected president, his domestic life could unravel. Columba Bush is no Jackie Kennedy. At a time when the world is not secure and in much turmoil, and America is open for attack, Columba could be a major impediment to Jeb's presidency.

CHAPTER 4

THE CYNTHIA HENDERSON AFFAIR

I told Barbara, "As long as the girl hangs a sign around her neck that says 'Bush,' she'll be fine."

—columnist Ymelda Dixon regarding
Jeb's marriage to Columba[iv]

There have always been rumors of Jeb having a troubled marriage. The consensus in Tallahassee, Miami, and into the Beltway long has been that Jeb and Columba lived "separate lives" during much of Jeb's years profiting off his brother's presidency and his own governorship. Jeb has dealt with public scandals in the past.

Early into Jeb's first term as governor on a Thursday in May, 1999, the *Tallahassee Democrat* reported "about a rumor of an affair involving two high-ranking but unidentified public officials." Two days later during the weekend, two other papers— the *St. Petersburg Times* and the *Orlando Sentinel*—wrote about the alleged affair involving Bush and Cynthia Henderson and said Bush had denied them.[56]

Jeb's alleged affair involved Cynthia Henderson. Henderson, a lawyer turned lobbyist, was appointed by Jeb as secretary of the Department of Management Service in 1999, even though she did not have any proper experience or credentials. Jeb was forced to publicly deny the affair at a bill signing.[57] Henderson quietly left Jeb's administration soon after the denial, not finishing the first term.

Henderson did not remain outside the public eye for long. Three short years later, it was reported that she was forced to obtain a temporary restraining order from her husband of three months after "he found her in bed with another man and allegedly threatened them with a crowbar."[58] Henderson is no stranger to infidelity.

CHAPTER 5

JEB GOES TO VENEZUELA

Jeb's early work in Venezuela and South Florida is much more troubling than Dubya pretending to be on active duty in Texas while he was actually off in Alabama helping a GOP U.S. Senate campaign and getting sloppy drunk in redneck bars.

—Investigative reporter Wayne Madsen[v]

One of the last things then–Central Intelligence Agency director George H. W. Bush did for Jeb was to have him hired by the international division of the Texas Commerce Bank as a CIA "non-official cover" officer or "NOC." Texas Commerce Bank was an optimal cover for CIA activities. The family of James Baker, a man for whom I have the utmost respect, founded the bank. All the elder Bush had to do was to place a call to Baker to have his son hired by the bank's international division, the usual branch where CIA NOCs were placed within banks and investment firms. Other banks used by the CIA for NOC embeds included Bank of America, Chase Manhattan Bank, and Manufacturers Hanover.[59]

Texas Commerce Bank, bought by Chemical Bank in 1987 and which is now part of J.P. Morgan Chase, had the right pedigree to enable it to work closely with the CIA. In 1977, its board members included Lady Bird Johnson and the recently defeated President Gerald Ford. In the 1980s, Kenneth Lay, who founded the CIA-connected Enron, became a board member of Texas Commerce Bank. Howard Hughes's CIA-linked Summa Corporation used Texas Commerce Bank to purchase a number of properties on the Las Vegas strip.[60]

In 1977, a short time after his father left the CIA as director, Jeb, fluent in Spanish as a result of his time as an exchange student in Guadalajara, was sent, along with his Mexican wife Columba, to Caracas, Venezuela to work as a "branch manager" and "vice president" at the young age of 24. But Jeb was no ordinary "branch manager." He was, officially, Texas Commerce Bank's top point man in the Venezuelan capital and, unofficially, the CIA's main financial liaison to the Venezuelan oil industry and the Colombian narcotics cartels. Jeb would regularly report to his CIA "official cover" counterpart attached to the U.S. embassy in Caracas as a State Department "diplomat."[61]

Jeb helped lay the groundwork for the future Reagan-Bush administration's 1980s covert war against Nicaragua and leftist guerrillas in El Salvador by establishing banking and money laundering links between the CIA and the Medellin and Cali drug cartels. Jeb's friends in the Colombian cartels, particularly Medellin cartel boss Pablo Escobar, would help finance the Nicaraguan contras in return for CIA-supplied weapons. While in Venezuela, Jeb cleverly managed to hide the Colombian cartel's drug revenues as oil industry revenues of "front" companies. Texas Commerce Bank was the bank of choice for Latin American drug cartels. It was later discovered to have stashed $7 million in drug profits for the Gulf cartel of Mexico.[62]

Baker sold Texas Commerce Bank's Houston skyscraper to the head of the National Commercial Bank of Saudi Arabia, Sheikh Khalid bin Mahfouz, in 1985. Bin Mahfouz was later identified as a key member of Saudi Arabia's support network for the 9/11 terrorist attacks against the United States, which is noted in the still-classified 28 pages of the U.S. Senate Intelligence Committee Report on 9/11 intelligence failures. Bin Mahfouz, who lived in the River Oaks section of Houston near George H. W. Bush, died suddenly in 2009 at the age of 59. Bin Mahfouz, who was also an Irish citizen, threatened with confiscatory lawsuits any publication that reported his links to 9/11 and his family ties to Osama bin Laden.[63]

Jeb had no problems with the Venezuelan government in providing financial support for the Colombian cartels. For much of Jeb's stay in Venezuela, the extremely corrupt Carlos Andres Perez, known as "CAP," was president. His extravagant spending using Venezuela's revenue from the recently nationalized oil industry earned his government the nickname of "Saudi Venezuela." Although CAP nationalized the oil industry and created the *Petroleos de Venezuela* (PdVSA) state-owned oil firm, he also was generous to American firms bidding for work with PdVSA. One of them was Bechtel Corporation, the firm of future Reagan-Bush Cabinet members George P. Shultz and Caspar Weinberger. With a number of Bechtel employees in Venezuela, Jeb was not the only CIA "NOC" present in the country, but he was the most influential.

During CAP's second term as president from 1989 to 1993, a young army officer named Hugo Chavez attempted to overthrow the corrupt government in a coup. Many of Venezuela's elite who Jeb befriended during his days as Langley's main NOC in Caracas later became involved with repeated CIA attempts to overthrow Chavez and his successor, Nicolas

Maduro. Today, they and their progeny live in the Miami-Dade area, particularly in Doral, nicknamed "Doralzuela," and are among Jeb's strongest and most deep-pocketed political supporters.

In 1989, CAP crushed popular protests against his government by killing as many as 3,000 protesters. The massacre is known as the "Caracazo" massacre. After leaving office the second time, Andres Perez was convicted of corruption and sentenced to 28 months in prison.

After leaving Venezuela in 1980 to help with his father's presidential and vice presidential campaigns, Jeb hooked up with Cuban-American Miami businessman Armando Codina, who had his own connections with CIA-supported anti-Castro Cuban exiles in South Florida. Codina helped Jeb make millions of dollars in the real estate business. Jeb, as a principal of the Codina Group, was able to arrange the sale of high-priced condos and mansions in the Miami area to his elite friends in Venezuela, with Jeb receiving handsome sales commissions.[64]

One of Jeb's close Miami associates was Cuban terrorist Orlando Bosch. Bosch was a key figure in the CIA's Operation Condor, which was an alliance of Latin American military dictatorships that targeted leftist leaders for assassination across international borders. Bosch helped carry out the October 1976 bombing of Cubana Airlines Flight 455, which was en route from Barbados to Jamaica. All 73 passengers and crew were killed in the attack, including children and the Cuban fencing team.[65]

The Cubana bombing plot was discussed at a 1976 meeting in Washington between Bosch; another Cuban terrorist, Luis Posada Carriles; and Michael Townley of the CIA. Jeb's father, the CIA director, was fully aware of the plot, as well as another plot to kill former Chilean foreign minister Orlando Letelier.

Letelier and Roni Moffitt, his American associate, were killed when their car exploded on Sheridan Circle in front of the Irish embassy in Washington on September 21, 1976, a few weeks before the Cubana airliner was blown out of the sky off Barbados.

Codina, Bosch, and Posada Carriles were all part of Jeb's inner circle of friends, which also included Cuban businessman Camilo Padreda, a former spy for Cuban dictator Fulgencio Batista, and Hernandez Cartaya, both later indicted for systematically embezzling funds from the Jefferson Savings and Loan of McAllen, Texas. Padreda and Cartaya were also identified as CIA agents who helped skim funds from Jefferson and other S&Ls to fund the Nicaraguan contras. Jeb's work for the CIA in Caracas in 1977 came a few months after the CIA's worst terrorism spree in history, which also happened to coincide with George H. W. Bush's single year as CIA director.

With his father as vice president, Jeb served as the liaison for the Nicaraguan contras. He arranged meetings between them and their supporters, and the White House point man for covert assistance to the Nicaraguan rebels, one Marine Corps lieutenant colonel by the name of Oliver North. Another one of Jeb's Cuban cronies, Miguel Recarey, received lobbying help from Jeb discussed elsewhere in this book. Recarey and his brother, who had close ties to the CIA, were also funded by Florida Mafia boss Santo Trafficante, Jr., a co-conspirator in several CIA plots to assassinate Fidel Castro and a suspected co-plotter in the assassination of President John F. Kennedy.

A Jeb Bush presidency would ensure the CIA's continued control of the White House. George W. Bush maintained the CIA's control over the presidency for eight years and before him, Bill Clinton, who had his own links to the CIA's contra-cocaine network through Mena, Arkansas, has seen his Clinton Foundation benefit from a $1 million contribution from one of Jeb's old Cuban-Venezuelan friends, Gustavo Cisneros, the multi-billionaire "Berlusconi of Venezuela." Cisneros, now exiled in the Dominican Republic, was involved in the CIA's 2002 abortive coup against Chavez.[66]

CHAPTER 6

THE S&L SCANDAL
BENEFITS THE BUSHES

Both Mr. Bush and Mr. Codina expressed surprise that the settlement of the loan could be interpreted as the use of taxpayers' money to make good a loan whose proceeds went for their building. Asked if they were aware that the funds for the repayment of the Broward Federal loan came from the taxpayers, both men said no.

—Jeff Gerth, *New York Times*[vi]

The Savings and Loan Crisis (S&L Crisis) was one of the largest thefts by the banking industry on the American taxpayer. During the 1980s and into the 1990s, over a thousand savings and loan associations, small banks known as thrifts, which specialize in accepting savings deposits and making mortgage and other loans, failed due to excess lending and fraud by insiders and employees. The S&L Crisis was a major impetus for the 1992 recession, which helped usher George H. W.'s 1992 defeat. While the S&L Crisis happened under H. W.'s watch, two of his children had significant roles in the fraud and abuse of the private sector. And neither faced any legal consequences—in fact, both were bailed out.

While the Bush family is among dark sheep in American political history, Neil Bush (son of Poppy Bush) is the present generation's darkest. In 2004, during W.'s re-election year, Neil went through an embarrassing very public and very messy divorce. Court documents revealed that Neil had sex with women in his hotel rooms in Asia; had an affair and may have fathered a child out of wedlock; and was cashing in on businesses with which Neil had zero expertise—including a computer-chip company managed in part by the son of former Chinese president Jiang Zemin.[67] Of course it is no coincidence that China's trade deficits with the United States, theft of American jobs, leverage on American debt, and membership into the World Trade Organization were all hallmarks of the W. presidency. W. was good business for China and Neil profited as well.

While Neil is not an expert in computer chips, he certainly specializes in bank fraud and taxpayer bailouts. During the 1980s, Neil was a director of the Silverado Banking, Savings and Loan Association. During Neil's three-year tenure "Silverado was the victim of sophisticated schemes and abuses by insiders, and of gross negligence by its directors and outside professionals," according to Douglas H. Jones, senior deputy general counsel of the FDIC who headed the government's lawsuit.[68] Neil approved loans to business associates. Silverado collapsed in 1988 with over $2.3 billion in assets. It cost taxpayers over $1 billion. While Neil initially insisted he was innocent, he settled out of court for a paltry $50,000. And his legal costs were financed by a major Republican donor. It pays to have Daddy in the Oval Office.

Neil escaped any criminal charges from his illicit actions at Silverado, and Jeb profited from the S&L Crisis. In 1983, Jeb and his business partner Armando Codina secured a first mortgage of $7 million from an insurance company and another $4.565 million loan from the thrift Broward Federal Savings and Loan for the purchase of 1390 Brickell Avenue in downtown Miami. Broward Federal Savings and Loan became "insolvent in 1988 because of what regulators said were poor lending practices on commercial loans in the mid-1980's." Jeb and Codina reached a settlement on the Broward loan and $505,000 and retained control of the building.[69] The taxpayers foot the bill on over $4 million for Daddy's little boy.

Codina also introduced Jeb to nefarious individuals. One was even a tenant in 1390 Brickell Avenue—Alberto Duque. Duque frequently flew Jeb on his private plane. He "showered Bush with attention." Unfortunately for Jeb, Duque got indicted and was unable to continue treating him like a prince. In 1986, Duque was convicted on 60 counts of bank fraud involving up to $100 million in loans. After serving seven of 15 years in prison, he fled from a halfway house and remains a fugitive.[70]

If the S&L Crisis was just a mention in H. W.'s presidency then it could be glossed over. However, with Neil escaping jail and Jeb profiting off the bailouts, the Bushes proved once again that their government "service" is an illicit and lucrative business. And business during the 1980s was good.

CHAPTER 7

JEB'S SHADY PARTNER, FUGITIVE MIGUEL RECAREY

Kevin, I only want to make sure that Mike Recarey gets a fair hearing.

– Jeb to Bush family friend Kevin Moley[vii]

The U.S. government is the largest spender, creditor, and debtor in the history of the world. The president is largely responsible for a behemoth which spends $4 trillion a year. Washington is a cesspool notorious for its waste, fraud, and abuse. Washington is a cesspool. In announcing his candidacy, Jeb said "he would take on the papered elite of Washington." The records show, however, that he is the papered elite. His business dealings with Miguel Recarey, Jr. prove this point.

In 1985, Recarey hired Jeb, who was building a real estate business, to assist in locating office space in South Florida. Recarey was president and CEO of International Medical Centers (IMC), the largest health maintenance organization (HMO) for the elderly in the U.S. Recarey had a checkered past that included "jail time for income tax evasion in the 1970s. He bragged about his ties to Florida crime boss Santo Trafficante Jr."[71]

IMC had been supported with over $1 billion in Medicare payments, but Recarey ran into a problem. Under federal regulation, an HMO cannot receive over 50 percent of its revenue from Medicare. Recarey needed a waiver from the Department of Health and Human Services (HHS) so IMC could receive increased payments. He spent over $1 million on Washington lobbyists including my firm Black, Manafort and Stone. The waiver was worth millions.

But Recarey had an ace in the hole, the son of the sitting vice president. Recarey's IMC received the waiver after lobbying efforts by Jeb in 1985. However, Recarey was running a Ponzi scheme, stealing over $100 million of the Medicare funds. Federal regulators began a search for the missing funds. Recarey was later indicted in April 1987 and again in October 1987 on racketeering and wiretapping charges. He fled the country, initially to Venezuela and later to Spain, where he currently resides, escaping extradition.

In 1992, as H. W. ran for re-election, his involvement with IMC became an issue. Bush claimed that he only spoke to a lower-level official named Kevin Moley. Moley "became concerned" when he heard Bush was helping Recarey. In sworn testimony, Moley said he asked "'Jeb, this is something, you know, you probably don't want to be involved in.' And (Jeb) said, 'Kevin, I only want to make sure that Mike Recarey gets a fair hearing.'"[72] Jeb also admitted to being paid $75,000 from Recarey for consulting "but said it was tendered for real estate consultation. (However) the deal he consulted on was never closed."[73]

The authors have scoured the federal reports; Jeb was never registered as a lobbyist, which is required under federal law when seeking federal funds.

Jeb Bush denied having reached out to HHS secretary Margaret Heckler on Recarey's behalf, a denial he maintains through a spokeswoman in 2015. However, Heckler told the *Huffington Post* that Bush not only called her but her then chief of staff. Jeb has been lying about his participation for over 20 years.[74]

As a member of the lobbying team for IMC, I participated in multiple conference calls along with the future governor of Florida. Jeb played a heavy hand in lobbying HHS for the valuable waivers. There was no doubt, "Mike" Recarey was an extremely demanding client and pushed relentlessly for Jeb to intercede with Heckler, a liberal Republican from Massachusetts who had served in Congress after improbably defeating Congressman Joseph W. Martin who had served as Speaker of the House in the 1940s. Jeb did not need much prodding. I marveled at how subservient the vice president's son was to the pushy and bombastic Cuban executive. I asked my partner, Nick Panuzio, a former mayor of Bridgeport, Connecticut, who was the managing partner of the IMC account, why Jeb was jumping through hoops for Recarey. Panuzio replied "Jeb's on the board and he has stock options. This could be worth millions."

To avoid a national scandal in 1987, it was vital for the Bushes to spirit Recarey out of the country. Three hours after a warrant was issued for his arrest, Recarey was driven to Miami International Airport in a car owned by the Bush Realty Corporation of Miami. Recarey also took a private plane at Miami International Airport, which the flight records listed as a flight for Bush Realty.[75]

In 1995, Recarey was interviewed by ABC's *20/20*. Recarey admitted that the $75,000 consulting fee was being paid to "buy influence in Washington." When asked whether he was paying for Bush's influence, Recarey responded, "Sure. Obviously not enough."[76]

CHAPTER 8

HOW JEB MADE HIS MONEY

Project Verde was unsuccessful.

—Jeb in an email to a Lehman Brothers colleague
in early July 2008[viii]

Leveraging Family and Florida Connections

When Jeb Bush left office in 2007, he set out to make money.[77] Bush joined over a dozen corporate boards, and he founded a consulting firm that would rake in $33 million by the time he started running for president.[78] He made that money the Bush way: by leveraging family ties and exploiting relationships forged through old-fashioned political patronage.

In Florida, the governor has more authority than his or her counterparts in most other states over how the state pension invests public employees' money, as one of three trustees tasked with overseeing the pension agency. Bush capitalized on that power, using the pension fund as a political piggy bank. His administration poured almost $2 billion into financial firms whose executives were top fundraisers for his brother's presidential campaigns.[79] A huge chunk of that money, $275 million, was sent to the private equity firm Carlyle Group, where Bush's father was working. Another $150 million went to an alternative investment fund run by Goldman Sachs, while Bush's cousin, George H. Walker IV, ran the firm's alternative investment division. And $250 million of the money was invested in a fund run by Lehman Brothers.[80]

It was the first time the state pension had invested in Lehman, which would soon hire cousin Walker. When Bush left office in 2007, Lehman quickly hired the former governor at a rate of $1.3 million a year, paid to his consulting firm, Jeb Bush and Associates. Florida continued to send money to Lehman, buying up increasingly risky products. Two months after Jeb's arrival at the firm, Lehman sold Florida hundreds of millions of dollars of toxic, mortgage-backed securities.[81] The securities defaulted within months, eventually costing the state of Florida more than $1 billion.[82]

Bush has denied playing any role in Lehman's sale of toxic securities to the state pension—as should be expected. He has not commented publicly about Florida's initial investment in Lehman while he was governor. But the sequence of events with Lehman is par for the course with Jeb.

In 1999, Bush's administration and local politicians lured the timber company Rayonier to Jacksonville with a $2.6 million package of tax incentives. Two years later, Bush and other state officials approved a plan to buy logging rights on roughly 7,500 acres of swampland near Jacksonville from Rayonier for $4.6 million, for the purpose of conservation.[83]

The state had already purchased the underlying land there from a trust—and Bush had expressed concern that the state was getting ripped off then. "Man, I can't wait to get back into the real estate business and sell property to the state," Bush told his colleagues at the time. A few years after the state bought the timber rights from Rayonier, a state audit questioned the cost of the new purchase. The state's valuation "contained questionable assumptions related to future timber rights that may not have supported" the price it paid, the audit said.

Florida paid Rayonier nearly $100 million to buy land and timber rights while Bush was governor. Two years after he left office, Rayonier rewarded Jeb with a seat on its board of directors. He kept that cushy job for six years, earning $1 million for his work. It wasn't the last time Jeb used the connections he forged as governor for his own financial benefit.

In 2005, one of George's top fundraisers and patrons, Randy Best, pitched Jeb on getting into the for-profit education business.[84] Best had been a top fundraiser for George's 2004 re-election campaign, and both the federal government and schools in Florida had contracted with his company, Voyager, to run reading programs while the brothers were in office.

When Jeb left office in 2007, he quickly cashed in on his connections with Best. A company run by Best paid Bush for a speech that year.[85] Soon, Bush started pushing a new venture from Best, called Academic Partnerships, which manages online classes for universities. Bush has repeatedly insisted as he runs for president that he did not become a lobbyist, or a consultant who acts like a lobbyist, when he entered the private sector. But his work with Academic Partnerships reeks.

As Jeb began his work with Academic Partnerships, he relied heavily on the friends he made in the governor's office. Jeb helped introduce Academic Partnership to two of Florida's state universities—Florida International University in Miami, and University of West Florida in Pensacola.

Bush made an introduction between Academic Partnerships and Florida International University before the public, state school signed its first contract with the firm in 2009.[86] Under that agreement, the university promised to pay the company 70 percent of each student's tuition per class. FIU later negotiated that percentage down to 45 percent. The university has paid Academic Partnerships nearly $20 million since the first contract.

After Bush officially became an adviser to and investor in Academic Partnerships, he tried to shake more money out of the company's pact with FIU. Bush regularly pressed the university's president, who had been hired by Bush's appointees, to "expand the relationship" with Academic Partnerships, or give his company more business.[87] FIU announced in 2013 it would launch a new degree program with Academic Partnerships, but the university backed away from the plan following outcry from professors who saw political motivations.[88]

In the case of UWF, Bush was in frequent communications with Janice Gilley, who served as a policy director in his office as governor before she became a lobbyist for UWF.[89] State records show that, before UWF's first contract with his company, Bush checked in with Gilley to ensure Academic Partnerships would be meeting with the school. They would continue to chat regularly about Best and about the prospects for additional deals. Academic Partnerships has been paid $5 million by the UWF.

Jeb and the Nigerian Export-Import Bank

In February 2015 during an appearance at the Club for Growth's winter conference in Palm Beach, Florida, Jeb called for a "phase out" of the Export-Import Bank (Ex-Im).[90] The Ex-Im provides taxpayer-backed funding to overseas businesses and foreign governments to buy U.S. products.

Though the Ex-Im was originally intended to specifically benefit American small businesses, in 2013, 87 percent went to three companies—Boeing, General Electric, and Caterpillar. Jeb's newfound opposition to the Ex-Im Bank is surprising considering that he profited off of one of the greatest frauds of the Ex-Im Bank.

In 1989, the year after H. W. was elected president, Jeb formed a partnership with J. David Eller, the CEO for Moving Water Industries (MWI), called Bush-El Corp. to market MWI's pumps overseas. Eller was a top Republican fundraiser who heavily supported H. W. during his contentious primary and the general election. Eller's support paid off. In 1992, Bush-El secured $74.3 million from the Ex-Im to sell MWI water pumps to Nigeria.

MWI had been working on the prospective deal since 1988. Jeb's involvement was crucial for MWI. Eller frequently suggested that Jeb had major influence in Washington. Eller even made a low-budget promo video "for the company's prospective Nigerian clients that touted his connections to the 'highest levels' of the US government and even prominently featured photos of him posing with Ronald Reagan and George H.W. Bush."[91] The $74.3 million loans were authorized to Nigerian states despite Nigeria's poor credit history.

In 2002, the Justice Department brought a whistleblower lawsuit against MWI for "fraudulently conceal(ing) that the deal would include a 'highly irregular' $28 million in commissions for the company's Nigerian sales agent."[92] Justice also brought a civil lawsuit against MWI that in 2013 resulted in a federal jury fining the water pump company. Jeb was never called as a witness in either trial.

Jeb claims that he only earned $650,000 from his partnership with Eller and none of the income came from the

Nigerian deal. But he travelled to Nigeria on behalf of MWI in 1989 and 1991 with large delegations. H. W.'s State Department even issued a cable celebrating the 1989 visit "as the grandest celebration of U.S.-Nigeria friendship we have seen in recent memory." Yet neither Jeb's name nor Bush-El Corp were ever cited in either case. Jeb was also never even called as a witness.

In February, 2015 Matt Dixon of the *Naples Daily News* reported MWI employee Mike Carcamo told the FBI that "Bush-El had a contract with MWI to receive 3 percent on projects in a handful of countries, including Nigeria."

Lehman Brothers, Carlos Slim, and BushObamaPhones

Jeb's tenure as governor of Florida was profitable for Lehman Brothers. Towards the end of Jeb's term, records show that Lehman Brothers was put in charge of $250 million worth of pension funds for Florida cops, teachers, and firefighters in 2005 and 2006. Lehman made over $5 million in fees on these deals alone. Lehman also gained additional contracts to manage another $1.2 billion of Florida's money.[93]

Jeb earned millions once he left the governor's mansion. The vast majority of his wealth came from Lehman. In 2007 and 2008, Jeb was paid over $1.3 million a year and made "it clear he wanted work as a hands-on investment banker."[94] Only weeks after Bush went on Lehman's payroll, the Florida State Board of Administration (SBA), a three-member body that makes investment decisions about state pension funds, purchased over $842 million worth of separate investments in Lehman's mortgage-backed securities. From June 2007 to June 2008, the SBA shifted another $420 million of pension money into the same fund.[95] Lehman reaped immediate rewards from its investment in Jeb.

In 2008 Lehman started the financial crisis as its mortgage-backed securities, the very ones that Jeb advised the SBA to heavily invest in, were being called in. Lehman faced bankruptcy and Florida's pensions were potentially exposed to over $1 billion in losses. Lehman launched "Project Green" in an effort to raise new capital and dispose of all those bad assets.

Lehman expected that Jeb would be able to deliver. His brother was president. Yet Jeb could not secure a bailout from the Treasury Department. Next he approached Carlos Slim, the Mexican billionaire and telecom giant. Bush called this "Project Verde" ("verde" is Spanish for "green"). Charlie Gasparino of Fox Business has exposed that "(o)n July 5, 2008, Bush reported that the meeting had been unsuccessful because Slim 'did not express interest in jv (joint venture) or stock purchase.'"[96]

Jeb denies that he ever asked Slim for an investment in Lehman. His longtime advisor Kristy Campbell claims "Bush met with Carlos Slim. It was regarding a specific telecom project. It was not regarding [a] general Carlos Slim infusion of cash to save Lehman Brothers." It is possible that Jeb is simply lying to save the embarrassment and potential voter exposure that he was unable to secure funding to save Lehman and therefore played a critical role in the financial crisis that the end of his brother's administration brought to the world.

If Jeb was indeed discussing a telecom deal with Slim, it would involve TracFone—which Slim owns. While the public believes that the federal program that distributes cell phones to low income voters started under the Obama administration, it was in fact initiated by President George W. Bush. The ObamaPhone is actually the BushObamaPhone. The FCC allowed wireless carrier Tracfone to join the program's list of approved providers under the W. administration in 2008.

Jeb is a shareholder in TracFone. Prior to becoming a presidential candidate, he transferred his stock to his son to avoid having to disclose his ownership in his federal financial disclosures. The *New York Times* has never disclosed the partnership between Bush and the Mexican billionaire.

While Jeb was unable to get Slim to invest in Lehman in that July 2008 meeting, he still succeeded in keeping his multi-million dollar job. Barclays, a British investment house, acquired Lehman. Jeb remained on Barclay's payroll at an increased consultant fee of $2 million a year until he resigned in 2014 in anticipation of his presidential candidacy.

CHAPTER 9

JEB CASHES IN ON OBAMACARE AND COMMON CORE

We've created a monstrosity.

—Jeb on Obamacare[ix]

In October 2015, Jeb Bush released a healthcare plan in New Hampshire which pledges to repeal Obamacare. Bush's plan promised to defer power to the states. This premise is antithetical Obamacare, the top-down federal takeover the Obama regime pounded on the states as an egregious attack on the Republic's founding principle of federalism.

Obamacare has made premiums and costs skyrocket for many Americans. However the insurance companies, drug companies, and hospital chains have all reported record profits—crony capitalism. Jeb, whose net worth is reported at $21M, made more than $2M directly off of Obamacare, legislation he now wants the public to believe he will repeal as president.

In 2007 after Jeb left the governor's mansion, he joined the board of Tenet Healthcare, the third-largest publicly traded hospital chain in the country. Tenet in particular reaped the awards of Obamacare and Jeb shared in those profits. As a result of the Affordable Care Act's Medicaid expansion, Tenet saw its share of unpaid care drop to $78 million in the second quarter of 2014. In the third quarter of 2015, Tenet's "revenue was up 6 percent over the previous year, to $4.18 billion, with the company attributing 40 percent of the gain."[97] On June 15, 2015 Tenet's stock price shot up $6 a share, which by no coincidence was the same day the W.-appointed Chief Justice Roberts delivered his second nonsensical decision legalizing Obamacare.

Jeb wants the public to believe that he no longer has any interest in Tenet because he stepped down from the board in 2014 in anticipation of his presidential run. But from 2007 through 2013, Tenet paid Bush $2.3 million. A large part of the compensation was in the form of stock awards. In 2013, Bush sold over $1 million in Tenet shares. A proxy statement from 2014 showed Bush still holding another $3 million in Tenet stock. This gives Jeb a vested interest in Obamacare.[98]

Jeb's pledge to repeal the Affordable Care Act is as reliable as Obama's promise that "if you liked your doctor you can keep your doctor." In fact, Jeb's healthcare plan is Obamacare Light. As Taylor Millard of Hot Air explained, "Bush's plan isn't bold. It's got some good parts sure, but instead of doing a smaller government-involved health care proposal, Bush should be willing to let the free market loose . . . it simply doesn't go far enough." In essence, Jeb is simply moving the Medicaid expansion and cost control onto the states. His friends at Tenet will still reap record profits off of crony capitalism.

Jeb Bush and Common Core
When Ronald Reagan became the 40th president of the United States in 1981, he wanted to abolish the Department of Education. The Department of Education was created late in Jimmy Carter's

presidency and President Reagan foresaw a federal power grab over local education. President Reagan famously said, "The most terrifying words in the English language are: 'I'm from the government and I'm here to help.'" The Department of Education is a perfect example. It has become a bloated bureaucracy and federal funds are used to build government, not schools.

As a big-government pseudo-Republican, W. expanded the Department of Education with his signature early initiative "No Child Left Behind." The program marked an unprecedented extension of federal authority over state education. Of course when the government makes a power grab, it will always seek more. Hence Common Core.

Common Core is the federal takeover of all education at the local level. Its supporters describe Common Core as benign and only seeking universal standards. This strains credulity—if ever fully implemented, Washington will control all curricula, including home school. Parents will lose control over their children's education. Common Core's biggest proponent in the Republican primary is Jeb Bush.

Jeb argues that Common Core's "universal standards" are essential to keep America competitive in the 21st century. But in fact Common Core forces all states to adapt a universal curriculum that is in line with the federal standards which No Child Left Behind made necessary. Without No Child Left Behind, Common Core would not be threatening the rights of parents nationwide.

Common Core is anathema to the vast majority of Republicans—especially primary voters who are more conservative. Jeb tried to spin his continued support of Common Core in the face of flagging poll numbers as a sign of leadership, noting that he would not waiver or flip-flop for political gain. Jeb has remained vocal about his support for Common

Core, another hot-button issue that voters of all stripes feel strongly about. Republican voters are particularly opposed to Common Core, but they're not the only ones.

Parents and teachers, even those who generally vote for Democrats, are rallying against Common Core around the country, and the anti-Common Core movement likely to continue gaining steam. Once again, Jeb is on the wrong side. Yet Jeb says he's "totally committed" to Common Core.[99]

Of course there is more to Jeb's position—Jeb has already made millions off of the program, and the big donors and special interests supporting his campaign stand to make billions in perpetuity should Common Core ever be passed through Congress. After leaving office, Jeb founded and was chair of the Foundation for Excellence in Education (FEE), which served as a platform to mainly push education reforms. In 2015 Jeb disclosed the major donors to include Learning.com and testing and textbook giants McGraw-Hill and Pearson. Both companies have major financial interests in Common Core. FEE collected over $46 million in its eight years of existence.[100]

Jeb stepped down as chair of FEE in 2014 in anticipation of his presidential run. His successor was Condoleezza Rice, W.'s national security advisor and secretary of state.

PART 2

SAMUEL AND PRESCOTT BUSH

CHAPTER 10

SAMUEL CASHES IN ON WORLD WAR I

There is such a thirst for gain [among military suppliers] . . .
that it is enough to make one curse their own Species, for
possessing so little virtue and patriotism.

—George Washington

A Crime Family's Beginnings on the Rails

The branches of any tree evolve from a central point of power,
a root if you will. In order to understand the tree, one must
understand the root, or origin. In the case of the American
Cosa Nostra, it's been traced back to its origins in Sicily, at the
dawn of the 20th century. To trace the Bush criminal/political
dynasty, one has to go back to the same era. Every enterprise
whether criminal or legitimate has a beginning, and the Bush
dynasty is no different. Every crime family has in its past one
patriarch who started it all. For the Bushes that man was Samuel Prescott Bush.

Samuel was born on October 4, 1863 in Brick Church, New
Jersey, the son of Harriet Fay and the Reverend James Smith
Bush, an Episcopal priest at Grace Church in Orange, New

Jersey. In the 1850s James attended Yale University, a tradition which resumed when James's grandson Prescott attended Yale in 1913. Samuel grew up in New Jersey, Staten Island, and San Francisco but spent the majority of his adult life in Columbus, Ohio. Back in Hoboken, New Jersey, Samuel graduated from the Stevens Institute of Technology in 1884. At the institute, he played on one of America's earliest regular college football teams. Upon graduating, Samuel accepted an apprenticeship with the Pittsburgh, Cincinnati, Chicago and St. Louis Railroad at their Logansport, Indiana shops.

By 1888 Bush became the assistant manager of railroad operations at the company's Dennison shop and in 1894, superintendent of all its Columbus lines. On June 20, 1894, Samuel married Flora Sheldon, who gave him six children: Prescott, Robert (who died in childhood), Mary, Margaret, Clement, and James. Prescott would be the one to continue the dynasty started by his father. In 1899, they moved to Milwaukee, Wisconsin where he took the position of superintendent of motive power with the Chicago, Milwaukee & St. Paul Railroad.[101]

Samuel Bush and Buckeye Steel
Buckeye Steel Castings was a Columbus, Ohio firm named for the Ohio buckeye tree. It was founded in Columbus as the Murray-Hayden Foundry, which made iron farm implements. In Mansel Blackford's book about Buckeye steel, *A Portrait Cast In Steel*, he writes that Buckeye's business was failing due to their inability to find a niche. That changed when the company switched to making automatic couplers that were stronger and safer than manual linchpin couplers. The Murray-Hayden Foundry changed its name to the Buckeye Automatic Car Coupler Company and began manufacturing iron railroad car couplers. Eventually demand for stronger coupling assemblies

led to a switch to steel and the name to Buckeye Steel Castings. With the growth in production of steel for the railroads, Buckeye Steel bought property which in time would cover 86 acres, and it employed thousands of workers at its huge plant along Parsons Avenue.

In 1901, Samuel Bush was hired as vice president and general manager. At the time, the president of Buckeye was none other than Frank Rockefeller, younger brother of Standard Oil tycoon John D. Rockefeller. After seven years, Frank Rockefeller stepped down and Samuel Bush became president and general manager of Buckeye Steel. During his time at Buckeye, the company held a 15 percent share of the coupler market and was the third largest producer in the country with annual net income of $350,000 on sales exceeding $2.3 million. By 1917, net income reached $1 million. Bush was to hold this position until 1928.[102]

Some of Buckeye's biggest accounts were railroads owned by the fabulously wealthy E. H. Harriman, future father of W. Averell Harriman. Edward H. Harriman was born in 1848 in Hempstead, New York. Like Samuel Bush, Harriman was the son of an Episcopal clergyman. When he was 14, he began working as an office boy in a New York brokerage house for a broker named Dewitt C. Hays. Harriman's uncle, Oliver Harriman, was a director of the Mutual Life Insurance Company, the Bank of America, and the New York Guaranty and Indemnity Co. When Harriman was 21 he borrowed $3,000 from uncle Oliver to buy a seat on the Stock Exchange. In 1879 he married Mary Averill, daughter of the president of the Ogdensburg & Lake Champlain Railroad. In 1881, Harriman bought control of the Sodus Bay and Southern Railroad, and after making improvements, sold it to the Pennsylvania Railroad. His next purchase was for the Illinois Central Railroad. Harriman died in 1909. [103]

As we'll see, the Harriman and the Bush families, along with the Rockefellers, would continue a relationship that would last for decades. The Harriman/Bush connection would cement itself with their sons, Averell Harriman and Prescott Bush. That tale is coming with the next generation of the Bush criminal dynasty.

At this point we must bring in another character that would become both enabler and codependent in the Bush saga: George Herbert Walker. The Scottish-bred Walkers arrived in New England before the American Revolution. George Herbert Walker's great grandfather, David Walker, had built up the largest dry goods import firm west of the Mississippi. By 1917, Samuel Bush was not only a major supplier of steel couplers for most of the nation's railways but was director of the Federal Reserve Bank of Cleveland. He was also director of the Pennsylvania Railroad's Ohio subsidiaries, of the Hocking Valley Railway and the Norfolk and Western Railway, and of the Huntington National Bank.

George H. Walker had by 1917 become wealthy beyond measure. His investment firm G. H. Walker and Company, founded in 1900, had become one of the more important investment firms in the Mississippi Valley. Walker was in on the ground floor of investment banking. He used his links to midwestern industry to become advisor to J.P. Morgan & Company, banker E. H. Harriman, and St. Louis businessman Robert Brookings, founder of the conservative think tank, the Brookings Institute.[104]

By 1910 Bernard Baruch (1870–1965) had become one of Wall Street's financial leaders. Born in 1870 in Camden, South Carolina, Baruch had worked his way up from runner to major player in just 20 years. In 1907 he purchased H. Hentz and Company, an international commodity firm with offices on

Wall Street and in Paris, London, Berlin and other cities. When Woodrow Wilson was re-elected president and war was looming, he called on Baruch for advice because Baruch understood the nation's economy and industrial resources. He won the position of chairman of the War Industries Board, which controlled the industrial establishment of the country during the war years.[105]

Spoils of War

As the United States prepared for war, Buckeye Steel broadened its operations to include the manufacture of rifle barrels for Remington Arms, controlled since 1914 by Percy Rockefeller. In 1915 a new Remington Arms plant was constructed and was operational by 1916 for the First World War. As a result of Buckeye Steel's new arms manufacturing plant, Samuel Bush was asked to become chief of the prestigious Ordnance, Small Arms, and Ammunition Section of the War Industries board by Bernard Baruch, the board's chairman. Another point of interest is that in 1914, Great Britain chose J. P. Morgan & Company as its commercial agent for purchasing war supplies from the United States. Allied wartime purchases through Morgan ultimately came to an astounding $3.2 billion, four times the entire federal budget in 1914.[106]

The new plant was finished just in time to fill a million rifle order from Russia. Sixty-seven percent of all the rifles used in World War I by the United States, Britain, and Russia were provided by Remington. The War Industries Board, at the end of World War 1, had profited in excess of $200 million.[107]

The year 1916 was an important one for Samuel Bush and Averell Harriman. Prescott Bush, son of Samuel Bush, and Roland Harriman, brother of Averell Harriman, were chosen for membership at Yale's Skull and Bones Society.[108]

Prescott was a huge man—six foot four and 250 pounds, a giant to his children. His voice was a gravelly baritone and carried quite a noticeable volume. He wore a coat and tie to dinner, even on those hot summer nights at Kennebunkport. He was charming and overbearing at the same time. His children feared and admired him. He was not an affectionate man, and used fear as a means of establishing unquestioned respect from his children, who described him as distant, scary, stern, and righteous. He demanded that his grandchildren call him "Senator." He drank heavily and was described as a mean drunk. Apparently Prescott enjoyed two activities: playing golf, which he was quite good at, and singing.

The Yale Skull and Bones Society helped Wall Street financiers seek active young men of "good birth" to form a kind of imitation British aristocracy in America. These young men were considered near "royalty" in America. Later, Prescott Bush, Roland "Bunny" Harriman, and several other Bonesmen would comprise the core partners of Brown Brothers Harriman, the world's largest private investment group.[109]

The Yale Skull and Bones Society will continue to play an important role, as we shall see. Bonesman Percy Rockefeller, chief of Remington Arms, supplied machine guns and Colt automatic pistols; millions of rifles to Czarist Russia; over half the small-arms used by the allies in World War I; and 69 percent of the rifles used by the United States in that conflict.[110] Between 1914 and 1917, Wall Street financiers lobbied heavily, twisting U.S. government police functions. With J. P. Morgan as its purchasing agent for Great Britain, these financiers wanted a great war and they wanted the companies they were linked with to benefit (profit) from the U.S. and British involvement in the war. This was business as had never been seen before, outside of the Civil War. Back then the Civil War offered financiers and bankers the first opportunity to fund a controlled conflict. The aim would be the erosion of democracy on a state level, the elimination of state chartered "free banking," and the establishment of centralized "national" banking and therefore a few private "national" banks that could be controlled and owned by a handful of elite families. From the start of the Civil War, these private banks loaned money to both sides of the conflict.

The National Banking Act of 1863 and a subsequent law passed in 1865 put free banks out of business forever. The control of "National Banks" was put, as hoped, in the hands of members of the Order of Skull and Bones. The Guaranty Trust Company, established in 1864, was one of these banks, owned by J. P. Morgan.[111]

This truly was the beginning of the "military industrial complex" as so eloquently put by President Eisenhower when he retired from office. Interestingly enough, when the United States entered World War I, the British purchases no longer went through the Morgan Company but were handled by the Allied Purchasing Commission, which was directly affiliated with the War Industries Board. St. Louis millionaire businessman Robert Brookings (mentioned earlier) went to Washington to become chairman of the War Industries Board Price Fixing Committee. As we see, the players are positioning themselves for maximum control and therefore maximum profit.

With Bush at the head of the Ordnance, Small Arms and Ammunition section of the War Industries Board, Bernard Baruch as chairman, and Brookings heading the Price Fixing Committee, it's not surprising that Averell Harriman put aside his railroading to build ships for the war effort. He set up near Philadelphia with a contract to build 40 freighters for the Federal Emergency Shipping Corporation. In 1917 Harriman, former St. Louis mayor, current ambassador to Russia, and close friend of Baruch, gave the Russian revolutionary government a $325 million credit to be spent on war materials from the United States.[112]

These men, born in the Midwest, were true American visionaries, yet there was something deeply un-American about enabling a war to spill out of control and envelop the entire world. I dare say that without the influences of these warmongering financiers, World War I would have developed quite differently. (Years later, in 1934, hearings by a committee led by U.S. senator Gerald Nye brought charges against the members of the War Industries Board and labeled them "Merchants of Death." War profiteering had not gone unnoticed. Interestingly, some of the same members of the "Merchants of Death" were brought up on charges 20 years later. In 1917, under President Woodrow Wilson, the U.S. Congress passed the *Trading With the Enemy Act*. The objective was to stop any American from trading with our enemies and the allies of our enemies during World War I. For now, all was well in the world of Bush, until Prescott brought embarrassment and shame to the family. Samuel Bush's wartime relationship to these businessmen would continue after the war and would especially aid Prescott's career in service to the Harrimans.

Prescott's Big Military Lie

Not one to be left out of his chance at glory and valor, Prescott did his honorable duty and joined the United States Army, and in June 1918, went to Europe with his unit. At the same time, Samuel Bush, Prescott's father, took over responsibility for relations of the government with the private arms producers. On August 8, 1918 an article appeared on the front page of the *Ohio State Journal*, Bush's home town newspaper, under the heading of "3 High Military Honors Conferred on Capt. Bush." The article went on to describe how Prescott had received the Distinguished Service Cross, the Cross of the Legion of Honor, and the Victoria Cross. The story then described how Prescott had been standing near three Allied leaders, General Ferdinand Foch, Sir Douglas Haig, and General John J. "Black Jack" Pershing, when a shell fired from an enemy position was coming right at them. Quickly drawing his bolo knife, he stuck it up in the air as if it were a ball bat and the shell glanced off of the knife causing it to change direction enough to save all of those who were in the sure path of death just moments before. Quite a story! The problem is that it was nothing more than a story: false from beginning to end. In fact, Bush did not see any action until September. The following month a letter, written by Prescott's mother Flora (Mrs. Samuel Bush), apologized for the false information written "in the spirit of fun."[113]

> Editor State Journal: A cable received from my son, Prescott S. Bush, brings word that he has not been decorated, as published in the papers a month ago. He feels dreadfully troubled that a letter, written in a spirit of fun, should have been misrepresented. He is no hero and asks me to make explanations. I will appreciate your kindness in publishing this letter . . . Flora Sheldon Bush, Columbus, Ohio.[114]

The news media, after laying so much honor and praise upon Captain Bush, responded with a fury of articles, cartoons, and editorial opinions against the lying Bush. How dare he try and glorify himself when others had given their lives in service to their country? This caused Prescott a considerable amount of humiliation when he returned to Columbus, in mid-1919.

Apparently the humiliation was so intense that he could no longer live there, and looking for some small measure of support, went to the 1919 Skull and Bones Society reunion in New Haven, Connecticut. Skull and Bones patriarch Wallace Simmons, closely tied to the arms manufacturers, offered Prescott a job in his St. Louis railroad equipment company. The humiliated Bush accepted the offer and moved to St. Louis, and as some have said, his destiny.[115]

CHAPTER 11

AN INDIFFERENCE TO ETHICS

I never heard him fart.

–Johnny Bush, the third son of Prescott Bush[x]

Harriman, Walker, and Thyssen

In 1919, Averell Harriman, son of railroad tycoon E. H. Harriman, persuaded his friend George Herbert "Bert" Walker to become president of a new Wall Street investment banking firm, W. H. Harriman and Company. With Walker as president and chief executive, Averell Harriman as chairman and controlling co-owner with his brother Roland, Percy Rockefeller was director and founding financial sponsor. Along with the help and cooperation of the Rockefeller-headed National City Bank, and the Morgan-connected Guaranty Trust, George Herbert Walker slipped easily into his new position. A deal was struck where Walker would support Averell's plans, which included participation in Germany's once prosperous Hamburg-Amerika steamship line, and oil and manganese interests in the Russian Caucasus. Moving to New York, Walker helped run W. A. Harriman and Company, but also family investment vehicles such as Harriman 15 Corporation, the Silesia-American Corporation, and Harriman International.[116]

Going back just a bit to 1904, Walker and his father had built a summer house on a lovely parcel of land in Kennebunkport, Maine. The stretch of land became known as Walker's Point. In 1901, Walker's eldest and favorite child, Dorothy, was born there. By 1919, Dorothy had been living in St. Louis where she met the very charming Prescott Bush. George Walker took Prescott under his wing, so to speak, and seemed to warm to the idea of a Bush in the Walker house. The Bushes were by no means as wealthy as the Walkers, but they were definitely the right sort of "American Royalty" type and seemed to be moving in the right direction. With his background at Yale, his membership in Skull and Bones, and his history, if only on the sidelines of the Walker, Bush, Harriman network, Prescott was deemed a good catch for Dorothy. In 1921, Prescott and Dorothy were married, cementing one of American history's crucial family ties.

These were exciting times for Prescott, with the exception of one terrible tragedy; his mother, Flora was killed in a car crash in 1920. Sadly, she would not see her "war hero" son climb the ladder of power and fortune. Perhaps she was better off. The Bush Walker marriage was more than a doubling of powerful families; it was the creation of the next generation of Bush criminals. The Bush seed, like an infection or a virus, would grow stronger than the previous generation, masking themselves as serving for the betterment of humanity, while they plotted to enrich themselves on huge profits made from the misery and suffering that came from the wars they fueled. Each future generation, nourished by the blood of those less fortunate, drew from an ever deepening well of sociopathic behavior.

Walker and several of his cronies had an interest in horse breeding. (It had most certainly crossed Walker's mind that breeding Prescott with his own Dorothy would prove to be a winning combination for offspring.) The idea of breeding only the strongest male would lead to a much more dangerous idea with humans replacing horses as breeding material. During the 1904 St. Louis World's Fair, which by the way was organized and funded by Walker, Brookings, and Missouri governor David Francis, they featured a "human zoo": live natives from backward jungle regions. These poor souls lived and were shown in cages under the supervision of an anthropologist, William J. McGee.[117]

To the elite bankers and financiers, these jungle people were less than human. No doubt the early seeds of eugenics had already started forming in the minds of these "superior" men. We'll be looking into the eugenics movement and its relationship to the Harrimans and Bushes a bit later.

Happily married, Prescott's career seemed to be at a standstill. True, he had married the daughter of one of America's wealthiest and well-connected financiers. But Prescott was only a minor executive of the Simmons Co., a railroad equipment supplier. In a short time, the couple moved back to Ohio where he worked at his father Samuel's rubber products company. They moved again, to Milton, Massachusetts, and it was here, on June 12, 1924, that Prescott and Dorothy had their first child, a son, whom they named George Herbert Walker Bush. Through the kindness of Roland Harriman, Prescott was brought in to the Harriman-controlled U.S. Rubber Company, in New York City. He moved again, this time to Greenwich, Connecticut, not far from New York and New Haven/Yale. Finally on May 1, 1926, Prescott joined W. A. Harriman & Co., as its vice president under Herbert Walker, his father-in-law and president of the company.[118] Prescott Bush certainly owed a great deal to the Walkers and the Harrimans.

While Prescott's career was taking shape, Samuel Bush maintained his position as president of Buckeye Steel until 1927. He was also the first president of the Ohio Manufacturers Association, and co-founder of the Scioto Country Club and Columbus Academy. Samuel served on the board of the Federal Reserve Bank of Cleveland and the Huntington National Bank of Columbus.[119]

With Prescott firmly in the family, the first order of business was to orchestrate a means whereby the Harriman firm could get a financial hold in Germany. Germany of course lost World War I, but that didn't mean they were useless to certain American interests. Those interests just happened to already control most of the Hamburg-Amerika commercial steamships. The ships had become the property of Harriman and Company at the end of the war, and Harriman brokered a deal that would put those ships back into service for a huge profit. In addition, the Harrimans would have the right to participate in 50 percent of all business originated in Hamburg, and for the following 20 years, the Harrimans had almost complete control of the German-based steamship line.[120]

The specifics of the deal were never made public. The deal was however reported in glowing terms in the *St. Louis Globe Democrat* on August 7, 1921. The story celebrated the merger of two big financial institutions in New York: the firm of Harriman and Co. and Morton and Company, a private bank. George Walker had positioned himself as founder and president of Harriman and Co, and he was prominent in the affairs of the Morton bank, which was connected to the J. P. Morgan controlled Guaranty Trust Company. With that merger in place, W. A. Harriman and Co. opened its European head-quarters in Berlin. As was their practice, Walker and Harriman sought and conducted business not only with Germany, but with Russia as well. Russia had been devastated by the Bolshevik Revolution and the Harriman crew stepped in to help them rebuild their oil industry. In addition, they contract-ed to mine manganese, essential in steelmaking production of the day. Some of these contracts were negotiated directly with Leon Trotsky, famed Marxist theorist, Russian politician, and founder of the Red Army. Trotsky was one of the seven origi-nal founders of the Politburo and eventually rose to a place of power second only to Josef Stalin. This was not to last as Trotsky veered away from the ever-increasing bureaucracy until he was expelled and later assassinated. When Trotsky fell out of favor with Stalin, the Harriman's Russian negotia-tor taking Trotsky's place was Feliks Dzerzhinsky, founder of the Russian secret police.[121]

The practice of American investment in both Germany and Russia was not without its problems. Harriman, Walker, Bush, and the Dulles brothers were criticized and accused of reckless lending and even aiding previous or potential enemies. (The Dulles brothers, John and Allen, were American diplomats and lawyers and worked at Sullivan and Cromwell, a New York firm where brother John was a partner. In 1927 Allen be-came director of the Council on Foreign Relations. In the 1920s and 1930s, he served as legal advisor to the delegation on arms limitation at the League of Nations, where he met with Adolph Hitler, and Benito Mussolini among others). Ignoring this potential liability of international trade, the Harrimans continued with investments on a scale unknown thus far. They set up a bank in New York to serve the Germans' Thyssen steel interests, purchased one-third interest in the principally

German-owned coal and zinc mines in Poland, and took a position in Germany's transatlantic cable company. Often these associations were cloaked behind smaller Harriman-controlled companies such as the Silesian-American Corporation, which handled the Poland coal and zinc purchase.[122]

This period proved advantageous for Prescott. He had taken over management of the gigantic personal investment funds of Averell and Roland Harriman. This was the beginning of the Bush family fortune. The real Bush fortune would be made from an international project that would bring both fortune and trouble for Prescott Bush.[123]

All the players were falling into place for an international power that would shape American foreign policy, influence world events, and at the same time, result in huge profits for the men at the top. It must have seemed like a dream come true for these giants of industry. They had created the genesis of the "shadow government" long before anyone had a name for it. One has to realize that America during this period was largely an isolationist country, not overtly wanting interaction with foreign powers. Even as World War I raged across Europe, there were mass demonstrations against joining the war. This was the perfect window to make deals and make money, big money. Harriman, Bush, Walker, and the Dulles brothers were not only building, step-by-step, an international entity capable of influence on a world scale, but they were creating what would later morph into the beginnings of the intelligence community. As you will see, some of the members of this elite banking community later became members of OSS, the Office of Strategic Service, forerunner of the Central Intelligence Agency. As a matter of fact, many of the early OSS members were Yale men, and members of Skull and Bones. Corporations and attorneys who represented international businesses often employed associates in their firms as private agents to gather data on competitors and business opportunities abroad.[124]

The connection between banking and espionage would establish itself and continue to this very day, shaping foreign policy, funding secret wars, and involving some of the biggest criminal fraud cases in American history.

Between 1929 and 1931 the crash of securities values nearly wiped out the small fortune Prescott had gained since 1926, but due to his unwavering support and devotion to the Harrimans, they staked him to what he had lost and put him back on his feet.[125]

It also set the tone for certain American industrialists to entertain the idea that America would be better off with a different form of government. 1931 started off with one of the most important mergers in American history. On January 1, 1931, Harriman Brothers & Co. and W. A. Harriman & Co. merged with one of the oldest investment houses in America, Brown Brothers and Company.

Prominence at Brown Brothers

Established in 1825 on Pine Street in New York, and moving in 1833 to Wall Street,[126] Brown Brothers were at the top of the food chain. Merging with the two Harriman companies, the new Brown Brothers Harriman & Company would become the oldest and largest private bank in the United States. An article in *Time* magazine's December 22, 1930 issue proclaimed that 11 out of 16 BB&H partners were Yale graduates, [127] and of those, eight were Skull and Bones members.[128]

Prescott Bush and Thatcher M. Brown became the new firm's senior partners. The Brown Brothers' British branch had fueled the American slave trade back in the 1860s during the

Civil War, by carrying southern slave cotton from the American South to British mill owners. In fact, as much as 75 percent of slave cotton was carried on Brown Brothers ships.[129]

Brown Bros. also had their share of criticism from America's press. On June 7, 1922, the *Nation* published an editorial titled "The Republic of Brown Brothers." The op-ed attacked the "new imperialism" of the United States in Central America and the Caribbean and called it "dollar diplomacy." The editorial went on to say that over the past dozen years, the American government had reduced Haiti, Santo Domingo (later the Dominican Republic), and Nicaragua, "to the status of colonies with at most a degree of rather fictitious self-government." The United States had "forced ruinous loans, making 'free and sovereign' republics the creatures of New York banks." In effect, the U.S. government had been "agents for these bankers, using American Marines when necessary to impose their will." The Brown Bros. argued that it was the other way around; they, were doing the bidding of the American government.[130]

In any event, regardless of public sentiment, Brown Brothers Harriman & Co. would continue their business expansions in whatever direction they pleased. It's important to understand that this tradition of the Bush family and their obvious indifference to ethical business practices started long ago. When one combines political power with corporate power on a large scale, and especially when generations of that type of criminal behavior have gone unpunished, there is little reason to change. In fact, as each generation provides a new layer of international and domestic criminal activity, the acts become more audacious, more sociopathic, and devoid of guilt or responsibility. The point here is that to these people (Bush, Harriman et al.) crime *does* pay.

By 1933, it was more than obvious that Germany, although forbidden by the Treaty of Versailles, signed in 1919, was gearing up and arming themselves for another attempt at military aggression. This time, they would have even more support from American businesses. It would make American investments for the First World War look like pennies. This time would be big. This time American bankers would invest heavily on numerous fronts to support the German machine. Germany was ready to make a move. They would need money and a lot of it. They would need armaments, pig iron, universal plate, galvanized sheet, wire, explosives, pipes and tubes, and they would need American bankers to set up a series of banks, corporations, and industrial firms to supply and arm the German war machine. Brown Brothers Harriman and Prescott Bush were ready and able to finance and support Germany in this second attempt at war. There was one more thing the Germans had that they didn't have last time: Adolph Hitler.

Merchant of Death

As events progressed, certain rumblings could be heard in the nation's capital. Those financiers and industrialists who rendered support to Germany and Russia in the First World War were under scrutiny. On the morning following Labor Day in 1934, hundreds of people had gathered in the Caucus Room of the Senate Office Building to witness the opening of an investigation that many were calling "historic." Officially known as the Special Committee on Investigation of the Munitions Industry, it was commonly referred to as the Senate Munitions Committee. Now, years later it is mostly remembered as the Nye Committee, after the name of its lead investigator, 42-year-old North Dakota senator Gerald P. Nye. The Nye Committee came about after widespread reports that manufacturers of armaments had unduly influenced the American decision to enter the war in 1917. These weapons' suppliers had reaped enormous profits at the cost of more than 53,000 American battle deaths. As local conflicts reignited in Europe through the early 1930s, suggesting the possibility of a second world war, concern spread that these "merchants of death" would again drag the United States into a struggle that was none of its business. The time had come for a full congressional inquiry.

Over the next 18 months, the "Nye Committee" held 93 hearings, questioning more than 200 witnesses, including J. P. Morgan, Jr., and Pierre du Pont. Committee members found little hard evidence of an active conspiracy among arms makers, yet the panel's reports did little to weaken the popular prejudice against "greedy munitions interests."[131]

As a leading manufacturer of arms and munitions via Remington Arms, Samuel Bush, Prescott's father, was attacked by the committee, and along with others, he would be forever labeled as one of the Merchants of Death for his role in supplying arms to 75 percent of the World War I combatants on both sides. Prescott could not possibly have missed the similarity in how his father was being portrayed at the very moment of his own activities as a Merchant of Death. The importance of this cannot be overstated. Here we have Samuel Bush, the grand architect of the Bush family, publicly being dragged before the United States Senate and accused of what amounts to Trading With the Enemy war crimes, and at the very same time, Prescott Bush, without regard for the consequences, engaging in the very same acts of treason. The point here is that a complete and utter disrespect for the laws of this great nation had been handed down from father to son. The criminal conspiracy to profit from war would continue.

Skull and Bones Finances German Rebuild

Hitler became absolute ruler of Germany in 1933. Prescott Bush would become deeply involved in what has become known as "The Hitler Project." He would do this with the help of several key persons: Fritz Thyssen, Friedrich Flick, George Walker, Averell Harriman, Barons Kurt and Rudolph Schroeder, and Allen and John Dulles. Germany had always held a special place for many of the gentlemen mentioned above. It certainly held an almost mythical significance for those of the Skull and Bones Society of Yale. To understand that, we have to go back, back before World War I, before the Civil War, to 1823 when Samuel Russell, a child of the Wall Street banking establishment, founded "Russell & Company," the largest opium smuggling operation in the world. From 1831 to 1832, William Russell, cousin of Samuel, went to Germany to study at Berlin. At the time Berlin was the center for a new way of thinking called the "scientific method." This ideology stressed the state over the person. Basically the ideology taught that true freedom could only be found by serving the state with total obedience. "The state has supreme right against the individual whose supreme duty is to be a member of the state."

When Russell enrolled at the University of Berlin, he became a member of a secret order called the Order of Skull and Bones, which embraced and incorporated these very ideas. Before he returned to the United States, he sought and obtained permission to form an American chapter of the secret German Order of Skull and Bones: chapter 322, The Brotherhood of Death. When he returned to Yale in 1832 he, along with his close friend Alphonso Taft (father of future president William Taft), and thirteen other privileged children of Wall Street elite, founded the American branch of the Order. For many years members made a pilgrimage to Berlin and the university where the German Skull and Bones originated.[132]

So it comes as no surprise that these gentlemen, many of them from Skull and Bones, felt it was their duty as Bonesmen to finance the German state. They believed that if sufficiently supported, and if Hitler went to war, there would be a good chance for an alliance with Hitler and the promise of a Hitler-aligned government in the United States. Hitler, of course, subscribed to the "scientific method" and all good Germans swore their lives to their divine "fuehrer."

Prescott's Dealings with Hitler's Main Financier

When we examine the men listed above (Thyssen, Flick, Walker, Harriman, Dulles, etc.) and how, along with Prescott Bush, they helped finance Hitler's reign of power and death, we must start with Fritz Thyssen. Thyssen was rumored to be a member of the secret German Skull and Bones Order or possibly the Illuminati of Bavaria, another secret order. In any event, in 1924, Thyssen was introduced to Hitler by Rudolph Hess, his friend, and after hearing him speak, was mesmerized by him. He saw Hitler as Germany's savior and began to finance the Nazi Party.[133]

Thyssen came from a wealthy industrialist family already producing steel. His father was August Thyssen, and during World War I, the Thyssen Company employed 50,000 workers and produced 1,000,000 tons of steel and iron a year. In 1926 Thyssen's father died and Fritz inherited the family fortune. In 1928, he formed United Steelworks, controlling more than 75 percent of Germany's ore reserves and employing 200,000 people. Averell Harriman visited Thyssen in Berlin in 1922, setting up the Union Banking Corporation in 1924 in New York to handle Thyssen's banking interests in America through a

Dutch bank (Bank voor Handel en Scheepvaart) controlled by Thyssen. By putting up $400,000, the Harriman organization would be joint owner and manager of Thyssen's banking operations outside of Germany. The Union Banking Corp. and the Dutch Thyssen bank acted as Nazi fronts and served to launder funds for Thyssen and the Nazis, money that could be used to buy guns, arms, favorable publicity, and dozens of U.S. senators, congressmen, and newspaper editors.[134]

In 1926 when Prescott became vice president of W. A. Harriman & Co., Clarence Dillon, of Wall Street's Dillon Read Co., an old friend of Prescott's father Samuel Bush, organized the German Steel Trust, the largest industrial corporation in Germany. Fritz Thyssen was president of German Steel Trust and partnered with Prescott Bush's Union Banking Corporation. In return for putting up $70 million to create German Steel Trust, Thyssen gave the Dillon Read Company two or more representatives on the board of German Steel Trust.[135]

Fritz Thyssen became Hitler's main financier and used his associations at Brown Brothers Harriman, Union Banking Corp., and the Harriman 15 Corp. to finance Hitler's war machine. In 1929 American investors were concerned that the demands by France on German war reparations were eating into their profits, and so called a meeting to decide what could be done. In attendance were members of the Federal Reserve bank, and leading American bankers from Guaranty Trust Company, Rockefeller, and a member of the Royal Dutch Shell. The consensus was that the only way to free Germany from French financial clutches was through revolution, either Communist or German National. Rockefeller argued that money should go to Hitler. In due course, $10 million was transferred to the Nazis. For Hitler this was not quite enough and soon he requested an additional $500 million. Rockefeller's reply was that this amount was out of the question and would shatter the financial market. After additional negotiations, another $15 million was sent from American banking and oil interests. Another payment of $7 million was paid in 1933.[136]

By the mid to late 1920s, George Herbert Walker and Averell Harriman's firms had sold an incredible $50 million worth of German bonds to American investors. Germany was a hot investment. Thyssen enlisted the partnership of Friedrich Flick, another wealthy German industrialist with coal and steel industries throughout Germany and Poland. One of the reasons for the merger was suppressing the new labor and socialist movement. Part of the massive steel conglomerate was the Consolidated Silesian Steel Corporation and the Upper Silesian Coal and Steel company located in the Silesian section of Poland. Thyssen and Flick paid Bush and Walker generously to manage that part of the corporation and according to fellow business associates, the four men and their rapid success astonished the business world. Once again Hitler was in need of funding, this time to purchase and remodel the enormous Barlow Palace. Hitler envisioned this to be the new Nazi National Headquarters. Thyssen shelled out the equivalent of $2 million for purchasing and remodeling the building.

Back in New York, Harriman and Bush organized a holding company called Harriman 15 Corporation and with it came one-third ownership of stock in Consolidated Silesian Steel Company. The other two-thirds were owned by Thyssen's friend and partner Friedrich Flick. When in 1934 Hitler came to power, he contracted Thyssen and United Steel Works to upgrade Germany's military machine. Thyssen and Flick's profits soared into the hundreds of millions and Thyssen's Dutch bank and Bush's Union Banking Corporation of New York were overflowing with money.

With things going so well for Union Banking Corp., it was a bit of a shock when Prescott showed Harriman an article in the *New York Times* about how the Polish government was applying to take over Consolidated Silesian Steel Corp. and Upper Silesian Coal and Steel Company from German and American interests. Roughly 45 percent of Poland's steel and coal production came from those two companies. The Polish government accused the Americans and Germans of gross mismanagement, excessive borrowing, fictitious bookkeeping, and gambling in securities. Eventually Bush and Harriman hired John Foster Dulles to cover up any improprieties that might arise under investigative scrutiny.[137]

Bush Profits from Auschwitz

When Hitler invaded Poland, any fears that Prescott or Averell may have had about losing their Polish steel and coal operations vanished like the Jews, Communists, and Gypsies being transported to the brand new concentration camp near the Polish town of Oswiecim. The camp was called Auschwitz. Prisoners at Auschwitz who were able to work were shipped to other companies who benefited from the slave labor work force. One of those companies was the Consolidated Silesian Steel Corporation.

The reason Auschwitz was built there was the rich coal deposits, which could be turned into either coal or additives for aviation gasoline. Harriman/Bush until that time had only one-third interest, but soon Thyssen/Flick wanted out and Bush/Harriman agreed to buy their shares, giving them complete ownership of a forced labor steel camp. They quickly changed the name to Silesian American Corporation, which became part of Union Banking Corporation and Harriman 15 Corporation. According to a Dutch intelligence agent, Prescott Bush managed a portion of the slave labor force from Auschwitz. Slave labor had become a critical part of the Nazi war machine, and the coal produced at Silesian allowed the Nazis to continue fueling their sweep across Europe. Prescott was an active participant in the murder of innocent men, women, and children in his slave labor camp, as these souls were literally worked to death. With free labor, his profits must have been substantial.[138]

When the Japanese attacked Pearl Harbor on December 7, 1941 and we were officially at war with Japan and thereby with Germany, President Franklin D. Roosevelt, Secretary of the Treasury Henry Morgenthau, and U.S. Attorney General Francis Biddle signed an amendment to the Trading With the Enemy Act of 1917 banning Americans from doing business with enemies, and those supporting the enemies of the United States. Prescott Bush must have thought that the law did not apply to him. He was, after all, Prescott Bush, son of Samuel Bush and one of New York banking elite's most powerful members. And yes, he was Skull and Bones. As we have seen, the majority of employees of the vast Harriman/ Brown/ Union Banking firms were members of the Skull and Bones Society, and as such we must consider the political and sociological kinship between these Yale men and the repressive regimes they financed. It is of interest that Samuel Bush was never punished, other than public humiliation, for his acts of treason during World War I. So it really comes as no surprise that Prescott Bush ignored the Trading With the Enemy Act and continued, with fervor, his criminal and treasonous acts.

The actual instances of criminal acts of treason against the United States that Prescott Bush can be linked to with verifiable facts are many. Whether through W. A. Harriman & Company, Brown Brothers Harriman & Co., Union Banking Corporation, the Harriman 15 Holding Company, the Guaranty Trust Company, the Hamburg-Amerika Line, the Holland America Trading Company, the Seamless Steel Equipment Company, or the Silesian-American Corporation, the trail of Prescott Bush is glaringly evident. In addition to these corporations, Prescott maintained long-standing relationships with men who not only had aligned themselves with the Nazi movement as sympathizers and supporters, but were actual Nazis.

CHAPTER 12

RUSSIANS AND NAZIS MAKE STRANGE BEDFELLOWS

This was the mechanism by which Hitler was funded to come to power, this was the mechanism by which the Third Reich's defense industry was re-armed, this was the mechanism by which Nazi profits were repatriated back to the American owners, this was the mechanism by which investigations into the financial laundering of the Third Reich were blunted.

—former US attorney John Loftus on the purchase of Nazi stocks by Prescott Bush[xi]

When the Bolshevik Revolution took control of Russia, an important component was the Baku oil fields. Yet through mismanagement and political chaos, the oil fields all but ceased production in 1921 and 1922. The chairman of the Soviet Oil Production Trust, or Azneft, put forward a program for its recovery. The program required equipment and technology not yet available in Russia. In an article published in *Pravda* (the Russian national newspaper) on September 21, 1922, Chairman Serbrovsky states: "But just here American capital is

going to support us. The American firm International Barnsdall Corporation has submitted a plan . . . Lack of equipment
prevents us from increasing the production of the oil industry of Baku by ourselves. The American firm . . . will provide
the equipment, start drilling in the oil fields and organize the
technical production with deep pumps.[139] The International
Barnsdall Corp. signed the contracts October 1922 and twice
in September 1922, despite the fact that Federal Authorities
prohibited trading in Russian credits in the United States."[140]

How is all of this connected to Prescott Bush? Because
the Guaranty Trust Company and the W. A. Harriman & Co.
owned the Barnsdall Corporation, which owned 75 percent
of the International Barnsdall Corporation. Although Prescott
was not brought into the Harriman firm until 1926, it shows a
pre -established pattern of business that Prescott adhered to
and aligned with.[141]

Another pre–Prescott Bush corporation which acted crimi-
nally was the Georgian Manganese Company, formed by W. A.
Harriman and Mathew C. Brush, one of the directors on the
board at Harriman & Co., and incidentally one of the only non–
Skull and Bones men on the Harriman board. In 1925, an agreement was made with the Russians for Georgian Manganese
Co. to provide loans and foreign exchange for the purpose of
exploitation of the Chiaturi manganese deposits and the introduction of modern mining and transportation methods. Four
million dollars was spent to bring these important upgrades
to the antiquated Russian mining machinery. It is important to know that both the Barnsdall Corp. and the Georgian
Manganese Corp. were in direct violation of the official 1920
State Department policy towards Russia. This policy prevented the extension of credit towards Russia and permitted only
pre-approved trading. Since neither the activities of Barnsdall

or Georgian were pre-approved, the two Harriman-controlled companies were committing illegal and treasonous acts.[142]

An overview of American banks doing business with Russia at a time when it was illegal under U.S. law shows that Harriman et al. were not the only ones violating statutes. For the sake of thoroughness, National City Bank, Chase National Bank, Kuhn, Loeb and Company, and the Mechanics and Metals National Bank all conducted illegal business with Russia during and after the Bolshevik Revolution. None of those banks were staffed by members of Yale's Skull and Bones Society. Industrial corporations guilty of "trading with the enemy" were numerous as well. Daniel Williard of Baltimore & Ohio Railroad, Westinghouse Air Brake Company, General Electric, Henry Ford, and the Vacuum Oil Company were some of those who supported the Russians. Few if any Bonesmen were involved with these companies.[143]

But the Skull and Bones Society acted as a resource for the Harriman family of banks. Yale members who were chosen for Skull and Bones were groomed for service to a select "family" of banks, and as good Bonesmen were expected to carry out the furtherance of banking policy as set forth by generations before them. Prescott Bush applied himself in this very manner. Certainly we are not suggesting that Prescott was in any way better or worse than other Bonesmen in similar positions, the difference being that Prescott Bush just happened to father a president of the United States (George H. W. Bush), who in turn fathered another president of the United States (George W. Bush) and perhaps two (Jeb Bush).

These aren't just some top industrialists of our country; they are the "leaders of the free world" and as such should be held to a higher standing than everyone else. In modern times we can reflect on Hillary Clinton as secretary of state having to

uphold maximum transparency with regard to foreign investments, so that there could be not even a question of impropri-
ety. Instead, in examining the history of the Bush family we
see quite the opposite: corruption, fraud, rampant theft, lying,
and an addiction to secrecy that is unparalleled in the annals
of American political history. With the exception of the Mafia,
there is no other equal.

Bush Charged with Funding Nazis

In October 1942 the federal government charged Prescott Bush
with running Nazi front groups in the United States. President Franklin D. Roosevelt's alien property custodian, Leo T.
Crowley, signed Vesting Order Number 248 seizing the property of Prescott Bush. Under the Trading With the Enemy Act,
all the shares of the Union Banking Corporation (UBC) were
seized. All of UBC's shares were owned by Prescott Bush, Roland Harriman, and three Nazi executives: Cornelis Lievense,
H. J. Kouwenhoven, and Johann G. Groeninger. The Union
Banking Corp. was an affiliate of Brown Brothers Harriman
where Prescott Bush, Averell, and Roland Harriman were
partners. Once the investigators had access to UBC records,
the Nazi connections and fronts became evident. Over the next
few days, subsidiaries of UBC Holland American Trading Corporation and the Seamless Steel Equipment Corporation were
also seized. Not long after those seizures, the government
went after the Harriman 15 Holding Co., the Hamburg-Amerika Line, and the Silesia-American Corporation. The government's findings stated that huge sections of the UBC empire
was operated on behalf of Nazi Germany and had greatly assisted the German war effort and the rise of Adolph Hitler.[144]

At the time of seizure, the UBC was holding $3 million
for Fritz Thyssen. In fact, the *New York Herald Tribune*, on July

31, 1941 ran a front page article titled, "Thyssen Has $3 million Cash In New York Vaults: Union Banking Corporation May Hide Nest Egg for High Nazis He Once Backed" by J. M. Racusin. The relationship between Thyssen and UBC dates back to its creation in 1924 for the purpose of transferring funds between the United States and Germany via the Dutch Bank voor Handel en Scheepvaart (BHS). It is interesting to note that of the six directors of UBC, three were Skull and Bonesmen (Prescott Bush and Averell and Roland Harriman) and three were members of the German Nazi Party (H. J. Kouwenhoven, Cornelis Lievense, and Johann Groeninger). In addition it was found that UBC was an interlocking component of the German Steel Trust, owned by Fritz Thyssen and Friedrich Flick. Investigators found that 50.8 percent of Nazi Germany's pig iron was produced under the UBC and German Steel Trust concern, as well as 41.4 percent of Nazi universal plate, 36 percent of Nazi heavy plate, 45.5 percent of Nazi pipes and tubes, 22.1 percent of Nazi wire, 35 percent of Nazi explosives, and 38.5 percent of Nazi galvanized sheet."[145]

At the Nuremberg War Crimes Tribunal, the United States government said that Flick was "one of the leading financiers and industrialists who from 1932 contributed large sums to the Nazi party and to the S.S."[146]

The S.S. were also known as the Black Shirts. They were Hitler's private army and the ones who ran the death camps all across Europe. Flick was sentenced to seven years in prison for his role in supporting the Nazis. The connection between Thyssen and Bush/Harriman as well as the connection between Prescott Bush and the Silesian-American Corp. has been thoroughly examined in preceding pages.

As we have seen earlier, George Herbert Walker took control of the Hamburg-Amerika Line in 1920, when he was president of W. A. Harriman and Co. Walker then organized the American Ship and Commerce Corp. to have control over Hamburg-Amerika's affairs.[147] The Bush/Harriman shares in American Ship and Commerce Corp. were held by the Harriman 15 Corp., which was run by Prescott Bush and George Herbert Walker.[148]

The Hamburg-Amerika Line was used to ship American weapons to Germany. A key figure in these activities was Samuel Pryor, founding director of both UBC and the American Ship and Commerce Corp. Pryor was also the executive chairman of Remington Arms.[149] Interestingly a U.S. Senate investigation on arms trafficking began after Remington contracted to supply the German firm I.G. Farben with explosives. The senators found that, "German political associations, like the Nazis, are nearly all armed with American . . . guns . . . Arms of all kinds coming from America are transshipped . . . to river barges before the vessels arrive in Antwerp. They then can be carried through Holland without police inspection or interference. The Hitlerists and Communists are presumed to get arms in this manner. The principal arms coming from America are Thompson submachine guns and revolvers. The number is great."[150]

Under official Nazi supervision, the Hamburg-Amerika Line and the North German Lloyd Company merged on September 5, 1933. On November 4, 1933 Prescott Bush chose Christian J. Beck to be manager of freight and operations in North America for the new joint Nazi shipping lines.[151]

Bush Earned $1.5 Million from Nazi Stock

With all these facts, verifiable beyond question, the only conclusion that can be drawn is that Prescott Bush through his association with the larger Harriman banking group, which includes UBC, Harriman 15, and other companies, was guilty of treasonous and criminal acts under the Trading With the Enemy Act as set forth by the United States government. Who says crime doesn't pay? In 1943 Prescott resigned from UBC, although he retained his stock in the company. With the UBC assets frozen (since 1942) anyway, this was not as righteous a move as it may have seemed. As with his father Samuel before him, there were no criminal charges levied at Prescott. Fritz Thyssen wasn't so protected. By 1948 he had been jailed by the Nazis and jailed by the Americans as well as interrogated. Thyssen and Flick were ordered to pay reparations for their crimes against humanity. In February 1951, Thyssen died in Argentina at the age of 78. When he died, the U.S. alien property custodian released the assets of Union Banking Corporation to Brown Brothers Harriman. Prescott Bush received $1.5 million for his share of UBC. How could a man so obviously guilty of treason be awarded such a huge sum of money, blood money? That money enabled Prescott to fund his run for the Senate, as well as help his son, George Herbert Walker, to set up his first royalty firm, Overby Development Company, that same year.[152]

The magnitude of these crimes, gone unpunished, reinforced the criminal behavior of Prescott's son and future president, George Herbert Walker Bush. Family traditions are an important part of the Bush clan, and acts of high treason and crimes had now become the family tradition.

Bush, Genocide, and Hitler

The government must put the most modern medical means in the service of this knowledge . . . those who are physically and mentally unhealthy and unworthy must not perpetuate their suffering in the body of their children . . . The prevention of the faculty and opportunity to procreate on the part of the physically degenerate and mentally sick, over a period of only 600 years, would . . . free humanity from an immeasurable misfortune.[153]

The per capita income gap between the developed and the developing countries is increasing, in large part the result of higher birth rates in the poorer countries . . . Famine in India, unwanted babies in the United States, poverty that seemed to form an unbreakable chain for millions of people-how should we tackle these problems? . . . It is quite clear that one of the major challenges of the 1970s . . . will be to curb the world's fertility.[154]

It's no accident that Hitler (whose words form the first quotation above) and George Bush (second quotation) would say just about the same things in their speeches regarding eugenics.

One of the more disturbing areas of Bush history is the American Eugenics Movement. Prescott was a believer and financier of the movement, which succeeded in the passage of sterilization laws in many states for anyone judged "unfit." These laws served as the basis of the Nuremberg Laws passed by the Nazis. Much of the Nazi eugenics research was funded, even during the war, with money from the Rockefeller Foundation and the Carnegie Foundation. The Harrimans were also major financial backers of the movement.[155]

As far back as 1910, Mary A. Harriman, Averell Harriman's mother, donated land, buildings, and $300,000 for the "Eugenics Record Office" at Cold Spring Harbor, New York. In fact the Eugenics offices are still there, now used by the Human Genome Project. On August 21–23, 1932, New York City hosted the Third International Federation on Eugenics, held at the American Museum of Natural History. One of the major topics was how to deal with the stubborn persistence of blacks and other allegedly "inferior" and "socially inadequate" groups in reproducing, expanding their numbers, and mixing with others. It was recommended that sterilization be used on a massive scale. It wasn't only racial purity the eugenics movement sought, but also the sterilization of the unfit, mentally inferior, sickly, execution of the insane, criminals, and the terminally ill. Mary A. Harriman's daughter, Mary, was responsible for the entertainment at this prestigious conference.[156]

Most Americans have heard the term "Master Race" and associate it with the Nazi belief that white, blond-haired, blue-eyed Aryans were the superior race and all others should be wiped out. It's true, this was the Nazis' vision; however it did not originate in Germany or from the Nazis. It was created in the United States, and cultivated in California, decades before Hitler came to power. In 1909, California became the third state to adopt eugenics laws. Eugenics practitioners forcibly sterilized some 60,000 Americans, barred the marriage of thousands, segregated thousands in "colonies,"and persecuted untold numbers in ways we are just learning. Elements of eugenics philosophy were enshrined as national policy by forced sterilization and segregation laws, as well as marriage restrictions, and were enacted in 27 states. The Harriman railroad fortune paid local charities such as the New York Bureau of Industries and Immigration to seek out Jewish, Italian, and other immigrants in New York and other crowded cities and subject them to deportation, confinement, or forced sterilization.

The goal was to eliminate Negroes, Asians, Indians, Hispanics, East Europeans, Jews, dark-haired hill folk, poor people, the mentally ill, criminals, and anyone who didn't fit the genetic lines drawn up by the pseudo scientists.[157]

In addition to giving some financial support for the eugenics movement, Prescott Bush was a friend and supporter of Margaret Sanger, founder of Planned Parenthood and firm advocate of forced sterilization. She coined a term for these misfortunates, calling them "human waste." Here are two quotes from her own book. "Stop our national habit of human waste" (*from Woman and the New Race,* by Margaret Sanger, 1920, Chapter 6). and "By all means, there should be no children when either mother or father suffers from such diseases as tuberculosis, gonorrhea, syphilis, cancer, epilepsy, insanity, drunkenness, and mental disorders. In the case of the mother, heart disease, kidney trouble and pelvic deformities are also a serious bar to childbearing. No more children should be born when the parents, though healthy themselves, find that their children are physically or mentally defective." (*Woman and the New Race,* 1920, Chapter 7).

There is no question that Margaret Sanger was a racist. Eugenics was the popular vehicle at the time for portraying widespread sterilization of "human waste" as a means of cleaning up the human species. In fact Prescott was the treasurer of Planned Parenthood Federation of America, Inc. In a fundraising letter drive called First Nationwide Planned Parenthood Campaign of 1947, Prescott Bush's name is clearly visible. Dated January 8, 1947, and signed by Sanger, the letter states: *"Friends and supporters of Planned Parenthood throughout the nation will be delighted to know of the plans for the first nationwide campaign which will begin February 10. This means the "coming of age" of our organization—made possible by the loyal interest and support of friends like you."*

She goes on to say, *"I believe, (the fundraising efforts) will not only mean obtaining sufficient funds but will mark the first major step in integrating Planned Parenthood in the health and welfare services of our country."*

Hitler himself wrote, "There is today, one state in which at least weak beginnings toward a better conception of immigration are noticeable. Of course, it is not our model German Republic, but the United States." He went on to say, "I have studied with great interest the laws of several American states concerning prevention of reproduction by people whose progeny would, in all probability, be of no value or be injurious to the racial stock."[158]

It's frightening to realize how seriously many influential Americans took such discussions of eugenics. In 1946, it was decided that a sterilization experiment should be conducted using school children. Under the guise of the Human Betterment League, the Sterilization League of America chose North Carolina as the state where this was to take place.

Already in place as a leading eugenics center was the Bowman-Gray Memorial Medical School in Winston-Salem. The experiment worked as follows. "All children enrolled in the school district of Winston-Salem, N.C. were given a special 'intelligence test.' Those children who scored below a certain arbitrary low mark (70 IQ) were then cut open and surgically sterilized."[159]

Not only was the American Eugenics Society headquartered at Yale University, but all parts of this movement had a busy home at Yale. The coercive psychiatry and sterilization advocates had made the Yale/New Haven Hospital and Yale Medical School their laboratories for hands on practice in brain surgery and psychological experimentation. And the Birth Control League was there, which had long trumpeted the need for eugenical births—fewer births for parents with inferior bloodlines.[160]

Prescott's association with the eugenics movement may have made him popular with wealthy, white industrialists;

however this wouldn't last. It would come back to haunt him and do some damage, although as usual, nothing that he wouldn't be able to ride out. He was a very charming man.

Prescott's father, Samuel, died at his home, Ealy Farms, in Blacklick, Ohio, on February 8, 1948. Prescott received an inheritance of $55,779 from Samuel's estate.[161]

Between 1948 and 1950, his old boss Averell Harriman was making moves. He had been sent by President Harry Truman to Europe to act as "ambassador at large." He was the non-military commander and administrator of the multi-billion dollar Marshall Plan, a plan to rebuild Europe after the devastation of World War II. The European countries would need to borrow huge sums of money and equipment from the U.S., loans which would take decades to pay off. The money was rolling in. Prescott was entering the political arena.

In 1947, he served as chairman of the Connecticut Republican State Finance Committee, and as delegate-at-large to the 1948 Republican National Convention.[162]

CHAPTER 13

POLITICIAN PRESCOTT AND (SOMETIMES) WILD ACCUSATIONS

One of the members of the group was reported to be none other than Prescott Bush.

—BBC report on a fascist group that plotted a coup against the Roosevelt White House[xii]

Continued Eugenics Concerns

In June of 1950, North Korea invaded South Korea and Harriman came back from Europe to serve as President Truman's advisor, to oversee national security affairs. 1950 was also an exciting year for Prescott: He ran against Connecticut's William Benton for a seat in the U.S. Senate. Following the untimely death of the previous senator, Prescott felt this was a golden opportunity to fill the vacated two-year term. Unfortunately, his association with eugenics would cost him the election. World War II had ended just a few years before and the horror of the holocaust and Hitler's race cleansing had turned the American public against the Eugenics Movement. Late in the 1950 senatorial campaign, Prescott was publicly exposed for being an activist and supporter of the fascist Eugenics Movement.

According to Jacob Weisberg of the *New York Times*, "Bush was running even with William Benton, the Democratic nominee. But on the Sunday before the election, the muckraking columnist Drew Pearson asserted on his radio show that Prescott was treasurer of the Birth Control League. In the days before Griswold v. Connecticut, birth control remained illegal in the majority-Catholic state. Prescott and wife Dorothy strongly denied the accusation and rather than tell the truth, they lied. While the family has long decried this as a smear, it was in fact a minor distortion—carefully orchestrated for maximum harm. Prescott was listed as treasurer on a letterhead for Planned Parenthood, a successor organization to the Birth Control League, which had closed up shop in 1942. Though he denied the charge, Prescott lost by 1,102 votes."[163]

In his foreword to a population control book, George H. W. Bush wrote about that 1950 election: "My own first awareness of birth control as a public policy issue came with a jolt in 1950, when my father was running for United States Senate in Connecticut. Drew Pearson, on the Sunday before Election Day, revealed that my father was involved with Planned Parenthood . . . Many political observers felt a sufficient number of voters were swayed by his alleged contacts with birth controllers to cost him the election."[164]

There were other issues that Prescott needed to address. According to his friend Connecticut House of Representatives member John Alsop, "he really didn't understand them [ordinary people] very well. He'd just never had been one." His son, Prescott Jr. confided, "My father . . . had been a little stiff and a little awkward in (that) campaign . . . he didn't quite relate to people as warmly as he could."

A rather amusing exchange during the campaign occurred when he campaigned in Democratic strongholds. Josephine

Evaristo shouted, "Now all of a sudden you're a lover of labor? I'm just talking about the members of my family that caddied for you. You never paid them on time, and you never gave them a tip. So since when now have you become a lover of labor?"

"I'm not a millionaire," Prescott replied, "I have a high earning power, but I never did have any capital."[165]

After his defeat, he waited until he could get revenge for the "smear" from the press. He would no longer leave the outcome of his political future to the whims of the public or a blistering press. In 1952, Connecticut's senior senator, James O'Brien McMahon, died at the age of 48. Coincidentally, McMahon had been the assistant U.S. attorney general in charge of the Criminal Division, from 1935 to 1939. McMahon had been privy to information about all the Nazi era crimes relating to the seizure of Union Bank assets and the Trading With the Enemy investigations. News of his Nazi ties would have been extremely embarrassing and politically destructive for Prescott Bush. Stopped temporarily by the 1950 Pearson revelation, he could not afford a second "smear" by anyone, including Senator McMahon. There is no proof, and no one has accused Prescott Bush of having anything to do with the death of McMahon, but the timing allowed Prescott to practically step into his now vacant Senate seat, without hardly any resistance. What a remarkable coincidence! The events of his decision to run are as follows.

In 1952, when Prescott was at his vacation home on Fishers Island, several members of a GOP delegation arrived and implored him to run again. Still stinging from his public humiliation and political loss, he told the men, "Listen fellows, I've had it. I'm not going around that state again with my hat in my hand." Prescott Jr. remembers the state chairman telling his father, "We'll do everything we can to make sure you win." The delegates assured Prescott that with Eisenhower as the nominee, the Republicans could sweep the state in '52. Prescott said he would give it some thought. As they left, Meade Alcorn, one of the delegates, was heard to say, "The stupid bastard can't lose this one unless, of course, he shits in his damn straw hat."[166]

And so Prescott ran in a special election for the suddenly vacant Senate seat of the dead James McMahon. The GOP delegates had predicted that Prescott would be a shoo-in, riding on Ike's coattails, and they were correct. Prescott now had a clear run until the next Senate election in 1956 (when McMahon's term would have ended), and Prescott could run again in that presidential election year, once again on Ike's coattails. During his senatorial career, Bush served as a member of the Senate Committee on Banking and Currency, the Senate Committee on Public Works, the Committee on Armed Services, a congressional Joint Economic Committee, and the Special Committee on Aging. Some may find it surprising that he supported a 1954 move to censure Wisconsin senator Joseph McCarthy. McCarthy, he felt, had been attacking the U.S. Army and the Eisenhower administration. Prescott thought he had gone too far. Bush said that McCarthy "has caused dangerous division among the American people because of his attitude and the attitude he encouraged among his followers: that there can be no honest differences of opinion with him. Either you must follow Senator McCarthy blindly, not daring to express any doubts or disagreements about any of his actions, or, in his eyes, you must be a Communist, a Communist sympathizer, or a fool who has been duped by the Communist line."[167]

He left a legacy as a moderate in the Northeast, supporting civil-rights legislation, larger immigration quotas, and higher taxes while opposing increasing senators' salaries. In his vision, either an independent income or a monastic lifestyle was required for elected officials. Prescott instilled the importance of trusting only your family, and this was never more true than in 1952. Averell Harriman, Prescott's longtime friend and business partner, had placed the name of his opponent for the Republican Senate seat, Abe Ribicoff, in nomination. This perceived betrayal from one of his closest friends perfectly illustrated his feeling that one can never fully trust anyone but family.

Supporting Nixon, and Propping Up His Son

The next presidential election year, 1960, Prescott would not have the advantage of running with an incumbent president, and so he retired from public office and returned to Brown Brothers Harriman.[168] Apparently, the rift between Harriman and Prescott was not an issue. Although publicly Prescott was no longer actively involved in politics, he wielded a lot of clout among members of both parties and was involved in securing future president Richard Nixon's early political career. According to Nixon's biography, it was Prescott Bush and the Orange County Republican Party that placed an ad in an L. A. newspaper to recruit someone willing to run against a Democratic congressman. Nixon answered the ad, won the congressional seat, and later was Prescott Bush's personal pick for vice president on the 1952 Republican ticket.

George Bush's father was the upright and tough Prescott Bush, a banker, internationalist, and golfing buddy of Dwight Eisenhower. ("A fine golfer," Ike said.) Prescott had first brought Nixon to the attention of his friend Tom Dewey, the "Dean" of the Eastern Establishment. Prescott had raised money on Wall Street for Nixon's 1946 campaign. Nixon's opponent Jerry Voorhis was a critic of big business and big banks.

Voorhis wanted to close the Federal Reserve. "Prescott Bush is one of the men who made Dick Nixon," political strategist Murray Chotiner told me (Stone). "Dewey looked at Nixon because of Bush's suggestion and after Nixon got the short list of 'acceptable' candidates for Ike's running mate. Prescott urged Ike to take Nixon on the ticket on a golf course in Greenwich, Connecticut. Nixon owed Bush."[169]

Although Prescott had retired from the political main stage, he still had a few tricks up his sleeve. In 1966 when son "Poppy" Bush arrived in Washington, DC in the House of Representatives, Prescott used his influence to get his son a seat on the House Ways and Means Committee. The powerful committee wrote all the tax legislation and was the gatekeeper against attempts to eliminate the oil depletion allowance. The oil depletion allowance greatly reduced taxes on income derived from the production of oil. In 1931 the giant East Texas oil fields were discovered and Texas oilmen fought vigorously to keep their oil depletion allowance.[170] (By the 1960s, it was estimated that the allowance had cost the American taxpayer an estimated $140 billion in lost revenue.)[171]

Young Poppy was a freshman congressman and no freshman since 1904 had ever gotten a seat on such an important committee. Not only had Prescott personally called the committee chairman, he had gotten Gerald Ford to make the request himself.[172]

In doing this, Prescott had positioned Poppy where he could provide Nixon with financial support from the Texas oil cabal. It was Prescott's understanding that if Nixon won the Republican nomination, he would then show his gratitude by selecting the young Bush as his vice presidential running mate. To this end, Prescott worked furiously to align support for his son. Within days, some of the most influential members of the Republican Party sent letters to Nixon urging him to choose Poppy as his running mate.

Nixon must have been impressed as he read the names on the letters: the CEOs of Chase Manhattan Bank, Tiffany & Co., and J.P. Stevens and Company; and, executives from Pennzoil and Brown Brothers Harriman.[173]

It must have come as quite a shock when instead of young Bush, Nixon picked Maryland governor Spiro Agnew in 1968. Prescott wrote to his friend Thomas Dewey, " I fear that Nixon has made a serious error here. He had a chance to do something smart, to give the ticket a lift, and he cast it aside."[174]

Did Prescott Attempt to Overthrow Roosevelt?

There are many accusations of criminal wrongdoing against Prescott, and to a lesser extent, his father, Samuel. I am assuming that the reader is not gullible enough to believe everything that one can find on the Internet. In fact, I hope that while reading this book, the reader takes the time to do a little fact checking of his own. It's not hard. Check the endnote and see what the source is. Just because something is written in a book or has been made into a documentary on YouTube, doesn't mean it's true. People love to exaggerate, if only to draw attention to themselves.

One of the more recent accusations about Prescott Bush is that he was involved in the planning of a coup d'etat against the American government. When Franklin D. Roosevelt was president, supposedly Prescott, along with several other banking types, had the support of 500,000 ex–World War I soldiers. In the YouTube video, the "investigative reporter" is very convincing as he describes finding "documents" which prove that Prescott was not only financing this coup, he was up to his neck in the planning as well. It's a great story, and most of it is true. It's just that there has never been any evidence that Prescott Bush was involved. The best article on this subject is "The Fascist Plot to Seize Washington" by John Spivak, from his book *A Man and His Times* (1967, http://coat.ncf.ca/our_magazine/links/53/Plot1.html). Spivak was the reporter who investigated the plot and had the good sense to report the events truthfully and accurately. In an accompanying article titled "The American Liberty League" by Richard Sanders, there is a detailed list of the right wing fascist bankers and the name Prescott Bush is nowhere to be found. Yet, there are dozens of websites and investigative pieces that accuse Prescott Bush. With each new discussion/blog, the involvement of Bush gets deeper and deeper until the website headings are "Bush's Grandfather Planned Fascist Coup in America." Even the normally accurate BBC is calling Bush the "planner" and stating that "one of the members of the group was reported to be none other than Prescott Bush, the grandfather of George W. Bush and father of George H. W. Bush." The word "reported" is key here. It doesn't say he was involved, it doesn't say who reported it or even if the report was validated. There are no footnotes, no sources, just the one reference, bolstered by an account of his financing the Nazis and the seizing of his assets under the Trading With the Enemy Act.

My point in all this is that we don't need people making up or spreading fanciful stories illustrating how evil and greedy Prescott Bush was. Stories like that can be easily disproved as baseless accusations. The damage is done when this occurs, leading the reader to assume "all the other Bush stories must be lies as well"—an obvious disinformation plant. We don't need false charges because the truth is bad enough, and the truth in the case of Samuel and Prescott Bush is that many people felt that they were criminals, guilty of treasonous acts, like selling guns and other weapons to our enemies, and financing the Nazi war machine, profiting from the slave labor of thousands of men, women, and children at Auschwitz. They—the elite of American banking and industrial society—seem blessed with a separate set of rules that allow them to operate without fear of criminal prosecution. The Bushes and other privileged families emerged from the world wars believing that the rules that were meant to govern all people in our society did not apply to them. They were and are considered by some as America's royalty, and as every king wants an heir, Samuel's heir was his son Prescott, and Prescott's heir was his son, George H. W. Bush.

PART 3

GEORGE HERBERT WALKER BUSH (AKA "POPPY")

CHAPTER 14

GROWING UP POPPY

I'm sure I could have done a lot of things better.

—George H. W. Bush[xiii]

Unaffected by the Depression

Born in Milton, Massachusetts, on June 12, 1924, George Herbert Walker was the second child for Prescott and Dorothy Walker Bush. Their first child was Prescott Jr., daughter Nancy, would be the third, and two more sons, Jonathan and William, would follow. Continuing with the tradition of family names, George Herbert Walker Bush was named after his grandfather on his mother's side whom she affectionately called "Pop." To avoid confusion, she called her son "little Pop," or "Poppy," and it stuck. For the purpose of clarity I will continue this tradition and refer to the future president as Poppy.

Just five years after he was born, the stock market crashed, sending this nation into one of the worst depressions in history. In the next few months, over a thousand banks failed, farm prices fell, factories closed, and millions of Americans lost their jobs and homes. People stood in lines ten blocks long for a bowl of soup and a little bread.

In 1931, as America continued to struggle in its free fall, Prescott bought an eight-bedroom Victorian house situated on two acres of rolling lawns, to accommodate his growing family. Dorothy's parents financed the purchase of the new home, and Prescott in his new position as full partner in the newly merged Brown Brothers Harriman and Co. was doing well enough to handle all the payments and other expenses.

He joined a second country club where Poppy could take swimming and tennis lessons and little Nancy could take piano lessons. Life was good for the Bush clan, and the children never knew of the hard and miserable life that most everybody else was having to deal with. The elegance of their homes, and the lifestyle that they had already become accustomed to, was proof that they, along with the Walkers, Harrimans, Morgans, Rockefellers, and others, belonged to a separate class, a privileged class that would shape and guarantee the future of their kind. While the rest of the country was starving, the Bushes were attended to by four servants and a chauffeur.

When Poppy turned five, he joined his older brother Prescott Jr. at the prestigious Greenwich Country Day School. The children were following a proven and well-traveled path where everything was part of a grand plan that groomed them to be members of America's elite. But don't you dare think for a minute that the Bush children were coddled. Mother Dorothy was a hard woman and she expected her children to be hard. She instilled in them an almost maniacal drive to win, without appearing to care about winning. "His mother was the most competitive living human," according to *Simply Barbara Bush* by Donnie Radcliffe.[175]

Father Prescott was known for his detachment and hard drinking. He favored corporal punishment and often used a belt, razor strap, and even a squash racket to beat the boys.[176]

In 1936 when Poppy was 12 years old, he transferred, as his brother had done, to the Phillips Academy in Andover, Massachusetts. This was a top of the line New England boys' prep school where students went on to Yale or Harvard and became important leaders of business and society. As a matter of fact, Phillips Academy was known to be Yale's biggest feeder, and shared many similarities including secret societies. Poppy wasn't considered a top student, although he did maintain an above average C+. He was listed in the 1942 yearbook as belonging to 25 associations and was captain of baseball, soccer, basketball, and just about every other sport offered.[177] In fact Poppy seemed to take sports much more seriously than studies. In 1989, Poppy told the Andover Alumni Bulletin that "what really drove me and what I loved back then was sports. The competition of athletics—I loved it . . . I wasn't a particularly good student." He was nearly flunked out of his English Composition class by his professor, Hart Leavitt. "He just sat in the class and handed in papers . . . I had very little respect for his mentality . . . he showed no imagination or originality. In my class, he was a non-entity . . . a nice guy, but that's about all."[178] He had to repeat his senior year, but that wasn't due to poor study habits. Poppy had become very ill from a staph infection in his shoulder that developed into hepatitis. [179]

It's All About Daddy's Connections

As President Franklin D Roosevelt stated so well, "December 7, 1941 [is] a date which will live in infamy." War had come knocking on America's door and Poppy embraced the idea of joining up and serving his country. He would have to wait, of course, until he graduated. Just before the Christmas holidays, he attended a "cotillion at the Round Hill Country Club in Greenwich, Conn. It was a social affair attended by upcoming débutantes and acceptable young men, according to Hyams' book *Flight of the Avenger*."[180] It was here that Poppy met a pretty 16-year-old brunette named Barbara Pierce. Young Poppy didn't know how to waltz, and so they sat most of the time talking, and smiling. Although Barbara's background wasn't quite as aristocratic as Poppy's, she was considered to have good breeding. In fact, she was a distant relative of President Franklin Pierce. Back then Barbara could best be described as a tomboy.

After the holidays Poppy's graduation day approached. It's interesting to note that Henry Lewis Stimson gave the graduation speech to Poppy and his fellow seniors. Stimson was president of the board of trustees for Andover as well as the secretary of war of war under Roosevelt. During the speech Stimson told the class that the war would be long, and they, the elite, should go on to college. Poppy had already made up his mind, against his parents' advice, to enlist in the Navy's Air program. There was one problem with that plan: It wasn't legal. The Navy had high standards for its men, and one of these standards was having to complete two years of college if you wanted to become an aviator. Thousands of men wanted to enlist in the Navy's aviator program but were denied for that reason. Poppy however, was no ordinary wannabe; he was a Bush. Here's where Daddy stepped in. One of Prescott Bush's banking partners was currently assistant secretary of war for Air. Another connection was that Prescott had launched the career of the current assistant navy secretary for Air.[181] Throw in Secretary of

War Stimson as a Bush ally, and suddenly the two years of college as criteria for enlistment vanished.

This is strong evidence of preferential treatment. The rules just don't apply if you have money and connections. Although Prescott didn't want his son to join, he saw how committed Poppy was, and by George, if his son wanted to be an aviator, then by God he would. It may have crossed their minds that Poppy would be crawling through the mud on the battlefield, or polishing the deck on some battleship. While those thousands of "regular" men had to either wait until they finished two years of college, or join now, and feed the fields of glory with their blood, Poppy enlisted without fulfilling any of those pesky requirements, and became the youngest pilot in the Navy.[182]

On Poppy's eighteenth birthday, he joined the Navy and reported for training as an aviation cadet at the base in Boston. By February 1943 he moved to Corpus Christi, Texas for additional training. In June of 1943, almost two years after he enlisted, he was given his commission as an ensign, and in August, he was flying the Grumman TBF Avenger at Fort Lauderdale, Florida. He flew his first combat mission against Japanese forces in the Marianas archipelago in June of 1944. He named his Avenger the "Barbara." It was on that first mission that he lost oil pressure and had to make an emergency landing at sea. After floating in the water for a few hours, he was rescued.

To his credit, he flew 14 missions during that year near Guam. He named his second plane the Barbara II. Interestingly, his rear seat gunner was a Skull and Bonesman from Yale named Ted White, whose father was a classmate of Prescott Bush. The radioman-gunner's name was John Delaney.[183]

At this point Poppy's only crime was to knowingly and willingly jump to the head of the line, bypassing the "normal" requirements. As fate would have it, World War II would give the as yet barely tainted Poppy an opportunity to immerse himself in a very suspicious and ungentlemanly matter. There was a story, one of courage and bravery in the face of extreme danger. It was also a story of loss. Three servicemen died, and although Poppy came out squeaky clean, his fellow airmen didn't.

CHAPTER 15

BUSH ABANDONS HIS MEN TO DIE

It still plagues me if I gave those guys enough time to get out.

—Bush on ditching the plane he was piloting
during a World War II bombing raid[xiv]

The Official Story, and What Really Happened
Here's one of several "official" versions of George H. W. Bush's plane crash: "On a run toward the island, Bush's plane (the Barbara II) was struck by Japanese antiaircraft shells. One of his two crewmen was killed instantly as the aircraft was set on fire. Bush was able to score hits on enemy installations with a couple of five-hundred pound bombs before he wriggled out of the smoking cockpit and floated towards the water. The other crewman also bailed out but died almost immediately thereafter because, as the fighter pilot behind Bush's plane was later to report, his parachute failed to open properly. Bush's own parachute became momentarily fouled on the tail of the plane after he hit the water."[184]

Sounds good, except the official account, according to a *New York Post* article report on Bush's debriefing aboard the submarine *Finnback* after his rescue, makes no mention of any fire aboard the plane.[185]

In his campaign autobiography published in 1987, Bush gave this account: "Once over water, I leveled off and told Delaney and White (the other crewmen) to bail out, turning the plane to starboard to take the slipstream off the door near Delaney's station."[186] In another account, this time from a book, Poppy says: "I looked back and saw that my rear gunner was out. He had been machine-gunned to death right where he was."[187]

Yet another version, this time found on a taped interview he did with author Doug Wead, Bush clearly says: "One of them jumped out and his parachute streamed. They had fighter planes over us and they could see the chute open, and the other one . . . he was killed in the plane . . . he was just slumped over."[188]

The story stuck and later on was a nice little brag in his campaigns. It wasn't until 1988 that the story was challenged. But how could Bush be expected to remember what happened after all these years? As luck would have it, the rear turret gunner in the plane directly in front of Bush's saw it all. As he became increasingly disturbed by Poppy's changing stories to the press, he decided to go to the *New York Post* and tell them what he saw. His name was Chester Mierzejewski, and this is what he said. "That guy's not telling the truth.

The biggest discrepancy was that Chester, who had a clear and unobstructed view of no more than 100 feet, states that there was no fire. He did say he saw a very slight puff of smoke, and it quickly dissipated. He asserted that after that, there was no more smoke visible, that Bush's "plane was never on fire" and that "no smoke came out of his cockpit when he opened his canopy to bail out." He stated that only one man got out of that plane and that was Bush. "I was hoping I would see some other parachutes. I never did. I saw the plane go down. I knew the guys were still in it. It was a helpless feeling."

" I think Bush could have saved those lives," Mierzejewski said, "if they were alive. I don't know that they were, but at least they had a chance if he had attempted a water landing."[189] Back on the ship, Chester Mierzejewski was debriefed by an intelligence officer named Kilpatrick. Until 1988 Mierzejewski never saw the intelligence report, which supported Bush's version, the one with the fire. Stunned, Chester said, "I told him what I saw. I don't understand why it's not in the report."

There was one more witness, gunner Lawrence Mueller on the same plane with Chester, who made notes in his log book following the incident. "White and Delaney presumed to have gone down with the plane." "No parachute was sighted except Bush's when the plane went down." He also recalled that no one in the debriefing room said anything about a fire. "I would have put it in my log book if I had heard it."[190]

The accusation is clear: George H. W. Bush abandoned his crew to die. What's important is the claim that Bush has made regarding the fire. The fire is needed in the story because if there is a fire, it hastens your decision to bail out. If there is no fire, you make a water landing. A water landing offers more hope for the rest of the crew. If it's true that Bush bailed out of the aircraft rather than trying to make a water landing, he is guilty, and should have been court-martialed and jailed. Instead, he used this tale of heroism to bolster his "macho image" during his campaign. Bush, the brave warrior!

With so many influential people having pulled strings to get Bush into the Navy, it wouldn't have been difficult for any of them to ensure that the "official" version remained undisputed. It's one of Poppy's dirty little secrets. One may remember that

Prescott had his moment of shame when his tale of heroism about saving the lives of General Ferdinand Foch, Sir Douglas Haig, and General John J. "Black Jack" Pershing was revealed to be false. There would be more to come.

In his book *Flight of the Avenger* author Joe Hyams concludes with this disturbing and chilling note: "When flying his Avenger off the deck of the San Jac, Bush was responsible for his own fate as well as his crewmans'. As president, he is responsible for the fate of all Americans as well as that of much of the world." That's not such a comforting thought.[191]

Daddy's Connections . . . Again

As the rest of the war continued without incident, Poppy was delivered from the Navy in December 1944. Things were moving quickly in his life, and in January 1945, he and Barbara Pierce were married in the Rye, New York Presbyterian church. For their honeymoon, they enjoyed swimming, tennis, and golf at the five-star luxury hotel on Sea Island, Georgia, The Cloisters. Poppy, it was assumed, would go to Yale as many of his relations had. Yale was the purpose of all the education, grooming, and planning that had governed much of his life, and he was excited to go. Just to make sure that Poppy didn't get lost in the freshmen class of over 1,100 students at Yale, on October 11, 1945, Prescott wrote to Yale president Charles Seymour suggesting they have lunch.

> I called your office this morning and in your absence left word with
> your secretary that I hoped very much that you could have lunch at
> Mory's at one thirty with Brig. Gen. Charles M. Spofford (Yale 1924),
> and myself tomorrow. Chuck and my son, George, who has just got-
> ten out of the Navy after more than three years of service in naval
> aviation, are going to play golf in the morning at the Yale golf course,

and I have set one thirty so as to be sure we will not keep you waiting . . . I will also bring my son, George, to lunch. He left Andover in June 1942 and went directly in the Navy on his eighteenth birthday. Now, at twenty-one and a half years, he is married and entering Yale on November 1st in the special school for returning servicemen.[192]

With Prescott being a member of the Yale Corporation, and serving on every committee that had to do with securing and spending funds (he had also undertaken the university's $80 million expansion drive), it's clear that George H. W. Bush's time at Yale would not go unnoticed.[193] College life went quickly for Poppy, and he was able to finish college in two and a half years, thanks to special arrangements for veterans. He graduated in the top 10 percent and was tapped for membership in Yale's Skull and Bones Society for 1948. Each year Skull and Bones selects 15 third-year students to replace them in their senior group the following year.

Although Poppy was the last of the 15 to be chosen, his father Prescott had a good deal of notoriety in that very secret club. In 1983 or early 1984, a Skull and Bones member revealed that in 1918, Prescott Bush, along with five other Bonesmen, stole Apache chief Geronimo's skull from its grave at Fort Sill, Oklahoma. A lot of speculation as to whether this ever happened or not can be avoided when one reads the contents of the Society's own internal history document, Continuation of the History of Our Order for the Century Celebration, 17 June, 1933, by The Little Devil of D'121. The account is as follows:

Six army captains robbing a grave wouldn't look good in the papers. . . . the ring of pick on stone and thud of earth on earth alone disturbs the peace of the prairie. An ax pried open the iron door of the tomb and Patriarch Bush entered and started to dig. We dug in turns . . . Patriarch James turned up a bridle . . . at the exact bottom of the small round hole, James dug deep and pried out the trophy itself . . . Patriarch Mallon's room where we cleaned the bones. Mallon sat on the floor liberally applying carbolic acid.[194]

CHAPTER 16

RECRUITED BY THE CIA?

Poppy Bush's own role with intelligence appears to date back as early as the Second World War, when he joined the navy at age eighteen.

—Journalist Russ Baker

Career Opportunities for the Graduate

When Poppy graduated from Yale, with all the backing and prestige of a Yalesman and a Skull and Bonesman, he went about looking for a job. In letters to his friend Gerry Bermiss, he confides: "I could work for Herby Walker in St. Louis-G.H.Walker & Co. investments etc . . . but the people I'd be doing business with in the investment business, I know to some degree now. I am not sure I want to capitalize completely on benefits I received at birth—that is on the benefits of my social position . . . doing well merely because I have had the opportunity to attend the same debut parties as some of my customers does not appeal to me."[195] Although Poppy may have wanted to distance himself from his birthright, in the end, he relied on the connections that his father Prescott provided. The first attempt at finding a job failed after he was turned down by Procter and Gamble even though Prescott had set up the interview. "No soap," he reported back to his father.[196]

There is one area of much discussion and presumption: whether or not Poppy was recruited by the CIA during his stint at Yale. While it is true that Yale was the major recruiting campus for Allen Dulles's Office of Policy Coordination (renamed Office of Strategic Services and then Central Intelligence Agency), and Skull and Bonesmen were the preferred candidates, there is no proof that Poppy was actually recruited. Here's what other authors and investigators have written. In *American Dynasty,* author Kevin Phillips states that at Andover, "Poppy's history teacher, Arthur Burr Darling, was a known intelligence community asset." In 1950 he wrote (in secret) the agency's own history of its formation and early years, *The Central Intelligence Agency: An Instrument of Government to 1950.* It is unlikely that Darling would have been recruiting from Andover's 17- and 18-year-olds. However, after graduating from Andover, "he could have been directly commissioned into an extremely flexible OSS as a way of easing him into navy flight school."[197]

In *Presidential Puppetry,* author Andrew Kreig states: "In *American Dynasty,* mainstream biographer Kevin Phillips highlights evidence pointing to George Bush's CIA connections while he was at Yale in the late 1940's."[198] Yet when we go back to the Phillips book, we get a *"could have."* In Russ Baker's *Family of Secrets,* he quotes CIA officer and ex Yale man Osbourne Day (class of 1943), "In my class alone there were thirty-five guys in the agency." That's an interesting quote but has actually nothing to do with Poppy Bush. Later, Baker states: "Bush, with naval intelligence work already under his belt by the time he arrived at Yale, would have been seen as a particularly prime candidate for recruitment." Here again, a *"would have."* Baker clarifies his information by stating that "Poppy Bush's own role with intelligence appears to date back as early as the Second World War, when he joined the navy at age eighteen. On arrival at his training base in Norfolk, Virginia, in the fall of 1942, Bush was trained not only as a pilot of a torpedo bomber, but also as a photographic officer, responsible for crucial, highly sensitive aerial surveillance. On his way to his ship, the USS San Jacinto, Bush stopped off in Pearl Harbor for meetings with military intelligence officers assigned to the Joint Intelligence Center for the Pacific Ocean Areas (JICPOA)." This would be Naval Intelligence, not CIA.

From the research I've done, George H. W. Bush was a man bent on making money when he left Yale. I think him too selfish to give his life over to the CIA. However, we shall see that Poppy was not averse to allowing the CIA to use him for his various businesses, and by the same token, he was not averse to using the CIA when it benefited him. This sort of scratch my back and I'll scratch yours started early in his career with Zapata Petroleum. But for now, we'll get back on course with his first job after being turned down by Procter and Gamble.

The Oil Business

Prescott made a call to one of his close friends and fellow Yale Skull and Bonesman, Henry Neil Mallon. Mallon had been part of the clandestine group as mentioned, along with Prescott Bush, that was responsible for stealing Geronimo's bones back in 1918. He had been the one to remove tufts of hair with carbolic acid. After Yale, he, like many Bonesmen, went into military service, and when the war ended, became a factory manager at the huge Continental Can Company. Throughout, he remained in good standing and in close contact with his pals

Prescott Bush and Roland "Bunny" Harriman of W. A. Harriman & Co. In 1928 Harriman & Co. had acquired ownership of an Ohio firm called Dresser Industries. Dresser Industries had been a leading manufacturer of drill bits and other oil drilling equipment. In an often told story, Prescott, Bunny Harriman, and Knight Wooley were sitting around the Harriman office discussing the reorganization of Dresser, and who best to run it. In a remarkable stroke of good fortune, in walked Mallon, who was returning home from a mountaineering vacation in the Alps. Suddenly, Bunny Harriman pointed at Mallon and exclaimed "Dresser! Dresser!" In due time, Mallon was interviewed by George Herbert Walker, the president of W. A. Harriman & Co., and immediately made president of Dresser Industries. This stroke of good fortune clearly shows just how important pedigree papers were to the elite. The fact that Mallon had absolutely no experience in the oil business made no difference. What was important was that he was a Yalesman, and Skull and Bones Society member, and therefore could be trusted. In 1930, Prescott became a member of the board of directors of Dresser Industries and held that position for 22 years until 1952 when he entered the Senate.[199] Under Mallon, Dresser began expanding into military strategic manufacture. While still engaged in manufacture of oil drilling parts, it was moving closer to the center of the new and rapidly growing military-industrial sector as a defense contractor and subcontractor.[200] It seems that Prescott was more than a member of the board of directors. In an interview he stated: "I was Neil Mallon's chief adviser and consultant in connection with every move that he made."[201]

Mallon, whom Poppy referred to as "Uncle Neil," agreed to hiring the young Bush and sent him, along with his wife and child, out to Odessa, Texas. This begins the relationship between the Bushes and Texas. Dresser, at the time, was the largest oil-equipment company in the world, and had moved into oil and gas exploration around the globe. Before departing for Odessa, Mallon had explained that oil and gas exploration was the 20th century's new frontier. In several accounts, Poppy's move to Odessa was in the new red Studebaker his parents had given him for graduation. Other accounts which seek to mystify the move as further evidence of a pampered and spoiled Bush have him flying in a Dresser Industries executive plane.[202] The tale is much simpler and less suspicious. In January 1949, Prescott, along with his wife Dorothy, flew to Texas on a Dresser inspection trip. The young Bush family, Poppy, Barbara, and a very young George W. Bush, posed in front of the plane with parents Prescott and Dorothy.[203]

And so, Poppy accepted employment at another Dresser subsidiary, IDECO, International Derrick and Equipment Company. Although his initial duties included sweeping floors and repainting oil machinery, it wasn't long before the family was transferred out to California to work at various Dresser subsidiaries including Pacific Pump Works. Pacific Pump Works had become an important part of the war effort and was producing hydraulic-actuating-assemblies for airplane landing gear, wing flaps, and bomb doors, like those used in the bombing of Hiroshima and Nagasaki.[204]

Dresser Industries provided another brush with the CIA. It was well known in the right circles that Dresser provided a handy cover to CIA operatives. Three former CIA officials, one a former Bonesman, confirmed the arrangement to author Joseph Trento.[205] Another transfer some months later saw them back in Texas, this time to Midland, some 20 or so miles from Odessa. Midland/Odessa had a curious population of recently graduated eastern college types. Here they socialized with the high society graduates of Princeton, Harvard, and Yale. Midland even boasted of having a Yale Club, a Harvard Club, and a Princeton Club.[206] Also present were Amherst graduates J. Hugh and William Liedkte, the Liedtke brothers. It seems that the oil business was where the Eastern establishment wanted their younger emissaries to be. Just down the street from young Bush's house lived John Overbey.

Taking Advantage of Poor Ranchers

Overbey was what Texans called a landman. A landman is someone who tries to identify potential land parcels that might contain oil. He would do this by learning of a parcel that a major oil company showed interest in, or he may have been privy to leaked geological information, or he may have paid insiders to keep him informed of hot spots. The landman would scout the property and attempt to get the owner to sign away mineral rights in the form of a lease. The landman would play down the potential for finding oil and try to get the owner to sign for the smallest dollar amount, usually, a one-time payment. Then the landman's job was to try and broker the lease by selling it off to a major oil company or another buyer, at an inflated price. Bear in mind that once oil was found, if it was, the money pouring out would never wind up in the original owner's pocket. Basically, these heartless landmen preyed on poor uninformed farmers and conned them out of the land. Not the type of business one thinks that George H. W. Bush would consider joining. But that's exactly what happened. Poppy offered Overbey capital if he would make him a partner. Suffering from a lack of capital, Overbey immediately agreed, and so Bush was now in the landman's game.[207]

Poppy and Overbey flew to New York and within a week were back in Midland, with $300,000 of capital, courtesy of

Herbert Walker and his many connections. The list of investors read like a "Who's Who," with $50,000 coming from James
Gammell of Scotland, $50,000 from Eugene Meyer, owner of
the *Washington Post*, and $50,000 from Poppy's own father,
Prescott. The rest came directly from "Uncle" Herbert Walker
of G. H. Walker & Co. of Wall Street.[208] Not much is written
about whether this influx of cash served to elevate the landman business, but I think it sad for those that were swindled
out of their land rights by none other than our future president.

With a firm sense of financial support from Walker back
east, Poppy was confident that he could do even better and so in
1953 he joined forces with two brothers from Tulsa, Oklahoma.
As mentioned earlier, these were the Amherst graduates, the
Liedkte brothers, William and J. Hugh. Bush and the brothers formed Zapata Petroleum. As usual G. H. Walker & Co.
became the principal underwriters of the stock and Uncle
Herbert himself purchased a large portion of stock along with
Gammell. Whenever the new company needed a cash infusion, Walker would float the necessary bonds. Initially about
$1 million was invested in Zapata Petroleum. At first they hit
paydirt when Zapata surmised that the six big oil rigs pumping oil from a property in Coke County called Jameson Field
were all pumping not from six wells, but from one gigantic
well. Zapata drilled 127 new wells on the same field and all of
them were gushers. Zapata stock rose from 7 cents a share to
$23 per share.[209] Poppy was doing well, and I'm sure his inves-
tors were pleased. Up until 1957, Zapata Petroleum did fairly
well. They suffered their first loss in '57 and the downward
spiral continued with greater losses each year. Realizing that
land-based oil speculation might have reached its limit, a new
consideration was on the table: offshore oil drilling. In 1954 the
United States government began to auction the mineral rights

to vast offshore areas in and around the Gulf of Mexico and the Caribbean. With a new sense of direction, Poppy and company formed Zapata Offshore.

Basically this was a drilling for hire business, and with the Seven Sisters oil cartel hungrily searching for offshore oil, there was little chance of failure. The Seven Sisters was a term coined in the 1950s by Italian businessman Enrico Mattei, head of the Italian state oil company Eni, to describe the seven oil companies which formed the "Consortium for Iran" cartel. The Seven Sisters dominated the global petroleum industry from the mid 1940s until the 1970s. The group consisted of Anglo-Persian Oil Company (now BP), Gulf Oil, Standard Oil of California (SoCal), Texaco (now Chevron), Royal Dutch Shell, Standard Oil of New Jersey (now Esso/Exxon) and Standard Oil Company of New York (Socony/Exxon/Mobil).[210]

CHAPTER 17

CONNECTIONS

> We had to pay off politicians in Mexico, Guatemala, Costa Rica, and elsewhere . . . Bush's company was used as a conduit for these funds under the guise of oil business contracts.
>
> —John Sherwood, chief of CIA anti-Castro operations in the early 60s[xv]

The Bush / Zapata / CIA Connection

1954 was a good year for the CIA. Or as Frank Sinatra sang, "It was a *very* good year." The top project for the CIA in that year was the violent overthrow of the government of Guatemala. Jacobo Arbenz was the elected president and he won his election by promising agrarian reform. Up until that time millions of acres of land were controlled by U.S. interests, most notably United Fruit Company, of which John Foster Dulles, brother of CIA chief Allen Dulles, sat on the board of directors.

As we well know, the Dulles brothers had been close friends of the Bush family for decades. By June 1954, Arbenz had already expropriated and distributed around 1.4 million acres back to the workers whose families had toiled in the jungles for generations. The CIA decided that Arbenz's land reform was simply a communist expression, and with a small guerrilla army and a psychological warfare program run by notorious CIA agent E. Howard Hunt, the CIA was able to successfully overthrow Arbenz and install a brutal dictatorship. I only mention this because this is an area where Poppy's Zapata Offshore and the CIA converge. Zapata's first oil platform, Scorpion, was located just 54 miles from Cuba, another simmering hot spot. On the board of directors at Zapata Petroleum and Zapata Offshore was Thomas J. Devine, a CIA staffer who had "resigned" his position at the CIA in order to go into business with George H. W. Bush. Resigning from the CIA in order to go into "private business" is a common CIA tool as evidenced by the "resignation" of CIA officer E. Howard Hunt in order to enter employment at the White House under Richard Nixon. It's a common CIA method of taking someone off the books, while secretly continuing their covert relationship. Devine would later "rejoin" the CIA and continue a relationship with Poppy Bush through 1975.[211]

There is more to the possibility—probability—of a Bush/CIA connection. In *Family of Secrets*, author Russ Baker writes: "Zapata Offshore, which provided perfect cover for activities in a host of hot spots around the world, may have been the brightest stone in Allen Dulles's crown." "On April 10, 1953, exactly two weeks after Zapata Offshore's land-based sister, Zapata Petroleum, was launched, Neil Mallon wrote to CIA director Dulles about an upcoming meeting at D.C.'s Carlton Hotel." "In addition to Bob Johnson, I have invited a close personal friend, Prescott Bush. We want to talk to them about our pilot project in the Caribbean and have you listen in."[212] The current thinking is that the pilot project was Zapata Offshore. Another clue appeared in *The Nation* magazine in 1988, stating

that a "source with close connections to the intelligence community confirms that Bush started working for the agency in
1960 or 1961, using his oil business as a cover for clandestine
activities."[213] By the way, this is the same issue that broke the
story of an internal memo, dated November 29, 1963, reporting that "Mr. Bush, of the Central Intelligence Agency, was
briefed by the Bureau about the reaction of the Cuban exile
community in Miami to the Kennedy assassination."[214] There
has been much discussion of this memo and we shall get into
it in the next chapter. There are a few more clues to reveal.
In 1988, Project Censored, a journalistic consortium based in
California, chose the probability of George H. W. Bush being a
CIA asset in 1963, when he ran Zapata Offshore, as "one of the
top 10 censored stories of the year."[215]

That Zapata's Scorpion platform, located just 50 some
miles from Cuba was used by the CIA, is supported by this
quote from the book *Prelude to Terror*: "George Bush would be
given a list of names of Cuban oil workers we would want
placed in jobs . . . The oil platforms he dealt in were perfect
for training the Cubans in raids on their homeland."[216] More
than using the oil platform as a training area for the Cubans,
there is evidence that Zapata's real purpose was as paymas-
ter. According to John Sherwood, chief of CIA anti-Castro operations in the early 1960s, "We had to pay off politicians in
Mexico, Guatemala, Costa Rica, and elsewhere . . . Bush's company was used as a conduit for these funds under the guise of
oil business contracts."[217]

These accounts of Bush/CIA connections are important
because they show the relationship between big business and
the intelligence community—in other words, the military-industrial complex that outgoing president Dwight Eisenhower
so clearly warned us about. What's more, as Eisenhower was

warning us, Prescott Bush had been one of his closest advisors and friends, in fact his favorite golf partner. Eisenhower may have just been warning us about the very people that had been closest to him. With Poppy Bush, there can be no mistake that he took this budding relationship between big oil and CIA to its utmost conclusion when he became CIA director and later president of the United States. Was our 41st president a big oil crony or was he a CIA boss? Me thinks they be one in the same. For now, we'll follow Poppy's rise to power. In doing so, we come to Poppy's Mexican connection.

The Bush / PERMARGO Lie

During 1960, Poppy and Mexican businessman Jorge Diaz Serrano secretly set up a Mexican drilling company called Perforaciones Marinas del Golfo, or PERMARGO. Serrano had worked for Dresser Industries, where he may have come into contact with Bush. Serrano met an American business-man named Edwin Pauley. Pauley at the time represented Pan American Petroleum Corporation. When Serrano wanted to buy drilling equipment from Dresser, they insisted that he take on George H. W. Bush as a partner. It was a meeting of two men with one purpose: drilling in Mexico. Unfortunately, Mexi-can law dictated that drilling rights would only be awarded to Mexican nationals. Bush never mentioned this deal with PER-MARGO, and as such his dealings with them, and his secrecy about the deal, was dishonest, if not illegal. PERMARGO was in direct competition with Zapata. As it turned out, the filings with the SEC between 1960 and 1966, when Bush was in total control, were destroyed by the SEC. Later, in the 1980s, Serrano was con-victed of defrauding the Mexican government of $58 million.[218]

Although Zapata Offshore was at best a company of mod-est dimensions, it created a network of subsidiaries which for some, seemed unnecessarily complex. These would be Zapata de Mexico, Zapata International Corporation, Zapata Lining Corporation, Zapata Oil Company, Zapata Overseas Corporation, and Amata Gas Corporation, which Zapata owned 41 percent. Nothing really sinister about these. It is, however, common for any really large money laundering and distribution operation to use as many subsidiaries as one can have. Therefore, this web of smaller connected businesses fits right in with the allegations that Zapata was, in fact, a money distribution point for CIA operations in the Caribbean. As we've shown, the SEC records for these companies during this time period are forever gone. In 1959, Bush moved his family and his company from Midland, to Houston, Texas. In these first early years of the 1960s, Poppy's quest for political legitimacy would become the hallmark of a man bent on nothing short of attaining the highest office in the White House.

After the failed Bay of Pigs operation in 1961, President John F. Kennedy promised to "splinter the CIA into a thousand pieces." As promised, he forcefully retired Allen Dulles from the CIA. This must have been a hard pill to swallow. The Dulles and Bush families had gone back decades. Dulles had been director since 1953, and had steered the agency through two successful covert operations, Iran and Guatemala. For Kennedy to blame Dulles for the failure at the Bay of Pigs, when anyone who was there knew it was Kennedy's nerve that failed, was unforgivable. As super spy E. Howard Hunt said about Dulles, "a remarkable man whose long career of government service had been destroyed unjustly by men who were laboring unceasingly to preserve their own public image."[219] As late as 1969, Prescott Bush wrote to Dulles's widow about the Kennedys, "I have never forgiven them."[220]

In 1962, Prescott announced that he would not be seeking another term in the Senate, citing health issues. That same year he spoke, in no uncertain terms, to Harris County GOP chairman James Bertron, demanding that Bertron find a place in the organization for Poppy. Bertron replied, "Senator, I'm trying. We're all trying."[221] What Prescott wanted, Prescott got, and in 1962, his son, Poppy, was named finance co-chair of the Harris County Republican Party. Just months later, Bertron announced his retirement and Poppy announced his intention of filling that post. After another party member, who had expressed interest in the position, had a change of mind, Poppy won the slot.[222] George H. W. Bush was on his way. In the next few years, Poppy would mount a campaign to run for Senate (as his father had) that would ultimately fail. But that wouldn't be until 1964.

CHAPTER 18

POPPY/JFK/1963

A man who identified himself as George H. W. Bush phoned the FBI in Houston a few hours after President John F. Kennedy's assassination in Dallas to report that a right wing Young Republican, James Milton Parrott, had been talking about killing the president.

—memo from FBI agent Graham Kitchel

The Bush / Dallas / JFK Question
1963 would be a tricky year for Poppy. Not so much at the time, but in later years, as there has been a great deal of speculation regarding Poppy's whereabouts on November 22, 1963. So, where was Mr. G. H. W. Bush on that fateful day? A simple enough question, but without a simple enough answer. If one were to look at the number of YouTube videos alleging Poppy's involvement with the assassination of JFK, one would think it's an open and shut case. Here are some of the links to these videos, if you're interested.

https://www.youtube.com/watch?v=jWdv2BsShwE
https://www.youtube.com/watch?v=-NlJQJUUqR4

https://www.youtube.com/watch?v=FWAQlztaFIA

I have given fair share to those who insist that Poppy Bush was involved, responsible, or otherwise hiding facts that could be traced back to his "involvement." To my knowledge, there are only two individuals of public notoriety, that can't seem to remember, or have changed their recollection, of where they were on that day. One of those is CIA spy E. Howard Hunt, and the other, George H. W. Bush. I won't concern myself with Hunt's case, as this book is not concerned with his shifting answers. We will, however, explore, to some extent, the case of G. H. W. Bush. In *Family of Secrets* by Russ Baker, he writes, "Jack Kennedy's death in Dallas on November 22, 1963, was one of the most tragically memorable moments in the lives of those who lived through it. So Poppy Bush's inability or un-willingness to say where he was on that day is extremely odd, to say the least."[223]

Backstory—Poppy's Polished Persona and His Path to the White House

No one acted more curiously than future president George H. W. Bush on the day President Kennedy was shot. For over 20 years, Bush claimed he couldn't remember where he was on that day. In fact, he went out of his way to create an alibi and dissemble about where he really was on November 21 and 22, 1963.

I have a unique experience with George H. W. Bush: I helped bar his ascent to the presidency in 1980, as I was work-ing for the Reagan GOP campaign. It would be a major mistake to view Bush's unfailingly polite, friendly, affable, and some-times goofy style as benign. Don't fall for the vapidity and ob-fuscation. Underneath them lie consuming political ambition, steely determination, boundless energy, and remarkable physical discipline for relentless travel to pursue his political goals. Barbara Bush brings a vindictive streak; she remembers everyone who was not for her husband.

Despite his "nice guy" image, George Bush is high-handed, secretive, and fueled by an incredible sense of entitlement. He is also disciplined and extremely well organized. He was a model candidate, traveling relentlessly, shaking hands, writing notes, and building his friends list. He was always collecting: people, addresses, supporters, and money. Only Richard Nixon was a more indefatigable campaigner.

I first met George Bush when I was Young Republican National Chairman and he addressed the group's national leadership conference. He was cordial. I heard later that my introduction of him as "George Herbert Walker Bush" was taken as a slight as if I was mocking his four-part patrician moniker. I wasn't. I grew up in Connecticut's Fairfield County when the Bushes still lived in Greenwich. I saw Senator Prescott Bush speak to the 1966 Republican state convention. I rooted for George Bush in his 1970 campaign for the U.S. Senate. Back then, I had only three posters in my room: Jim Buckley (New York) for Senate, John Lupton (Connecticut) for Senate, and George Bush ("He Can Do More for Texas"). I also knew the seeds of a family feud between the Bushes and Lowell Weicker, which would play out in the 1980s.

Bush was not a conservative, but, like Nixon, he knew when he had to sound like one. He always accommodated the "kooks" as Harris County GOP chair and even worked with them. He treated everyone with bonhomie. He knew the buzzwords and dutifully repeated them: UN, Gun Owners, Civil Rights. After the 1988 election, he famously swept a copy of Bill Buckley's *National Review* off a coffee table in his

Kennebunkport, Maine home and said "well we don't need this shit anymore."

I had the chance to observe George Bush up close when I worked against him in the Northeast during the 1980 presidential campaign. The states that I handled for Ronald Reagan had GOP establishments still dominated by the Eastern moderates and were thought to be Bush strongholds. In fact, Bush's campaign manager James A. Baker would later tell me that I was "a pain in the Bushes' ass."

Baker admitted that Bush was counting on delegate votes in New York and New Jersey, where Reagan swamped him, seizing all the delegates. In Bush's native Connecticut, Reagan victories in three congressional districts forced Bush to split the 35 delegates down the middle.

"Barbara hates your ass," Lee Atwater told me. He was Bush's campaign manager, later Republican national chairman, and my friend of 20 years.

When I saw presidential candidate George W. Bush, whose campaign for governor I had financially supported at a fundraising reception in New Jersey, he told me "My father always said you stole those New Jersey delegates from him."

Secretary to the Eisenhower Cabinet and New Jersey Republican National Committeeman Bernard "Bern" Shanley, who ran for the Senate in New Jersey, told me "the Bushes hate you." As a soldier in the service of Ronald Reagan, I still wear their scorn proudly.

Bush's 1980 campaign was hampered when it hired his longtime mistress, Jennifer Fitzgerald, as his scheduler. Fitzgerald hoarded information; power struggles plagued the campaign. Barbara Bush once famously exploded at Fitzgerald in the back of a limousine when she touched

Bush's knee. Senior campaign aides plotted to remove Fitzgerald, and eventually Bush's savvy campaign chief James A. Baker III gave Bush a "her or me" ultimatum. Fitzgerald would leave the campaign, only to be hired later to handle the vice president's schedule (she was kept in the vice president's ceremonial Capitol Hill office rather than the White House). Fitzgerald let it be known that she had a trove of love letters from the vice president and wouldn't be going anywhere.

George Bush was sinking into political obscurity when he was defeated for president in 1980, after losing two U. S. Senate races. Only his elevation to the vice presidency by Ronald Reagan gave him a chance to later become president. His unwillingness to defend Reaganomics, which had given the nation its largest economic boom in history, was a stunning display of disloyalty to the "Gipper."

Perhaps his lack of prominence in Washington was because George H. W. Bush, underrated within his own party, had no fixed ideology. Nixon and Kissinger considered Bush a lightweight; in his book *Being Poppy*, Richard Ben Cramer would say that Nixon believed Bush "lacked the killer instinct." In his 1970 Senate race, he said "I realize this is a politically sensitive area. But I believe in a woman's right to choose. It should be an individual matter. I think, ultimately, it will be a constitutional question. I don't favor a federal abortion law as such." He would switch to oppose abortion to run for vice president with Reagan. Deriding Reagan's tax cuts as "voodoo economics," Bush himself ran on a no-new-taxes pledge in 1988—a pledge he would promptly break.

CIA in '63?

As we've seen, George Bush may have been associated with the CIA as early as 1953. Fabian Escalante, the chief of a Cuban counterintelligence unit during the late 1950s and early 1960s, describes a plan called "Operation 40" that was put into effect by the National Security Council and presided over by Vice President Richard Nixon. Escalante said that Nixon, as operation director or "case officer," had assembled an important group of businessmen headed by George Bush and Jack Crichton, both Texas oilmen, to gather the necessary funds for the operation. Operation 40, a group of CIA assassins, was subsequently brought into the Bay of Pigs invasion. Interestingly, CIA official Fletcher Prouty delivered three Navy ships to agents in Guatemala to be used in the invasion. Prouty claims that he delivered the ships to a CIA agent named George Bush. Agent Bush named the ships Barbara J, Houston, and Zapata.

In 1963, Poppy was serving as chairman of the Harris County (Houston) Republican Committee and was warming up for a 1964 U.S. Senate bid. There, he presided over a rift in the local GOP between the country club moderates who had migrated to Houston and a deeply conservative faction aligned with the John Birch Society. Despite the Bush family's longtime closeness to the Rockefellers, Bush would join his fellow Texans supporting Barry Goldwater in 1964 and asked his senator father to withhold his endorsement of Rockefeller.

In the 1964 Republican Senate primary, Bush was opposed by Jack Cox, who had made a valiant run as the Republican candidate for governor in 1962, and Robert Morris, who served on the chief counsel of the Senate Judiciary Subcommittee on Internal Security through the 1950s. Morris ran for the Republican U.S. Senate nomination in 1964 and 1970 and was defeated both times. Bush defeated Cox in the 1964 runoff, 62 to 38 percent, to win the GOP nomination. Morris endorsed Cox nonetheless.

Bush waged a spirited and peripatetic campaign. To his credit, he refused to write off African-American or Mexican-American votes. Bush ran to the right: He denounced the United Nations and pledged to vote against Johnson on civil rights. Like Barry Goldwater, he argued federal enforcement of civil rights was a violation of states' rights. Although Bush got 200,000 more votes in the state than Barry Goldwater—more than any Republican ever had—Texans voted the ticket led by their native son Lyndon Johnson. Bush was trounced by Senator Ralph Yarborough.

In 1985, a memo dated November 29, 1963 from FBI director J. Edgar Hoover came to light in which he discussed reactions among Cuban exiles to the JFK assassination. Hoover said, "George Bush of the CIA had been briefed . . . " In 1988, reporting for the *Nation*, Joseph McBride asked Vice President George Bush's office for comment. Bush's representatives claimed that he "didn't know what you are talking about." Bush also said it "must be another George Bush."

At first, the CIA said that there was no employee named George Bush at the CIA in 1963. After McBride wrote his story, the CIA would change theirs. There was a George William Bush detailed from another agency in 1963, but the CIA could not find him. McBride didn't have trouble finding him—he was still on the payroll. George William Bush said that he had been detailed only briefly to the agency and denied knowing anything about a briefing regarding anti-Castro elements and what they might do in the wake of Kennedy's murder. In fact, George William Bush was a lowly clerk. Did the CIA plant this George Bush as a "cut-out" to shield the real George Bush?

The Bush/Parrott Smear/Lie

An article in the *San Francisco Examiner*, written by Miguel Acoca, appeared in 1988 with the headline: "Documents: Bush Blew Whistle on Rival in JFK Slaying." A second FBI document mentioning George Bush was revealed. In a memo from Houston FBI agent in charge, Graham Kitchel (whose brother George Kitchel was a Bush political supporter and friend), it was reported that "A man who identified himself as George H. W. Bush phoned the FBI in Houston a few hours after President John F. Kennedy's assassination in Dallas to report that a right wing Young Republican, James Milton Parrott, had been talking of killing the president." Allegedly, before leaving for Dallas, Bush called the Houston FBI field office and promptly identified himself and his location in Tyler, Texas, this only six minutes after Walter Cronkite would announce to the world that JFK was dead. This memo makes Bush's claim that he could not remember where he was on November 22, 1963 all the more incredible.

In the article, Acoca, unable to locate Parrott, noted that an address on the FBI report was listed, which just happened to be the address of Bush, now the current vice president of the United States.[224] The entire memo was declassified in 1993 and reads as follows:

> Mr. George H W Bush, President of Zapata Offshore Drilling Company, Houston, Texas, residence 5525 Briar, Houston, telephonically furnished the following information to writer by long distance telephone call from Tyler, Texas. Bush stated that he wanted to be kept confidential but wanted to furnish hearsay that he recalled hearing in recent weeks, the day and source unknown. He stated that one James Parrott has been talking of killing the president when he comes to Houston. Bush stated that Parrott is possibly a

student at University of Houston and is active in political matters in this area. He stated that he felt Mrs. Fawley, telephone number SU2–5239, or Arline Smith, telephone number JA9–9194 of the Harris County Republican Party Headquarters would be able to furnish additional information regarding the identity of Parrott. Bush stated that he was proceeding to Dallas, Texas, would remain in the Sheraton-Dallas-Hotel and return to his residence on 11–23-63. His office telephone number is CA2–0395.

In short order, the FBI dispatched agents to the Parrott residence. Parrott, who was not home at the time, had to rely on his mother for an alibi. "She advised that James Parrott had been home all day helping her care for her son Gary Wayne Parrott whom they brought home from the hospital yesterday." She also mentioned another person who could provide an alibi. "Mrs. Parrott advised that shortly after 1:00 pm a Mr. Reynolds came by their home to advise them of the death of President Kennedy, and talked to her son James Parrott about painting some signs at Republican Headquarters on Waugh Drive."

Later in the investigation, both Reynolds and Parrott put the time of Reynolds' visit at between 1:30 and 1:45 p.m. The case seems airtight, yet still rather bizarre. When interviewed in 2007 by Russ Baker, Reynolds denied having gone to Parrott's home that day. In fact, he said, he had been asked to accompany Parrott down to the local Secret Service office:

> There was a young man who came around headquarters . . . and somebody said that he had made a threat against Kennedy and this was, I believe, this came up after the assassination. . . . The end result was, it was suggested that I contact the Secret Service, the local Secret Service, and I accompanied this young man . . . And

we went down, and this was kind of a strange kid, mild mannered, quiet kind of, seemed to be living in another world, and I took him down one day, escorted him down there.[225]

During questioning, Parrott acknowledged that he had been active in picketing members of the Kennedy administration. He also insisted that he had not threatened the president's life. He was a member of the ultra-rightwing John Birch Society and had vigorously opposed Bush during his campaign for GOP chairman of Harris County—a major offense to Bush running for a minor office, and Bush never forgot the offender. Parrott had been painting "Bush for Senate?" signs when the FBI arrived to question him. Ironically, Parrott would surface again—as a volunteer for George Bush's 1988 presidential campaign. Was Parrott also a patsy?

In any event, the FBI cleared James Parrott. But what to make of all this? Why was Poppy accusing a mild-mannered youth of such things? Bush dropped a dime on an unemployed 24-year-old Air Force veteran who had been honorably discharged.

It appears the only benefit that Poppy's phone call to the FBI served was to place in an FBI official file the whereabouts of one Poppy Bush. By making that call, Poppy was inserting into the record that he was calling from Tyler, some 200 miles away from Dallas. In fact, he was witnessed by the Kiwanis Club, placing him there at his scheduled speaking event at 12:30 p.m., the time of the shooting. The reader can decide whether the supposed photograph of George H. W. Bush in Dealey Plaza at the time of the shooting is really him. The laws of physics and the many Kiwanis Club witnesses say it can't be. It *does* resemble him though.

Duck and Cover

Here's how Poppy covered his tracks in Dallas: George registered himself and Barbara Bush for a two-night stay at the Dallas Sheraton November 21 and 22. On the morning of November
22, after their first night in Dallas, they flew by private plane to
Tyler, Texas, about 100 miles away, where the GOP Senate candidate was to speak at a local Kiwanis Club luncheon.

According to an eyewitness account published in Kitty
Kelley's book *The Family: The Real Story of the Bush Dynasty*,
Bush had just started to speak when news of the shooting
reached the club. "I gave the news to the president of the club,
Wendell Cherry, and he leaned over to tell George that wires
from Dallas confirmed President Kennedy had been assassinated," Aubrey Irby recalled in the book.

"George stopped his speech and told the audience what had
happened. 'In view of the president's death,' he said, 'I consider
it inappropriate to continue with a political speech at this time.
Thank you very much for your attention.' Then he sat down."

Who could forget such a moment? More importantly, why
would Bush lie about it? Because he was attempting to cover
his trail and make a plausible denial case against personal involvement, just as CIA agents are instructed?

In 1994, Barbara Bush published *Barbara Bush: A Memoir*,
in which she revealed the actual "letter" that she had written
on the very day, at the very moment, that Kennedy was shot.
The letter has plenty of details, but curiously does not mention
George H. W. Bush's call to Hoover's boys in Houston.

> On November 22, 1963, George and I were in the middle of a sev-
> eral-city swing. I was getting my hair done in Tyler, Texas, working
> on a letter home.

"Dearest family, Wednesday, I took Doris Ulmer out for lunch. They were here from England, and they had been so nice to George in Greece. That night we went to. . . .

"I am writing this at the Beauty Parlor, and the radio says that the president has been shot. Oh Texas—my Texas—my God—let's hope it's not true. I am sick at heart as we all are. Yes, the story is true and the Governor also. How hateful some people are.

"Since the beauty parlor, the president has died. We are once again on a plane. This time a commercial plane. Poppy picked me up at the beauty parlor—we went right to the airport, flew to Ft. Worth and dropped Mr. Zeppo off (we were on his plane) and flew back to Dallas. We had to circle the field while the second presidential plane took off. Immediately, Pop got tickets back to Houston, and here we are flying home. We are sick at heart. The tales the radio reporters tell of Jackie Kennedy are the bravest I've ever heard. The rumors are flying about that horrid assassin. We are hoping that it is not some far-right nut, but a "commie" nut. You understand that we know they are both nuts, but just hope that it is not a Texan and not an American at all.

"I am amazed by the rapid-fire thinking and planning that has already been done. LBJ has been the president for some time now—two hours at least and it is only 4:30.

"My dearest love to you all, Bar"

Exactly to whom this letter was mailed has never been made clear and the original is not known to exist.

Note the jab at LBJ. Bar had no idea. The documents reversing JFK's Vietnam policies were drafted before his death and were executed on November 23.

On the night of November 21, 1963, Poppy attended an oil contractors' association meeting in Dallas, and he stayed for drinks afterward. This would seem to preclude his presence at a party at the home of Clint Murchison, which Oliver Stone made iconic in his movie *Nixon*. I believe this Murchison affair did take place, and I believe that Nixon was there but left early. I think LBJ did come late. Jack Ruby would supply the girls to entertain the business and government titans, according to reported LBJ mistress Madeleine Brown.

Barbara said that their friend Zeppo's private plane transported them to Tyler. This was, in fact, oilman Joe Zeppa, partners with Bush friend John Alston Crichton in a private offshore drilling company. Swashbuckling right-wing oilman Jack Crichton had deep ties to Army intelligence and the events of November 22, 1963. Fabian Escalante, the chief of a Cuban counterintelligence unit during the late 1950s and early 1960s, along with George Bush and Jack Crichton, both Texas oilmen, gathered the necessary funds for the operation to assassinate Castro. In fact, Crichton is woven into the fabric of the Kennedy assassination. (Read on.)

The Bush's entertaining a spy and his wife is yet another curious CIA tie. According to Barbara Bush, she and her husband had lunch with longtime CIA operative Alfred Ulmer and his wife Dorothy during the week of November 22. Thus, George and Barbara were drinking Bloody Marys with an expert on assassination and coup d'état only days before the assassination of JFK. This is particularly curious in view of the fact that Bush would deny any connection to the CIA prior to him becoming director in 1975.

The de Mohrenschildt Lie

There's more to the Bush/JFK scenario. The name of George de Mohrenschildt may not be as well known as Lee Harvey Oswald, but the two are entwined in the events surrounding the assassination and by virtue of their relationship, we have to look at a third entanglement, that of George H. W. Bush. Let's jump forward, from 1963 to 1976, when Poppy was director of the CIA. A letter arrived one day addressed to him from a desperate sounding man named George de Mohrenschildt. The letter read:

> Maybe you will be able to bring a solution into the hopeless situation I find myself in. My wife and I find ourselves surrounded by some vigilantes; our phone bugged; and we are being followed everywhere. Either FBI is involved in this or they do not want to accept my complaints. We are driven to insanity by this situation . . . I tried to write, stupidly and unsuccessfully, about Lee H Oswald and must have angered a lot of people. . . . Could you do something to remove this net around us? This will be my last request for help and I will not annoy you anymore. (signed by G de Mohrenschildt)[226]

George Bush wrote back:

> Let me say first that I know it must have been difficult for you to seek my help in the situation outlined in your letter. I believe I can appreciate your state of mind in view of your daughter's tragic death a few years ago, and the current poor state of your wife's health. I was extremely sorry to hear of these circumstances. In your situation, I can well imagine how the attentions you described in your letter affect both you and your wife. However, my staff has been unable to find any indication of interest in your activities on the part of federal authorities in recent years. The flurry of interest that attended your testimony before the Warren Commission has long subsided. I can only speculate that you may have become "newsworthy" again in view of the renewed interest in the Kennedy assassination, and thus may be attracting the attention of people in the media. I hope this letter had been of some comfort to

you, George, although I realize I am unable to answer your question completely.

When questioned by the FBI in 1988 regarding de Mohrenschildt, Poppy responded in a memo:

"I do know this man de Mohrenschildt. I first met him in the early '40's. He was an uncle to my Andover roommate. Later he surfaced in Dallas (50's maybe) . . . Then he surfaced when Oswald shot to prominence. He knew Oswald before the assassination of Pres. Kennedy. I don't recall his role in all this."

This loss of memory has surprised many readers but for others more acquainted with Bush strategy, this is a common occurrence.

To give some background on de Mohrenschildt, he was born in Russia, 1911, to a family of wealth and nobility. His family's money came from oil. His father, Baron Sergey Alexandrovich von Mohrenschildt, was governor of the province of Minsk for the czar and along with an uncle ran Branobel Oil Company in Baku. George de Mohrenschildt emigrated to the United States in 1939 and found employment with Humble Oil, which was co-founded by Prescott Bush. In 1952, de Mohrenschildt moved to Dallas and joined the exclusive Dallas Petroleum Club as well as becoming a regular in attendance at the Dallas Council on World Affairs, launched in 1951 by Bush friend Neil Mallon.[227] Throughout the 1950s, de Mohrenschildt traveled on oil business to many of the same locations where CIA interests were being developed. In fact, he was instrumental in expanding American oil interests in Cuba during the late 50s while working for the Cuban-Venezuelan Oil Voting Trust Company. The CVOVT had managed to corner the rights of over three million acres on the island. A *New York Times* article from November 30, 1956 read:

> The Cuban Stanolind Oil Company, an affiliate of the Standard Oil Company (Indiana), has signed an agreement with the Cuban-Venezuelan Oil Voting Trust and Trans-Cuba Oil Company for the development of an additional 3,000,000 acres in Cuba. This is in addition to the original agreement covering 12,000,000 acres. Stanolind has agreed to start drilling within 120 days and maintain a one-rig continuous drilling program for three years.[228]

It was during this time when de Mohrenschildt met J. Walton Moore, local CIA man in Dallas and Jack Crichton, an oil man who began negotiating with Cuban dictator Fulgencio Batista. In 1961, de Mohrenschildt was invited to lunch by Moore and according to Edward Jay Epstein, Moore told de Mohrenschildt about Lee Harvey Oswald living in Minsk (city in Russia). From that time until Oswald was accused of killing JFK, de Mohrenschildt was as close a friend to Oswald as anyone could ask for. Epstein also adds that de Mohrenschildt told him that Moore had asked him (de Mohrenschildt) to find out about Oswald's time in the Soviet Union. In return, he was given help with an oil deal he was negotiating with Haitian dictator Papa Doc Duvalier. In March 1963, de Mohrenschildt got the contract from the Haitian government. He had assumed that this was because of the help he had given to the CIA.[229]

So by 1962, de Mohrenschildt had befriended Oswald. Author Edward Jay Epstein (*The Assassination Chronicles: Inquest, Counterplot, and Legend*), who interviewed de Mohrenschildt in March of 1977, states: "Then, this morning, I asked him (de Mohrenschildt), about why he, a socialite in Dallas, sought out Oswald, a defector. His explanation, if believed, put the assassination in a new and unnerving context. He said that although he had never been a paid employee of the CIA, he had 'on occasion done favors' for CIA connected officials. In turn, they had helped in his business contracts overseas. By way of example, he pointed to the contract for a survey of the Yugoslavian coast awarded to him in 1957. He assumed his 'CIA connections' had arranged it for him and he provided them with report on the Yugoslav officials in whom, they had expressed interest."[230] De Mohrenschildt told Epstein that he had been ordered by CIA operative J. Walton Moore to meet Oswald, and he said that he would not have done so if he had not been ordered to.

Later that afternoon, George de Mohrenschildt was found dead, an apparent suicide, only a day before he was to testify before the House Select Committee on Assassinations. In his address book found in his personal possessions was a listing for *George H W Bush at 1412 W. Ohio*; also *Zapata Petroleum, Midland*. There is much here to establish that de Mohrenschildt knew Poppy Bush and as CIA director, Poppy was not being completely candid about what he knew of George de Mohrenschildt. Once again, Bush would have a memory lapse. He insisted that he had never asked for CIA files and records on the JFK assassination. Yet the agency would release eighteen documents (under the Freedom of Information Act) that showed he had, as the director of Central Intelligence, requested information from agency files—not once, but numerous times—on a wide range of questions regarding the Kennedy assassination.

Was George Bush trying to find out if his name was in the CIA Kennedy assassination file?

Was John Crichton Also Involved?

If Bush's actions on November 22, 1963 are curious, consider the case of his friend and 1964 Republican running mate John Alston Crichton, a former World War II spy, Cold War military intelligence officer, and Big Oil millionaire.

Born in Louisiana in 1916, Crichton served in the Army after graduation and landed in the Office of Strategic Services, the forerunner to the Central Intelligence Agency. Soon after World War II, he used his intelligence and business contacts to build an international network of companies, which were the epitome of "Big Oil" during the era.

By most accounts, Crichton first encountered Poppy Bush in 1964 when he earned the Republican nomination for governor in an uphill challenge to popular incumbent Democrat Governor John Connally, Jr. Bush had the nomination for the Senate—both men went down in defeat. Still, they formed a friendship sharing many political stages across Texas.

Fabian Escalante, the chief of a Cuban counterintelligence unit during the late 1950s and early 1960s, describes in his 1995 book a National Security Council plan called "Operation 40," a CIA assassination squad debuted at the Bay of Pigs. Escalante charges that Vice President Richard Nixon assembled an important group of businessmen headed by George Bush and Jack Crichton to gather the necessary funds for the operation. At the time, Crichton had big investments at stake in Cuban oil rights.

An owner, investor, and board member in innumerable companies, Crichton knew or worked with nearly every player in Texas. A founder of the Dallas Civil Defense, he was a popular figure in Texas's growing right-wing movement. He was also director of Dorchester Gas Producing Co. with D. H. Byrd, who owned the Texas School Book Depository building and was a close friend of Lyndon Johnson. Clint Murchison, Sr., a connected oil man who hosted an assassination-eve party at his Dallas mansion, served on a Crichton company board.

Crichton also became commander of the 488th Military Intelligence Detachment in 1956, an Army Reserve unit based in Dallas. According to him, dozens of the men in his unit worked in the Dallas Police Department. Some of them were in Dealey Plaza on November 22.

Crichton would actually be involved in the arrangements for President Kennedy's trip to Dallas. His close friend, Deputy Police Chief George L. Lumpkin, a fellow member of the the Dallas Army Intelligence unit that Crichton headed, drove the pilot car of Kennedy's motorcade. Also riding in the car was Lieutenant Colonel George Whitmeyer, commander of all Army Reserve units in East Texas. Crichton himself was thought to be in a command-center bunker established by Crichton's Army Intelligence unit.

Also, after Oswald's arrest, the Dallas Police Department would contact Crichton to provide an interpreter for a distraught Marina Oswald. According to the Warren Commission report, Ilya Mamanto translated for Oswald during her initial questioning by the Dallas authorities in the hours immediately after her husband had been arrested. According to author Russ Baker in *Family of Secrets*, these "were far from literal translations of her Russian words and had the effect of implicating her husband in Kennedy's death."

Incredibly, Crichton was never questioned by the Warren Commission.

Every way the JFK assassination story turns, you see the specter of the swashbuckling Crichton. A very public man, he died in 2007, a pillar of his community. He was 91 years old.

Today, John Alston Crichton's papers are stored at the George Bush Presidential Library in College Station, Texas. They are sealed.

So, Did Bush Have a Role in Dallas?

Although it would be interesting to cover all of the connections linking Poppy with JFK's murder, it would take up far too much of readers' time on an issue that has been written about in much more detail in other books, particularly in *Family of Secrets* by Russ Baker. According to a list compiled by Baker:

1. Poppy Bush was closely tied to key members of the intelligence community including the deposed CIA head with a known grudge against JFK (Allen Dulles); he was also tied to Texas oligarchs who hated Kennedy's politics and whose wealth was directly threatened by Kennedy (Texas big oil); this network was part of the military/intelligence elite with a history of using assassination as an instrument of policy (Guatemala, Castro, etc.).

2. Poppy Bush was in Dallas on November 21, and most likely the morning of November 22. He hid that fact, he lied about knowing where he was, then created an alibi based on a lead he knew was false. And he never acknowledged the closeness of his relationship with Oswald's handler George de Mohrenschildt.

3. Poppy's business partner Thomas Devine met with de Mohrenschildt during that period, on behalf of the CIA.

4. Poppy's eventual Texas running mate in the 1964 election, Jack Crichton, was connected to the military intelligence figures who led Kennedy's motorcade.
5. Oswald got his job in the building through a friend of de Mohrenschildt's with her own intelligence connections, including family ties to Allen Dulles (Ruth Paine).[231]

CHAPTER 19

STRUGGLING TO BE RELEVANT IN DC

Nixon: How about Bush?
Kissinger: Absolutely not, he's too soft and not sophisticated enough.
Nixon: I thought of that myself.[xvi]

Snubbed by Nixon

In 1966, Texas Republicans won a surprise victory in court mandating congressional redistricting. A new Houston district was carved for Bush—it was "country club" and heavily Republican. George H. W. Bush would go to Congress and quickly become a water-carrier for Big Oil, a defender of the oil-depletion allowance, and a proponent of the Texas defense contractors. Prescott Bush pulled strings to get his son appointed to the powerful Ways and Means Committee, a key assignment with real fundraising potential for another Senate race.

Bush and his father were major backers of Richard Nixon in his 1968 comeback bid. Bush and Nixon had been supporters of each other with Nixon campaigning for Bush in 1964 and 1966. Poppy ran unopposed for his seat in the

Congress, and he hoped he could deliver Texas electoral votes to Nixon. Together with Texas business associates Hugh Liedtke and Robert Mosbacher, the Bushes raised big money for Nixon's bid.

Once Nixon was nominated, Poppy and Prescott worked every connection they could, and within a few days some of the most influential members of the Republican Party sent letters to Nixon urging him to choose Poppy as his running mate, although George had only been in Congress four years. Prescott Bush would get Tom Dewey, instrumental in Nixon's own selection as vice president, to urge Nixon to take the young Texan on the ticket. Texas senator John Tower, elected in a special election to fill Johnson's senate seat in 1961, pushed Bush with Nixon. So did the CEOs of Chase Manhattan, J. P. Stevens, and Pennzoil. Of course, Brown Brothers Harriman weighed in.

William Middendorf II, a longtime GOP fundraiser for Barry Goldwater, Nixon, Gerald Ford, and Reagan who later served as secretary of the navy, claimed that he had worked the 1968 GOP convention to line up support for Bush. On the day after Nixon was nominated, Middendorf said that his associate, New York financier Jerry Milbank, went to Nixon's hotel room to talk about the vice presidential choices. "It was pretty early, I think it was about 7:30, I think it was his bedroom, actually, reading the paper. I said we've got delegates pretty much lined up for George, and it looks like he'd be a very popular choice among the delegates," Middendorf recalled. "That's when he told me that, 'Oh, gee, fellas, I'm going with my man Spiro T. Agnew,'" the little-known governor of Maryland who would later resign in a scandal.

Nixon promised Poppy that he would support his run for a seat in the Senate in 1970. He also assured Poppy that if he won, he would consider him as his vice presidential running mate in the 1972 presidential election. If he lost, Nixon would find him a desirable Cabinet position.[232] As history shows, he lost his Senate bid. Nixon sent him a letter of condolence, but no offer of a desirable appointment. When Poppy was tipped off that Treasury Secretary David Kennedy was leaving, Poppy wasted no time and called Nixon with a pitch; he asked Nixon if he could be undersecretary. Nixon's response was to tell Poppy that his new secretary of the treasury would be John Connally, a conservative southern Democrat from Texas. Connally, it was assured, would not pick Bush to be undersecretary. Now, Bush was being snubbed by a man he had supported, and for a *Democrat*? It was unforgivable! Bush rallied himself and suggested another job to Nixon: ambassador to the United Nations! Not only was he appointed to the position, Nixon upgraded the post to that of full ambassador, something usually held by envoys to foreign states. Nixon even made Bush a member of his Cabinet, another highly unusual turn of events.[233] Behind closed doors, Poppy was thought of as weak, as this short discussion between Nixon and Henry Kissinger shows when considering a mission to China:

> **Nixon:** How about Bush?
> **Kissinger:** Absolutely not, he's too soft and not sophisticated enough.
> **Nixon:** I thought of that myself.[234]

Bush held this post until 1972 when during a meeting at Camp David with Nixon, he was offered a different job. This must have seemed like a grand day for Poppy! Before he left that day for Camp David, John Ehrlichman, Nixon's chief of Domestic Affairs, had asked Poppy to stop by the office of Secretary of the Treasury George Shultz. Shultz offered Poppy the post of undersecretary of the treasury, which Poppy assured Shultz he would take under consideration.[235]

Losing the Senate Seat . . . Again

Warming up for a rematch with Yarborough in 1968, Bush courted LBJ on the theory that, once out of office, LBJ would rally the Texas Bourbon Democrats against his hated enemy. There was a secret meeting in early 1969 at LBJ's ranch—Bush was the only Republican member of the Texas congressional delegation to see LBJ off at Andrews Air Force base rather than attend Nixon's inaugural festivities. Bush sought Johnson's "advice" about leaving his House seat to challenge Yarborough.

"I got right to the point," George recalled to friends. "I said, 'Mr. President, I've still got a decision to make and I'd like your advice. My house seat is secure—no opposition last time—and I've got a position on Ways and Means. I don't mind taking risks . . . I'm not sure it's really worth it.'" Johnson looked George in the eye and spoke slowly and deliberately. "Son, I've served in the House, and I've been privileged to serve in the Senate too. So I wouldn't begin to advise you on what to do, except to say this: that the difference between being a member of the Senate and a member of the House is the difference between chicken salad and chicken shit. Do I make my point?"

LBJ wanted the meeting kept secret. Bush, however leaked it to the press in a May 28, 1969 press conference. He thought it would boost his status among the conservative Democrats. George decided to run, and lost. He received no help from LBJ.

After Bush landed a seat on the House Ways and Means Committee, many of the oil barons who had financed LBJ's

Prescott Bush lost the 1950 Connecticut Senate race when his ties to Planned Parenthood were exposed. (Getty)

Prescott Bush won a U.S. Senate seat on his second try. (Wikimedia Commons)

It seemed Poppy was working for the
CIA as early as 1961. (Associated Press)

George Bush ran for the Senate as a Goldwater conservative in 1964 and was
crushed. (Associated Press)

Date: November 29, 1963

To: Director
             Bureau of Intelligence and Research
             Department of State

From: John Edgar Hoover, Director

Subject: ASSASSINATION OF PRESIDENT JOHN F. KENNEDY
             NOVEMBER 22, 1963

        Our Miami, Florida, Office on November 23, 1963, advised that the Office of Coordinator of Cuban Affairs in Miami advised that the Department of State feels some misguided anti-Castro group might capitalize on the present situation and undertake an unauthorized raid against Cuba, believing that the assassination of President John F. Kennedy might herald a change in U. S. policy, which is not true.

        Our sources and informants familiar with Cuban matters in the Miami area advise that the general feeling in the anti-Castro Cuban community is one of stunned disbelief and, even among those who did not entirely agree with the President's policy concerning Cuba, the feeling is that the President's death represents a great loss not only to the U. S. but to all of Latin America. These sources knew of no plans for unauthorized action against Cuba.

        An informant who has furnished reliable information in the past and who is close to a small pro-Castro group in Miami has advised that these individuals are afraid that the assassination of the President may result in strong repressive measures being taken against them and, although pro-Castro in their feelings, regret the assassination.

        The substance of the foregoing information was orally furnished to Mr. George Bush of the Central Intelligence Agency and Captain William Edwards of the Defense Intelligence Agency on November 23, 1963, by Mr. W. T. Forsyth of this Bureau.

1 - Director of Naval Intelligence

VIN:gct (12)

DEC. 9 1963

62-109060-1396

This FBI memo from Director J. Edgar Hoover identified George Bush as working for the CIA in 1963 (see bottom paragraph). (Wikimedia Commons)

UNITED STATES GOVERNMENT

Memorandum

TO   :   SAC, HOUSTON   DATE: 11-22-63

FROM   :   SA GRAHAM W. KITCHEL

SUBJECT: UNKNOWN SUBJECT;
           ASSASSINATION OF PRESIDENT
           JOHN F. KENNEDY

At 1:45 p.m. Mr. GEORGE H. W. BUSH, President
of the Zapata Off-shore Drilling Company, Houston, Texas,
residence 5525 Briar, Houston, telephonically furnished
the following information to writer by long distance
telephone call from Tyler, Texas.

BUSH stated that he wanted to be kept confidential
but wanted to furnish hearsay that he recalled hearing in
recent weeks, the day and source unknown. He stated that
one JAMES PARROTT has been talking of killing the President
when he comes to Houston.

BUSH stated that PARROTT is possibly a student
at the University of Houston and is active in political
matters in this area. He stated that he felt Mrs. FAWLEY,
telephone number SU 2-5239, or ARLINE SMITH, telephone
number JA 9-9194 of the Harris County Republican Party
Headquarters would be able to furnish additional information regarding the identity of PARROTT.

BUSH stated that he was proceeding to Dallas, Texas,
would remain in the Sheraton-Dallas Hotel and return to his
residence on 11-23-63. His office telephone number is
CA 2-0395.

ALL INFORMATION CONTAINED
HEREIN IS UNCLASSIFIED
DATE 10-15-93 BY 9803 ___/KSR
(JFK)

GWK:djw
(2)

Schmidt -

Jackson -

62-2115-6

NOV 16 1963
FBI - HOUSTON

Oswald's handler, George deMohrenschildt, killed himself after being subpoenaed to testify about JFK's murder. Bush's phone number was found in his address book. (Corbis)

Poppy won a House seat in a district especially drawn for him. (Corbis)

GEORGE BUSH
For United States Senator

Bush was slickly packaged as a more conservative John Lindsay in 1970—he lost anyway. (Wikimedia Commons)

Attorney General and Nixon political advisor John Mitchell told me he directed the White House's 1970 illegal, dark money Townhouse operation to put hundreds of thousands of laundered money into George Bush's 1970 presidential campaign. It was called the "dress rehearsal for Watergate." (Wikimedia Commons)

Retired Senator Prescott Bush wanted to be president himself. He lined up big Eastern and Wall Street money for both failed Bush Senate bids. (Wikimedia Commons)

The UN was Poppy's consolation prize from Nixon after losing the 1970 Senate race. (Corbis)

George H.W. Bush perjured himself in his CIA confirmation hearings. (Corbis)

Senate Democrats confirmed Bush as CIA Director only after President Gerald Ford agreed to rule him out as a Vice Presidential candidate. (Wikimedia Commons)

Bush mistress Jennifer Fitzgerald (right) blackmailed Poppy with his love letters. (Corbis)

As Ronald Reagan's Northeast Political Director, I opposed putting Bush on the Reagan ticket. (Nydia Stone)

Selecting George Bush for Vice President was perhaps Reagan's greatest error. (Getty)

CIA drug smuggler Barry Seal was murdered weeks after threatening to expose Jeb and Dubya in drug dealing. He also died with George H. W. Bush's personal phone number in his wallet. (Wikimedia Commons)

OLIVER L NORTH
DOB 10 7 43

VP Bush chaired a restricted access group to traffic millions of dollars worth of cocaine into the U.S. to illegally raise money for Iran-Contra. Rumors continue to swirl around whether Oliver North had any role in the killing of Barry Seal. (Wikimedia Commons)

ROGER JASON STONE, JR.
Eastern Regional Campaign Director, Reagan-Bush Committee

I learned at the knee of Dick Nixon, and helped to elect Ronald Reagan (Nydia Stone)

Reagan was shot six days after signing a secret "transfer of power" agreement with Vice President Bush. Secretary of State Al Haig was opposed. (Wikimedia Commons)

A second gunman can be seen on the balcony, and the trajectory of the bullet that hit Reagan matches this downward angle. (Getty Images)

Bush family "friend" John Hinckley fired five bullets—none of them hit Reagan. (Wikimedia Commons)

Bush was superficially cordial despite the fact that I orchestrated his defeat in the New York and New Jersey Republican primaries in 1980. We split the delegates in Connecticut. (Nydia Stone)

Will Jeb restore the House of Bush? Will Jeb's son? (Wikimedia Commons)

Paul Manafort (left) is the best convention and floor manager in the Republican party. Lee Atwater (right), former Republican National Chairman confirmed that Bill had a mixed race son he abandoned. (Wikimedia Commons)

Jeb dealt drugs at Andover and allegedly in Houston. (Wikimedia Commons)

Jeb and his Grandfather Prescott Bush, who made his fortune selling arms to the Nazis. (Wikimedia Commons)

Was Jeb a CIA cut-out in Venezuela? (Wikimedia Commons)

Miguel Recarey fled the country in a private jet chartered by Bush Realty. (Wikimedia Commons)

Neil Bush used the family name to defraud investors. (Wikimedia Commons)

Just because Michael became president, doesn't mean we have to elect Fredo. (Corbis)

Dubya kisses the head of faux reporter and gay callboy Jeff Gannon. (Wikimedia Commons)

The Bushes and Clintons profiteer together. (Getty)

President Nixon backed all of George Bush's losing campaigns because Prescott Bush was instrumental in getting him on the Eisenhower ticket. Privately he said, "Poppy was a lightweight." (Wikimedia Commons)

career became Bush donors. As he had in 1964, Bush also raised hundreds of thousands from well-connected donors back East.

Finally, On to the Senate . . .?

Bush's election to the Senate in 1970 was considered a cakewalk. The Ways and Means seat brought vast fundraising capability, Texas had moved right, the Republican Party in Texas had grown, and Yarborough was out of step with the new Texas. Bush was again opposed in the Republican primary by Robert Morris. This time, the primary was a rout. Bush won with 96,806 votes (87.6 percent) to Morris's 13,654 ballots (12.4 percent). Morris would move back to New Jersey where he had already run once in the Republican primary for the Senate in 1958 against Representative Robert W. Kean, veteran congressman and father of future New Jersey governor Tom Kean. Morris ran again in 1982—and lost again—to the stunning Hungarian-American mayor of Montclair, Mary Mochary.

Bush had the nomination, but LBJ and his protégé John Connally were lying in wait to sandbag him.

Lloyd Bentsen, a conservative Democrat who served in the House with Johnson and was his neighbor on the Pedernales River, jumped into the Democratic primary. John Connally made 30-second TV ads endorsing Bentsen. LBJ told Bush that he was "neutral," but Johnson's friends did his bidding. Yarborough lost the Democratic primary in an upset.

Poppy had prepared for six years for a race against Yarborough. Now, he faced a smooth Bourbon Democrat to his right. An attempt to get liberal Democrats to cross over for Bush fizzled. Bentsen ran well with Mexican-Americans and blacks yet held conservative Democrats, who would have deserted Yarborough.

Bush brought in Harry Trealeven who, with the skillful Roger Ailes, remade Nixon's TV image in 1968—no small feat. Trealeven staged the ultimate modern media campaign, showing Bush as handsome, friendly, energetic, and glamorous. This "Kennedyesque" appeal was devoid of substance to attract both pro–Nixon conservatives and liberals upset with the Yarborough loss. Bush's slogan "He Can Do More" boasted of his "connections." Bush was depicted as dashing here and there, jacket slung over his shoulder, playing touch football. He outspent Bentsen— even Nixon sent $100,000 from his secret Townhouse fund. This particular gift would come back to bite "Poppy."

Bush's brother Jonathan Bush said that George was "getting in position to run for president." Peter Roussel, Bush's highly regarded press aide from 1970 to 1974 said "There were high hopes for him in that race. It was one of the premier races of that year, and a lot of people thought, well, Bush is going to win this Senate race, and there's probably a good chance that'll be the stepping stone for him ultimately going to run for president." Bush lost, however.

I attended John Jay High School in Katonah, New York with Marvin Pierce II, or "Peter" Pierce as he was called. I ran with Peter—he was a crazy mother. George H. W. Bush was Peter's uncle—his father, Jim Pierce, was Barbara Bush's brother. I drank a lot of beer, smoked a lot of marijuana, and drove a lot of cars too fast with "Pete," who was a big supporter of his uncle in the 1970 Texas Senate race.

I was volunteering for the New York campaign of Jim Buckley for the Senate at the time, and I recall spending election night with Pete. We were in his car, drinking beer and listening to returns on the radio. I was exultant because

Conservative Party nominee Buckley was winning a three-way race with liberal Republican Charles Goodell and Democrat Richard Ottinger. Bill Brock won in Tennessee. J. Glen Beall snagged a Senate seat in Maryland, Lowell Weicker (then a Nixon man) won in Connecticut over Reverend Joe Duffy, a far-left anti-war Democrat, and disgraced incumbent Tom Dodd running as an Independent. Then came the news out of Texas: Bush had lost to Lloyd Bentsen, a creation of LBJ and John Connally.

Peter was inconsolable. "My uncle said LBJ is a prick. Years of kissing his ass, and he decides to settle an old score—and screw George Bush in the meantime," he said. I was a Bush man, too, and had written him a letter telling him that I would come to Texas in the summer to volunteer for his Senate campaign. I got a response from his assistant Tom Lias brushing me off, so instead I did volunteer work for Buckley all summer.

"My uncle is going to be president someday," Pete said. At that time, I doubted he was right. (Pete was later badly injured in a car crash in which his female passenger died. He passed away in 2012.)

Overlooked Again

As a victim of two unsuccessful Senate campaigns, Bush's political future was in doubt. For the next 18 years, he would not be in control of his political career. He was well suited to advance his career by serving others in administrative posts, but it seemed a dead end. When Nixon offered him an insignificant job as assistant to the president, Bush made his case for more.

When Bush served as UN ambassador, he got to brush up his foreign policy credentials and attend endless cocktail

THE BUSH CRIME FAMILY

parties. He wrote notes, kept in touch with his friends, and bided his time.

Kissinger and Nixon both considered Bush a lightweight. He was never told of the back channel communiqués with the Communist Chinese. He staked himself out at the UN as a hardliner for Nationalist China and against the Reds. Poppy was kept in the dark about Nixon's visit to China. George and Barbara Bush lived blissfully ignorant in a sumptuous double apartment at the Waldorf Towers, with Herbert Hoover and Mrs. Douglas MacArthur as their neighbors.

Bob Dole served Nixon well as chairman of the Republican National Committee. Day-to-day operations were run by co-chair Thomas B. Evans Jr., later a Delaware congressman and an important early supporter of Ronald Reagan in 1980. Nixon decided to sack Dole for no other good reason other than he had gotten beaten up for attacking Democrats on behalf of Nixon. The president asked Bush to take Dole's place. "Dole is still pissed about it," Scott Reed, the Kansas senator's 1996 campaign manager, told me in 2013.

Bush mounted his second bid to be chosen for vice president. A boiler room run by Nebraska Republican National Committeeman Richard "Dick" Herman was set up in a suite of rooms at the Statler Hilton Hotel in Washington. There, Herman and two assistants began calling through George Bush's deep Rolodex. Senator Howard Baker, Elliot Richardson, Governor William Scranton, Melvin Laird, Senator Bill Brock, Governor Dan Evans, Donald Rumsfeld, Governor Nelson Rockefeller, and Senator Barry Goldwater were all under consideration.

My friend, syndicated columnist Robert Novak, reported that "as the new president [Ford, following Nixon's resignation] was sworn in, Rockefeller had become a considerably less likely prospect than either Senator Howard Baker of Tennessee or George Bush, the gregarious patrician and transplanted Texan who heads the Republican National Committee." Bush's elevation seemed assured.

On August 10, Ford announced that he would poll Republicans with the Republican National Committee to tabulate the results. Many Republicans who didn't favor Bush didn't want to tell him that, given George and Barbara's reputation for vindictiveness. RNC members and Republican members of the House overwhelmingly supported Poppy. The matter of the poll itself was the subject of a complaint by Delaware Republican National Committeeman Thomas B. Evans Jr., who attacked the poll in the press and also wrote to Ford. Evans, a former RNC co-chair, wrote:

> No one should campaign for the position, and I offer these thoughts only because of an active campaign that is being conducted on George Bush's behalf, which I do not believe properly reflects Republican opinion. Certainly, one of the major issues confronting our country at this time is the economy and the related problems of inflation, unemployment, and high interest rates. I respectfully suggest that you need someone who can help substantively in these areas. George is great at PR, but he is not as good in substantive matters. This opinion can be confirmed by individuals who held key positions at the National Committee.

Those favoring Rockefeller would counterattack, as. Webster G. Tarpley and Anton Chaitkin reported in *George Bush: The Unauthorized Biography*.

By August 19, the eve of Ford's expected announcement, the *Washington Post* reported that unnamed White House sources were telling *Newsweek* magazine that Bush's vice presidential bid "had slipped badly because of alleged irregularities in the financing of his 1970 Senate race in Texas." *Newsweek* quoted White House sources that "there was potential embarrassment in reports that the Nixon White House had funneled about $100,000 from a secret fund called the 'Townhouse Operation' into Bush's losing Senate campaign against Democrat Lloyd Bentsen four years ago." *Newsweek* added that $40,000 of this money may not have been properly reported under the election laws. Bush was unavailable for comment that day, and retainers James Bayless and C. Fred Chambers scrambled to deliver plausible denials, but the issue would not go away.

Bush's special treatment during the 1970 campaign was a subject of acute resentment, especially among Senate Republicans whom Ford needed to keep on board. Back in 1970, Senator Mark Hatfield of Oregon had demanded to know why John Tower had given Bush nearly twice as much money as any other Senate Republican. Senator Tower had tried to deny favoritism, but Hatfield and Edward Brooke of Massachusetts had not been placated. Now, there was the threat that, if Bush had to go through lengthy confirmation hearings in the Congress, the entire Townhouse affair might be dredged up once again. According to some accounts, there were as many as 18 Republican senators who had gotten money from Townhouse but whose names had not been divulged. Any attempt to force Bush through as vice president might lead to the fingering of these senators, and perhaps others, mightily antagonizing those who had figured that they were getting off with a whole coat. Ripping off the scabs of Watergate wounds in this way conflicted with Ford's "healing time" strategy, which was designed to put an hermetic lid on the festering mass of Watergate. Bush was too dangerous to Ford. Bush could not be chosen.

The CIA, By Way of China

Poppy became Ford's envoy to China and, recognizing conservative animosity towards Rockefeller, he began focusing on the 1976 vice presidential nomination. That effort was short-circuited by Ford's request that Bush become director of the Central Intelligence Agency. Bush believed that White House Chief of Staff Donald Rumsfeld, soon to become secretary of defense, had maneuvered Bush into the CIA post to eliminate him from consideration as Ford's 1976 running mate. Indeed, Senate Democrats sought and received a commitment from Ford that Bush would not be considered as a condition of Senate confirmation. The 1980 Bush operative David Keene—later national chairman of the National Rifle Association—told me "Bush thought Rummy screwed him."

Rumsfeld details the situation in his book *Known and Unknown*. "The circumstances surrounding George H. W. Bush's nomination to be director of the CIA is a particularly stubborn chapter of the myth that I had stage-managed Ford's staff reorganization," he writes, according to *Politico*. "By repeating the myth instead of setting the record straight, Bush in effect endorsed it."

The tension between Rumsfeld and George H. W. Bush was still alive in 2006. *Salon* reported that "Former President George H. W. Bush waged a secret campaign over several months early this year to remove Secretary of Defense Donald Rumsfeld. The elder Bush went so far as to recruit Rumsfeld's potential replacement, personally asking a retired four-star general if he would accept the position, a reliable source close to the general told me. But the former president's effort failed,

THE BUSH CRIME FAMILY

apparently rebuffed by the current president. When seven retired generals who had been commanders in Iraq demanded
Rumsfeld's resignation in April, the younger Bush leapt to his
defense. 'I'm the decider, and I decide what's best. And what's
best is for Don Rumsfeld to remain,' he said. His endorsement
of Rumsfeld was a rebuke not only to the generals but also to
his father.

CHAPTER 20

THE LEOPARD DOESN'T CHANGE HIS SPOTS

Prescott Bush established three essential myths that Bush men live by. The first is: I made it on my own. The second is: I'm not really rich. The third is: I'm running to serve my country.

—Political journalist Jacob Weisberg[xvii]

Same Old Racist

As we mentioned briefly before, in 1964 Bush set his sights on politics. To that end, after help from father Prescott, he landed a seat as chairman of the Republican Party for Harris County, Texas. Chairman of the Republican Party for the county may have been an achievement for others less driven, but Poppy had set his sights higher, much higher. He decided to run for a Senate seat from Texas.

After winning the Republican primary, he lost to Democrat Ralph W. Yarborough. "That was a vicious campaign," recalled Alex Dickie Jr., an aide to Yarborough. "Bush tried to make Ralph look like a nigger lover . . . Bush played that racial card over and over and appealed to the lowest common denominator in people. He did it then, and he never stopped."

Bush's racism is clearly shown in speeches that Bush made during the Senate campaign. "The new Civil Rights Act was passed to protect 14 percent of the people," George said. "I'm also worried about the other 86 percent . . . I am for the great traditions of this state and those of the Senate itself, and it irks my soul to see a man turn his back on his own people."237 Clearly Bush was not in favor of the Civil Rights Act, nor was he in favor of the Nuclear Test Ban Treaty. In fact, Bush went on record, following Goldwater's lead, to advocate the use of "small tactical nuclear weapons if militarily prudent."238

The Emperor's "New" Clothes

The years 1965 and 1966 would be for Poppy a time spent in self-evaluation and distancing himself both ideologically and personally from the extremist rhetoric he had espoused on the '64 campaign trail. This was "the new Bush." 1966 was the year that he left his position at Zapata Offshore to devote himself full-time to his quest for political power. He told the *Wall Street Journal*, "I want conservatism to be sensitive and dynamic, not scared and reactionary."239 Bush ran a successful campaign for a seat in the House of Representatives in 1966, becoming the first Republican to represent Houston in the U.S. House.240

Although the exterior of Bush may have received a new white wash, there were plenty of issues which showed his true colors. During his time in Congress, Bush was given the nickname "rubbers" for his unrelenting view of population control for the lower masses.241 The nickname was given to him by then chairman of the Ways and Means Committee, Wilbur Mills, Democrat from Arkansas. Mills was being forced

out of the chair due to his alcoholism. A phone call from father Prescott asked Mills to use his connections with other
Republicans, notably Gerald Ford, to treat this as an opening
for Poppy. Mills called Ford and John Byrnes of Wisconsin, the
ranking Republican on the Ways and Means, and quick as you
can say "Daddy Warbucks," Poppy was in.[242]

In 1969, Bush told the House of Representatives that, unless the menace of human population growth were "recognized and made manageable, starvation, pestilence and war
will solve it for us." Poppy repeatedly compared population
growth to a disease.[243]

One only has to remember that Prescott was an ardent supporter of race eugenics, something that cost him an election
way back in the day. Like father, like son, I would say. It's also
obvious that Poppy may have had a much different political
career if not for his father making calls and pressuring the
right people. Poppy had always said that he wanted to make
his own way and not rely on his upper class society standing
and connections to powerful family members and friends, yet
it is clear that this was not really so.

The Bush Oil Depletion Charade

There was another area that Poppy Bush was adamant about:
the oil depletion allowance. Here we'll see Poppy's masterful
technique of seeming to be in favor of a change, yet secretly
attempting to minimize the oil depletion allowance to the benefit of his cronies in the oil industry.

In 1926 the oil depletion allowance was set at 27.5 percent, allegedly to strengthen the new American oil industry.
This may have been a smart move in 1926, but by 1969, the
oil industry could hardly use the excuse of its being in its
infancy. It was estimated that the nation had missed out on

roughly $140 billion in tax revenues since the depletion had been set. In 1950, President Harry Truman declared that no tax loophole was "so inequitable" as the depletion, and cited the example of one oilman who enjoyed a tax-free income of almost $5 million thanks to this provision. Truman wanted to cut the allowance to 15 percent.[244]

In 1969, Poppy was in the perfect political position to influence this critical situation. In July, the Ways and Means Committee reported a measure to cut the allowance to 20 percent. Poppy seemed to be on board, yet according to him, "unrefuted" expert testimony had proven that a tax incentive was necessary for oil and gas exploration, "due to the serious gas reserve shortage in this country."[245]

Late in August 1969, Congressman Bush and Texas senator John Tower flew to San Clemente to meet with President Nixon on this issue. Bush instructed Nixon that the oil cartel was willing to accept some reduction of the depletion allowance, and that Nixon's administration should just say that it was willing to accept whatever Congress approved.[246] In the end, the Senate passed an allowance of 23 percent, which was a pittance, only amounting to a tax revenue of just $175 million a year. You see, Bush was never interested in really creating new legislation to increase the tax to these oil billionaires; his job was to minimize the amount and thereby keep any proposals for increased allowance from the books for years to come. Minimize the damage in favor of the oil companies, while appearing to be a champion of the people. In fact, an aide to Senator William Proxmire, Democrat from Wisconsin complained, "If the committee cuts back the depletion allowance by a modest amount—say to 23 percent–it may represent a low enough profile that Senate liberals will have a more difficult time cutting it further."[247]

The Bush World Genocide Program

One of the programs that Poppy engaged in during his brief time as the U.S. ambassador to China was the National Security Study Memorandum 200 (NSSM 200), Implications of Worldwide Population Growth for U.S. Security and Overseas Interests. The plan, developed by Henry Kissinger, Poppy's boss, and General Brent Scowcroft, detailed a "hit list" of 13 developing countries whose population, for national security reasons, and special U.S. political and strategic interests, should be reduced or limited. Sounds familiar? This hearkens right back to Prescott's eugenics movement, and Poppy's efforts at world population control (for poor folks, of course). Another thinly veiled attempt at genocide.

The idea was that population growth in third world countries would eventually threaten the United States by placing demands on limited strategic raw materials. Population growth in these countries would also mean increased strategic and military power for the countries in question. More people, bigger armies. The countries on the list included India, Bangladesh, Pakistan, Nigeria, Mexico, Indonesia, Brazil, the Philippines, Thailand, Egypt, Turkey, Ethiopia, and Colombia. In 1975, China, along with Kissinger and Bush, teamed up with Cambodia to create a model demonstration of NSSM 200. What followed was Cambodia's worst nightmare In the end, tens of thousands of peasants were starved to death.[248]

CHAPTER 21

BUSH AND WATERGATE

Keep George Bush, he'll do anything for us.

—President Nixon to H. R. Haldeman

RNC and the Road to Watergate

At his Camp David Meeting with Nixon in 1972, the president talked to Bush in the following terms: "George, I know that Shultz has talked to you about the Treasury job, and if that's what you'd like, that's fine with me. However, the job I really want you to do, the place I really need you, is over at the National Committee running things. This is an important time for the Republican Party, George. We have a chance to build a new coalition in the next four years, and you're the one who can do it."[249] After conferring with wife Barbara, who did not want him to take the job, he accepted Nixon's offer saying, "Boy, you can't turn a President down."[250] This sudden request from Nixon was a crafty move. The outgoing RNC Chairman was Kansas senator Bob Dole, someone that Nixon was not happy with. Why? Because Dole would not take orders from the White House.[251]

This is important when one takes into consideration that Nixon was already battling the accusations surrounding the Watergate break-in, which happened in June of that year. Bush was now in an important position to help Nixon, by stemming the flow of the investigation. Bush began his new role in January 1973 and at a press conference pledged that the Republican Party, from Nixon on down, would do "everything we possibly can " to make sure that the GOP was not involved in political dirty tricks in the future.[252]

Much has been written about Watergate; many researchers have put forth a variety of answers to the questions of why did it happen, who was responsible, and what did Nixon know and when? There are a few gems about Watergate that are still relatively unknown. One of these gems is the money trail that takes us from the Watergate burglars, all the way up to, you guessed it, George H. W. Bush. Really? Poppy Bush linked to Watergate?

The White House Special Investigations Unit, better known as "the Plumbers," can be traced to the demands of Henry Kissinger who in 1971, constantly complained to Nixon that something had to be done to stop the leaks of the Pentagon Papers. The Pentagon Papers were a secret study by the Department of Defense on U.S. involvement in Vietnam from 1945 to 1967. What the papers revealed was that the Johnson administration had systematically lied to the public and to Congress. It also made clear that despite the political rhetoric, the war could not be won. Why should Nixon worry about a war that he didn't start? Kissinger's angle was that it could undermine the secret talks with North Vietnam as well as show weakness in allowing the leaks to continue.

And so, the "Plumbers" were conceived as an alternate investigations unit free from FBI and CIA oversight. In fact,

Nixon had asked many times for help from the FBI and the
CIA, only to be denied. Out of sheer frustration, he gave life
to his own intelligence team. Top of the list was E. Howard
Hunt. Hunt had just retired from the CIA (that was the cover
story) and was looking about for work. Charles Colson, special counsel to the president, knew of Hunt as being a graduate, as he was, of Brown University. Hunt's name was well
known, almost legendary, as someone who was not afraid to
get the job done. In fact Nixon was also quite familiar with
Hunt. They met for the first time back in 1957 in Montevideo,
Uruguay, when Nixon was traveling on a South American
good-will tour for Eisenhower. Hunt had spotted Nixon (then
vice president) at a swanky restaurant and approached the
VP. He complimented Nixon on his dealings with Alger Hiss
back in the 40s. Nixon was so pleased, that he asked Hunt
to join him. The two spent an hour and a half in a spirited,
but like-minded discussion of foreign policy. Later on, Nixon
found out that Hunt was a man of action, and after that,
Hunt's reputation grew into a fearsome legend as well as
one of a sophisticated world traveler. Hunt was the first to
insist that coincident to an invasion of Cuba, Castro had to
be assassinated. As an outcome of this, Hunt met with Mafia
godfathers Santos Trafficante of Tampa and Johnny Roselli,
of Las Vegas. Hunt organized a special group of willing and
trained assassins named Operation 40, who were charged
with murdering foreign diplomats, dictators, heads of state,
embassy heads . . . anyone who didn't fall into line with the
CIA's overall plan to conquer wherever policy demanded.
This was during the Eisenhower presidency, and Richard
Nixon was the White House liaison that gave the green light
to assassinate leaders. (We spoke about Operation 40 before,
and I will mention more in a later chapter.)

Nixon must have felt in good hands knowing that a CIA covert ops master agent was running things. Although Nixon never really had the stomach for knowing the details of a hit, he was fascinated by the likes of Hunt and his band of assassins. Hunt had a very special status at the CIA and co-wrote Allen Dulles's memoir, *The Craft of Intelligence*. CIA director Dick Helms, too, fell under the Hunt spell and counted Hunt as more than just an agent; they often lunched together and Helms confided many personal details of his life to Hunt. Helms was also a big fan of Hunt's spy novels and did his best to promote the man, often keeping a stack of Hunt's books in his office, handing them out.

The Bush/Watergate Money Trail

Back to the money trail. The money used to finance the plumbers unit was provided by George H. W. Bush's business partner and lifelong friend, Bill Liedtke, from days of old, in the oil business. Liedtke was president of Pennzoil. In 1972, Liedtke raised $700,000 in anonymous contributions, including what appears to have been a single contribution of $100,000. According to Harry Hart, part of the money came from Bush's good friend, Robert Mosbacher, his former secretary of commerce, and head of Bush's re-election campaign. One account revealed that "two days before a new law was scheduled to begin making anonymous donations illegal, the $700,000 in cash, checks, and securities was loaded into a briefcase at Pennzoil headquarters and picked up by a company vice president, who boarded a Washington-bound Pennzoil jet and delivered the funds to the Committee to Re-Elect the President (CREEP) at ten o'clock at night."[253] The Mexican checks were turned over to Maurice Stans of CREEP, who gave them to Watergate burglar G. Gordon Liddy. Liddy then passed them to Bernard

Barker, aka "Macho." Macho Barker had been Hunt's right-hand man since the Bay of Pigs, and before that he headed Cuban President Batista's secret police. Barker was a short, stocky, bland-looking man who no one would suspect was a killer. On the night of the Watergate break-in, he was one of the five who were caught. It was some of the Bush money that Barker had on his person.[254]

At this point, the U.S. House of Representatives Banking and Currency Committee started to investigate the money financing the break-in. Chaired by Texas Democrat Wright Patman, the committee soon discovered the money trail. Patman was relentless, and soon more than a few "donors" were sweating it out. Patman, although not having specific authorization by his committee, reported that the largest amount of money, $100,000, had been sent by Bush ally and partner Texas CREEP chairman William Liedtke to a Mexican bank where it was laundered and then sent back to Barker's account in four smaller checks totaling $89,000, plus $11,000 in cash, which was found on Barker. Originally the $100,000 had come from a Robert H. Allen, a nuclear weapons material executive. Allen was also chairman of Gulf Resources and Chemical Corporation in Houston. As it turned out, Allen was Texas CREEP's chief financial officer. In addition, it was learned, in 1982, that the H. L. Hunt family owned 15 percent of Gulf resources shares. In 1977 they hired George Bush to be the executive committee chairman of their family enterprise, the First International Bank in Houston.[255] Although indirectly, Bush's name and connection was all over much of the money used to finance the Watergate break-in. It was looking like Poppy might be swept in with the rest of the lot.

On October 3, 1972, a vote was cast in the House Banking and Currency Committee to decide if the investigation would continue (as Patman wanted) or not In a 20–15 count against Patman, the investigation into the financial aspects of Watergate was ended. This prevented the issuance of 23 subpoenas for CREEP officials to come to Congress to testify. This was a blow to uncovering the truth, and a resounding victory for George H. W. Bush. In describing how and why the vote turned out like it did, CREEP chairman Maurice Stans said, "An all out campaign was conducted to see that the investigation was killed off, as it successfully was."[256]

Bush Mentioned on the "Smoking Gun" Recording?

There was one last concern for Poppy Bush. On August 5, 1974, the White House released the transcript of what has been called "the smoking gun" tape. This is the absolute proof that Nixon, despite all his rationalizations that he didn't directly approve, or know of the details of the break-in, was obstructing justice. What most people don't know, yet what Nixon and Poppy knew, was that during the conversation recorded between Haldeman and Nixon, where they reference "the Texans," they are actually referring to George H. W. Bush, among others.[257]

Here is a section of the "smoking gun" recording, from June 23, 1972, with H. R. Haldeman being the first speaker (emphasis added): [P = President]

H: That's the way to handle this now is for us to have (CIA Deputy Director Vernon) Walters call Pat Gray (FBI Director) and just say "Stay the hell out of this—this is ah, business here we don't want you to go any further on it." That's not an unusual development, and ah, that would take care of it.
P: What about Pat Gray—you mean Pat Gray doesn't want to?

H: Pat does want to. He doesn't know how to, and he doesn't have, he doesn't have any basis for doing it. Given this, he will then have the basis. He'll call Mark Felt in, and the two of them—and Mark Felt wants to cooperate because he's ambitious.

P: Yeah.

H: He'll call him in and say, "We've got the signal from across the river to put a hold on this." And that will fit rather well because the FBI agents who are working the case, at this point, feel that's what it is.

P: This is CIA? They've traced the money? Who'd they trace it to?

H: Well, they've traced it to a name, but they haven't gotten to the guy yet.

P: Would it be somebody here?

H: Ken Dahlberg.

P: Who the hell is Ken Dahlberg?

H: He gave $25,000 in Minnesota and, ah, the check went directly to this guy Barker.

P: It isn't from the committee though, from Stans?

H: Yeah. It is. It is directly traceable and there's some more through some *Texas people* that went to the Mexican bank which can also be traced to the Mexican bank—they'll get their names today.

P: Well, I mean, there's no way—I'm just thinking if they don't cooperate, what do they say? That they were approached by the Cubans. That's what Dahlberg has to say, the *Texans* too, that they—

H: Well, if they will. But then we're relying on more and more people all the time. That's the problem, and they'll stop if we could take this other route.

P: All right.

H: And you seem to think the thing to do is get them to stop?

P: Right. Fine.

There it was. Poppy's dirty secret that was nearly found out. How many secrets was Poppy keeping? The abandoning of his plane and the certain death it caused to his mates, the lies he told to cover it up, the fact that Poppy relied on his father's connections for all of his appointments in government, his secretive relationship with the CIA and Zapata Oil, his secret deal with the Mexican Jorge Diaz Serrano and PERMARGO, his faulty memory as to where he was on the day Kennedy was killed, his framing of an innocent man just to establish his alibi, and now this, the money that funded the Watergate plumbers. He was a slick character. Though seemingly weak and timid to most, for those that knew him, he was ruthless and would go to any lengths to gain what he felt was his birthright, the presidency. There's more, much more.

The Bush Watergate/Bellino Lie

There is evidence of another instance where Poppy injected himself into the Watergate Hearings. By July 1973, the Hearings were following a route that would keep Bush safe from exposure as to the funds he donated and also keep the culpability for Watergate squarely on Nixon. Deep in the secrets and origins of the JFK assassination and Watergate are allegations that Watergate was not a Nixon operation at all, but "a deep cover operation against Nixon, seeking to protect the prerogatives and secrets of a group accountable to no one."[258] There was only one committee member that could pose a potential threat to the safety of this secret group and his name was Chief Watergate Investigator Carmine Bellino. So, in July 1973, Poppy issued a statement accusing Bellino of ordering electronic surveillance of the Republicans in 1960.

At a press conference on July 24, 1973, Bush said, "This matter is serious enough to concern the Senate Watergate Committee, and particularly since its chief investigator is the subject of the charges." Bellino admitted that in 1960 he had sought to investigate the source of anti-Catholic literature during the Kennedy campaign, but he denied ever engaging in any illegal wiretapping or surveillance. Yet the damage to Bellino was done. Within days of his press conference, 22 Republican senators signed a letter to committee chairman Sam Ervin, urging that Bellino be investigated. The investigation of Bush's charges lasted two and a half months before Bellino was cleared of any wrongdoing. Bellino said, "Mr. Bush has attempted to distract me from carrying out what I consider one of the most important assignments of my life."

Shortly before his death, Bellino said, "I think it was a terrible thing that George Bush did. His charges were absolutely false. Bush was doing the bidding of the White House. His real reason was to disrupt my work because I had all the financial records of H. R. Haldeman, John Ehrlichman, and Charles Colson."[259] The accusations misdirected valuable time and resources away from more important matters and successfully neutralized Bellino from digging into deeper Watergate/JFK connections. Much like the accusation Bush had made against James Parrott back in 1963, Bush was using the same tactic to disable Bellino from digging where he shouldn't.

On August 7, 1974, George H. W. Bush delivered a letter to his embattled president.

Dear Mr. President,

It is my considered judgment that you should now resign. I expect in your lonely embattled position this would seem to you as an act of disloyalty from one you have supported and helped in so many ways. My own view is that I would now ill serve a President whose massive accomplishments I will always respect and whose family I love, if I did not now give you my judgment. Until this moment resignation has been no answer at all, but given the impact of the latest development, and it will be a lasting one, I now firmly feel resignation is best for the country, best for this President. I believe this view is held by most Republican leaders across the country. This letter is much more difficult because of the gratitude I will always have for you. If you do leave office, history will properly record your achievements with a lasting respect.[260]

The next day, Nixon delivered his resignation.

With Nixon out of the White House, and Gerald Ford, his vice president, assuming the presidency, there was a vacancy in the White House: the vice presidency Once again Poppy mounted a full scale effort to win Ford's choice. However, just as in Poppy's other attempts to slip into that chair, he failed. Ford called upon Nelson Rockefeller. A few hours before Ford made the VP announcement, he telephoned Bush and assured him that he would be able to offer Bush a prime post as a consolation, in the ensuing days.

Bush accepted a post as ambassador to China. He recommended this post for himself because he wouldn't be subject to a Senate confirmation hearing. God forbid they ask questions about his past that he didn't want asked. President Ford had offered him a post in either London or Paris, but both would have entailed an examination of his past. Bush said: "The United States didn't maintain formal diplomatic relations with the People's Republic at that time, so my appointment wouldn't need Senate confirmation. Because I'd been ambassador to the United Nations, I carried the title 'ambassador' to China."[261]

And so, once again Poppy stepped into a high-level government position, without any questions asked. His boss was Henry Kissinger, who as we have seen, considered Poppy weak. In fact Kissinger retained full control over Bush, and all decisions were made by Kissinger. Bush's job was to see that Kissinger's programs were carried out. And to see that Bush's agenda was kept in order was Jennifer Fitzgerald, Poppy's personal assistant. There is much evidence to show that Jennifer and Poppy were having an affair. From The Family *by Kitty Kelley:* "It wasn't just another woman, it was a woman who came to exert an enormous influence over George for many, many years . . . She became in essence his other wife . . . his office wife." This prompted Barbara Bush to pack up and leave for three months, burn her love letters, and eventually lead to her severe depression. Jennifer Fitzgerald arrived in Peking on December 5, 1974 and the next day she and Poppy left for 12 days in Honolulu to attend the Chief of Missions Conference.[262]

Need I say more?

CHAPTER 22

THE CIA IN THE '70S

I do know this man de Mohrenschildt

—CIA Director Bush[xviii]

Shake-Up at the Agency

On November 1, 1975, Bush received a telegram from Kissinger informing him that President Ford was planning to announce some major personnel shifts in the administration. This became known as the Halloween Massacre, in which Secretary of Defense Schlesinger was replaced by Donald Rumsfeld, and CIA Director William Colby was replaced by Bush. Colby was thought to have cooperated too openly with the Church and Pike congressional investigations. The Pike Committee (named after New York representative Otis G. Pike) or Select Committee on Intelligence delved into all aspects of the CIA and the intelligence community.

The Church Committee (named after Idaho senator Frank Church) was the Senate Select Committee to Study Governmental Operations with Respect to Intelligence Activities. Colby had been embroiled in both these investigations, and willingly and openly responded to questions that Kissinger and Ford felt should not have been answered. Colby believed that the CIA had a moral and legal obligation to cooperate with the Congress and demonstrate that the CIA was accountable to the Constitution. Now, it makes sense why George H. W. Bush was picked to direct the CIA. Obviously Kissinger understood that underneath Poppy's milquetoast exterior was a man who subscribed thoroughly to keeping secrets and avoiding exposure. He quickly accepted.[263]

There was an uproar on Capitol Hill concerning Ford's appointment of Bush as CIA director. Bush would now have to face scrutiny in the upcoming confirmation hearings. Even before the hearings began, there was outrage and opposition to Bush. There were references made to the "Townhouse fund," of which Poppy Bush was a main benefactor.

The Nixon / Bush Townhouse Slush Fund

The "Townhouse Operation" came into being when President Nixon wrote a memo to senior aide H. R. Haldeman saying, "One of our most important projects in 1970 is to see that our major contributors funnel all their funds through us." In carrying out Nixon's orders, Haldeman and Commerce Secretary Maurice Stans set up a secret fundraising enterprise, the "Townhouse Operation," designed to bypass the Republican National Committee. By doing so, Nixon intended to ensure that financial contributions were handed out to those candidates loyal to him. It turns out that George H. W. Bush was a main beneficiary of the secret fund, totaling about $106,000.

The Townhouse fund and the Bush money found in Watergate burglar Bernard Barker's pocket were two issues that tainted Bush. At a time when the public outcry against CIA misdeeds was at a peak, many thought that Bush was the least likely candidate to bring peace and confidence back to the CIA and the American people.

The *Washington Post* came out against Bush in an editorial titled "The Bush Appointment." The editorial commented that the position "should not be regarded as a political parking spot" for then-Ambassador Bush, especially at a time when public confidence in the CIA needed to be restored.[264] Frank Church spoke out very vocally against Bush. In a statement he issued as a response to Ford's attempt to impose a black-out on the Church Committee's report about CIA involvement in assassinations, he viewed the appointment of Bush as part of a plan of concealment and suppression. Asked by reporter Daniel Schorr about the appointment, Church responded with "There is no question in my mind but that concealment is the new order of the day."[265]

Negative mail was coming in from both houses of Congress. One of the main issues was that Bush would likely campaign for the vice presidency in 1976. Another was that he was a man with a recent partisan political past. Still another was his involvement with the Townhouse slush fund and the Barker money. GOP congressman James Collins of Texas wrote to Ford: "I hope you will reconsider the appointment of George Bush to the CIA. He is not the right man for the CIA."[266]

Democratic congressman Lucien Nedzi of Michigan wrote to Ford: "The Director of CIA must be unfettered by any doubts as to his politics. He must be free of the appearance, as well as the substance, that he is acting, or not acting, with partisan political considerations in mind . . . Accordingly, I respectfully urge that you reconsider your appointment of Mr. Bush to this most sensitive of positions."[267]

With so much negativity, it must have felt uplifting when of all people, Richard Nixon reached out to Bush in a letter of support: "You will be tempted greatly to give away the store in assuring the members of the Senate Committee that everything the CIA does in the future will be an open book. I think you will be far better off to stand up and strongly defend the CIA and the need to maintain, particularly, its covert activities."[268] Bush wrote back: "I couldn't agree more. We must not see the Agency compromised further by reckless disclosures."[269]

The Bush / Ford Letter Lie

Bush's confirmation came down to whether he was planning to seek the vice presidential nomination or not. Although Bush remained ambiguous, stating that he would not deny his "birthright," he realized that he would have to choose one or the other. The decision was made for him. On December 18, 1975 he was summoned to the Oval Office for a meeting with the president. Ford had, he explained to Poppy, written a letter to the committee chairman assuring the committee that Bush would not be offered the vice presidential nomination. In other words, Bush had been ruled out, and that was that. Realizing that he had no choice in the matter, he convinced Ford to amend the letter to make it look like it was Bush's desire to remove himself from the VP ticket. The last part of the letter that was delivered to Chairman Stennis reads as follows: "He [Poppy] and I have discussed this in detail. In fact, he urged that I make this decision. This says something about the man and about his desire to do this job for the nation . . ." Bush was approved to head the CIA the next day, December 19, 1975. Still, he had to pass the Senate vote. He passed by 64–27. On January 30, 1976 Poppy was sworn in.[270]

This really *does* say something about the man. It says that George H. W. Bush is a slippery opportunist, a man always scheming for his own gain. This had been true of his father, and his grandfather, and soon it would be true of his son. Now that Bush was in place, we can see how his reply to Nixon's letter was true to his words.

The CIA / Media Payroll Lie

The Church Committee was still going strong and the current issue at hand was the use of journalists on the CIA payroll, to shape and disseminate the news to the CIA's needs. Some of the senators wanted the names of these CIA-controlled journalists revealed to the public. Bush had made a statement, on February 12, that he would remove all "full-time or part time news correspondents accredited by any U.S. News service, newspaper, periodicals, radio, or TV network or station" from the CIA payroll. Yet in April the Senate Select Committee on Intelligence Activities found that there were at least 25 journalists and reporters still paid by the CIA. When questioned about his outright lie, Bush replied that his statement referred to correspondents "accredited" by U.S. news services. It did not account for the huge number of freelance reporters, editors, news executives, and foreign news organizations. These journalists apparently were free to be controlled by the CIA. So when Senators Huddleston and Mathias drove out to CIA headquarters in Langley, Virginia, to meet with Bush to demand he release the names of these CIA/media personnel, he flatly stated, "the CIA was not at liberty to reveal the names."[271]

New Policies for the CIA

In spite of his short tenure at the CIA, Poppy implemented some changes which would have a lasting effect. In fact, a Ford-approved reorganization of the agency's authority to conduct controversial operations and its director's authority over the greater intelligence community prompted the *New*

York Times to report that "Bush now had more power than any other director of Central Intelligence since its creation."[272] Another change that came while Bush was at the wheel was Executive Order 11905, which authorized the agency to conduct foreign counterintelligence activities in the United States.

Yet another venture that Poppy Bush was responsible for was to enlist the Saudis to provide financing for covert operations that Congress had refused to fund. This privatizing of covert ops enabled CIA to go around Congress if need be. As CIA director, Poppy Bush worked closely with his Saudi counterpart, Kamal Adham, who in addition to being chief of the Saudi General Intelligence Division, was also head of a separate agency charged with protecting the Saudi royal family. Poppy put his CIA resources to use in working with Adham to protect the royals. There had been threats on the king's life when a mullah had issued an edict proclaiming the Saudi royal family to be corrupt. Protection or not, at a conference in March 1975, one of King Faisal's nephews shot and killed the king.[273] Bush's CIA quickly launched an investigation into the assassination, working closely with Kamal Adham's intelligence apparatus. It was in this climate of fear that the CIA/Saudi pact was spawned. Yet years later, when Adham was caught up in a banking scandal, Poppy denied ever knowing Kamal Adham. "I don't know anything about this man except I've read bad stuff about him."[274]

Assassination Attempts in Jamaica

In Bush's first few months as director, the CIA launched a ruthless campaign to destabilize Jamaica for the purpose of preventing the re-election of Prime Minister Michael Manley. Included in this campaign were rallies to foment violence, illegal shipments of arms into the island, and three attempts to assassinate Manley. The CIA spent roughly $10 million on that secret campaign.[275]

To further deepen the horror, there has been talk that these same CIA-sponsored assassins were responsible for attempts on the life of reggae star Bob Marley. In 1976 Marley was setting up a huge outdoor concert with the least amount of political tone possible. However, he was in favor of Manley, a socialist, who represented the greatest threat to the United States. Manley's party was the People's National Party (PNP). The CIA-backed Jamaican Labour Party (JLP) was headed by Edward Seaga. Marley had noticed the island was full of guns, more than usual. With his free concert coming up, he was approached by the JLP and the PNP, both seeking his support. Marley wanted a non-aligned concert. Manley jumped on it with full endorsements, and to most people it seemed that Manley's endorsement amounted to a Marley/Manley union. The JLP, feeling that Marley had lied to them, had revenge on their minds. Three gunmen burst into Marley's home on December 3rd and shot Bob Marley. Although it's still argued as to who was behind the shooting, most people are willing to point the finger at the CIA-backed JLP.[276]

Lying for the CIA

Poppy harbored a hyper-interest in CIA files relating to the Kennedy assassination, requesting JFK files from the CIA vaults time and time again. However, in later years when he became president, he would deny ever making any requests to review such agency files. This lie would come right back and bite him when the agency released 18 documents that showed he had indeed, as CIA director, requested information on several occasions regarding the Kennedy assassination.[277] In one memo, dated September 15, 1976, he asked his deputy director to look into the news accounts that linked Lee Harvey Oswald's assailant, Jack Ruby, to mobster Santos Trafficante. "A recent Jack Anderson story referred to a CIA cable, the subject matter of which had some UK journalist observing Jack Ruby visiting Trafficante in jail (in Cuba). Is there such a cable? If so, I would like to see it."[278]

In another memo dated September 9, 1976, he asked about a Jack Anderson column that said CIA records showed the former CIA director John McCone had briefed Lyndon Johnson about the JFK assassination and suggested that "Cubans may have been behind the assassination." In the margin of the column Poppy wrote: "Is this true?"[279] It's probable that he kept tabs on JFK-related items, in case his own questionable involvement in JFK matters surfaced.

The Consummate Liar

As CIA director, Poppy testified 51 times before Congress. According to Kitty Kelley's bio book, *The Family*: ". . . he had perfected the bending and stretching of truth . . . George was as smooth as an eel slithering through oil. His lies on behalf of the CIA ranged from outright falsehoods and adamant denials to obfuscations and evasive omissions."[280] A more accurate portrait of Poppy Bush I have not seen. He stalled in providing information to the Justice Department prosecutors in their case against former director Richard Helms for lying to Congress about the CIA's role in the 1973 military coup in Chile. He buried the CIA's lies to Congress about Cuban involvement in Angola, and he denied the CIA had planted false propaganda in the U.S. press about Soviets in Angola. He refused to cooperate with the investigation into the Washington, DC, car bombing of former Chilean ambassador to the United States, Orlando Letelier. The car bomb took the life of

Letelier and the wife of his assistant, Michael, Ronni Moffitt. He had good reason to cover up that dirty little secret: the CIA knew that two of the assassins were in the United States at the time of the bombing, and knew that Chilean dictator Augusto Pinochet's secret service was behind it.[281] As detailed in the next section, George H. W. Bush knew much more about the bombing.

The Letelier Bombing Lie

Salvador Allende's former ambassador to the U.S. Orlando Letelier, and Ronni Moffitt, the wife of his assistant, Michael, were murdered on September 21, 1976, when a remote-controlled bomb ripped apart Letelier's car as they drove down Massachusetts Avenue, a stately section of Washington known as Embassy Row. Allende, the world's first democratically elected Marxist president, was ousted in a bloody CIA-backed coup that led to his assassination in 1973. The attack on Letelier was later attributed to CORU (Coordination of United Revolutionary Organizations).

Within four months of forming in 1976, CORU claimed to have killed 76 people in North and South America, including Letelier. CORU was later described as a terrorist group that had "the active support of the CIA." CORU members also had close links with Chile's feared secret police, DINA, which was also implicated in the murder of Letelier. Two Cuban exiles and a U.S. citizen were later charged with Letelier's murder.[282] Many CORU members served with the CIA's contra terrorist movement in Nicaragua.

One of the assassins was CIA agent Michael Vernon Townley. Townley had been working "off the books" for the Chilean secret police, DINA. At this time DINA was engaged in its Operation Condor, a plan to assassinate opponents of the Pinochet dictatorship. George Landau, the ambassador to Chile, sent a cable to the State Department requesting that two agents of the DINA be allowed entry into the United States on Paraguayan passports. The assassins requested to meet with General Vernon Walters, the outgoing deputy director of Central Intelligence. The cable was read by Walters and Poppy Bush. Once in the United States, the two assassins met with Frank Terpil, an associate of Ed Wilson, one week before the bombing. The bomb that killed Letelier and Moffitt was the same type that the FBI claimed Ed Wilson was selling, with the same timer mechanism.[283] In the ensuing investigation, Bush stonewalled and did everything he could to divert culpability away from his CIA. He flew down to Miami on November 8, and warned the Miami FBI against allowing the investigation to go any further than the lowest-level Cubans. In the end, some low-level Cubans were convicted and Agent Townley got off with a plea bargain for a lighter sentence. Strangely, the records of the July-August cable traffic with Vernon Walters and Bush were expunged.[284]

Under George Bush, the CIA leaked a false report that not only cleared Chile's military dictatorship, it pointed the FBI in the wrong direction. The bogus CIA assessment spread through *Newsweek* magazine and other American media outlets, was planted despite CIA's now admitted awareness at the time that Chile was participating in Operation Condor, a cross-border campaign targeting political dissidents, and the CIA's own suspicions that the Chilean junta was behind the terrorist bombing in Washington, according to the author Robert Parry writing on the website consortiumnews.com.

In a 21-page report to Congress on September 18, 2000, the CIA officially acknowledged for the first time that the mastermind of the terrorist attack, Chilean intelligence chief Manuel

Contreras, was a paid asset of the CIA. The new report was issued almost 24 years to the day after the murder of Letelier and Moffitt. In the new report, the CIA also acknowledged publicly for the first time that it consulted Contreras in October 1976 about the Letelier assassination. The report added that the CIA was aware of the alleged Chilean government role in the murders and included that suspicion in an internal cable the same month.

Bush has never explained his role in putting out the false cover story that diverted attention away from the real terrorists. Nor has Bush explained what he knew about the Chilean intelligence operation in the weeks before Letelier and Moffitt were killed. In 1988, Parry said that when then–Vice President Bush was citing his CIA work as an important part of his government experience, he submitted questions to him asking about his actions in the days before and after the Letelier bombing. Bush's chief of staff, Craig Fuller, wrote back, saying Bush "will have no comment on the specific issues raised in your letter."

Echoes of Lockerbie

By far the most serious act of terrorism alleged against the CIA, when Bush was its chief, was the blowing up of a Cuban Airlines plane shortly after it took off from Barbados on October 6, 1976. The attack, which was claimed by the aforementioned Cuban exile terrorist group called CORU, killed 73 people, including the entire Cuban Olympic championship fencing team.

Proof has recently emerged of the lengths that the CIA would go to carry out acts of terrorism against civilian targets and, even more pertinently, how the agency was prepared to fabricate evidence "providing irrevocable proof" that Cuba was responsible for terrorist actions which they knew Cuba was not involved in. The *Guardian* reported the existence of Operation Dirty Trick—a plan to blame Cuba for any mishap during John Glenn's pioneering Earth orbit flight on February 20, 1962. This would be accomplished by "manufacturing various pieces of evidence" that would "prove" electronic interference by Cuba. This evidence was among 1500 pages of classified documents released by the Assassination Records Review Board—the agency that oversees the release of papers connected with the murder of President Kennedy in 1963.

A U.S. Army memorandum from March 1962 entitled *Possible Actions to Provoke, Harass or Disrupt Cuba* suggested "downing a US plane and blaming it on Mr. Castro," or showing "convincingly that a Cuban aircraft has shot down a chartered civilian airliner." It also proposed sinking a U.S. warship—and presumably killing their own servicemen—"which could be blamed on Cuba." The CIA would use Cuban exile terrorists who would fly close to the island to "distract local pilots with radio conversations with the aim of causing the crash."

The memo also proposed developing a strategy of tension with exile groups that involved a plan to "sink a boatload of Cubans en route for Florida." The U.S. government was planning acts of treason and piracy on the high seas as well as indiscriminate terrorist acts against civilian airliners in its ambition to remove the popular government of President Castro and replace it with the mobsters and autocrats who supported the Batista regime until the revolution in 1959.[285]

Carter's Premonition

Jimmy Carter was elected president in 1976, and Poppy went down to Plains, Georgia, to pitch the importance of letting him stay on at the CIA. Bush's point was that in 1960 and 1968, CIA directors were retained during presidential transitions. Carter apparently was not impressed and Bush had to step down. During one of the last intelligence briefings with Carter, one of Poppy's deputies outlined a long-range national security problem due to surface. Carter, as if in a psychic premonition calmly said, "I don't need to worry about that. By then George will be president and he can take care of it."[286]

CHAPTER 23

ON TO THE (VICE) PRESIDENCY

Why the hell can't he speak English? He acts like one of those goddamn country clubbers.

—Former President Nixon complaining about George H. W. Bush to co-author Roger Stone

The Busy Corporate Executive

Once Bush left the CIA, he embarked on a maniacal quest to assert himself among corporations and the banking industry. In February 1977, Robert Stewart III, chairman of the holding company for First International Bankshares of Dallas, announced that Bush would become the chairman of the executive committee of First International Bank of Houston, and at the same time, become a director of First International Bankshares Ltd. of London. Poppy also became a director of First International Bankshares, Inc., and he joined the board of Purolator Oil Company, Eli Lilly and Co., a huge pharmaceutical company, and Texas Gulf, Inc. Bush also became a director of Baylor Medical College, a trustee of Trinity Medical College in San Antonio, and a trustee of Phillips Academy in Andover, Massachusetts.[287]

Assembles a Campaign Staff via the CIA

As if all this wasn't enough, Poppy Bush slowly built his political machine to carry him to the presidency. One of Poppy's main allies in this effort was James Baker III. Baker came from Baker & Botts, a Houston law firm that dated back to the end of the Civil War. Baker & Botts were connected to Bush by Pennzoil. A Baker & Botts partner became president of Pennzoil and in 1979, partner B. J. Mackin became chairman of Zapata Corporation. Baker was one of the Houston attorneys for First International Bank of Houston when Bush was chairman. In 1980, Baker became the chairman of the Reagan-Bush campaign committee.

Another member of Bush's support team was ex-CIA Taiwan station chief, Ray Cline. Cline served as station chief in Taiwan from 1958 to 1962, and deputy director of Central Intelligence from 1962 to 1966. He then went on to direct the intelligence gathering operation at the State Department. In 1979, Cline was approached to organize a "CIA-type staff" for Bush's campaign. Stefan Halper was Ray Cline's son-in-law and a former official in Nixon's White House. Halper was in charge of Bush's "research" (dirty tricks) staff. A member of Halper's staff was CIA veteran Robert Gambino. In his CIA days, Gambino acted as director of CIA's Office of Security. The Office of Security manages CIA needs with all the country's law enforcement branches. Every law enforcement branch, state, county, city, etc., has to cooperate to protect the security of CIA buildings and personnel.

Other spooks that filled George H. W. Bush's campaign ranks were Gen. Sam V. Wilson and Lt. Gen. Harold A. Aaron, both former directors of the Defense Intelligence Agency. The *Washington Post* noted in an article by Bill Peterson, "Simply put, no presidential campaign in recent memory—perhaps ever—has attracted as much support from the intelligence community as the campaign of former CIA director George Bush."[288]

The Debate and Poppy's Tantrum

On May 1, 1979, Bush announced his candidacy for president. In Poppy's mind, his Republican opponent, Ronald Reagan, was no threat at all. He assumed he would grab the nomination of his party. Early on, Reagan and Bush were running about the same, but a debate changed all that. When a local newspaper, the *Nashua Telegraph*, agreed to sponsor a one-on-one debate between the Republican front-runners, the FCC ruled the paper's sponsorship was an illegal campaign contribution. Reagan offered to split the cost with Bush, but Bush, the penny-pinching miser, refused. Reagan ended up paying his share and Bush's, to the tune of $3,500. Reagan felt that since he was paying the entire cost, he should be able to change the event from a Bush/Reagan debate to one including the other candidates.

On the night of the debate, there were only two chairs on the stage. In the wings, at Reagan's invitation, were Senator Bob Dole of Kansas, Senator Howard Baker of Tennessee, Representative Phil Crane of Illinois, and Representative John Anderson, also of Illinois. When the other candidates showed up, they requested a meeting in a back room to discuss opening up the debate to all the candidates. Reagan was happy to oblige, yet Poppy sat at the edge of the stage as if in a trance, refusing to even discuss the idea with the other candidates. From the room behind the stage, Reagan sent Senator Gordon Humphrey out to urge Bush to talk to the other candidates. Humphrey said, "If you don't come now, you'll be doing a disservice to party unity." Bush snapped back, "Don't tell me about unifying the Republican Party, I've done more for this party than you'll ever do!" Like a spoiled child, he sat there, refusing to even acknowledge the others.

Meanwhile, out in the audience, people were stamping and shouting for the debate to get going with ALL the candidates. Reagan spoke into the microphone saying that the debate should commence with all the candidates. When the newspaper editor John Green yelled "turn Mr. Reagan's microphone off!" Reagan replied, "I'm paying for that microphone, Mr. Green." The crowd broke into wild applause for Reagan, while Bush just sat there, stewing in his childish temper tantrum staring straight ahead.[289] To most people he looked weak and according to William Loeb, "He looked like a small boy who had been delivered to the wrong birthday party."[290] The debate finally went on, and Poppy got his way, but the outrageousness of his behavior caused him damage beyond repair. Reagan came out of it looking like a man of action. Nobody seemed to remember the debate itself, only that Poppy Bush behaved like a spoiled, spoon-fed child.

After spending $3 million on the campaign, Bush won only four states to Reagan's 29. In May 1980, he bowed out and gave his support to Reagan. As the number one contender, Bush thought that surely Reagan would offer him the vice presidency. It was, as he had said so many times before, his "birthright." Poppy had been passed over three times before: once by Nixon and twice by Ford. It would seem the odds were in his favor. Reagan, however, didn't want Bush, and even worse, Nancy Reagan could not abide him. Reagan wanted Ford. Ford confided to Reagan that stepping down to the position of VP was not something that he would accept. Ford suggested Bush. Just how unwilling Reagan was to have Bush on the ticket is best illustrated by a counter-offer Reagan made, wherein Ford would be more like a "co-president." Again, Ford pushed for Bush. It's true, the polls all showed that a Reagan/Bush ticket would not only be the ideal choice, but would also unite the party. Reagan was still unhappy about Bush, saying, "Why can't I pick someone I like?"[291] Finally, bowing to the consensus of the pollsters, he phoned Poppy, who accepted immediately.

The October Surprise

With the November elections coming up, the Reagan/Bush team went into high gear. The biggest threat was that Jimmy Carter would resolve the Iranian hostage crisis just before the election, guaranteeing another four years in the White House.

The Iranian hostage crisis grew out of the overthrow of U.S. puppet dictator Shah Reza Pahlavi in 1979. The Shah had come into power through an American-backed coup in 1953 when the democratically elected Mohammad Mosaddeq nationalized the British Anglo-Iranian Oil Company. This act was viewed as a direct threat against British national interests. The Brits wanted America's CIA to mount and carry out the coup, and we did just that. In order to keep the Shah in power, the CIA trained a secret police force for him, known as the SAVAK. The Shah's regime was murderous and brutal and finally in 1979, was overthrown in an armed revolution by the people.

The Iranians made no secret of their hatred of the United States, calling us Satan. The fleeing Shah, and his fortune, sought sanctuary in the United States and Carter, ostensibly for humanitarian reasons (the Shah needed medical treatment) allowed the Shah and family entry. As a result, the Iranian people stormed our embassy and took 52 Americans hostage. Carter, at the urging of the Rockefellers, froze all the Iranians' petrodollars and the Shah's looted billions that were then being held in the Rockefellers' Chase Manhattan Bank in London. Chase was going through a shaky financial period and those billions served to bolster the bank's future outlook.[292] A year later, with the elections looming, the Reagan/Bush people sought to undermine Carter's attempts to win freedom for the hostages.

The Reagan/Bush camp needed to cut a secret deal with the Iranians not to release the hostages before the election. As it turned out, the hostages were not released as Carter had promised, and partly as a result of the year-long standoff with the Iranians, Carter lost the election. On January 20, 1981, the very day that Reagan and Bush were being sworn in, the hostages found themselves on a plane to freedom. Coincidence? The accusations that Reagan and Bush had somehow thwarted the Carter/Iranian deal to free the hostages by election time, thereby winning the election for Carter, were rampant. How much of a role did Poppy play? That's the million dollar question.

A preliminary congressional investigation was initiated and in 1992 a Special Report appeared in the *Executive Intelligence Review*, titled "Treason in Washington: New Evidence on the October Surprise." The report revealed through FBI and CIA documents released under the Freedom of Information Act that Bush played a personal role in keeping the hostages in Khomeini's hands until after Election Day 1980, and that Bill Casey, Reagan's campaign manager, CIA director, and a close personal friend of Bush, coordinated the operation.[293] The report was published by Lyndon LaRouche, a longtime Bush critic, so it's no surprise, October or otherwise, if the findings seem a slight bit biased.

Since the October Surprise is well known but often argued, we'll try to sort out the allegations and see what the truth is.

Basically, we know the outline of events. According to the allegations, the Reagan administration rewarded Iran for its participation in the plot by supplying Iran with weapons via Israel and by unblocking Iranian government monetary assets in U.S. banks. Presented here are the details.

- March 1980: Jamshid Hashimi, international arms dealer, is visited by William Casey at Washington's Mayflower Hotel, who asks that a meeting be arranged with "someone in Iran who had authority to deal on the hostages."[294]
- April 1980: Donald Gregg, a National Security Council aide with connections to George Herbert Walker Bush, meets Cyrus Hashimi in New York's Shazam restaurant, near Hashimi's bank. Former Iranian president Banisadr said in his 1991 book *My Turn to Speak* that he had "proof of contacts between Khomeini and the supporters of Ronald Reagan as early as the spring of 1980."[295]
- In the last week of July 1980: At a meeting in Madrid arranged by the Hashimi brothers that includes Robert Gray, a man identified as Donald Gregg, and Iranian reformist politician Mehdi Karroubi, William Casey says that if Iran could assure that American hostages were well treated until their release and were released as a "gift" to the new administration, "the Republicans would be most grateful and 'would give Iran its strength back.'" Karroubi says he has "no authority to make such a commitment."[296]
- About August 12, 1980: Karroubi meets again with Casey, saying Khomeini has agreed to the proposal. Casey agrees the next day, naming Cyrus Hashimi

as middleman to handle the arms transactions. More meetings are set for October. Cyrus Hashimi purchases a Greek ship and commences arms deliveries valued at $150 million from the Israeli port of Eilat to Bandar Abbas. According to CIA sources, Hashimi receives a $7 million commission.[297]

- On October 21, Iran, for reasons not explained, abruptly shifts its position in secret negotiations with the Carter administration and disclaims "further interest in receiving military equipment."[298]

- Between October 21 and the 23, Israel secretly ships F-4 fighter-aircraft tires to Iran, in violation of the U.S. arms embargo, and Iran disperses the hostages to different locations.[299]

- On January 20, 1981, the hostages are released into United States custody after spending 444 days in captivity. The release takes place just minutes after Ronald Reagan is sworn in as president.

Let's look at the evidence to support or disprove the timeline allegations. A key point of dispute was an allegation made by Iranian arms dealer Jamshid Hashimi that he had arranged for William Casey to meet Ayatollah Karroubi in Madrid on the 27 and 28 of July 1980, telling *ABC News' Nightline* of the meetings in 1991. *Nightline* discovered that Casey had attended a World War II historical conference in London around that time and therefore could not have been in Madrid. *Newsweek* journalist Craig Unger warned, prior to publication, that the conference records had been misread and did *not* prove that Casey could not have been in Madrid. A reporter for *Frontline*, Robert Parry, later discovered that in 1993–1994, "senior officials in Iran had informed intermediaries close to President Clinton in '93-'94, that the House task force had gotten the story all wrong." The Iranians asserted that they had indeed collaborated with Casey and other Republicans in 1980. Clinton chose not to reopen the "closed" investigation.[300]

Another key point of evidence was the claim that Casey attended a meeting with Karroubi in Paris on October 19, "an assertion supported by four French intelligence officials, including the French spy Alex de Marenches who described the meetings to his biographer."[301] George H. W. Bush was also said to be at the meeting, but has repeatedly denied it. During investigations in the early 1990s, Bush provided several alibis that fell apart, before maintaining that he was visiting a private residence in Washington. Bush refused to disclose the person visited, except to members of the House October Surprise Task Force on condition that they did not disclose the name or interview the person. (Then, I ask, what would be the point?) This person ultimately proved to be Richard Anthony Moore (Ambassador to Ireland 1989–1992), but he had died by the time this fact was disclosed.[302] That's convenient!

Political researcher Robert Morrow interviewed retired admiral Bobby Ray Inman in 2009 in Austin, Texas. Inman, who was involved in intelligence for over 25 years, told Morrow that he was convinced that the Reagan campaign made a deal with the Iranians to not release the American hostages until after the 1980 general election. Inman said he was completely convinced Reagan campaign chair William Casey was involved in such a deal, but he said he did not think G. H. W. Bush was involved because Casey hated Bush. Inman worked at high levels of the Office of Naval Intelligence and the Defense Intelligence Agency while Bush was CIA director in 1976 and they developed a close working relationship.

So, as with so many other "facts," we come to our own conclusions. Do we believe that our candidate was honest and would never dream of co-opting a presidential deal for his own gain? No, I say.

In 1981, an unrelated matter of great concern, and now relief for Poppy, was that the Security and Exchange Commission filings for Zapata Oil for 1960–1966 were found to have been "inadvertently destroyed." That's convenient!

The Reagan Assassination Attempt: "No Conspiracy"

George H. W. had observed the JFK assassination cover-up and learned from it, despite being perhaps the only person on earth to claim he could not remember where he was the day Kennedy was killed. Still bitter about losing the presidential nomination to Reagan, H. W. felt, as many in the GOP did, that he would have a very hard time getting elected president. Many of Poppy's CIA pals also felt that things would go better for them if their former boss was in the Oval Office. As in Dallas, there would be a lone nut gunman, a number of odd coincidences, curious personal connections, and unlikely physics.

Reports immediately after the shooting mentioned shots heard from a position above and to the right of Hinckley's, which covered the exit from which Reagan walked. NBC correspondent Judy Woodruff said that at least one shot was fired from the hotel above Reagan's limousine. Photos and footage related to those shots have rarely been seen, seemingly having vanished after being shown once. In the photo reprinted here, we can clearly see something or someone on the balcony above and behind Reagan. This photo has been reprinted many times, but almost always cropped to remove the figure on the balcony. Is it just a coincidence, or is this another grassy (Bushy) knoll?

On March 24, six days before the shooting, President Reagan signed an order putting Vice President Bush in charge of crisis management. Bush was the victor in a power struggle against Secretary of State Alexander Haig, over Reagan's signing of that order. Many of Reagan's top advisors opposed it. In that role, Bush was supported by Richard V. Allen's National Security staff. It was just six days later that the first crisis arrived when Reagan was shot.[303]

Haig was ridiculed for saying that he was "in control" of the White House after the shooting. As reported in the *New York Daily News* Haig actually said, "As of now, I am in control here in the White House, pending the return of the vice president."

As with Dallas, a lot of things about the Hinckley shooting bear closer examination. It is one of the least-scrutinized, under-investigated political events of the 20th century.

On the afternoon of March 31, 1981, an attempt to assassinate President Reagan was carried out on the streets of Washington, DC. The Secret Service, acting quickly, saved the president's life. It wasn't obvious that any bullets had hit the president until Reagan felt a sharp pain in his chest as the limousine sped off towards the White House. The car detoured and took the president to the hospital for a complete examination. One bullet entered his side, pierced his lung, and lodged just an inch from his heart. These are facts we all know. What's curious is that there are areas that Poppy Bush should have revealed to investigators, and instead tried to keep from the press and the public.

Bush had just delivered a plaque at the Hyatt Regency in Fort Worth, designating it a national historic site. Haig called Bush and informed him of the shooting. The vice president flew back to Washington to take control of the government. At around 7:00 p.m. that evening, Poppy calmly walked into the Situation Room and assumed control. Poppy asked for a condition report on (1) the president; (2) on the others wounded; (3) on the assailant; and (4) on the international scene. After the reports were handed over, Bush announced that there was "no conspiracy."

What's remarkable about this is that Bush announced that "no conspiracy" existed, either domestic or international, only five hours after the actual shooting. This was before Hinckley had been properly questioned, and before any thorough investigation had been started! How is it that a vice president, acting temporarily as president, could make such a sweeping statement without any investigation or evidence? From this point on, the "no conspiracy" assertion became the rule. One can only suspect that someone had something to hide. That someone was George H. W. Bush, and the something was the fact that the Bush family had been longtime friends and allies of the Hinckley family. The most immediate connection was that Neil Bush, Poppy's son, and Scott Hinckley, the assassin's brother, were scheduled for a dinner date at Neil's home the day following the attempted assassination.[304]

The Bush/Hinckley relationship went back at least 10 years to their shared conquest of the oilfields of Texas.[305]

Neil Bush told the *Houston Post* that "he knew the Hinckley family because they had made large contributions to the Vice President's campaign." He said he "could not recall meeting John Hinckley Jr.," who shot the president.[306] Sharon Bush, Neil's wife, stated, "They (the Hinckleys) are a nice family . . . and have given a lot of money to the Bush campaign."[307]

The very next day after these statements were made by Neil and Sharon Bush, Neil called a press conference and stated he wanted to set straight certain inaccuracies that appeared the previous day in the *Houston Post* article. The first inaccuracy was the statement made by both he, and Sharon regarding the "large contributions" to the vice president's campaign. According to Neil, the 1980 campaign records showed no money from the Hinckleys. (hmm, I say).[308]

Then they downplayed the scheduled dinner saying that Hinckley was there as a dinner date of a close female friend. In one more "clarification," Neil stated that he only met Hinckley once at a surprise party given to him by Sharon in January 1981.[309] Yet Neil's press secretary Shirley M. Green said, "I've spoken to Neil and he says they never saw Hinckley again . . . (after the party). They kept saying 'we've got to get together again,' but for some reason they never made any plans until tonight."[310]

That the vice president did not disclose the relationship between the families after learning the assailant's name is curious and at least a withholding of evidence. In view of these startling statements, and then their immediate about face, it seems pretty clear that the "no conspiracy" edict was meant to stave off any embarrassing revelations to this most curious and under-investigated family tie. Why, I ask, was Bush allowed to make such a sweeping determination of a matter not yet investigated? Why did the FBI agree with Bush's "findings"? There are some glaring inconsistencies in the official story. To offer a balanced perspective, I offer these points as outlined by Charles Overbeck, editor of *ParaScope*, in his essay entitled "Reagan, Hinckley and the 'Bushy Knoll' Conspiracy":

Reagan, flanked by Secret Service agents, was walking to his limousine when John Hinckley, Jr. surged forward, .22 pistol in hand, and opened fire. A bullet ricocheted off the limousine and took Reagan down, but he lived. One must wonder, then, why correspondent Judy Woodruff (now a CNN anchor), reporting for NBC News Special Reports immediately after the assassination attempt, insisted that at least one shot came from an overhang over Reagan's limousine. Woodruff later reported that the shot came from a Secret Service agent who was stationed on the overhang, which researcher John Judge dubbed "the Bushy Knoll."

Though John Hinckley Sr. was characterized repeatedly by the news media as "a strong supporter of President Reagan," no record has been found of contributions to Reagan. To the contrary, in addition to money given to Bush as far back as 1970, the senior Hinckley raised funds for Bush's campaign to wrest the nomination from Reagan. Furthermore, he & Scott Hinckley separately contributed to John Connally in late 1979 when Connally was leading the campaign to stop Reagan from gaining the 1980 nomination. The Bush & Hinckley families, of course, would do better under a Bush presidency.

According to author Barbara Honegger, a member of that group told Anderson he had warned the Secret Service about Hinckley's designs on Reagan 2 months before the shooting. In October 1980, Hinckley had flown to Nebraska to contact a member of the American Nazi Party. If Anderson's source is to be believed, the SS did nothing to stop the gunman. The day after his Nazi-seeking mission, Hinckley flew to Nashville to stalk Carter, but was arrested at the airport when authorities discovered 3 handguns in his suitcase. Oddly, after only 5 hours in custody, this unstable character—who had attempted to transport weapons over state lines & into a city to be visited by the president of the US—was fined and released without further ado.

Researcher John Judge has extensive notes and additional points regarding a Bush coup on ratical.org. In view of history, not the "official" history, but the actual history, a coup seems like a very natural occurrence, especially considering the coup on November 22, 1963. It worked then, why not again?

Reagan, at 70, was the oldest president ever elected in American history. He was already showing signs of limited focus. He was inclined to nap for several hours a day, and in doing so left the day-to-day matters of policy and control to his capable vice president. Reagan may have been unaware that he was surrounded by Bush loyalists, many from the CIA. During Reagan's recuperation from the attack, Bush tightened his grip around the few Reagan supporters, and asserted his power as the "shadow president," the one that called the shots. It's remarkable that Poppy can outwardly appear to have the temperament of milquetoast. At various critical moments he displays language and tone that hide his true character. Nixon and Kissinger both agreed that Bush was "too soft and not sophisticated enough." Bush employs this tactic to cause his political rivals to severely underestimate him. It's worked, every time. He's cagey, soft spoken, and a dangerous sociopath—sly like a fox. As we move into the next area of Poppy's quest for the presidency, we must address the deepening criminal acts supported and sustained by Poppy Bush.

CHAPTER 24

THE IRAN—CONTRA QUAGMIRE

What I have found is a snake pit without a bottom. They will do anything to keep this covered up.

—Ross Perot, American businessman and independent 1992 presidential candidate

The Iran-Contra Affair—First Layer

There are numerous accounts of the Iran-Contra Affair. For the purpose of this book we will try to limit ourselves to George H. W. Bush's involvement, which, by the way, is extensive.

As we've already discussed, Poppy was director of the Special Situation Group (SSG), charged with formulating plans for any anticipated crisis. This authority gave Bush total control over U.S. Intelligence. Under the SSG, another subgroup was formed, the CPPG, or Standing Crisis Pre-Planning Group. The CPPG's job was to work as an intelligence gathering agency, something that I thought was the CIA's job. In any event, these groups took care of every possible action or option related to clandestine activity, including diverting funds for ops, transportation of goods and services, control of the press, news media, and writers tasked with putting a spin on the story (if it were to come out), that the public would find favorable. In other words, the whole ball of wax, as never before.

Bush chose his staff carefully, calling on CIA veteran Donald P. Gregg to act as his principal advisor on national security. Gregg in turn brought along CIA assassinations specialist Felix Rodriguez. Felix was a high-level specialist who worked in the CIA's Phoenix Program in Vietnam. Phoenix was charged with destroying the Viet Cong's morale by killing and decapitating local villagers who may (or may not) have given aid to the communists. It wasn't important that most villagers were not aligned with the enemy; it was the body count that the CIA wanted. The more headless bodies—men, women and children—the better. In addition Felix was the CIA assassin who chased and eventually caught up with Che Guevara in the jungles of Bolivia. Killing Che was Felix's most treasured duty. Both Rodriguez and Gregg served under Bush during his brief tenure as CIA chief. Both men were completely loyal to the vice president.[311] Rodriguez reported to Gregg, who in turn reported directly to Bush. Nothing happened without Bush's approval.

In December of 1982, as a consequence for the CIA's rampant misdeeds and abuses in the 1970s, as brought to light by Senate hearings on CIA activities, an amendment was passed, entitled the Boland Amendment. This law stated that *"none of the funds provided in this Act may be used by the Central Intelligence Agency or the Department of Defense to furnish military equipment, military training or advice, or other support for military activities, to any group or individual . . . for the purpose of overthrowing the government of Nicaragua."*

Lt. Oliver North came to the vice president's CPPG from the National Security Council, where he had been for a couple of years after a distinguished service in Vietnam. North was ready to do whatever was necessary to support the CIA-backed Contra "freedom fighters" in their civil war with the communist-backed Sandinista rebel army. It was North who took partial responsibility for the idea of selling weapons to Iran, then using the profits to fund the Contras. The Iranians were gearing up for their invasion into Kuwait, and massive arms shipments were very much needed. The weapons were part of negotiations to purchase the release of American hostages who been kidnapped by pro-Iranians in Lebanon, and if a deal could be reached it was thought that moderate Iranian leaders would see America in a slightly better light.

By March 1983, Felix Rodriguez was having regular, although secret, meetings with Donald Gregg at the White House. Gregg had a plan for El Salvador–based military attacks against Nicaragua. At about the same time, plans were approved for a U.S. invasion of the tiny island of Grenada. The decision to wage war was approved without consideration of the War Powers Resolution, which requires the president to get congressional approval if U.S. troops are deployed for more than 60 days. Grenada was in the midst of a civil uprising. Rebels, led by Maurice Bishop, succeeded in overthrowing the pro-Western government of Sir Eric Gairy. The four-year reign of that Revolutionary Government ended when Deputy Prime Minister Bernard Coard overthrew Bishop and placed him under house arrest. Later, Bishop was murdered. Riots followed and requests for intervention came from the Organization of Eastern States, Barbados, and Jamaica. I mention these operations to illustrate the emergence of a "new" form of government in the United States. Rather than the president making foreign policy decisions with his advisers, it now seemed that the advisers, being CIA, steered policy towards CIA goals. In so doing, CIA goals became the president's goals.

In December 1983, Poppy Bush and Oliver North flew to El Salvador to meet with army officers. From January till March '84, the CIA, on approval from Bush, began launching coastal raids on Nicaragua, culminating in the mining of Nicaragua's harbors. Another Boland Act, Boland II, was passed. In meetings attended by President Reagan and VP Bush, the discussion was about risking third country financial support. The obvious elephant in the room was the fact that what was being discussed was illegal, yet the discussion quickly turned from "should we?" to "how can we?" do this. This is key to accepting the notion that both Reagan and Poppy Bush violated laws of our government, and laws of the sovereignty of other countries.

In January 1985, Felix Rodriguez met with Medellin Cartel money launderer Ramon Rodriguez who a year before had given Felix $10 million for the contras. In return, Felix promised to use his influence with Bush to drop charges against Rodriguez for smuggling cocaine. The timing of this is interesting because just a few months before, in November, a partner of Felix's was convicted of smuggling $10.3 million of cocaine into the States. Ramon Rodriguez had partied at the White House for Reagan's inauguration ceremony, but by May 1983, he was arrested aboard a Panama-bound boat with $5 million in cash. Over the next three to four months, Bush and North worked closely to outline a proposal in which they would supply arms to Iran for the hostages release, and use Israel as the middle man. In a memo from Poppy to North, he thanked him for "your dedication and tireless work with the hostage thing and with central America."[312] Congress passed yet another law limiting U.S. aid to the Contras. This was known as Boland III.[313]

In March of '85, Bush and Felix were back in Central America, delivering $110 million in economic and military aid to Honduran president Roberto Cordova. This was a "payment" for Cordova allowing the CIA to set up a military base where attacks against El Salvador could be launched from, and a large camp to train anti-Contras. The payment was in direct violation of the Boland Act: all three of them, in fact!

In January 1986 Reagan met with Poppy Bush, Donald Regan, NSA counsel McFarland, and Admiral Poindexter to discuss implementation of a draft that called for shipping arms to Iran through Israel. President Reagan signed the draft even though it openly, and by design, violated the National Security Act. Bush urged the president to sign a "counter draft" overriding the NSA. This counter draft also gave permission for the SCG (Bush's Special Crisis Group) to withhold and refrain from "reporting this finding to the Congress until I otherwise direct."[314]

The Contra resupply objective was going smoothly. Poppy felt that everything he, North, and Felix had worked so hard to put together, although illegal and an impeachable offense, was a success. He, Poppy, had circumvented the laws of the Congress of the United States, and damned if he was going to be told what or what not to do. Of course this was nothing new to Bush; after all, he was born and raised—cultivated you could say—to be the master of his world, controlling all things and bowing to none. This was the Bush story. He had carried on the family tradition of greatness and power begun by Prescott and Samuel Bush. He would never abide by the laws that the rest of society labored under. The Bushes made their own laws, if and when it served their agenda. His grandfather had done it that way, his father had done it that way, and he was doing it that way, the Bush way, the only way.

Poppy felt it was time for him to back off the day-to-day running of the Iran-Contra operation, and so he put it into the very capable hands of Oliver North. North, of course was honored that his vice president had such confidence in him. What a fool! Poppy, perhaps sensing that at some date in the future, these highly illegal activities might come to the attention of the press or the public, was stepping back to set North up as the fall guy. That would come later.

For now, Iran was getting their final delivery of 4,000 TOW missiles, and the hostages in Lebanon would be released. Down in Honduras, Felix was running the day-to-day unloading of weapons and other armaments for the Contras, and loading the plane full of marijuana to be delivered by pilot Michael Tolliver for delivery to Homestead Air Force Base in South Florida. (Actually, all Tolliver ever said was that he worked with someone named Hernandez who he believed was Rodriguez.) Tolliver completed this assignment and the next day Felix paid him $75,000. It wasn't just pot that Tolliver was flying back to the States; on several return flights Tolliver carried tons of cocaine.[315] After all, for the same space needed to transport marijuana, you could increase your profit by tenfold. Bush sought donations for the Contras from numerous sources. Accordingly the Sultan of Brunei donated $10 million to the Contras. In a strange twist, after it was deposited in a Swiss bank account, the money was "lost." On the night of October 5, 1986, another CIA pilot, Eugene Hasenfus, was flying a C-123k cargo aircraft over El Salvador in preparation for a drop. He was carrying around 10,000 pounds. of small arms, ammunition, and hand grenades, when it was struck by a missile fired from a handheld ground-to-air missile launcher. Hasenfus parachuted out, but lost his three crew members. The next day, Felix made a call to Poppy Bush to inform him that one of the aircraft had not returned as scheduled.[316]

Immediately the disinformation campaign was set into motion. Several attempts were concocted to divert ownership of the downed plane away from Bush's SSG. The Contras were ordered by Bosco Metamoros (senior Nicaraguan Democratic Force, FDN) in Washington, DC, to "take responsibility for the Hasenfus plane because we need to take the heat off the vice president."[317]

From Oliver North's diary: "Felix is talking too much about the Vice President's connection."[318] Reagan and Bush both wanted to deal arms directly to Iran and cut Israel out of the picture completely. So what to do? Write a proposal. A draft of this proposal was shown to Reagan, who immediately signed it into law: National Security Decision Directive (NSDD) 207.[319] Bush's SSG, also called Bush's Terrorism Task Force, was a 24-hour operation with no accountability.

Poppy was right to have started distancing himself from the responsibility of this secret anti-terror group. Things were starting to unravel. After Bush sent Oliver North down to El Salvador to assess the damage, control the press, and create an alternate explanation as to the plane crash, it wasn't long before the *Washington Post* ran a story titled: "Captured American Flyer to be Tried in Nicaragua." Worse was the press interview with pilot Eugene Hasenfus where he revealed Felix Rodriguez's involvement and close relationship with the vice president.[320] Bush answered the many press questions by stating: "To say I'm running the operation . . . it's absolutely untrue." In an interview with Mike Wallace of *60 Minutes*, Hasenfus stated that "Vice President Bush was well aware of the covert arms supply operation . . . he was backing this 100%." Heads began to roll.

The majority of blame for the Contra issue was placed on Oliver North and Donald Regan. Bush was heard to say that White House Chief of Staff Donald Regan should resign. There was no way out for Regan, so with much bitterness, he resigned. Five weeks later, CIA Director William Casey resigned. Casey was a witness to all the meetings and knew first-hand of Regan's and Bush's involvement. Within a few weeks, he was dead. A couple days later Robert "Bud" McFarlane supposedly attempted suicide by overdosing on drugs.

An investigating commission was convened with three members: Senator John Tower, Senator Ed Muskie, and Brent Scowcroft. Named the Tower Commission, it "investigated" the allegations that Regan and Bush had knowledge of the Contra supply effort, and gave them a clean bill of health. Some members of the press asked Tower how he had been paid off.[321] When Bush became president, he rewarded Tower by appointing him secretary of defense. The Senate refused to confirm him, most likely due to the favoritism he showed Bush during the "investigation." Tower died in 1991 in a plane crash.

President Reagan called on Bush to reconvene his Terrorism Task Force to evaluate the current Task Force program! Bush, evaluating himself for wrongdoing? As expected, he released this statement to the press: "Our current policy as articulated in the Task Force report is sound, effective, and fully in accord with our democratic principles, and national ideals of freedom."[322] Once again Bush got away clean. At least, so far.

Once Poppy became president, he nominated his Iran-Contra co-conspirator Donald Gregg for U.S. ambassador to Korea. During the grueling confirmation hearings, Senator Alan Cranston questioned Gregg on his relationship with the then Vice President Bush as well as his longtime friendship with Felix Rodriguez. Despite overwhelming evidence showing that Felix, Gregg, and Bush had many meetings at the time the Contra re-supply project was planned and discussed,

Gregg denied that either he or Bush knew of the "intricacies" of the illegal and criminal undertaking. At one point, when showed a memo about re-supplying the Contras, Gregg stated that it must have been a misspelling. Gregg stated, under oath, that the meeting was about resupplying "copters": helicopters, not Contras. This explanation caused laughter to break out among the senators.

It was more than obvious that Gregg was protecting Bush. In its closing statement, the committee lambasted Gregg and openly accused him of lying under oath, and making a mockery of the investigation:

> . . . when you (Gregg) are confronted with written evidence undermining your story, you point the finger of blame elsewhere. At our last meeting you said the (Gorman) cables were wrong, North's notebooks were wrong, Col. James Steele, U.S. Military official in El Salvador was wrong, North's sworn statements were wrong, you concocted a story that your secretary erred by writing Contras instead of helicopters. When we confront you with documented evidence which undermines your testimony, you accuse us of concocting conspiracy theories. The National Security Agency has rejected our legitimate inquiries out of hand. The Central Intelligence Agency provided a response with access restrictions so severe as to be laughable. The Department of Defense has given an unsatisfactory response, two days late. The State Department response was utterly unresponsive. The Committee has been stonewalled by Oliver North too. No member of the Senate can escape the conclusion that these administration actions are contemptuous of this committee.[323]

George H. W. Bush certainly had some loyal friends. He would not suffer nor accept blame for any part of the Iran-Contra criminal re-supply effort. In 1984, the Sandinista government filed a suit in the International Court of Justice (ICJ) which resulted in a 1986 judgment against the United States. The ICJ held that the U.S. had violated international law by supporting the Contras in their rebellion against the Nicaraguan government and by mining Nicaragua's harbors.

In 1986, the Reagan a acknowledged that funds from cocaine smuggling helped fund the Contra rebels. An FBI probe found that there had been a limited number of incidents in which known drug traffickers had established drug activity with the Contra rebels.[324]

The Iran-Contra Affair: Cast of Characters

- *Barry Seal:* pilot, drug smuggler, contract agent for the CIA, DEA informant, biggest smuggler in American history, murdered after threatening George H. W. Bush. (more details in the next chapter)
- *Al Martin:* retired U.S. Navy lieutenant commander and Office of Naval Intelligence, key witness to many Iran-Contra meetings, author of *The Conspirators.*
- *Jeb Bush:* Son of President George H. W. Bush, laundered money for the Iran-Contra affair, along with Oliver North; set up Barry Seal for assassination.
- *George H. W. Bush:* Vice president under Reagan and later president of the United States, formed and implemented plans to illegally fund Contras, worked closely with Felix Rodriguez and Oliver North, came under blackmail threat by Barry Seal.
- *Oliver North:* former Marine, assigned to National Security Council; worked directly with George H. W. Bush to set up and implement illegal funding of

232

the Contras; along with Jeb Bush, set up Barry Seal for assassination by Colombian hit men.

- *Medellin Cartel:* at the time, the world's largest cocaine producers and traffickers, attached to the drugs for arms sales to fund the Contras, headed by the Ochoa family.
- *Richard Secord:* former advisor to Vietnamese government, Air Tactical operations, war profiteer selling arms to terrorist groups, defrauded the U.S. government of money and services by overcharging and diverting extra profits for himself.
- *Felix Rodriguez:* Cuban-born original member of Operation 40, member of subgroup inside Op 40 which concerned assassination, member of anti-Castro brigade 2506, tracked and killed Che Guevara, trained members of Operation Phoenix in Vietnam, ran the supply depot in El Salvador for Iran-Contra, worked with Oliver North and George H. W. Bush.
- *Terry Reed:* Vietnam vet, recruited by Oliver North and Barry Seal to secure planes for Nicaraguan Contras, trained Contra pilots, set up warehouse in Mexico used for transshipment of drugs and arms for Contras, worked out of Mena, Arkansas, confidant of Barry Seal.
- *Ted Shackley:* CIA Miami station chief during Bay of Pigs; member of Operation 40; head of the "Secret Team" within Op 40 with Thomas Clines, Frank Sturgis, Felix Rodriguez, Rafael Quintero, Luis Posada Carriles, David Morales, and Edwin Wilson; head of Phoenix Program which in two years murdered 28,978 civilians; number two man in CIA;

negotiated arms for hostages deal with Iran, an important player in Iran-Contra affair.

- *Tom Clines:* with Ted Shackley at Miami station, placed in Laos as deputy to Shackley, headed CIA operations in Chile, worked with Rafael Quintero in Cuba plots, assigned to Nicaraguan project to aid Sandinistas, conspired to sell arms to Contras.

The Beginning

One can trace the Iran-Contra model all the way back to 1959 and Richard Nixon. After Castro successfully overthrew the CIA- and Mafia-backed Batista regime in Cuba, he deported all the Mafioso, closed their casinos, and kept the millions still in Cuba. He next deported all American embassy officials, workers, and military personnel. In Miami, they gathered with Richard Nixon to discuss ways of deposing Castro and regaining control of Cuba. To this end, a special off-the-shelf group was formed within the National Security Council to train and supply a private army engaging in terrorist acts against Castro and Cuba. These acts included guerrilla tactics such as economic destabilization, poisoning water supply systems, burning and bombing sugar cane fields, assassination of local village leaders, dropping anti-Castro/pro-American leaflets, and destroying radio and communication installations. This very special group became known as Operation 40 because there were at one time 40 members. Some of the members were Felix Rodriguez, Luis Posada Carriles, Antonio Veciana, Frank Sturgis, Orlando Bosch, Virgilio Gonzales, Carlos Bringuier, Eugenio Martinez, Barry Seal, and Rafael "Chi Chi" Quintero.[325]

But there was another even more secret group within Op 40. This group was specifically charged with assassination. In that assassinations group were Felix Rodriguez, Luis Posada

Carriles, Rafael "Chi Chi" Quintero, Frank Sturgis, and Rolando Martinez. The Op 40 group was run by E. Howard Hunt on orders from CIA deputy director Tracy Barnes. Richard Nixon, as vice president, was the White House point man for the secret team. Hunt was the first to insist that any successful invasion of Cuba would have to coincide with the assassination of Fidel and Raul Castro along with several other top Cubans.[326]

According to Fabian Escalante, a senior officer of the Cuban Department of State Security, Nixon recruited a group of businessmen headed by George H. W. Bush and Jack Crichton, both Texas oilmen, to raise money for the group.[327] This claim of Poppy Bush's involvement with Operation 40 is also supported by Reinaldo Taladrid and Lazaro Baredo in their book *The Bush Family and the Kennedy Assassination* 2006). The CIA basically used the same team that successfully ran the Guatemala coup just a few years before. That team was Tracey Barnes, Richard Bissell, David Morales, David Atlee Phillips, and E. Howard Hunt, all of them CIA. In addition to these seasoned agents were added Ted Shackley, Tom Clines, and William Harvey. According to author Daniel Hopsicker, Edwin Wilson, Barry Seal, William Seymour, Frank Sturgis, and Gerry Hemming were also involved in Op 40.[328]

The model for Iran-Contra came when Shackley and Tom Clines were transferred to Laos in 1965. Previously they were involved in the Cuba Project. With them they brought Felix Rodriguez, Chi Chi, and Posada. Together they formed the Special Operations Group also known as Joint Task Force on Unconventional Warfare. In charge of the military end of things was Maj. Gen. John Singlaub, who later became President Reagan's administrative chief liaison in the "private" Contra supply efforts. Once Shackley's group established itself in Laos, they became involved in the drug trade. The leader of anti-communist forces in Laos was General Vang Pao, who also happened to be one of several opium producers and heroin traffickers. Vang Pao wanted help to finance his anti-communist rebels. Shackley used his CIA connections, weapons, and tactics, to sabotage Vang Pao's competitors. In short order Vang Pao was left as the only producer and supplier of heroin in Laos. Shackley and Clines also helped Vang Pao obtain financial backing to form his own Air Transport Company in 1967. According to Alfred McCoy, author of *The Politics of Heroin: CIA Complicity in the Global Drug Trade*, Shackley and Clines set up a meeting with Vang Pao and Florida Mob chief Santos Trafficante to establish a heroin operation between Laos and the United States. As part of the deal, a percentage of the profits from the sale of heroin went to Shackley and Clines, who set up a bank in Australia named the Nugan Hand Bank, to deposit their personal wealth.[329]

Thus the model for dealing with drug traffickers and using profits from the sale of drugs to finance anti-communist guerrillas has its history in the early Vietnam period. When one realizes that many of these same people keep coming up as involved in illegal drugs and assassinations on a huge scale, it all fits together.

CHAPTER 25

POPPY AND THE MURDER OF BARRY SEAL

I love my dad. I'd kill for him. I'd go to prison for him because, I love him so much.

—Jeb Bush[xix]

The Murder, Bush, and the CIA

Barry Seal was an ace pilot who had been flying since he was 15. In 1955 he joined the Civil Air Patrol and took part in joint training missions in New Orleans run by David Ferrie. According to Tosh Plumlee, another pilot and friend of Seal's, Seal started working for military intelligence around 1956 at the age of 17. By 1958 he was flying weapons to Fidel Castro, who was fighting to overthrow the corrupt dictatorship of Mob- and CIA-backed Fulgencio Batista. (The CIA funded and supported both sides until Castro gained power and aligned himself with communism.) As we have noted, Seal was a member of Operation 40. Plumlee also adds that Seal worked closely with Ted Shackley in Laos and Vietnam. In 1972, Barry Seal was arrested in New Orleans and accused of sending C-4 explosives to anti-Castro Cubans in Mexico. The plane Seal was using, a DC-4, was loaded with almost seven tons of the C-4, 7,000 feet of explosive primer cord, and 2,600 electric blasting caps. It took two years to bring Seal to trial. It was ruled a mistrial and Seal was let go. According to Deborah Seal, his wife, Seal became involved in drug smuggling in 1975. In 1979 Seal was arrested in Honduras after arriving from Ecuador with 40 kilos of cocaine. He spent nine months in prison.[330]

While in prison he met and became friends with Roger Reeves, who worked for the Ochoa family cartel of Medellin, Colombia. Upon release he worked for the Ochoas, now known as the Medellin Cartel. The CIA saw that the Medellin Cartel could be used to help fight the spread of leftist or communist ideology in Latin America. To that end, Felix Rodriguez persuaded the Medellin Cartel to donate $10 million to fund the Contras.[331]

By 1982, Seal had moved his base of operations from Louisiana to an obscure airport in Mena, Arkansas. This was the loading and unloading center for drugs and military hardware. With Governor Bill Clinton's approval and his protection, the CIA set up an area, chain link fenced, including some large hangars. The flights went on 24 hours a day. Anyone who questioned the unusual activity was quickly told never to speak of it, ever.

It seems Barry Seal couldn't stay out of trouble. In March 1984, Seal was indicted in Fort Lauderdale, Florida, for smuggling Quaaludes and laundering money. In December 1984, Seal was arrested again, this time in Louisiana after flying in a cargo of marijuana. He paid a $250,000 bond. Trying to avoid a 10-year sentence, Seal reached out to George H. W. Bush to make a deal. He appeared in a secret session of Bush's Task Force on Drugs in Washington, DC, where he testified that the Sandinistas were directly involved in drug trafficking into the United States. He claimed that the Medellin Cartel cut the Sandinistas in for a share of profit in exchange for the use of airfields in Managua. Pressure was put on the DEA by Ronald Reagan and G. H. W. Bush to enlist Seal as an undercover agent and get photographic evidence of Sandinista drug trafficking. In accordance with those wishes, Seal's transport aircraft was outfitted with secret video cameras. Seal did get photographic evidence: a blurry photograph purportedly showing Pablo Escobar directing Nicaraguan soldiers loading 1,200 kilos of cocaine on a C-123 military cargo plane. The *Washington Times* (July 17, 1984) broke the story; the *New York Times* and the *Washington Post*, along with major wire services also gave abundant coverage of the Sandinista/drug trafficking story. Reagan was happy. He had his "evidence" of Sandinista cocaine trafficking and went on national television in March 1986 to plead to the American public to aid the Contras, that the Sandinistas, in addition to being Communists, were drug smugglers as well, and that this endangered the lives of our children. "I know every American parent concerned about the drug problem will be outraged to learn that top Nicaraguan government officials are deeply involved in drug trafficking." Sounds pretty convincing, except it was a lie.

Congressman William Hughes (D-NJ), chairman of the House Judiciary Sub-Committee on Crime, announced that he had uncovered evidence that the entire Sandinista connection was a U. S. Intelligence fabrication. During testimony, DEA agent Ernest Jacobsen stated under oath that White House officials undermined a DEA probe of the Colombian cocaine kingpins by blowing an undercover informant's cover when they leaked information in an attempt to link Nicaragua to the drug trade.[332] We know now that the informant was Barry Seal, and the person who leaked his identity was Oliver North.[333]

In articles dated March 18 and March 19, 1986 Joanne Omang of the *Washington Post* and Joel Brinkley, *New York Times* quoted DEA officials saying that they had no information implicating the Nicaraguan government in the drug trade. In Oliver North's handwritten notes (8/9/85) he states: "DC-6 which is being used for runs to supply the Contras out of New Orleans is probably used for drugs into the US."

In a December 27, 1985 deposition given to Assistant U.S. Attorney Bradley C. Meyers, IRS Special Agent William C. Duncan, and Arkansas State Police Investigator Russel Welch, along with his attorney Louis Unglesby, Barry Seal testified that between March 1984 and August 1985, he had made over a quarter of a million dollars smuggling up to 15,000 kilos of cocaine while working for the DEA, and another $575,000 when the DEA let him keep the money from one shipment.

As a result of Seal's exposure by North, the Medellin Cartel had put a $500,000 price on his head. Yet Seal confided to his co-pilot and friend Terry Reed that he wasn't worried about the Medellin Cartel. On their last flight together Seal also confided that if there was anyone to fear, it was the people he had been working with. Just prior to takeoff, Reed had overheard Seal on the phone with someone saying:

> Well, I'm sorry Leroy, if they feel like I'm blackmailing them. But this is business and I just gotta do what I gotta do . . .

When they were airborne, Seal started talking:

> There ain't nothin' in this world more powerful than blackmail, Terry, and don't let anybody tell ya different. Jeeeesus Christ, I got some good shit on some big people. Ever hear of that expression, it's not what you know, it's who you know? Well, whoever said

that just hadn't caught the Vice President's kids in the dope business, 'cause I can tell you for sure what you know can definitely be more important than who you know. It seems some of George Bush's kids just can't say no to drugs, ha ha ha ha . . . Well, ya can imagine how valuable information like that would be, can't ya? That could get you out of almost any jam. It's like a get out of jail free card. I got names, dates, places . . . even got some tape recordings. Fuck, I even got surveillance videos catchin' the Bush boys red handed. I consider this stuff my insurance policy.

Seal was referring to George H. W. Bush and son Jeb Bush picking up a couple of kilos of cocaine.[334]

The End Is Near for Barry

In reality, Barry Seal's sense of security was an illusion. Far from being an asset, he had become a liability. His boasting of having damning material on the Bush boys, and his increasingly reckless behavior—not to mention his cover being blown, his mounting criminal charges, and the fact that now the IRS was after him—all came to undermine his value as a DEA informant and CIA asset. Seal's lawyer, Louis Unglesby, was with Barry when the IRS showed up at his home and seized all his property. The IRS agent said: "You owe us $30 million for the money you made drug dealing." Seal replied, "Hey, I work for you, we work for the same people." To which the IRS agent said, "You don't work for us, we're the IRS."[335]

Seal's lawyer testified that when they told Barry he had to report to the halfway house, Barry told them it was a death warrant. Seal went back to Unglesby's office, where they called George Bush directly, who was then both Vice President and coordinator of the Drug Task Force. Barry threatened to blow the whistle on the Contra guns-for-drugs deals. Barry had openly said to many people that he had hired and trained a lot of the pilots on that operation, and he had the goods on Bush and others. After the IRS agents showed up at his house, he called Bush again and told him to get the IRS off his ass. 'If you don't get these IRS assholes off my back I'm going to blow the whistle on the Contra scheme.' He wouldn't let the IRS agents in the house, so they came back with a warrant. He was burning things in the toilet. This testimony came from IRS agents in the sentencing phase when we were trying to prove the government was involved. Shortly before he was killed, they were threatening to take away his house. The IRS was able to seize most of Seal's aircraft, while his million-dollar offshore bank accounts were also mysteriously emptied out.[336]

Unglesby has another interesting story to relate. He recounts when he had a confrontation with Barry Seal over the fact that Seal was keeping him in the dark about matters Unglesby considered crucial to defending him:

> Barry pushed the phone across the desk to me and said, "You wanna know what's going on? Here. Dial this number. Tell 'em you're me."
>
> When I did what he requested, a female voice answered the phone, sayin' "Vice President Bush's office, may I help you?"
>
> I said, "This is Barry Seal." She asked me to wait while she transferred the call, which was immediately picked up by a man who identified himself as Admiral somebody or other, who said to me "Barry, Where you been?"
>
> That's when I told him that I wasn't Barry Seal, I was his lawyer. Immediately he slammed down the phone.[337]

On February 19, 1986, Barry Seal was shot to death in a hail of automatic gunfire. In the immediate aftermath, Barry's girlfriend was murdered in Miami as well. The FBI stepped in and confiscated everything in Barry's trunk. It was known that Seal carried all his important papers (including his blackmail evidence) in the trunk of his car. Six Colombian hit men were rounded up in the next few days, and they had an interesting story to tell.

Richard Sharpstein, the defense attorney for Miguel Velez, one of the gunmen said: "All three Colombians who went on trial always said they were being directed, after they got into this country, on what to do and where to go by an 'anonymous gringo,' a US military officer, who they very quickly figured out was Oliver North." As we learned before, Seal wasn't afraid of the cartel; he had worked out a deal with them. Dandra Seale, no relation, was Seal's secretary, and she said that she never believed the cartel carried out the assassination. "The CIA people allowed it to happen. He had a chart, he had dirt on anybody and everybody." Barry Seal was murdered by Colombian hit men on orders from George H. W. Bush and Jeb Bush that were carried out by Oliver North. Oh, and by the way, Barry Seal died with Vice President Bush's phone number in the trunk of his car.[338]

A Liability, Now Gone

The following allegations have appeared only in author Al Martin's book, and only he can confirm if they are true. According to Martin, he had been at a meeting with Jeb Bush in February 1986 to discuss the text of Martin's upcoming grand jury testimony:

"I said to Jeb, 'Isn't it convenient that Barry Seal was assassinated when he was? And now suddenly all the information and documents he had are gone missing?'

"Jeb had a rather broad smile on his face, and he concurred that it was convenient. He added a little snicker—as he often had a tendency of doing. Also little beads of sweat formed on his forehead, as when he gets nervous. It's something you can notice when he's on television. He still has a tendency to have little beads of sweat around his forehead, when he is either lying about something, or he's nervous about what someone is saying.

"My conversations with Jeb at this meeting were overheard by the two Secret Service agents who were always assigned to Jeb when he was in his office at 1390 Brickell Avenue in Miami. I had intimated that if certain parties in Washington were not prepared to come to my aid pursuant to my grand jury testimony, that it would be entirely possible that certain details of a certain meeting occurring in September of the year [Sept., 1985] before might be leaked out to the press. Jeb asked me what I was talking about. I specifically mentioned a September meeting of the Dade County Latin America Chamber of Commerce, which Jeb chaired, and which, of course, was not used as a Chamber of Commerce meeting at all. It was essentially used as a political meeting for covert operational planning pursuant to Iran-Contra."[339]

Although there are no corroborating sources, Al Martin has also alleged that Oliver North, Richard Secord, Dewey Clarridge, Sam Watson, and Fred Ikley were directly or indirectly entangled in the murder of Barry Seal. As he writes, "I had recounted to Jeb—as if he didn't know what the text of that meeting was that he chaired—the conversations he had with Oliver North and Richard Secord and Dewey Clarridge, all of whom attended that meeting. Dewey seldom attended the meetings, but this time the four of them were discussing the assassination of Barry Seal and how it was to be carried out, since Barry was becoming an increasing liability. I had told Jeb that I had substantial corroboration of that meeting.

And I think Jeb understood what I meant. It would certainly place him into a conspiracy to assassinate a CIA drug runner for the sake of political expediency. When I was through speaking, Jeb became quiet and his demeanor became serious and changed. He became flushed, as he often does when he's frightened. Jeb responded by telling me that it would be most unfortunate if I were to do that, since I might wind up like George Morales or Johnny Molina."[340] George Morales was a pilot in the Contra drug trafficking scheme, and went to prison for drug smuggling. According to Al Martin Jeb Bush said, "Of course, Morales will never leave prison alive."[341]

In an article in the *Los Angeles Times*, Morales testified that he contributed $4 million to the Nicaraguan Contras and flew weapons to them after two Contra leaders promised to use their CIA connections to get him out of trouble with U.S. prosecutors. He testified that the CIA and the DEA were "very, very aware" of the flights, which encountered virtually no efforts to interdict them. Both agencies denied the charge. Morales said that he made six flights to landing strips on land owned by John Hull, an American farmer. In a videotaped interview with the Contra leaders, they confirmed Morales's story.[342] The day before he left prison, he "slipped on a bar of soap, hit his head, and died." Johnny Molina was found dead the next day with an entire 20-round clip fired into his own body. It was ruled a suicide. Jeb Bush was right. The funny thing is that Jeb was telling Martin about Molina's death about *eight hours before it happened*.[343]

In one more incident recounted by author Martin—and only Martin, so some may question its veracity—he refers to a meeting he attended that included Oliver North, Jeb Bush, Dewey Clarridge, and Joe Fernandez. "Dewey Clarridge and Joe Fernandez were there and Jeb was whining about how they were importing so much cocaine for the purposes of maintaining illicit covert revenue streams that, in fact, they were depressing the street value of the price of cocaine." Revenues were in fact diminishing. And North chuckled, and said that he had already made arrangements, that he, Dewey, Fred Ikley and Clair George had made arrangements. What they were referring to by "arrangements" was the opening of the so-called sea routes to substantially increase the amount of cocaine that was being imported. Jeb Bush said to Oliver North, "All you would manage to do is to further the price of cocaine." North's attitude was, "Well, we'll simply bring in more and more of the stuff to maintain revenues." As has been pointed out in the past, CIA-assisted enterprise narcotics trafficking managed to depress the street price of a value of cocaine from $30,000 in early 1985 to $12,000 by mid-1986. Later in the conversation, Jeb, wanting to be helpful, threw out a suggestion regarding the separate Guns-For-Drugs Operation being run out of Mena Airport in Arkansas. He suggested that North start changing the fraction *vis-à-vis* the Contras. Instead of one M-16 rifle, 1,000 rounds of ammunition, and the full field kit in exchange for one kilogram of cocaine, Bush suggested that North inform Enrico Bermudez and Eden Pastora that henceforth it was going to be two kilograms of cocaine for the same weapons delivery as it had been in the past. North rebuffed this suggestion, reminding Bush that the one M-16 rifle, ammunition, and field kit cost them a total of $1,000 net delivered and the value of the kilogram of cocaine was still $17,000 or $18,000.[344]

"Chip" Tatum was a pilot in Vietnam, a member of the first elite combat controllers (CCT), and contract agent for CIA, codenamed "Pegasus," recruited to infiltrate the 498th Medical Company from Fort Stewart, Georgia, assigned to Honduras. Tatum's handler was Oliver North. He worked closely with

North and Felix Rodriguez and transported cocaine to Mena, Arkansas, where he delivered it to Dan Lasater and Governor Bill Clinton personally. Quoting from The Chip Tatum Chronicles:

> We landed at Santa Anna and met with Enrique Bermudez and other Contra leaders. We were then taken to a processing area of some sort. As we approached, there was a strong smell of jet fuel and acetone. There were several tactical bladders, used for carrying fuels, sitting around the area. Six large fuel pods were on the ground but had the tops torched off. Inside there was fuel and ground-up coca leaves. Mr. North stated the following to the other passengers, "One more year of this and we'll all retire." He then made a remark concerning Barry Seal and Governor Clinton. "If we can keep those Arkansas hicks in line, that is," referring to the loss of monies as determined the week prior during their meeting in Costa Rica. I stood silently by the vat of leaves, listening to the conversation. General Alverez had gone with the Contra leader to discuss logistics. The other three—North, Rodriguez, and Ami Nir—continued through the wooden building, inspecting the cocaine. North continued, ". . . but he (Vice President Bush) is very concerned about those missing monies. I think he's going to have Jeb (Bush) arrange something out of Colombia," he told his comrades, not thinking twice of my presence. What Mr. North was referring to ended up being the assassination of Barry Seal by members of the Medellin Cartel in early 1986."[345]

In 1988, the day after Jeb Bush won the governorship in Florida, Al Martin got a phone call from Neil Lewis in Miami, an attorney who had previously represented Jeb and Martin, and who acted as a conduit for people like Martin to Jeb or whomever, a middle man messenger if you will. "Neil told me that he had a direct message from Jeb stating that if I wished to continue to be a resident of this state and to remain at large and with life that I best not reveal stories such as I have revealed here."[346]

The Iran-Contra drug trafficking operation went on officially till March 1987. In a March 1987 address from the Oval Office, Reagan admitted his responsibility for the scandal. "First, let me say I take full responsibility for my own actions and for those of my administration. As angry as I may be about activities undertaken without my knowledge, I am still accountable for those activities. As disappointed as I may be in some who served me, I'm still the one who must answer to the American people for this behavior. A few months ago I told the American people I did not trade arms for hostages. My heart and my best intentions still tell me that's true, but the facts and the evidence tell me it is not. As the Tower board reported, what began as a strategic opening to Iran deteriorated, in its implementation, into trading arms for hostages. This runs counter to my own beliefs, to administration policy, and to the original strategy we had in mind."[347] Poppy maintained that he was out of the loop.

Iran-Contra—The Living and the Dead

- **Caspar Weinberger**, Secretary of Defense, was indicted on two counts of perjury. He was pardoned by George H. W. Bush in 1992, before he was tried.
- **William Casey,** Head of the CIA, was stricken with a brain tumor and died hours before he would testify.
- **Robert McFarlane**, National Security Advisor, convicted of withholding evidence, was pardoned by George H. W. Bush.
- **Elliott Abrams**, Assistant Secretary of State, convicted of withholding evidence, was pardoned by G. H. W. Bush.

- **Alan D. Fiers,** Chief of the CIA's Central American Task Force, convicted of withholding evidence, was pardoned by G. H. W. Bush.
- **Clair George**, Chief of Covert Ops—CIA, convicted of two charges of perjury, was pardoned by G. H. W. Bush.
- **Oliver North**, National Security Council, convicted of accepting illegal gratuity, obstruction of justice, and destruction of documents. North's conviction was vacated because the appeals court felt that the trial was influenced by North's congressional testimony (as opposed to solely other evidence brought by the prosecutor), for which he had been given immunity. This grant of immunity put the prosecutor in a tough position, because there was a burden to prove that the trial was not influenced by the congressional testimony, an impossible hurdle.
- **Duane Clarridge**, ex-CIA official, indicted on seven counts of perjury, was pardoned by G. H. W. Bush.
- **Richard Secord,** ex–Major General who organized the Iran arms sales and Contra aid, pleaded guilty and was given two years probation.
- **Barry Seal**, pilot, covert DEA informant and drug smuggler for Bush, assassinated.
- **George Morales**, pilot, and CIA asset during Iran-Contra murdered
- **Johnny Molina**, pilot and CIA asset during Iran-Contra, murdered.
- **Olof Palme**, Prime Minister of Sweden who refused Oliver North's request that he provide false end-user certificates for the multitude of weapons that

were being purchased for the Contras. After refusing, he was dead within weeks.

- **Edmond J. Safra** died mysteriously when a fire swept his Monaco penthouse apartment. His banks had been used for laundering money by the Bush Iran-Contra traitors.

- **Charles M. McKee and Matthew Gannon:** McKee, ostensibly a military attache for the DIA in Beirut; Gannon, CIA Deputy Station Chief in Beirut; and three others were on board Pan Am Flight 103, which exploded over Lockerbie, Scotland. They were part of a counter-terrorist team in Beirut investigating the possible rescue of nine American hostages in Lebanon. The McKee team uncovered evidence that a rogue CIA unit called COREA, based in Wiesbaden, was doing business with a man called Monzer Al-Kassar, a Syrian arms dealer and drug trafficker. Al-Kassar was part of the covert network run by Lt. Col. Oliver North. Outraged that the COREA unit in Wiesbaden was doing business with a Syrian who had close terrorist connections and might endanger their chances of rescuing the hostages, the McKee team decided to fly back to Virginia unannounced. They never got there. "For three years, I've had a feeling that if Chuck hadn't been on that plane, it wouldn't have been bombed," said Beulah McKee, 75, Charles McKee's mother, to *Time* magazine. Four months after her son was killed for his efforts to expose the CIA, Mrs. McKee received a sympathy letter from George H. W. Bush. Mrs. McKee has never been satisfied with the government's version of events.

- **Don Aronow** was a close friend of George H. W. Bush. According to the book *George Bush, the Unauthorized Biography*, there is compelling evidence to conclude that Aronow was a drug smuggler and suspected drug-money launderer. He was murdered by professional killers on February 3, 1987. In the days before his death, he made many personal calls to George H. W. Bush.
- **Tommy Teagle**, a man interviewed by author Thomas Burdick, was afraid of being murdered by Bush because he had knowledge that Aronow and Jeb Bush had been partners in cocaine trafficking.
- **Michael Hand** was a Green Beret and an Army Colonel assigned to the CIA. He ran the Nugan Hand Bank, a front for CIA drug money, in Sydney, Australia. He was in frequent contact with George Bush after he became vice president, according to CIA operative Trento Parker. Hand was found in his car on a remote road outside Sydney, an apparent suicide. There were no fingerprints on the gun.
- **Danny Casolaro** was working on a book that tied together the scandals surrounding the presidency of George H. W. Bush. He told his friends he was going to "bring back" the head of the octopus. Instead, his body was found in a hotel in Martinsburg, West Virginia, on August 10, 1991, an apparent suicide. His wrists had been slashed 12 times. According to Casolaro's brother, Danny was extremely squeamish about blood; even a pin prick would have turned his stomach.
- **George H. W. Bush** was never listed as a conspirator in Iran-Contra; he became the 41st president.

- **George W. Bush** was never listed as a conspirator in Iran-Contra; he became the 43rd president.
- **Jeb Bush** was never listed as a conspirator in Iran-Contra, and is now running for president in 2016.

At least 30,000 people died as a direct result of the Contras. That war spilled over into El Salvador where another 75,000 were killed.[348]

During his election campaign of 1988, G. H. W. Bush denied any knowledge of the Iran-Contra Affair by saying he was "out of the loop." In fact, we know, as we have proven here in this book, that Poppy Bush *was* the loop!

CHAPTER 26

PRESIDENT 41— CARRY A LITTLE STICK

Sarah, if the American people ever find out what we have done, they would chase us down the street and lynch us.

—George Herbert Walker Bush to Sarah McLendon, 1992

President George H. W. Bush and Noriega

George Herbert Walker Bush, who had served as Ronald Reagan's vice president for eight years, and who had weathered the Iran-Contra scandal without so much as a stain upon the Bush name, was elected 41st president in November 1988. He won arguably by promising to the American people not to raise taxes. His famous quote was "read my lips, no new taxes." He knew at the time that he was lying, but he was prepared to do anything to get elected.[349] His popularity soon dropped and in midterm elections the Republicans lost nine seats. It was the lowest off-year turnout since Watergate. The talk around Capitol Hill was that Reagan had given in to the Democrats and that Bush was a "wimp." Even worse, Calvin Dooley, from California's 17th District, recounted a story of how Bush showed solidarity with the House of Representatives by coming to the Hill to use the gym. Dooley was there when Poppy showered, and as he looked over at Bush, "It's quite an experience to be a lowly freshman congressman in the shower with the President of the United States, and to look over and see the leader of the free world is . . . a . . . well . . . just an average little guy." Each time Dooley retold the story of Bush's "little stick," he got laughs, especially from the Speaker of the House.[350]

Once Bush became president, he could look back on his amazing rise to the office of the most powerful man in the world. Bush's tenacity had helped him reach his goal, even though he had lied in the face of overwhelming contrary evidence, ignored national and international law, subverted democracy, interfered in the free will of freely elected officials of foreign governments, allowed known drug traffickers to operate without fear, allowed the importation of drugs into our own country while campaigning a hard line against drugs, and sent American troops into wars as if they were his own personal fighting force. A greater criminal in United States politics had not been seen since Lyndon Johnson. One would think that at this point Poppy would have slowed down his megalomaniacal tendencies. (Megalomania as defined in Merriam-Webster's Dictionary: A delusional mental disorder that is marked by feelings of personal omnipotence and grandeur, a mania for great or grandiose performance.)

As has been well established, both in this text as well as countless books, articles, and court transcripts, the CIA has used its private army to depose freely elected officials when their policies cease to be profitable for American interests. The CIA has had on its payroll (that's our tax money) leaders of foreign countries who are ruthless, murderous drug trafficking criminals. Nothing new there, just business as usual.

Now we come to one of those CIA assets. His name was Noriega and his country was Panama. He was on the CIA payroll for upwards of $200,000 a year.[351]

Not only that, he laundered billions of dollars for the drug cartels and the U.S. turned a blind eye as long as he remained "friendly." As internationally respected author Noam Chomsky wrote, "It's all quite predictable, as study after study shows. A brutal tyrant crosses the line from admirable friend to 'villain' and 'scum' when he commits the crime of independence."

Noriega was an asset of the U. S. government for decades. It never bothered us as long as his drug dealing and money laundering were kept fairly quiet. In fact Bush had met with Noriega while he was director of the CIA. Things started to change when it was discovered that Noriega was also giving intel to the Soviets. Another factor was that in 1978, President Jimmy Carter had negotiated a treaty with then-President Torrijos to "give back" the Panama Canal. Torrijos had implemented plans for agrarian reform, education, economic restructuring, and establishing social services for his people. In 1981, President Torrijos was killed, and the U.S. backed General Noriega as president/dictator. Now Noriega was showing signs of diminishing returns. His grip on the country was slipping. Panamanians were tired of the corrupt dictator and they especially resented the yoke of the United States. They wanted freedom. Sounds familiar?

Yet there was another more sublime reason for the invasion, and this has to do with what is called "state criminality." The nation-state, through its own organizational structures and state managers, has historically engaged in numerous violations of its own criminal and civil laws, as well as various forms of international law. The United States, starting in the

Bush/Reagan era, utilized the concept of "rollback" to analyze U.S. foreign policy action. Rollback is the determination of U.S. policy elites to return to a pre-Communist world, with the final goals of eliminating communism and establishing free-market capitalism worldwide, or as Poppy called it, a "New World Order." This New World Order is designed to exploit third world countries for resources, cheap labor, markets, and opportunities for investments while remaining under political and economic control of the United States.[352] Panama was just such a country. Since the American occupation in 1903, the Panamanians had lived with American presence with varying degrees of toleration.

With Noriega losing control of the people, the United States decided it was time to make him go away. There was one more thing about Noriega; besides having concrete evidence of Bush's involvement in the Iran-Contra affair, there were rumors that Noriega ran a well-known "honey trap" at his home, inviting diplomats, including top CIA and other U.S. officials, to his home for parties where drugs were used and sex was provided with young boys and girls. Noriega, according to the U.K. *Daily Mail*, had these parties filmed.[353]

The Bush spin machine went to work and within days there were press releases from the White House stating that American citizens could be in danger in Panama. Noriega was now portrayed as a ruthless drug-dealing criminal! (Yes that was true, but he'd always been that way.) Bush outlined four reasons why we should invade Panama: to safeguard American citizens, to defend democracy in Panama, to apprehend Noriega and bring him to trial for drug trafficking, and to ensure the integrity of the Panama Canal Treaties. All lies. American citizens were never in danger, there wasn't democracy in Panama anyway, the Canal was never threatened, and the drug trafficking was not a concern because the U.S. was involved anyway.

The invasion codenamed Operation Just Cause went full steam ahead. Within Operation Just Cause was another operation called Operation Nifty Package, which was to prevent Noriega's escape and to bring him into custody on American soil. In other words, kidnap him.

The United States offered a $1 million reward for his capture. He found sanctuary, temporarily, at the Vatican diplomatic mission in Panama City.

On December 20, 1989, the U.S. invaded Panama with 27,684 troops and over 300 aircraft including F-117A Nighthawk stealth aircraft, and Apache helicopters. The invasion provoked international outrage.

On December 22, the Organization of American States passed a resolution condemning the invasion and calling for withdrawal of U.S. troops, as well as a resolution condemning the violation of the diplomatic status of the Nicaraguan Embassy in Panama by U.S. Special Forces who had entered the building.[354]

On December 29, the General Assembly of the United Nations voted 75–20 with 40 abstentions to condemn the invasion as a flagrant violation of international law. [355]

In January 1990, Noriega gave himself up and was flown to the U.S.

The casualties of the invasion were downplayed by U.S. authorities and put at around 516 Panamanian deaths; however The Commission for the Defense of Human Rights in Central America estimated 2,500–3,000 deaths. Around 20,000 people lost their homes and became refugees and an entire neighborhood (Chorrillo)was burned to the ground displacing

THE BUSH CRIME FAMILY

another 2,700 families.[356] Operation Just Cause ended on January 31, 1990.

Although there was substantial support for President Bush to invade, this was based on the lies that were given at his press conference. During the invasion, there were severe restrictions on the press. In truth, the Panama invasion was a clean-up act left from the Iran-Contra drug trafficking project.

The Gulf War

On March 31, 1989 an article appeared in the *Executive Intelligence Review* with the title "Is Bush Courting a Middle East War and a New Oil Crisis?" The article went on to say that a "worldwide pattern of events monitored on Palm Sunday by *Executive Intelligence Review* suggests that such a move may be in the works." In August 1989, Bush moved a battleship and a carrier to the eastern Mediterranean, and a carrier in the northern Arabian Sea, thus threatening Iran and Syria, whose forces went on alert.[357] Apparently, this was in response to the execution of Marine Lt. Col. William R. Higgins by the pro-Iranian Organization of the Oppressed of the Earth.

For the last eight years Iran had been at war with its neighbor Iraq, and due in part to U.S. Military Intelligence briefings on Iranian positions, Iraq had come out the victor. During the war Syria had closed its pipeline that had allowed Iraqi oil to reach tankers on the Mediterranean. This put tremendous pressure on Iraq. Kuwait, along with Saudi Arabia, kept Iraq from going bankrupt by providing an average of $60 billion per year in subsidies.[358] Saudi Arabia provided Iraq with $1 billion per month starting in mid-1982.[359] In a declassified 1991 report, the CIA estimated that Iran had suffered more than 50,000 casualties from Iraq's use of several chemical weapons, though current estimates are more than 100,000 as the long-term effects continue to cause casualties.[360]

For all indications, the U.S. was an ally to Iraq. That's why when in August of 1990, Iraqi forces under Saddam Hussein invaded Kuwait, we expressed little interest in the affair. In truth, we had been keeping a close eye on the Iraqi forces building up on Kuwait's border. On July 24, 1990, the State Department stressed that the United States had no commitment to defend Kuwait.[361] On July 25, Ambassador April Glaspie met directly with Saddam Hussein, and assured him that she was acting on direct orders from President Bush: "We have no opinion on the Arab-Arab conflict, like your border disagreement with Kuwait . . . I have direct instructions from the president to seek better relations with Iraq."[362]

By July 31, the *Washington Post* and the the *New York Times* expressed growing concern that hostilities could break out. Still Bush said and did nothing. Clearly the Iraqis had little to fear from Poppy Bush. The build-up of Iraqi troops along the Kuwait border was now reaching 100,000 men. After a meeting with Margaret Thatcher of Great Britain, Poppy's attitude changed. According to Kitty Kelley, Thatcher reminded Bush that she was almost defeated in England until the Falkland Island invasion took place. "I stayed in office for eight years after that." Thatcher, according to Bush's description of her was a "broad with steel balls." "Don't go wobbly on me George, don't go wobbly," Thatcher once famously said.[363]

During August meetings with Prince Bandar, the Saudi ambassador, Bush told him that the Pentagon had satellite photos showing Iraqi troops massing on the Saudi border. This was a lie. The photos did not show what the president claimed; Bush felt he needed to exaggerate the danger of an Iraqi invasion to obtain consent to deploy American troops on Saudi soil.[364] By August 7, the first U.S. troops began to arrive in Saudi Arabia. In a false news campaign designed to whip up a frenzy of hatred against Iraq, a young 15-year-old Kuwaiti woman, a volunteer at al-Aden hospital, testified before the Congressional Human Rights Caucus that Iraqi soldiers had ripped scores of babies out of incubators, leaving them to die on the cold hospital floor.[365]

Later, in 1992, it was found out that the young girl was the daughter of the Kuwait ambassador and that she had been coached by the firm Hill and Knowlton. In fact the entire story was false, designed to sell the war to the American people.[366]

The loss of life due to George H. W. Bush's invasion into Iraq is still somewhat of a mystery. Sources such as the Pentagon say that 100,000 soldiers were killed and Iraqi officials put the death toll of civilians at roughly 7,000.[367]

Ex-President George H. W. Bush accused of war crimes and political killings by Irish writer Seán Mac Mathúna.

George H. W. Bush has been accused throughout his life of being involved either with terrorism, the Mafia, or drug trafficking, either during his time as CIA director (1976–1977) or during his term as vice president (1981–1989) or president (1989–1993). Apart from his alleged involvement in the CIA at the time of the Kennedy Assassination, he is also said to have carried out violations of the Geneva Convention as a US fighter pilot during the war. He was alleged to have killed Japanese trawler men in a lifeboat while he was a fighter pilot during World War II. The latest person to make these allegations was the former Panamanian dictator and CIA stooge General Manuel Noriega, who is presently serving a 40-year jail sentence in the USA. Calling Bush a "cold blooded killer," he repeats the story that Bush had found Japanese trawler men in a lifeboat and shot them, even though they all had their hands up. According to the *Observer*, Bush has always refused to respond to accusations that he killed the Japanese trawler men whose ship he sunk in 1944.[368]

Japan Indicts Bush as War Criminal

In early 1997, Bush was indicted as an alleged war criminal by the Japanese government. This was in response to the U.S. decision to bar 16 Japanese citizens from the USA for alleged war crimes committed during the Second World War. Japanese Foreign Ministry spokesperson Hiroshi Hashimoto announced that 10 Americans would be barred from Japan for their "war crimes, crimes against humanity, and violations of human rights." Top of the list was George Bush for "the murder of hundreds of thousands of innocent civilians, including thousands of children, in attacks on Iraq and Panama" in 1988 and 1990. The other alleged war criminals were generals Colin Powell and "Stormin" Norman Schwarzkopf, former presidents Ronald Reagan and Gerald Ford, and other U.S. military and government figures such as Oliver North, Henry Kissinger, Robert MacNamara, CIA director John Deutch, and Elliott Abrams.[369]

CHAPTER 27

THE PEDOPHILE NETWORK

It means, it means, teaching troubled children through your presence that there's no such, that there's such a thing as reliable love. Some would say it's soft and insufficiently tough to care about these things. But where is it written that we must act as if we do not care, as if we are not moved? Well I am moved. I want a kinder, and gentler nation.

—George H. W. Bush at the 1988
Republican National Convention[xx]

Serious Allegations
George H. W. Bush and the CIA have their fingerprints on a nationwide pedophile network that was covered up in the late 1980s and early 1990s. One of the exploited children even implicated Bush as a pedophile, and a DC pimp implicated some of the men around Bush as pedophiles. Moreover, a CIA asset used the network as a honey trap to ensnare and then blackmail politicians who were seduced into partaking of its malevolent machinations. The Justice Department, FBI, and Secret

Service also immaculately covered up the network during 41's reign as president.

I realize that these are very serious allegations to lay at the doors of both Bush and the CIA, but two well-researched books and a suppressed documentary have documented the existence of the pedophile network that federal and state authorities declared did not exist. While these allegations have been known for many years, you the reader can speculate if there's either smoke or fire here. Journalist Nick Bryant spent seven years researching and writing *The Franklin Scandal: A Story of Child Abuse, Powerbrokers, and Betrayal*, which thoroughly documents the reality of the pedophile network, its cover-up by federal authorities during the Bush administration, and also its connections to a CIA asset, who actually took "call boys" on midnight tours of Bush's White House.[370]

The story of the "Franklin" pedophile network is indeed a leviathan of a story, because the network was nationwide in scope, and three grand juries were used to cover it up—two federal grand juries and a state grand jury. The network's ringleaders were a pair of Republican powerbrokers: Lawrence King of Omaha and Craig Spence of Washington, DC. King was a middle-aged, African American, and throughout the 1980s he was described as a Republican Party "high-roller."[371] He was vice chairman for finance of the National Black Republican Council, a sanctioned affiliate of the Republican National Committee.[372] King also ardently campaigned for the 1988 presidential bid of his personal "friend" George H. W. Bush, hosting a "$100,000 gala" for the newly nominated Bush at the 1988 Republican Convention in New Orleans.[373]

King's partner in pedophilic pandering and blackmail was Craig Spence, a Washington, DC–based lobbyist and powerbroker.[374] An article featured on the front page of the

Washington Times, "Power Broker Served Drugs, Sex at Parties Bugged for Blackmail," included extensive corroboration that Spence's home was bugged for audio-visual surveillance.[375] Craig Spence also confessed to being a CIA asset, and *Washington Times* reporters corroborated his claim.[376,377] Spence later confessed to *Washington Times* reporters that "friendly" intelligence agents had bugged his home.[378] And as previously mentioned, Spence took midnight tours of Bush's White House with male prostitutes in tow.

The pedophile network run by King and Spence was operational throughout most of the 1980s. King was based in Omaha, Nebraska, where he was the general manager of the Franklin Community Federal Credit Union. He acquired children from a variety of sources, including Boys Town, the distinguished Catholic orphanage on the outskirts of Omaha, and also through the foster care system.[379] King then routinely flew children into Washington, DC. In DC, Spence's home, which was wired for blackmail, would often be the setting for pedophilic orgies.

The first documented victim of Lawrence King–related child abuse to come forward was 16-year-old Eulice Washington.[380] She had been placed in the foster home of Jarrett and Barbara Webb as an 8-year-old—Barbara Webb was a cousin of Lawrence King. The Webbs eventually adopted Eulice and her two sisters as well as two other children. Three foster children also lived in the Webb home.

The children in the Webb home told social services personnel of repeated "beatings" and "whippings" at the hands of the Webbs.[381] In fact, a physician who treated one of the children said that a "rubber hose" most likely produced the welts on his back.[382] After years of social services documenting abuse by the Webbs, the children in the Webb household were ultimately placed in various foster homes, but child abuse charges were never leveled against the Webbs.[383]

After Eulice Washington's liberation from the Webb home, she told her new foster mother that her adopted father, Jarrett Webb, had repeatedly molested her. She even passed a polygraph administered by the Nebraska State Patrol (NSP) on her accusations, but Jarrett Webb was never prosecuted for his purported molestation of Eulice Washington.[384] Washington also told her foster mother that Lawrence King had flown her and several Boys Town students to pedophilic orgies in Chicago and New York City.[385]

Investigation Halted

In March of 1986, a Boys Town youth worker interviewed Eulice Washington and penned a very detailed report about her allegations regarding Boys Town students, Lawrence King, and the pedophilic orgies she had attended. She also told the youth worker that she had seen George H. W. Bush at one of the pedophilic orgies.[386] Boys Town allegedly informed the NSP and FBI about Eulice Washington's allegations, but no follow-up actions were taken by either law enforcement entity. Moreover, a social worker who started to investigate the abuse in the Webb household was reportedly threatened by FBI agents to back off from investigating the Webbs.[387]

Approximately two years after Eulice Washington unfurled her revelations regarding King and Bush, the Omaha Police Department (OPD) investigated Lawrence King and a photographer associated with King for "child pornography." But, despite the OPD uncovering leads and filing multiple crime reports, the investigation was inexplicably discontinued.[388]

About a month after the OPD's investigation of Lawrence King for child pornography, a 15-year-old girl at an Omaha psychiatric hospital disclosed to hospital personnel, including her psychiatrist, that she had been enmeshed in a child prostitution and pornography ring since she was nine years old. The girl's psychiatrist phoned the OPD, and an OPD officer was dispatched to the hospital to interview the girl, who related to the OPD officer that Lawrence King was "involved" in her abuse and the abuse of other children.[389] Although the OPD officer found the girl to be "credible," the OPD did not interview her again.[390] So, consequently, three investigations into Lawrence King–related child abuse had been inexplicably discontinued by state and local law enforcement in Nebraska.

In 1988, supervisors for Nebraska's foster care system became cognizant of the child abuse allegations whirling around King, and one of them submitted a report to the Nebraska Attorney General of a "child exploitation ring" on July 20, 1988.[391] However, the Nebraska Attorney General's office investigator who was assigned to investigate the child abuse allegations would ultimately confess that he did not interview a single alleged victim.

On November 4, 1988, approximately five months after foster care personnel alerted state authorities about their concerns regarding Lawrence King–related child abuse, federal agents descended on King's Franklin Credit Union, and the National Credit Union Administration would ultimately conclude that King had looted $39.4 million from the credit union. The raid occurred four days prior to the election of George H. W. Bush as president.[392] Individuals who are familiar with the nuances of this story postulate that King was a fire that Bush had to extinguish, because the pedophile network King oversaw was attracting too much attention.

A few weeks after the Franklin Community Federal Credit Union was raided by federal agents, Nebraska state senators in Lincoln, the state's capital, had seen enough Franklin Credit Union press about missing millions and cooked books to conclude that something was seriously awry. The senators unanimously approved a resolution that called for a state senate subcommittee, the "Franklin Committee," to investigate the credit union's failure. Senator Loran Schmit, who chaired the state senate's Banking Committee, drafted the resolution.

Shortly after Senator Schmit introduced the resolution, he said he received an anonymous phone call that foreshadowed the suppressive forces that the Franklin Committee would be challenging: the caller urged Schmit not to pursue an investigation into the Franklin Credit Union under the auspices of being a "good Republican," because he said it would "reach to the highest levels of the Republican Party."[393] Schmit, however, was undeterred.

Shortly after the Franklin Committee was formed, foster care personnel testified in front of the committee, and the committee members heard shocking tales of interstate child trafficking and extreme child abuse that had been perpetrated with impunity, even though authorities within law enforcement were aware of the allegations. The testimony of the foster care personnel ushered the King-related child abuse allegations into the public consciousness, and the *Omaha-World Herald*, *Lincoln Journal*, and *New York Times* followed with articles on the allegations. The *New York Times* described the allegations as "lurid."[394]

Senator Schmit and the Franklin Committee quickly found themselves navigating very treacherous waters. An *Omaha World-Herald* article reported that there was pressure to stop the investigation. In the article, Schmit confirmed the pressures: "I have gotten phone calls threatening me," he said. "I've been told to leave it alone or my kids were going to be orphans."[395] Schmit wasn't being overly dramatic about the death threat, because a number of people who were enmeshed in "Franklin" would experience premature, enigmatic deaths.

After the Franklin Committee formed, a group of Nebraska citizens who were aware of King plundering their community for children banded together and called themselves Concerned Parents. At one Concerned Parents' meeting, a woman stood up and said; "I think George Bush is involved in this child abuse case, and that is why all these people have been dying."[396] Another member of Concerned Parents was aware of a psychologist living in Omaha who had been formerly employed by the CIA, stating that rumors of Bush's pedophilic predilections were rife among CIA personnel when Bush headed the CIA.[397]

A Private Investigator Uncovers Details

The Franklin Committee ultimately hired Lincoln, Nebraska–based private investigator Gary Caradori to investigate the child abuse allegations. Caradori had a stellar record in both the military and the Nebraska State Patrol before forming Caracorp, his private investigation firm. Though Caradori was the chief executive officer of a large security and investigative firm, he was a seasoned and relentless detective, and his passion was finding missing persons, particularly abducted children and teenage girls enmeshed in drugs and prostitution. Over the years, various newspapers had published articles lauding Caradori's investigations.

From the onset of Caradori's investigation, several obstacles confronted him and his staff. He faced widespread distrust and a pall of fear as he attempted to cultivate confidential informants or simply interview individuals who had previously volunteered information. Caradori also encountered enemies that he had not anticipated. He suspected his phones were tapped, because when he arranged meetings over the phone FBI agents would already be at the designated place when he arrived. A friend of Caradori's who worked for the phone company checked out his phones and confirmed that they were tapped.[398]

Caradori managed to uncover scores of receipts from various air charter services used by Lawrence King. The flight receipts rarely listed passengers, or would merely list "Larry King." The receipts revealed that King charted planes on an almost weekly basis.[399] Though King jetted to numerous locations throughout the country, his favored destination was Washington, DC, where Craig Spence resided—King's partner in pedophilic pandering and blackmail.

Caradori also managed to find additional victims of King, who were willing to speak out about their abuse. He ultimately recorded four on videotape. They repeatedly corroborated each other and other victims who had previously come forward. They spoke of being sadistically abused by very prominent men in Omaha and around the country.

By mid-December of 1989, Caradori had accrued approximately 21 hours of victim testimony.[400] As the Franklin Committee members were confronted with Caradori's mounting evidence, they became increasingly perplexed about where to turn due to their distrust of state and federal law enforcement, because committee members felt that those agencies had not properly pursued the child abuse allegations. The Franklin Committee tendered its concerns to the U.S. attorney general's office, but they did not receive a response.

The committee ultimately submitted its 21 hours of videotaped statements to the offices of Nebraska's attorney general and Nebraska's U.S. attorney in December of 1989. State and federal law enforcement were now forced to act. They no longer had the luxury of defaulting to the position that the child-abuse allegations had no substance. In addition to pledging immediate action by the NSP, Nebraska's attorney general called upon the Douglas County judges (Omaha is located in Douglas County) to impanel a state grand jury to probe the child abuse allegations. The U.S. attorney for Nebraska later announced that a federal grand jury would probe the allegations too.

The announcement of the state grand jury coincided with a rather unexpected event involving Lawrence King when President George H. W. Bush visited Omaha to speak at a fundraiser for Nebraska's governor. King claimed President Bush was a personal friend, and he had previously hosted a "$100,000 gala" for the newly nominated Bush.[401]

An unnamed source informed Caradori that King had purchased a ticket to attend the fundraiser. This source also disclosed to Caradori that when the Secret Service discovered King's plan to grace the fundraiser, they either ushered him to the federal courthouse in Omaha or demanded that he make haste to the federal courthouse. Either way, King appeared at the federal courthouse in the early afternoon of February 7, 1990 before U.S. Magistrate Richard Kopf.[402] (In the U.S. federal court system, a magistrate judge is a judge appointed to assist a U.S. District Court judge in the performance of his or her duties.)

At the hearing, which Magistrate Kopf inexplicably called for without a motion from the prosecution or defense, Kopf ordered King to undergo an immediate "mental health evaluation" at the U.S. Medical Center for Federal Prisoners in Springfield, Missouri, even though sources close to King reported that he was not suffering from psychiatric impairment.[403] King waived a hearing on Kopf's unorthodox ruling, and that day he found himself en route to Springfield in the custody of two U.S. marshals. After King's "mental health evaluation," a U.S. District Court judge remanded him to a federal psychiatric hospital as a pretrial detainee, and King would be at the federal psychiatric hospital for the next five months. King would remain safely tucked away at a federal psychiatric institution as the state and federal grand juries investigated the child abuse allegations.

By June of 1990, after the state grand jury had been impaneled for three months, Caradori had been immersed in the "Franklin" case for nearly a year. His investigation included uncovering organized child abuse of an extreme nature, persistent media assaults, and a seemingly concerted effort by state and federal law enforcement and the media to sabotage his investigation. Two people had also informed Caradori that federal and state authorities were in the process of framing him to take the fall for scripting the child-abuse allegations.[404] Shortly after Gary Caradori realized that he was being "set up" for an arrest, he wrote a letter to renowned lawyer Gerry Spence, noting that the pedophile network he had uncovered extended "to the highest levels of the United States."[405]

The victims Caradori had interviewed discussed being the victims of child pornography, so Caradori set out to find child pornography of them. He felt that pictures would provide absolute proof of their victimization. Two of the victims named a child pornographer who worked for King named Rusty Nelson, and Caradori commenced a hunt for Nelson. Nelson maintains that Caradori contacted him through a family member when he was in New Mexico, and he agreed to meet Caradori in Chicago and slip him incriminating pictures that would exonerate the victims and expose the perpetrators.[406]

The Investigator's Demise

After Caradori reportedly made contact with Nelson, he flew his 1984 single-engine Piper Saratoga from Lincoln to Chicago. Caradori, accompanied by his eight-year-old son Andrew James (A.J.), ostensibly made the jaunt to attend the July 10 Major League Baseball All-Star Game.

After Caradori and A.J. landed at Chicago's Midway Airport, Caradori's hour-by-hour activities are unclear prior to the game, but four sources—*Washington Times* reporter Paul Rodriguez, Sandi Caradori (his wife), Loran Schmit, and a victim's mother—say they received phone calls from him.[407] Caradori called Rodriguez in Washington, DC, from a payphone, and their conversation was quite candid—Caradori unequivocally told him that he was on the verge of acquiring pictures and other materials that would corroborate the victims' stories.[408] Caradori's call to his wife cryptically conveyed to her that his Chicago trip had been a "success."[409] He also had a pithy conversation with Schmit that the latter relayed to a reporter: "Loran, we got them by the shorthairs."[410]

Caradori and his son flew out of Chicago's Midway Airport around 2:00 a.m. on July 11, and his plane crashed in a Lee County, Illinois cornfield where he and his son were killed.[411] Parts of the plane were scattered up to 1,800 feet from the fuselage, and the National Transportation Safety Board (NTSB) stated almost immediately that Caradori's plane broke up in flight, but the "exact mechanism" for the plane's breakup was never discovered. Five sources, including Rusty Nelson, corroborate that Caradori acquired what he was seeking—pictures—during his sojourn to Chicago, and the anomalies and inconsistences involved in the official account of his death are too numerous to explicate here.

Washington Times reporter Paul Rodriguez was in frequent contact with Caradori prior to the latter's death, because Rodriguez had uncovered Spence's illicit activities in DC, which quickly led him to Caradori's investigation and King. Rodriquez first came into contact with Spence's name when he salvaged credit card vouchers from a male escort service showing that Spence spent up to $20,000 a month on male escorts.[412]

The credit card vouchers offered *Washington Times* reporters a wormhole that delivered them to a parallel universe of illicit sex and blackmail. The *Washington Times* first major article on Spence, "Homosexual prostitution inquiry ensnares VIPs with Reagan, Bush 'Call Boys' took midnight tour of White House," discussed Spence taking male prostitutes on late night tours of the White House while George and Barbara Bush were supposedly sound asleep.[413] The *Washington Times* reporters eventually became aware of multiple late night tours of the White House that were arranged by Spence. Barbara Bush was questioned about the late night tours, and she responded that it had not raised security questions that worried the first family.

The day after the *Washington Times* published the story about Spence's midnight tour of the White House with male prostitutes in tow, the newspaper unfurled a story about Spence's blackmail enterprise that was complimented by a banner headline: "Power Broker Served Drugs, Sex At Parties Bugged For Blackmail."[414] The article elucidated the hidden cameras that were concealed around Spence's upscale DC home, and it also discussed his various connections to the CIA. Spence would tell *Washington Times* reporters that he was a CIA asset, and they would confirm his connections to the Agency.

Spence spent $20,000 a month on male prostitutes from an escort service that was owned by Henry Vinson, who published a tell-all book, *Confessions of a DC Madam: The Politics of Sex, Lies, and Blackmail*, which discusses the pedophilic pandering of Spence and King. In the book, Vinson claims that Spence personally showed him the blackmail equipment that was scattered throughout Spence's home, and Vinson also details how Spence and King attempted to coerce him into providing them with children, but he refused to succumb to their coercion.

Bush Friends Implicated

Although Vinson doesn't directly implicate George H. W. Bush as a pedophile in his book, he mentions that Donald Gregg, Bush's national security advisor when Bush was vice president, had compulsive homosexual appetites and was a frequent flyer of his escort service.[415] According to Vinson, Gregg used his government issued MasterCard to procure escorts from Vinson. These allegations about Gregg's patronizing a homosexual prostitution service have never been proved in court and thus remain allegations only, but they have been around for years and, to our knowledge, Gregg has never challenged anyone publishing these charges.

Gregg wasn't a run-of-the-mill government apparatchik. He had been a CIA agent for 31 years, and Gregg, Felix Rodriquez, and George H. W. Bush were the early architects of Iran-Contra. Gregg was also a very close friend of Bush. When Bush became president, he appointed Gregg to be the ambassador to South Korea. In fact, Spence told *Washington Times* reporters that it was Gregg who gave him late night access to the White House, which Gregg denied.

In *Confessions of a DC Madam*, Vinson discloses that the Government Accounting Office made inquiries to Vinson about Gregg's prolific use of his government-issued MasterCard to a front company that Vinson used to process credit cards.

According to Vinson, Spence and a member of George H. W. Bush's Cabinet attempted to pressure him into concocting a cover story for Gregg's prolific spending, but Vinson refused to take part in the subterfuge, despite threats from the Cabinet member.[416] Shortly thereafter, Vinson's escort service was raided by the Secret Service.

Spence had previously told Vinson that he provided the Cabinet member in question with young boys. If Vinson is being truthful, it's difficult to believe a man of immense power would put his Cabinet position, career, and family on the line to help a degenerate, blackmail artist like Spence. It only makes sense if the Cabinet member was in the same shadowy blackmail network as Spence or if that shadowy network had compromised him.

Earlier I mentioned that Nebraska senator Loran Schmit was warned to forgo an investigation into Lawrence King and the Franklin Credit Union, because it would "reach to the highest levels of the Republican Party." I also mentioned Gary Caradori writing a letter to attorney Gerry Spence in which he said that the pedophile network he had uncovered extended "to the highest levels of the United States." These may seem like absurd statements at face value, but the cover-up of King and Spence's pedophile network definitely demonstrates that it was orchestrated at the pinnacle of power, and it included the hijacking of three grand juries.

In Nebraska, six victims of King and Spence's pedophile network ultimately summoned the courage to come forward to give statements about their abuse to law enforcement and/or the Franklin Committee. The victims were then subjected to threats by FBI agents who attempted to coerce them into recanting their abuse. Eulice Washington was one of the victims who was subjected to FBI intimidation, but she never recanted her abuse accusation or her claim that she saw

George H. W. Bush at a pedophilic orgy in Chicago in 1984. Though Eulice Washington and three other victims wouldn't recant their abuse, the FBI agents were successful in coercing two additional victims into recanting their abuse.

As previously mentioned, after Caradori accrued 21 hours of videotaped victim testimony, a state and a federal grand jury were impaneled in Nebraska to ostensibly investigate the child abuse allegations. Although Caradori's videotaped statements of King's victims were the critical mass that launched the grand juries, he had died in the enigmatic plane crash before the state and federal grand juries rendered their verdicts.

Although the phrase "grand jury" has authoritative connotations, the grand jury process has the potential to be seriously flawed. A grand jury makes the initial decision to indict (formally accuse) a criminal defendant to stand trial. But unlike a standard trial, a grand jury proceeding is cloaked in secrecy: grand juries aren't open to the public, and the identity of the witnesses who testify and the content of their testimony are never disclosed. The special prosecutor of a grand jury calls the witnesses, questions the witnesses, and selects the evidence that is shown to the grand jurors, and grand jurors are normal, everyday citizens who have shown up for jury duty and have been funneled to a grand jury.

Generally, only witnesses and evidence deemed relevant by special prosecutors are presented to grand jurors, and special prosecutors are in a unique position to manipulate grand jurors' judgments in a particular direction. Commenting about the influence a special prosecutor has over grand jurors, a former chief appellate judge of New York State once famously remarked that a special prosecutor could persuade grand jurors to "indict a ham sandwich."[417] And the state and federal grand juries investigating the child exploitation of King et al.

were essentially a ham and swiss on rye. The state grand jury's report declared that the child abuse allegations were a "carefully crafted hoax," and the federal grand jury declared that not a single child had been transported across state lines for immoral purposes.[418]

In *The Franklin Scandal*, Bryant dedicates a chapter to the state grand jury, which declared that King et al. hadn't molested a single child. Bryant managed to acquire the sealed testimony and exhibits of the state grand jury, and excerpting witness testimony, he shows exactly how the special prosecutor deliberately hijacked that grand jury. Instead of indicting the perpetrators who abused the children, the state grand jury indicted two of the victims who refused to recant their abuse on perjury charges. Interestingly, Eulice Washington and a second victim who refused to recant their abuse were not indicted on perjury charges. The victims who were indicted on perjury would ultimately have to face jury trials to sanctify the grand jury verdicts, so it's reasonable to surmise that the state only indicted two of the victims on perjury charges, because trying two victims for "perjury" would be much easier than trying four victims for perjury. The state grand jury also ascribed striking incompetence and malfeasance to Gary Caradori, who was dead and couldn't defend himself.

Covered Up and Threatened

Alisha Owen, one of the victims who refused to recant her abuse, was indicted on eight counts of perjury by the state grand jury and eight counts of perjury by the federal grand jury. She was staring at over 300 years in prison from her perjury indictments. At the time of her indictments, she was 21 years old. A second victim who refused to recant his abuse was indicted on three counts of perjury by the state grand jury, and he was facing 60 years in prison due to his perjury indictments.

The state of Nebraska pulled out all stops, spared no expense, and deployed dirty tricks to rig Alisha's perjury trial, because her trial represented much more than a simple case of perjury—her jurors would also be deliberating the findings of the grand juries, which disavowed the pedophile network. In essence, Alisha Owen's guilt would protect the rich and powerful men who had been provided with children.

Although Alisha Owen's trial had all the makings of a corrupt kangaroo, she and her attorney put on a valiant effort to exonerate her of the trumped up perjury charges. Her trial lasted five weeks, and it was the longest criminal trial in Nebraska history. Despite mind-boggling malfeasance by the judge, prosecutor, and a vast supporting cast, the jurors deliberated Alisha Owen's fate for three days before finding her guilty. Alisha Owen was sentenced to between nine and 15 years for perjury, and she spent nearly two years in solitary confinement. Her 17-year-old brother also died under very mysterious circumstances in the lead-up to her trial. Because the state barely managed to convict Alisha Owen in a thoroughly corrupt trial, the state dropped the perjury charges leveled against the second victim who refused to recant his abuse.

Throughout the Franklin Committee's investigation, the grand juries, and Alisha Owen's trial, both the local and national media were obsequious to the government's cover-up. The *Omaha-World Herald* was the government's most vociferous cheerleader, and it even called the Franklin Committee a "disgrace" to Nebraska.[419] The *New York Times*, the *Washington Post*, and CBS' *48 Hours* also chimed in to propagate the government's dubious cover story.

The officers of both the state and federal judiciaries who participated in the cover-up experienced upward mobility within the judicial system. Gerald Moran, the Douglas County deputy attorney who prosecuted Alisha Owen, was appointed a Douglas County District Court judge after her conviction. Generally, District Court judges work on their judicial chops in a lower court, Omaha Municipal Court, before being appointed to the District Court. But Moran leapfrogged over all the Omaha Municipal Court judges to become a Douglas County District Court Judge.[420]

Thomas Thalken, Nebraska's first assistant U.S. attorney, who was the special prosecutor of the federal grand jury that found King et al. hadn't engaged in the interstate transportation of children for immoral purposes and also indicted Alisha Owen on eight counts of perjury, was bumped up to a federal magistrate.[421] And the federal magistrate, Richard Kopf, who was integral in depositing King in the Springfield, Missouri, federal psychiatric facility when George H. W. Bush visited Nebraska on a fundraiser and other facets of the cover-up was anointed a U.S. District Court judge, which carries a lifetime appointment.[422]

Gary Caradori's death, the corrupted grand juries in Nebraska, and Alisha Owen's conviction essentially concluded an immaculate cover-up in Nebraska of King and Spence's pedophile network. But a cover-up of their activities also had to be orchestrated in Washington, DC, due to the *Washington Times'* series of articles about Spence's blackmail operation and his CIA connections.

The cover-up in Washington, DC, shared a number of similarities to the cover-up in Nebraska, because it included a corrupt grand jury, media manipulation, and a fall guy— Henry Vinson. Although the Justice Department played a fundamental role in the cover-ups in both Nebraska and Washington, DC, the FBI in Nebraska was the principal heavy that issued threats and engaged in malfeasance to abet the cover-up in Nebraska, and the Secret Service was the principal heavy in Washington, DC.

Shortly after Henry Vinson's escort service was raided by the Secret Service, the U.S. attorney for the District of Columbia, Jay Stephens, impaneled a grand jury to ostensibly investigate Spence and also Vinson's escort service. In the wake of the newly impaneled grand jury, the *Washington Times* reported on a campaign of terror that the Secret Service unleashed on Vinson's family. Secret Service agents busted down the front door of Vinson's sister's home and held his brother-in-law at gunpoint.

The *Washington Times* also ran an article that questioned the validity of the grand jury.[423] The newspaper's reporters interviewed "a longtime acquaintance" of Spence's who had been called before the grand jury. The article mentioned that he "had spent considerable time as a guest" in Spence's home and he was "a participant in one of the late-night White House tours." The witness told the reporters that one of the grand jury's primary concerns was establishing if Spence had been in the possession of purloined White House china that dated back to the Truman administration.

Spence was involved in pandering children, pandering adults, blackmailing powerbrokers, etc., so it's rather mind-boggling that one of the grand jury's primary concerns was if Spence purloined some of the White House's Truman china. The *Washington Times* even commented about the grand jury being corrupt: "The grand jury investigation begun in June by U.S. Attorney Jay Stephens was described as a 'credit card' probe. It is not clear, however, how vigorous federal prosecutors have been nor where the case may be headed."[424] The *Washington Times* article that questioned the rigor of fed-eral prosecutors in the grand jury proceedings sought answers from U.S. Attorney Jay Stephens, but he refused to comment.

The Washington, DC, grand jury exonerated Spence of any crimes, including solicitation of prostitution, but Vinson was charged with a 43-count RICO indictment, and he was fac-ing 295 years in prison. RICO is an acronym for the Racketeer Influenced and Corrupt Organizations Act, and it was origi-nally designed to dismantle the Mafia, as RICO allows for Mob bosses to be tried for crimes that were sanctioned on their behalf. The U.S. attorney also threatened to indict Vinson's el-derly mother.

Facing a 295-year sentence, Vinson ultimately cooperated with the federal government. He opted to remain silent over the various illegalities he had witnessed, and he entered into a plea agreement of 63 months of incarceration. At the onset of his cooperation, government agents debriefed Vinson, and Vinson claims that he told the debriefing agents about the interstate pedophile network operated by King and Spence. However, federal officials never publicly acknowledged the purported network, and they sealed Vinson's evidentiary file, which may include Vinson's statements about the King and Spence pedophile network and whether or not these allega-tions were investigated. The *Washington Times* attempted to unseal Vinson's evidentiary file twice, but the government re-buffed each attempt. Documentation in Vinson's case remains sealed today—25 years after the fact.

Just as officers of the court in Nebraska who assisted in the cover-up experienced upward mobility within the judicial system, DC-based officials experienced that same phenom-enon. For example, Jay Stephens, the U.S. attorney for DC, whose office oversaw the corrupt grand jury that covered up the activities of Spence, was appointed United States associate attorney general by President George W. Bush in 2001.[425] But this position proved to be a two-year pit stop for Stephens, because in 2002 he became a vice president of the Raytheon Corporation, the world's fifth largest defense contractor.

The Justice Department and Secret Service had successfully covered up the exploits of King and Spence in Washington, DC, but they needed a little help from the *Washington Post* to put its imprimatur on the cover-up and seal it. Consequently, the *Washington Post* ran articles that disingenuously trashed the meticulous reporting of the *Washington Times*. According to the *Washington Post*, Spence didn't have a house that was wired for blackmail, and he wasn't a CIA asset. In fact, the *Post* portrayed him as a gadfly who was a society bottom feeder and merely a prodigious name-dropper. The newspaper also conscripted the *New York Times* and *Los Angeles Times* to jump on its bandwagon and bash the *Washington Times* reportage on Spence.[426]

The *Washington Post* aiding and abetting in the cover-up of Spence's blackmail activities might sound implausible, but the newspaper has a fabled history aiding and abetting the CIA. The book, *Katharine the Great*, written by former *Village Voice* journalist Deborah Davis, is a biographical sketch of *Washington Post* publisher Katharine Graham, and it focuses specifically on the clandestine connections between the CIA and *Washington Post*. According to *Katharine the Great* and numerous sources, the CIA's Frank Wisner tapped then-*Washington Post* publisher Philip Graham to be the CIA's point man to infiltrate the media—known as Operation Mockingbird.

In *Katharine the Great*, Davis quoted a former CIA agent who discussed meetings between CIA personnel and Philip Graham in which they conferred about the availability and prices of journalists: "You could get a journalist cheaper than a good call girl, for a couple hundred dollars a month."[427]

In the end, the *Washington Post* had little difficulty disparaging the *Washington Times*, because the Reverend Sun Myung Moon owned the newspaper. It's a rather pathetic commentary on the American media when a Moonie-owned media outlet is the only news source providing Americans with the truth about a blackmail enterprise that's subverting their political system.

So after three grand juries, profuse media manipulation, and the enigmatic deaths of Gary Caradori and others, the George H. W. Bush administration was able to cover up the "Franklin" pedophile network. Earlier I stated that the cover-up of King and Spence's pedophile network was orchestrated at the pinnacle of power, which certainly implicates George H. W. Bush, but a naysayer might argue that the cover-up could have been orchestrated by Bush's minions, and Bush himself probably wasn't cognizant of what was going on.

The naysayers, in this case, obviously aren't aware of how government bureaucracies function. In federal bureaucracies, cover your ass is a foremost consideration, so it is highly unlikely that the U.S. attorneys for Nebraska and Washington, DC, and also the FBI and Secret Service participated in the cover-up of a nationwide pedophile network without their decisions being sanctioned from the summit of the Justice Department. Richard Thornburgh was the attorney general during the period when the "Franklin" network was being covered up, but could Thornburgh have preemptively made the decision to cover up such heinous crimes? If the cover-up had backfired, Thornburgh's head would have ended up on the political chopping block. In this case, there was only one individual that Thornburgh answered to, and that individual was George H. W. Bush.

PART 4

GEORGE W. BUSH (AKA "DUBYA")

CHAPTER 28

GETTING STARTED
IN THE FAMILY BUSINESS

Families is where our nation finds hope. Where wings take dream.

—George W. Bush speaking in La Crosse, Wisconsin, 2000[xxi]

W. Joins Skull and Bones, and the Texas Air National Guard Lie
Following the elite path to power shaped by Prescott, Yale '17, and George H. W. Bush, Yale '48, before him, George W. Bush also became a member of the cryptic Skull and Bones. The secretive group, a fraternal order that has bonded power-elites into lifelong, mutually beneficial relations, welcomed the third generation of the Bush dynasty with open arms.

Bush, known in his college days as a lackadaisical C-student who preferred copious drinking to academic endeavor and never earned an A grade, seemed to regard his admission into the Skull and Bones with the same unenthusiastic demeanor. When W. was given the option to pick his codename, he made it known to the group that he couldn't think of one. W. was assigned the name "Temporary,"[428] perhaps an indication of what his fellow Bonesmen thought of his long-term prospects with the group. There is also an indication that young W.

regarded the generational secret society with disdain, perhaps a reminder of his troubled relationship with his father.

"Young George is as unlikely a Bonesperson as I've ever met," said Fay Vincent, a Bush family friend and the eighth commissioner of Major League Baseball.[429]

W. never returned for a reunion after graduating from Yale in 1968, and has made it known that he believes the school represents "a certain East Coast attitude" brimming with "intellectual arrogance."[430]

Despite his severe enmity towards elitism, Bush would use his father's connections shortly after leaving Yale to join the Air National Guard and obtain a preferential assignment at a base in Texas where he could safely wait out the Vietnam War. When later asked if he was assigned to the base in an attempt to dodge the draft, Bush stated, "No, I was becoming a pilot."[431]

A deeper look into W.'s military service revealed that the young Bush may not have had the right stuff to qualify for the post and he was aided by then–Speaker of the Texas House Ben Barnes.

"I would describe it as preferential treatment," Barnes told CBS. "There were hundreds of names on the list of people wanting to get into the Air National Guard or the Army National Guard. I think that would have been a preference to anybody that didn't want to go to Vietnam or didn't want to leave. We had a lot of young men that left and went to Canada in the '60s and fled this country. But those that could get in the Reserves, or those that could get in the National Guard—chances are they would not have to go to Vietnam."[432]

In 1973, Bush was honorably discharged from air service after he neglected to take his required annual physical. Following his time in the Air National Guard, W. would deny any special treatment.

"Any allegation that my dad asked for special favors is simply not true," said Mr. Bush. "And the former president of the United States has said that he in no way, shape or form helped me get into the National Guard. I didn't ask anyone to help me get into the Guard either."[433]

Candidate for the People of Midland

In the 1970s, the 19th District of Texas was arguably one of the most conservative, religious-right congressional districts in the nation. It had been represented for four decades by George Mahon, a powerful Democrat who rose to be chairman of the Appropriations Committee and dean of the House.

But in 1978, Mahon decided to retire. The newly minted, 31-year-old Texas oilman, George W. Bush, entered and won the Republican primary for the 19th District. Having flirted with the idea of running for the State Senate a few years earlier, George W. saw an opening—and jumped into it. Born in Connecticut and having spent most of his school years in a Houston prep school, Phillips Academy in Andover, Massachusetts, Yale, and Harvard, the eldest Bush son nevertheless tried to translate the few years he had actually lived in Midland into the image of a regular local businessman who just wanted to serve.

It almost worked. George W. carried his "hometown" and nearby areas, but didn't fare as well in the rest of the district, where his Democratic opponent, Kent Hance, was successful in pegging Bush as a privileged, less-than-authentic Texan. Hance defeated Bush by roughly 6,000 votes. It didn't help George W. that, with a history of alcohol-related episodes, some of his campaign volunteers organized and advertised a campuswide "Bush Bash" that offered free beer to students— just days before the election. Absent that blunder on the part of youthful supporters and Hance's broadcasting of it to thousands of Christian conservatives, the election would likely have been much closer.

A man of the people? That depends on what "people." George W. had barely finished his Ivy League education, was only 31 years old, and certainly hadn't established any of his own credentials in either business or politics. In one of his first appearances of the campaign, his Andover-Yale-Harvard upbringing slipped out when he greeted a rural crowd by announcing that "Today is the first time I've been on a real farm."[434]

That same young, inexperienced candidate—running against a well-known state senator—managed to secure financial backing from the likes of the chairman of Bank of America, Ford Motor Company's William Ford, and many others whose involvement could be attributed less to good government and the 19th District of Texas than to affection for the Bush family name and the influence it represented. The elder Bush was well into his preparations for a presidential primary battle against Ronald Reagan, and a win for George W. would certainly enhance the family brand within the Republican establishment.

Despite the family name and ample funding from his father's friends from Midland to New York, George W.'s congressional run fell short. Voters didn't quite buy his rapid transformation from privileged, partying Yalie to an instant Midland businessman, and his opponent successfully challenged his authenticity.

However, the problems that sank that first campaign for public office could be fixed, and they were. George W., with the help of his Midland crowd, would reenter the business world, find religion, stop drinking, visit a few more farms, and shape himself into a Texan who could assume a high-profile role in his father's presidential campaign, buy a baseball team, be elected governor twice—and become president.

His first try was probably doomed to fail, but George W. Bush would never lose another election after 1978.

$4.7 Million Sets Up W. and Arbusto

How does a 32-year-old aspiring oilman with virtually no tangible assets put together $4.7 million to jumpstart a drilling enterprise? In the case of George W. Bush, he does it the same way he finances a failed congressional campaign. He leverages his father's friends and position. And his son needs money to get into the oil business.

Apparently, having a father like that makes for a good set of bootstraps. Armed with some mineral rights, George W. was able to go to New York, Greenwich, and other financial centers and pull together enough money to create Arbusto Energy, the company that would eventually morph into Bush Exploration, Spectrum 7, and Harken Energy.

When he graduated from the Harvard Business School in 1976, George W. Bush was one of the only students who left the heavily recruited program without a job. He had $20,000 left in his education trust fund. Through his father, he was also well connected so getting into the oil business made good sense. He returned to Midland, Texas, a move some say was designed to prepare him for public office.

Bush organized his first company in 1977, an oil exploration company he called Arbusto Energy Inc.—a name picked because it was Spanish for bush. He took rent-free office space from his father's friends; he used empty crates as furniture. He became what is known in West Texas as a landman—he convinced local landowners to give him the mineral rights to their property. As one might expect, he didn't set the world on fire.

George W. had virtually no experience and precious little cash of his own, but he had the one asset that would open the doors of storied money men such as Lew Lehrman and Prudential-Bache's George Ball. That asset, obviously, was his name and lineage. Lehrman, who would later set spending records for his multi-million dollar failed campaign for New York governor, chipped in for almost $50,000, and Ball bought in for $100,000. They were joined by other Bush friends William Draper and FitzGerald Bemiss, as well as other investors any other 32-year-old entrepreneur could only dream of reaching.[435]

While most of the money for Arbusto Energy came from the Bushes' New York and New England circles, a reported $50,000 came from what ultimately became a rather inconvenient source: an agent for Salem bin Laden based in Houston, Texas. Salem was the half-brother of Osama bin Laden. When the bin Laden connection became known, the agent, James Bath, maintained that the $50,000 he invested in George W.'s business was his own money. However, Bath was widely known to represent Saudi interests and some have questioned whether he actually had the personal funds to make such an investment. What is known is that he represented Salem bin Laden's interests as his business agent in Texas.[436]

What is also known is that Bath and George W. served together in the Texas Air National Guard. And it is a safe assumption that Salem's investment funds came from the same source as the fortune his brother, Osama bin Laden, used to bankroll al Qaeda, and presumably the attacks on 9/11: their father's construction company that was built largely from contracts granted by the Saudi royal family.

Salem bin Laden was killed in a plane crash in 1988 in his adopted home state of Texas.

James Bath's mysterious business relationships were not limited to the bin Ladens. He also served as a director of BCCI, the Bank of Credit and Commerce International. Founded in 1972, BCCI experienced inexplicable growth into the 1980s, when investigations by regulators in several countries revealed that the bank was actively soliciting deposits from drug traffickers and engaging in large-scale money laundering.[437]

Likewise, one of Bath's other significant enterprises included an aircraft brokerage that arranged tens of millions of dollars' worth of deals with Middle Eastern interests. One of his companies, Southwest Airport Services, came under scrutiny in 2000 when the *Houston Post* revealed that the U.S. government was spending millions of dollars to buy fuel from the company despite the fact that less costly government fuel supplies were readily available at the same location.[438]

George W. Bush denied that he had a financial relationship with James Bath, despite the documented fact that Bath was an early investor in Arbusto Energy, and maintained an equity stake for several years.

Ironically, while George W. was impressively successful at bringing cash into Arbusto from investors who would have likely been unreachable absent his father's position and relationships, even his name wasn't enough to overcome falling oil prices—or make a profit. By 1982, the company's book value was less than 10 percent of the $4.7 million that had been invested by the Bushes' country club and Middle Eastern friends.

CEO of Spectrum 7 and the $3 Million Debt
With a losing oil market and the reality that George W.'s Arbusto simply wasn't finding enough crude, the company was in serious straits by 1982. Then, miraculously, an investor by

the name of Philip Uzielli decided to purchase 10 percent of the company for $1 million. That's $1 million for one-tenth of a business that was worth less than $400,000. Definitely an odd investment by a successful Panamanian businessman—unless that businessman is a college friend of Bush loyalist James Baker and George W.'s father happens to be vice president of the United States.

In the early 1980s, oil prices dropped and Arbusto was reeling. In a blatant attempt to further capitalize on the family name, George W. decided to rename the company as Bush Exploration. By 1984, the company was in dire need of capital. Apparently assuming the name change would have some appeal, W. also offered shares of the company to the public. The plan was to raise $6 million. The public offering brought in roughly $1 million, leaving Bush Exploration seriously short of what was needed to keep the doors open and the drills drilling.

Within a year, the company was on the ropes—again. Conventional investors were nowhere to be found, not surprisingly, given the performance of George W.'s enterprise up to that time. But the miracles kept coming. Another oil company, Spectrum 7 Energy Corp., owned by William DeWitt Jr. and Mercer Reynolds of Cincinnati, Ohio, was in need of a CEO, and the vice president of the United States had a son in the oil business who was available—for a price. That price was to buy Bush Exploration and bail George W. out once again. It was called a "merger." According to an April 1986 New York Times story, Spectrum 7 specialized in creating tax shelters—limited partnerships which generated lucrative write-offs.

Business or politics? The Spectrum 7 deal was the doing of two men who, like their predecessors in the Bush investment club, moved in the same circles as the Bush family and would be significant supporters. One of the Spectrum 7 owners, William

DeWitt, was a fellow Ivy Leaguer whose family had owned the Cincinnati Reds. His co-owner and partner in Reynolds, DeWitt & Co. was Mercer Reynolds III. Reynolds would later become the finance chairman of George W.'s campaign for the White House.[439] George W.? He became not only the CEO of a new and temporarily improved company, but its third largest shareholder (he received 1.1 million shares of stock, or 16.3 percent of the company). His new partners? They gained a losing business proposition, but became shareholders in a future presidency.

The original, early investors in George W.'s oil ventures? When all the deals were done, the money spent and the meager profits distributed, they lost a combined $3 million. The future president got a job as CEO for $75,000, and equity in a new company. His friends and backers, if they were fortunate, were left with some sizable tax write-offs.

As for George W.'s new partners, the balance sheet of their company would not improve much, but apparently not at the expense of their friendship. Mercer Reynolds would go on to co-chair Bush's inaugural committee and to become the ambassador to Switzerland and Liechtenstein, despite his striking lack of foreign service credentials. William DeWitt Jr. would similarly lick his financial wounds with an appointment to the President's Intelligence Advisory Board and his wife's appointment to the National Endowment for the Arts—all while buying and taking over the management of the St. Louis Cardinals.

CHAPTER 29

BUSH AND HARKEN

I still haven't figured it out completely.

—Bush on selling his shares in
Harken Energy just before the stock plummeted.[xxii]

Stepping Into It

Within two years, Spectrum 7 was in trouble. In the six months before Spectrum 7 was acquired in September 1986, it had lost $400,000. Still, Dallas-based Harken Energy, an independent oil and gas company, bought Spectrum, put Bush on the board, set him up with a comfortable $120,000 income, and gave him stock options that would later make him a wealthy man.

Why would Harken jump at the chance to buy a failing company and hire its CEO who had never succeeded in business? He may have been a good choice because his name lent prestige to the company. Harken assumed $3.1 million in debts and swapped $2.2 million of its stock for a company that was hemorrhaging money, though it had oil and gas reserves projected to produce $4 million in future net revenue.[440]

George W. Bush's value became obvious six months after he joined the company: When the company was crying for capital in early 1987, Junior brought Harken executives to meetings with Jackson Stephens, head of Stephens, Inc., a Little Rock, Arkansas, investment bank, and a financial supporter of Poppy's politics—he gave the Reagan-Bush campaign $100,000 in 1980 and another $100,000 to Bush in 1990.

As a result, Stephens encouraged Union Bank of Switzerland (UBS) to buy $25 million worth of Harken stock. Sheikh Abdullah Bakhsh, a Saudi real estate developer and financier, also joined Harken's board as a major investor. It's important to note that Stephens, UBS, and Bakhsh are all tied to the Bank of Credit and Commerce International (BCCI)—the notorious international bank accused of lending laws violations and laundering money for Saddam Hussein, Manuel Noriega, the Medellin Cartel and terrorist Abu Nidal (according to the Francisco Bay Area Independent Media Center, July 5, 2002).

While drawing a paycheck at Harken, Bush worked full time in Washington on his father's presidential campaign. He flew back to Midland for board meetings and assisted with corporate development.

It is during Bush's tenure at Harken that author Russ Baker first saw what he calls "The Quacking Duck"—clear indications that the company was entangled in intrigue far beyond its business model. "There always seemed to be something more going on: that overlay of peculiar money-moving, a general lack of profitability, the participation of foreign interests, and a hint of black intelligence operations," Baker wrote in his seminal work on the Bush clan, *Family of Secrets*. Harken started ed out as a fairly run-of-the-mill energy company, but after nearly ten years in operation, company founder Phil Kendrick sought buyers for an Australian subsidiary. The search turned up a shady character in Manila, Philippines: American expatriate attorney William Quasha, rumored to be the man who brought strongman Ferdinand Marcos to power. He was also said to be helping Marcos get his pilfered money out of the islands and laundered by taking positions in real companies.

While William Quasha never bought the Australian division, his son Alan was introduced to Kendrick via an investment banker working with Harken. Alan Quasha took a significant position in the company via a Bermuda trust named after his mother, joined the board, and Kendrick feels Quasha then crashed the company share price, that it was an intentional move to gain control of the company.

After Bush joined the company in 1986, the Harken business was transformed. Quasha family members took significant stakes in the firm and, according to SEC documents, his father William bought 21 percent of the stock. Billionaire George Soros swapped oil stocks to attain a significant position. Not twenty years later, Soros invested millions in leftist organizations devoted to defeating incumbent president George W. Bush.

Joining the Marcos crony, the Hungarian billionaire, and other mysterious Harken investors was an unlikely partner: Harvard University. And they showed up quite soon after Bush.

Harvard Management Company, the university's investment arm, agreed to invest $20 million in the firm and bought 1.35 million new Harken shares for $2 million. Harvard Management became one of its biggest backers, loaning it millions of dollars and transferring oil properties to it.

Harken had Harvard connections, beginning with business school graduates Bush and Alan Quasha, the investor and board member. Robert Stone Jr., who nearly controlled the university endowment for many years, was a Texas oilman and had the final say on energy investments. Some have speculated that he assured the fund invested in the Bush enterprise because of connections to the family.

Stone worked hard to distance himself from the Bush family, but the ties were there and longstanding. He married a Rockefeller and his in-laws were close friends with W.'s grandparents, Prescott and Dorothy Bush.[441] The Stones lived in Greenwich, Connecticut, and Houston, like the Bush family, and in 1979 he donated to Poppy's run for president along with his family and executives at his energy company, Stonetex Oil. He and his wife also donated to the 1988 race.[442]

Most interesting: Stone, who had apparent Central Intelligence Agency connections, was in business with CIA career officer Thomas J. Devine, who retired from the Agency to found Zapata Offshore, the energy company founded by George H. W. Bush. Devine even became Stonetex's treasurer. The more you know about Stone, the more sense Harvard's unusual investment in Harken makes.[443] The George W. Bush White House later insisted Harvard began talks with Harken in April 1986, well before the former president joined Harken. "The original relationship had nothing to do with President Bush," said spokesman Dan Bartlett.[444]

Throughout Bush's association with Harken, Harvard continued to invest. The university owned about 30 percent of Harken at the height of its investment, but began selling its shares in the early 1990s according to Harvard Management chief executive Jack Meyer. Meyer told the *Boston Globe* that Harvard made a "small profit." Even when he was in the White House in 2002, when the media examined Bush's Harken profits, Harvard owned 254,251 shares in the company.[445]

Harken continued to benefit from their well-connected director. While Bush was working for Harken, Rodrigo

Villamizar, a Bush friend since college days, became head of Colombia's bureau that supervised sale of state oil concessions. Bush had helped Villamizar get jobs early in his career and Villamizar returned the favor by granting Harken a series of oil contracts in the Magdalena Valley, the home of violent cocaine-connected death squads.

Later, Villamizar wrote policy briefs for the 2000 Bush campaign and declined the newly elected president's offer to serve as Assistant Secretary of State for Western Hemisphere Affairs. Soon after, Villamizar was accused of official corruption in his home country, was convicted, and went on the lam.[446]

In January 1990, Harken shocked the energy industry by winning drilling rights from the Bahrain government. Never—not once—had the tiny company that beat oil giant Amoco for the work dipped a drill bit in the water. Many suspected Bahrain was trying to win favor with the sitting president by selecting a company where his son served as a director. More cynical critics believe the George H. W. Bush administration exerted influence to assure Harken won the bid.

In June, Bush sold his shares in Harken and netted almost $850,000. The money covered a loan he had taken to join the group set to buy the Texas Rangers. Russ Baker revealed in *Family of Secrets* that the stock was likely purchased by Harvard Management Company—a trade ticket associated with the sale bore the name Michael Eisenson, president of Harvard Management Company and a Harken board member.

"Bush didn't even know who the buyer was at the time. He still doesn't know. No one but me ever knew who the buyer was. And no one ever will know," said Ralph Smith, the institutional trader who represented that buyer who bought Bush's shares. "It's nobody's business. There isn't anything there. And nothing was done wrong."[447]

Baker insists in his book that Harvard, which had already stepped up to save the company in 1986, came to the rescue again to help Bush get rich. Baker called this a "conflict of interest in the truest sense of the term."[448]

A week after Bush's insider stock sale, Harken announced a quarterly loss of $23.2 million and the stock dropped like a rock. There were indications that Bush and other company leaders knew of the loss, but Bush was the only one to liquidate his position. This led to a four-and-a-half month Securities and Exchange Commission investigation of Bush for insider trading that was eventually closed without charges. Of course, this was during Senior's presidency—and investigators never interviewed Junior.

The Bahrain deal did not improve the company's precarious finances. Six weeks after Bush sold his stock, Iraq attacked Kuwait and made regional oil exploration a risky venture. When the work was done, Harken subcontracted to an energy firm owned by the billionaire Bass family—big backers of George W. Bush in his future endeavors. In the end, no oil was found anyway, but the announcement of the surprising win boosted the company stock price.

Harvard may have later regretted their association with the oil and gas exploration company. In July 1990, Harken was mired again in financial trouble. To weather the storm, the firm, with Bush's assent, created an off balance sheet entity, similar to the shady moves that famously sank Enron, to move troubled assets and large debts off the company's balance sheet. The partnership with Harvard was formed at a time when the company's finances were dicey; Harken earned vital cash flow for managing the new entity and gained no debt.

The move was risky, but necessary. Edging up on bankruptcy again, the failing company threatened to tarnish Bush's business reputation—a record on which he hoped to run for office. The damage to his reputation had to be stopped. Was this why Harvard entered the precarious partnership? Regardless, the deal worked and Harken's share price recovered.[449]

George W. Bush came to Harken Energy a failed businessman and left a wealthy man with pumped-up business credentials. It's important to note that the SEC investigation into his timely stock sale did not find Bush innocent. Investigators simply concluded they did not have the evidence needed to prosecute him.

CHAPTER 30

SEEKING HIGHER OFFICE

Rarely is the question asked: Is our children learning?

—President George W. Bush[xxiii]

W. Runs for Governor

In 1994, George Bush ran against popular incumbent Texas governor Ann Richards. Richards was a firebrand, a progressive activist ahead of her time who fought for the rights of minorities, women, and gay people of both genders.

Richards had a disdain for the Bushes, whom she saw as pampered and imbecilic; they became a source of her pointed barbs. "Poor George, he can't help it," Richards said of then–Vice President Bush at the 1988 Democratic Convention in Atlanta, "He was born with a silver foot in his mouth."[450]

Though her dislike for the Bushes was apparent, it was nearly nonexistent in her race against W. Richards made the mistake of waging a non-campaign under the belief that her record would win over divisive politicking. Bush also avoided an attack-filled strategy, focusing more on widening his base. This was best summed up by Paul Burka in *Texas Monthly* shortly after the election:

Richards did nothing, and so it was Bush who defined the race. Her campaign had no battle plan, no theme, no message. She said little about her record—which was the best of any governor since John Connally—and even less about what she wanted to do in her next term. The Richards camp seemed to lack confidence. They used focus groups incessantly, trying to figure out the mood of the voters, while Bush's strategists operated more on instinct, using only one set of focus groups. Richards wanted just one debate, a limit to which the Bush strategists were thrilled to agree.

The Bush campaign had a game plan and stuck to it. Bush would be the candidate of change, the magic word in the nineties; attack Richards on nonpartisan issues of public discontent (crime, welfare, education); soft-pedal the generic Republican issues like taxes and spending; and avoid purely personal attacks. Mike Toomey, a wonkish former Houston legislator turned business lobbyist, helped form teams to develop Bush's policy positions. Bush learned his lines and stuck to the message. After the votes were counted on Election Day, Toomey exulted that the race had come down to "ideas over personality."[451]

Leading up to Election Day, experts said the contest was too close to call, yet Bush ended up claiming victory by eight points. W.'s win that year was aided by Republican success at the polls nationwide with the party winning both houses of Congress and a mass movement in Texas in which many of the state's Democrats shifted political allegiance.

The Recount
I was surprised when Lee Atwater called and said "pack your bags, Baker wants you to go to California." It was the first week of October 1988 and it was the first presidential election since 1968 in which I had had no general election role.

James A. Baker III was someone for whom I have great reverence and respect. Unlike George Bush, he was a real Texan, direct, earthy, and confident. He was also an excellent judge of people and his brief hallmark in national politics had been selecting skilled operatives for key jobs and supporting them to the hilt. After Gerald Ford's 1976 campaign listed badly under the incompetent leadership of former Georgia congressman Howard "Bo" Calloway, a crony from Ford's House days, and then former Maryland governor and Nixon's interior secretary Rogers C. B. Morton, Baker had been tasked with rounding up enough delegates to nominate Ford in a close and hard fought contest with Reagan. Baker had quickly assembled a highly capable team that included my longtime Young Republican colleague and future business partner Paul J. Manafort. The Ford campaign narrowly prevailed at the Kansas City convention after a deft move by Reagan campaign manager John Sears to require that the presidential candidates name their vice presidential running mate *prior* to the presidential nominating ballot. Sears knew that Ford had committed the vice presidency to both John Connally and Nelson Rockefeller among others, and that calling his hand in advance could only lead to a serious erosion in Ford's support. While the gambit was unsuccessful, it did mean that Reagan went to the Kansas City convention with the nomination still in doubt. Coupled with Reagan's surprise announcement that Pennsylvania senator Richard Schweicker would be his running mate, Sears's maneuver bought the Reaganites time to attempt to chisel enough delegates off of Ford in the Pennsylvania delegation to put Reagan over the top. Ford's Pennsylvania chairman Drew Lewis was able to hold the Ford delegates in the Keystone State in line, but the result was in doubt until the actual first balloting began.

Baker emerged from the Ford campaign with his reputation enhanced. In 1979 it was announced that he would helm Ambassador George Bush's long shot bid for the Republican nomination in 1980. After Reagan vanquished Bush, loyal soldier Baker would join the Reagan entourage. Nancy Reagan keenly remembered Baker's role in skillfully denying the nomination to her husband in 1976, and was also attracted by Baker's courtly Southern manners and obvious organization. With the recommendation of Michael Deaver and the support of Nancy Reagan, Bushite Baker would emerge as Reagan's first White House chief of staff over the bumbling but ideologically pure Edwin Meese.

After Reagan's 1980 election, I passed up the opportunity to join the administration, instead forming a political consulting and lobbying firm with Reagan campaign veterans Charlie Black and Paul Manafort. My first big client was former New Jersey House speaker Thomas H. Kean. I had met and courted Kean to be Reagan's campaign chairman in New Jersey as early as 1979, and although we had a series of promising meetings, Kean would ultimately beg off on the basis of a commitment to New Jersey public television to be a commentator on the race. In truth, I think that although Kean liked Reagan, he was feeling substantial cross pressure from his friend Nicholas F. Brady to helm the Bush campaign in the Garden State, just as he had chaired Ford's campaign in New Jersey in 1976.

Only New Jersey and Virginia had gubernatorial elections in the off year of 1981. Republican Marshall Coleman, the Virginia attorney general, was thought to be a strong front-runner over Richmond mayor Douglas Wilder, an African American. In New Jersey, Democratic congressman Jim Florio was considered a strong favorite and Republican prospects were not enhanced by a bruising nine-way primary for the

Republican nomination. Kean had run for governor in 1977, essentially as a moderate Republican, but this time I convinced him to tack right. He won the endorsement of Jeffrey Bell, who had upset incumbent U.S. senator Clifford Case in the 1978 Senate race in New Jersey, and a tax cut proposal put forward by Kean had won the avid endorsement of Congressman Jack Kemp. Despite a well-funded bid by multi-millionaire businessman Joseph "Bo" Sullivan, Kean won the primary but began the race trailing Florio by 20 points.

Through the late summer and fall, the likeable Kean doggedly campaigned to close the gap while Camden's Congressman Florio acted as if the election was over and he had already been anointed. Rife corruption in the Camden County Democratic machine and the spectacular unpopularity of New Jersey governor Brendan Byrne, coupled with Kean's likeability in two debates, allowed the former speaker to close within three points. In our private polling conducted by veteran Republican pollster Bob Teeter, I realized that a late campaign appearance by President Ronald Reagan could put Kean over the top. I had begun lobbying White House Chief of Staff Baker for a Kean appearance around Labor Day but had been told "we will win Virginia and lose New Jersey, we see no reason why the President should put his prestige on the line only to sustain a loss." Nonetheless, I had carefully kept Baker posted on our steady progress in closing the gap. I decided to make one final pitch to Baker, asking Teeter to follow up with a phone call nudging the Texan to put a New Jersey campaign stop on the president's schedule. This time Baker said, "I'll think about it." I called Teeter begging him to call the president's chief of staff. Two hours later, the ever efficient Margaret Tutwiler called to say, "Mr. Baker said to tell you that the president is going to New Jersey." Shortly thereafter the White House switchboard called to patch in a call from deputy chief of staff Mike Deaver. "Stone," he said, "the president is going to New Jersey. If we lose it's your ass." I hadn't had the nerve to ask for a Reagan endorsement TV spot. Instead I lined up a camera crew and wrote a 30-second script. The president's schedule showed that he would have a brief down time in a hangar at Newark airport after the landing of Air Force One. The plan was to have Tom Kean ask him on the spot to record a commercial, which we just happened to have a camera crew standing by for. Kean gutted up to the ask. Although Deaver shot me a dirty look, Reagan immediately said yes and I put the script in his hands. He scanned the paper before him. "How long," he said. "Twenty-eight seconds," I replied. The president was shepherded into an office within the hangar where he sat on the edge of a desk. The camera crew crowded into the room. "I'm not the kind of fella that tells other people how to vote, but I got to tell you, I like Tom Kean," Reagan said in his most winning and folksy style. Ever the Hollywood pro, Reagan knocked out the TV commercial in one take: "28 seconds on the nose," the cameraman said after looking at his camera.

Tom Kean would go on to win the governorship of New Jersey by 1200 votes out of 2.2 million votes cast. For weeks we were mired in a recount while the Democratic machine endeavored to somehow save the governorship for Jim Florio. With the help of lawyer Andrew Napolitano, whom Kean would later appoint to the bench, our narrow margin held. In the world of politics, I owed Jim Baker for victory in the first statewide race in which I was the lead strategist.

In 1988 the chit was called in. Baker's uber-capable associate Margaret Tutwiler summoned me to the Bush Headquarters to meet Baker. "Something's fucked up in California," he said.

"Every week I increase the media budget but Teeter (Bush's pollster) says the numbers aren't moving. We are in a dead heat. Get your ass out there and find out what is wrong," he said with his Texas drawl.

"Bush hates me," I said. "He's not going to like this."

"That's because you took those New Jersey delegates from us," he said referring to 1980. "You let me handle Bush, just get on the first plane to California."

I landed at LAX just before midnight, heading wearily to a beat-up hotel near the airport. I had scheduled breakfast with Bush's California campaign director Bill Lacey, a Dole man whom I knew to be highly capable and who had expressed some frustration over the phone about the state of affairs within Bush's California campaign. "Wilson and Deukmejian are at each other's throats and both think they know better how to carry California," said Lacey. "It's a shit show." (At the time, Deukmejian was Governor of California while Wilson was Senator.)

I flopped down on the big double bed with the sagging mattress in my hotel room and switched on the TV. In the space of two hours I knew exactly what the problem with Bush's California campaign was. I saw five different television spots for Bush. It wasn't hard to figure out that the campaign was running too many messages on television without putting sufficient repetition behind any one message. I would subsequently learn that Bush's media maven Roger Ailes, now the president of Fox News, had had his TV spot rotation instructions countermanded by first the Wilson and then the Deukmejian people. I called Ailes' media buyer, who confirmed that the rotation instructions were being changed back and forth almost daily.

My breakfast meeting with Lacey was perfunctory. He agreed with the root of the problem and told me he would back a recommendation that Ailes' instructions be untouched. Before boarding a plane back to Dulles International Airport in DC, I called Atwater and summed up the situation, suggesting he pass my recommendation on to Baker. "Call him yourself," Atwater said, "he's going to want to hear it from you." My conversation with Baker was short. I made my case, to which he said "got it," and abruptly signed off. Bush's California television spot rotation was corrected. Bush would defeat Massachusetts governor Michael Dukakis in the Golden State by 1 percent.

In 2000 the chit was called in again. By any measure George W. Bush should have easily defeated Vice President Al Gore in the state of Florida. George Bush's brother Jeb was the sitting governor with all the vast patronage and influence that that office brings. Yet on election night the Sunshine State seesawed back and forth between the Democratic contender and his Republican rival. It became clear that Bill Clinton would sit in the White House a little longer while Florida and the nation went through the agony of a protracted recount. Still I was surprised when Margaret Tutwiler called my office in Virginia. "Mr. Baker wants to know if you can go to Florida as soon as possible," she said. "He knows you know about recounts and said to tell you that you will only need to stay for a few days." While I was no great fan of Governor George W. Bush and even less of a fan of his Sancho Panza Karl Rove, I knew Baker was calling a chit. "Tell him I'll be on the next plane," I said.

I was somewhat shocked when the HBO movie *Recount* showed actor Tom Wilkinson playing Jim Baker turning to his assistant in a conference room of Republican lawyers and operatives and saying: "We're in a street fight for the presidency of the United States—get me Roger Stone."

Baker sent me first to Palm Beach County, where a substantial number of elderly voters had been confused by the elaborate "butterfly ballot" supposedly inadvertently casting their votes for Reform Party candidate Pat Buchanan while *meaning* to cast their votes for Al Gore. Democrats railed against the layout of the "butterfly ballot" until it was revealed that it had been used in Gore campaign manager Bill Daley's Chicago for decades. Looking back at it now and examining the ballot, I can only conclude that a voter would have to be really stupid to miscast a vote for Buchanan when meaning to vote for Gore. Overall, however, the Republican recount effort seemed well in hand if not overstaffed in Palm Beach County.

When I called Baker with my assessment, he reassigned me to Miami-Dade, where Democrats on the election board were attempting to recount the same trove of disputed ballots a *third* time. The recount was being conducted in a large open room in the county courthouse in full view of dozens of partisan lawyers as well as members of the news media. Sometime during the proceedings, one of the Democratic board members attempted to remove a sheaf of ballots in the company of a Gore campaign operative. I was in a trailer outside the courthouse following the proceedings by walkie-talkie, manned by a Bush-Cheney operative inside. The two Democrats headed down a narrow hallway attempting to take the ballots into an anteroom, which had neither windows nor any other observers. The scene was described to me. "What should we do," my panicked Republican colleague asked. "Don't let those ballots out of your sight," I barked. "Break down the door if you must." A large contingent of Republican operatives and Bush-Cheney supporters had seen this drama unfold and they accompanied my panicked liaison, crowding the narrow hallway. A shouting match ensued and thus the so-called Brooks Brothers riot was born.

Downstairs in the courtroom a large crowd had gathered, whipped into a frenzy by Spanish-language Cuban radio talk show hosts, who likened the effort to "find" more votes for Gore to the Cuban Revolution under Fidel Castro. My Cuban-American wife Nydia Stone, fluent in Spanish, had made the rounds of the Cuban radio talkers, spreading around dineros from the vast Bush-Cheney recount fund. In frustration, the Bush supporters had begun pounding on the metal doors to the courthouse, causing a horrific racket in the cavernous building and ratcheting up the pressure on the Democratic members of the election board. Finally, after much sturm and drang, the third recount was called off and thus George W. Bush would become president.

It is an action I would regret. While Bush had campaigned as a "compassionate conservative" and I thought him preferable to the stilted and insecure Al Gore, his leading the country into a costly and bloody war in Iraq and the erosion of our civil liberties with the Patriot Act stand in my mind as among the two most egregious acts committed by any American president.

In November of 2008, I told the *Daily Beast:* "There have been many times I've regretted it," . . . "When I look at those double-page *New York Times* spreads of all the individual pictures of people who have been killed [in Iraq], I got to think, 'maybe there wouldn't have been a war if I hadn't gone to Miami-Dade. Maybe there hadn't have been, in my view, an unjustified war if Bush hadn't become President.' It's very disturbing to me."

CHAPTER 31

43: WORST EVER?

You work three jobs? ... Uniquely American, isn't it? I mean,
that is fantastic that you're doing that.

—President Bush to a divorced mother of three, Omaha,
Nebraska, February. 4, 2005[xxiv]

The No Child Left Behind Scam
On January 23, 2001—three days after he was inaugurated—
President George W. Bush proposed the No Child Left Behind
Act. As a replacement and reauthorization of the comprehensive law that governs federal education programs, it was a
massive proposal that fundamentally changed the traditional
relationship between the federal government and state and local school administration.

For one of the new president's first and most heralded policy
initiatives, it was very non-Republican. After all, a great many
Republican governors, senators, and congressmen constantly
advocate less federal interference in education, not more. But
strangely enough, President Bush—himself a former governor and a self-proclaimed conservative—couldn't wait even a

week before urging Congress to enact a law that would require every public school in the nation to test all students. Any state that failed or refused to do so would be denied federal school funding. Even in small states, it was an extortion amounting to tens of millions of dollars each year.

The requirement for annual testing in every school of course carried with it a number of standards and mandatory measurements that would satisfy the feds and allow the dollars to flow from Washington, DC, to the states.

Despite the fact that a great many of George W.'s fellow Republicans were more than a little uneasy about such a dramatic expansion of the federal government's role in education, the White House put tremendous pressure on Congress to vote for the No Child Left Behind law. It was the newly elected president's signature initiative; he had a mandate from the voters, and loyalty demanded a Yes vote, the White House said. In Washington parlance, it was a "must have" vote for not only the president, but the congressional leadership. If a senator or congressman wanted their phone calls returned or committee assignments secured, voting No would not be a good idea. Their lobbying was successful. Only 45 members of the House and eight senators voted against it, and it was signed into law on January 8, 2002.

During his campaign and lobbying effort, George W. held up No Child Left Behind as a key piece of his particular brand of "compassionate conservatism," claiming it would reduce achievement gaps across ethnic and economic divides. He even insisted that it really wasn't a federal power grab—even though it expanded federal power on a historic scale.

And it was obviously personal. When a president has a major, complex legislative proposal ready to go three days after he is sworn in, it is clear that he intends to make it happen. He did.

How is it that a "conservative" Republican was so insistent about creating a federal testing requirement for every school in the nation, and obviously had the proposal in his pocket, ready to be introduced as soon as he unpacked his suitcase in the White House?

One explanation might be that in 1999, one year before the presidential election, George W.'s younger brother, Neil Bush, had co-founded Ignite! Learning, Inc., a computer company specializing in products designed to help prepare students for standardized testing. From insider trading issues to the Savings and Loan scandal that left him barred from the banking industry, Neil's business career has been colorful at best. But once again, the Bush family enterprise took care of its own, this time literally creating an industry that Neil was poised to exploit, along with the investors who ponied up more than $20 million to get the business up and running. Those funders include Barbara and George H. W. Bush, along with a variety of investors from Asia and the Middle East with whom the Bush family, including Neil, have long had business dealings.

The Bush family education enterprise didn't stop with the passage of a federal law and some strategic investments. In the wake of the devastating Hurricane Katrina, in 2006, Barbara Bush donated an undisclosed sum to the Bush-Clinton Katrina Fund and specified that her donation be spent to purchase Neil's software. Doubling down, Barbara and Neil solicited funds from others to do the same. While the full amount raised and spent with Neil's Ignite! company isn't clear, at least eight schools in Texas that took in students displaced by Katrina purchased the software, at a cost of $10,000 per school.[452]

President George W. Bush isn't the only elected education "reformer" in the family. As governor of Florida, Jeb made education one of his signature issues as well, including strongly supporting the Florida Comprehensive Assessment Test, known as FCAT and administered as part of the state's compliance with No Child Left Behind. One of the first companies to begin pitching its test-preparation programs to Florida schools, little more than a year after the passage of No Child Left Behind, was Neil's company, Ignite!. After offering no-cost trials of the software to a couple of Florida schools, the company was not shy about expressing its hopes to sell its program to other schools in the state—at a cost of $30 per student per year.[453]

One brother proposes the federal law and gets it enacted. Another brother complies with that law as governor of one of the nation's largest states, and yet another brother just happens to sell a computer package that makes it all work. And the mother and father chip in with their considerable fundraising ability.

Marvin Bush Provides Security for World Trade Center

Marvin P. Bush, the president's younger brother, was a top executive in a company once called Securacom, later named Stratesec, which provided security for the World Trade Center, United Airlines, and Dulles International Airport. Securacom was backed by KuwAm, a Kuwaiti-American investment firm on whose board Marvin Bush also served.[454]

According to its present CEO, Barry McDaniel, the company had an ongoing contract to handle security at the World Trade Center "up to the day the buildings fell down."[455]

The company lists as government clients "the U.S. Army, U.S. Navy, U.S Air Force, and the Department of Justice," in projects that "often require state-of-the-art security solutions for classified or high-risk government sites."[456]

Stratesec (Securacom) differs from other security companies, which separate the function of consultant from that of service provider. The company defines itself as a "single-source" provider of "end-to-end" security services, including everything from diagnosis of existing systems to hiring subcontractors to installing video and electronic equipment. It also provides armored vehicles and security guards.[457]

The World Trade Center was destroyed just days after a heightened security alert was lifted at the landmark 110-story towers. "Of course without power there were no security cameras, no security locks on doors and many, many 'engineers' coming in and out of the tower."[458] Marvin just happened to be in New York on 9/11. President Bush's cousin, Jim Pierce, was supposed to be in the World Trade Center when it was attacked. Pierce, managing director of AON Corporations, had arranged a business conference on the 105th floor of the South Tower where its New York offices were based. But his group was too large, so they decided to move across the street to the Millennium Hotel.[459]

In 1997, the World Trade Center and Dulles accounted for 55 percent and 20 percent of the company's earned revenues, respectively. The World Trade Center and Dulles projects figured largely in both Securacom's growing revenues from 1995 to 1997 and its decreases from 1997 to 1998. Stratesec continued to refer to "New York City's World Trade Center" as a former client through April 2001. The company had a contract from 1996 to 1998, involving security systems integrations. Neil Bush was with the company until 2000. Some filings indicate that the contract expired in 1998; however one company officially was widely quoted as saying they were responsible for WTC security "until the day they fell down."[460]

From 1993 to 1999, KuwAm held a large interest in Securacom. In 1996, KuwAm Corporation owned 90 percent of the company, either directly or through partnerships like one called Special Situations Investment Holdings and another called "Fifth Floor Company for General Trading and Contracting." KuwAm owned 31 percent of Securacom in 1998 and 47 percent of Stratesec in 1999. Marvin Bush was re-elected annually to Securacom's board of directors from 1993 through 1999. His final re-election was on May 25, 1999, for July 1999 to June 2000. Throughout, he also served on the company's Audit Committee and Compensation Committee, and his stock holdings grew during the period. Directors had options to purchase 25,000 shares of stock annually. In 1996, Marvin Bush acquired 53,000 shares at 52 cents per share. Shares in the 1997 IPO sold at $8.50. Records since 2000 no longer list Bush as a shareholder.[461]

Stratesec and KuwAm were closely connected at the leadership level. The former CEO of Stratesec is Wirt D. Walker III. For several years, Walker has also been chairman and CEO of an aircraft company, Aviation General, about 70 percent owned by KuwAm. Walker, while a principal at Stratesec (a director since 1987, chairman of the board since 1992, and formerly CEO since 1999), was also on the board of directors at KuwAm. Mishal Yousef Saud Al Sabah, the chairman at KuwAm, also served on Stratesec's board from 1991 to 2001. Walker and Al Sabah had major stock holdings in each other's companies. The sons of both also held shares in the two companies. Stratesec hired KuwAm for corporate secretarial services in 2002, at $2,500 per month.[462]

The Saudi Arabian embassy, the Kuwait embassy, and KuwAm have office suites in the Watergate complex, where both Stratesec and Aviation General held their annual shareholders' meetings in 1999, 2000, and 2001. Bush was re-elected to his annual board position there, across the hall from a Saudi Arabian Airlines office.[463]

Saudi princess Haifa Al-Faisal had her checking account at Riggs Bank, which has a large branch in the Watergate. Given that Jonathan Bush, the president's uncle, was a Riggs executive, it is difficult to understand any obstacle for American authorities pursuing the "Saudi money trail." The princess's charitable activities were processed through Riggs, which is just one of many troubling links between the Saudis and the Bushes.[464]

The Saudi 9/11 Cover-Up

The Bill, Hillary, and Chelsea Clinton Foundation has taken millions of dollars from foreign governments attempting to buy influence with a woman who might be the next president.

The $2 million contribution from Saudi Arabia, however, is the most troubling. Putting aside that the Saudis oppress women, denying them the most basic human rights, the self-styled "women's advocate" should still return that cash. Money from foreign nationals and foreign governments is illegal in U.S. political campaigns. So the Saudis are using their petro-dollars to buy future influence.

It is worth taking a moment to examine how the Saudis have used their vast wealth to affect U.S. foreign policy and have used their influence to hide the facts about the Saudis' actual role in the events of 9/11 from the American people. Infact, the Saudis have used their power and influence to cover up their involvement in the greatest terrorist attack in U.S. history and continue to do so today.

At least 11 members of the Bin Laden family were spirited out of the country in the 24 hours after the 9/11 attacks with the assistance of the George W. Bush administration. The FBI still denies knowing about the seven airplanes used to move the Bin Ladens out of the country when all private, commercial, and military air-travel was grounded.

Prince Bandar bin Sultan bin Abdul Aziz, the Saudi Arabian ambassador to the United States, orchestrated the exodus of more than 140 Saudis scattered throughout the United States. They included members of two families: one was the royal House of Saud, the family that ruled the kingdom of Saudi Arabia, perhaps the richest family in the world. The other family was the Saud's close allies, the Bin Ladens, who in addition to owning a multibillion-dollar construction company had produced history's most notorious terrorist, Osama Bin Laden.

Yet none of those spirited out of the country were questioned nor was a list of those leaving supplied. Dan Grossi, a former police officer recruited by the Tampa Police to escort the departing Saudis, said he did not get the names of the Saudi he was escorting. "It happened so fast," Grossi says. "I just knew they were Saudis. They were well connected. One of them told me his father or his uncle was good friends with George Bush Senior."[465]

The White House denied the flights even took place. Officially, the FBI says it had nothing to do with the repatriation of the Saudis. "I can say unequivocally that the FBI had no role in facilitating these flights one way or another," said FBI Special Agent John Iannerelli. Bandar, however, characterized the role of the FBI very differently. "With coordination with the FBI," he said on CNN, "we got them all out."[466]

Among those hustled out of the country were Osama's brother-in-law Mohammed Jamal Khalifa, thought by U.S. Intelligence to be an important figure in Al Qaeda and connected to the men behind the 1993 World Trade Center bombing and to the October 2000 bombing of the USS *Cole*. Also in the traveling party was Khalil Bin Laden, who boarded a plane in Orlando to leave the United States and whom Brazilian Intelligence suspected of having possible terrorist connections. According to the German wire service Deutsche Presse-Agentur, he had visited Belo Horizonte, Brazil, which was a known center for training terrorists. Neither was questioned before leaving the U.S.[467]

The erudite, Western-educated and Savile Row tailored Prince Bandar was an influential figure in the world of Islam and the power circles of Washington. His father, Defense Minister Prince Sultan, was second in line to the Saudi crown. Bandar was the nephew of King Fahd, the aging Saudi monarch, and the grandson of the late king Abdul Aziz, the founder of modern Saudi Arabia. So close to the Bush family was the Saudi ambassador that Barbara Bush dubbed him "Bandar Bush."[468]

The Bush and Bin Laden families have long-standing business dealings. These began in the late 1970s, as we discovered earlier, when Sheik Mohammed bin Laden, the family patriarch and Osama's father, had, through a friend of the Bush family named James R. Bath, invested $50,000 in Arbusto, the oil exploration company founded by George W. Bush with his father's help. The "investment" was arranged by Bath, an aircraft broker who had emerged as an agent for the House of Saud in political and business circles.[469]

In 1997, Prince Bandar gave $1 million to the George Bush Presidential Library and Museum in College Station, Texas.

In 1989, King Fahd gave $1 million to Barbara Bush's campaign against illiteracy. In 2002 Prince Alwaleed bin Talal gave $500,000 to Andover to fund a George Herbert Walker Bush scholarship. In 2003, Prince Bandar gave a $1 million oil painting of an American buffalo hunt to President Bush for use in his presidential library after he leaves the White House.[470]

On September 11, 2001, Shafiq Bin Laden, an "estranged" half-brother of Osama, gave to the Carlyle Group in Washington, DC an initial $38 million to manage. Carlyle is a $16 billion private equity firm that pays huge fees to "advisors" George H. W. Bush and former secretary of state James Baker.[471]

After former president George H. W. Bush, James Baker, and former prime minister John Major of Great Britain visited Saudi Arabia on behalf of Carlyle, the Saudis increased their investment in the Carlyle Group to at least $80 million.[472]

It's therefore not surprising that the BBC reported that FBI agents in London were pulled off an investigation of Bin Laden family and Saudi royals soon after George W. Bush took office. In addition to Osama Bin Laden, other members of the family had terrorist connections and were under investigation by the FBI.

Of the nineteen 9/11 hijackers, 14 were Saudi, yet after the attack on American soil FBI agent John O'Neill stated publicly he was blocked from investigating the Saudi connection for "political reasons." What political reasons are more important than the investigation of the World Trade Center destruction and the murder of 2000 Americans?

More recently, the *New York Times* and others have reported on an aborted investigation into Saudis who fled Florida two weeks before the 9/11 attack. The investigation into the prominent Saudi family's ties to the hijackers started on September

19, 2001, and remained active for several years. It was led by the FBI's Tampa field office but included the bureau's field offices in New York and Washington.

The FBI identified persons of interest, establishing their ties to other terrorists and their sympathies with Osama bin Laden, and documenting their anti-American remarks. They examined their bank accounts, colleges, and places of employment. They tracked at least one suspect's re-entry into the U.S. Yet incredibly, none of this was ever shared with Congress or the 9/11 Commission.

Now it's being whitewashed again, in a newly released report by the 9/11 Review Commission, set up in 2014 by Congress to assess "any evidence now known to the FBI that was not considered by the 9/11 Commission." Though the FBI acknowledges the Saudi family in Florida was investigated, it maintains the probe was a "dead end."

The 9/11 review panel included one local FBI report from the Florida investigation that said Abdulaziz and Anoud al-Hijji, the prominent Saudi couple who "fled" their home, had "many connections" to "individuals associated with the terrorist attacks on 9/11/2001." The panel's report also doesn't explain why visitor security logs for the gated Sarasota community and photos of license tags matched vehicles driven by the hijackers, including 9/11 ringleader Mohamed Atta.

Former Florida senator Bob Graham, former chairman of the U.S. Senate Intelligence Committee, has publicly accused the FBI of a "cover-up" in the Florida case. Graham said there was no evidence that the Bureau had ever disclosed the Florida investigation to his committee or the 9/11 Commission, which delivered their report in 2004.

There are still 28 pages of the 9/11 report regarding the Saudis that remain classified and were redacted, wholesale, by President George W. Bush. After reading it, Congressman Thomas Massie described the experience as "disturbing" and said, "I had to stop every two or three pages and rearrange my perception of history . . . it's that fundamental."

Intelligence officials say the claims in the secret 28 pages were explored and found to be "unsubstantiated" in a later review by the national commission. If that is the case, why not release them? The Saudis have covered their trail.

Both the Florida investigation and the hidden 28 pages of the 9/11 report received more attention this year when an Al Qaeda operative in custody described prominent members of Saudi Arabia's royal family as major donors to the terrorist network in the late 1990s. The claim by terrorist Zacarias Moussaoui prompted a quick statement from the Saudi Embassy saying the 9/11 commission rejected allegations that Saudi officials had funded Al Qaeda. But Senator Graham, who has seen the classified material, spilled the beans: "The 28 pages primarily relate to who financed 9/11, and they point a very strong finger at Saudi Arabia as being the principal financier," he said, adding, "I am speaking of the kingdom," or government, of Saudi Arabia, not just wealthy individual Saudi donors. "This is a pervasive pattern of covering up the role of Saudi Arabia in 9/11 by all of the agencies of the federal government which have access to information that might illuminate Saudi Arabia's role in 9/11."

U.S. Intelligence has sought to undermine the credibility of both Graham and Moussaoui, labeling Graham as a past-his-prime publicity seeker and Moussaoui as mentally unstable. Yet the *New York Post* reported, "sources who have seen the censored 28 pages say it cites CIA and FBI case files that directly implicate officials of the Saudi Embassy in Washington and its consulate in Los Angeles in the attacks"—which, if true, would make 9/11 not just an act of terrorism, but an act of war by a foreign government. The section allegedly identifies high-level Saudi officials and intelligence agents by name, and details their financial transactions and other dealings with the San Diego-trained hijackers. It zeroes in on the Islamic Affairs Department of the Saudi Embassy, among other Saudi entities.

In fact the Saudis are playing a dangerous double game, claiming to be U.S. allies in the war on terror while at the same time funding terrorist groups that espouse a violent Wahhabi Islamic ideology that is particular to Saudi Arabia. They have used their money and influence to shield the truth from the American people. With their huge contributions to the Clintons, they hope to do it again.

CHAPTER 32

WAGING WAR

I think war is a dangerous place.

—President Bush, Washington DC, May 7, 2003

The War on Terror

On September 9, 2001, President George W. Bush's approval rating was 55 percent, according to an ABC News poll. One month later, after the attacks of 9/11, it was 92 percent, the highest approval rating ever for a U.S. president since such polling has been done, going back to FDR.

That highest-ever rating was measured not only after 9/11, but also after President Bush declared the War on Terror, launched military attacks in Afghanistan, and work had begun in earnest on legislation such as the USA Patriot Act that was presented as crucial to the execution of the new brand of war.

Not only did Americans in their rightful fear and anger after 9/11 approve of Bush's declaration of an ill-defined war, but the president himself learned something.

He learned the political value of a crisis.

It wasn't just his historic approval rating. He and others in his administration, along with the politicians on Capitol Hill, figured out that they could do virtually whatever they wanted—as long as it was portrayed as part of the War on Terror.

On October 26, six short weeks after 9/11, George W. signed into law the Patriot Act, almost without objection. Few of the senators and members of Congress who voted for it even read it. They just said YES. What politician wanted to vote against something called the Patriot Act while the ruins of the Twin Towers were still smoldering? With the possible exception of the Civil War, this president was able to seize more power and enact more sweeping changes in government than at any time in history. Even a president with the best intentions could not possibly experience such power without using it, and wanting to keep it.

The War on Terror, much like the Civil War, had created an opportunity to fundamentally consolidate the power of the federal government over the states and American citizens. Likewise, it offered the politicians an excuse to expand, buy, and build virtually without regard or concern about cost. If it was needed for the War on Terror, or even if they just said it was needed, just do it. No questions asked, including the price.

George W. recognized the opportunities, and made the best of them.

The Revolutionary War was ignited in significant part by Americans' disgust with the British practice of knocking on random colonists' doors and demanding to search their homes for contraband, taxable items, and other illegalities they might stumble across—all with no cause nor a warrant. With the full blessing of Congress, President Bush gave himself a 21st-century version of precisely the same power. Using creative interpretations of both old and new laws, he commenced the practice of monitoring Americans' phone calls, emails, financial transactions, and even what books citizens were checking out of the library. It was all done, and continues today, under the guise of the War on Terror.

He gave himself the power to tell travelers how much deodorant or hair spray they can carry onto an airplane and created a new army known as the Transportation Safety Administration.

Overseas, he authorized the CIA and the military to assassinate "suspects," including American citizens, and put the U.S. in the business of "regime change"—a business that continues today under a different president who, like most before him, certainly doesn't want to give up the power he or his predecessor achieved. The War on Terror has become a license to kill, literally—and equally significantly, a license to throw the Constitution out the window.

Americans want to be safe. But George W. Bush seized and consolidated powers in the presidency that are unprecedented in American history—all in the name of a war that is undefined, never-ending and, unfortunately, probably never to be won. It is the ultimate crisis, and no politician will let it go unused.

One need look no further than the 2016 presidential campaign, in which virtually every potential president is pledging to pick up the baton and keep fighting the war that George W. Bush proclaimed. And the candidate who is perhaps most committed to continuing George W.'s power grab is a former governor by the name of Bush.

The Second Iraq War

The attacks of 9/11 shook America to its core. Americans were angry, defiant, and even vengeful, but they were also frightened and more aware than ever of their vulnerability.

Thanks to an endless line of reports from analysts, pundits, and the government itself assessing the potential threat of future attacks, America's fear quickly became especially acute with regard to "weapons of mass destruction", or WMDs.

At the same time, Americans were watching with approval as the U.S. military launched a devastating assault in Afghanistan, where the 9/11 masterminds were believed to be, along with an identifiable group—the Taliban—who comprised an enemy on which the U.S. could focus. These were bad guys and using American power to attack them was justifiably cathartic.

Then there was Iraq. George W. Bush's father had gone to war against Iraq in 1991 to turn back its invasion of Kuwait—and had won, thanks to a skilled military, a clear objective, and a meaningful coalition with other nations. But the elder Bush had chosen not to press his advantage and carry the war into Iraq. He drove them out of Kuwait, but stopped at the border. That, of course, left Saddam Hussein to live and fight another day.

Saddam licked his wounds, regrouped, and refocused his attention on the decades-long conflict with neighboring Iran. His regime was brutal. The United Nations and the West had condemned his invasion of Kuwait, and it was widely accepted that Saddam had used chemical weapons in the war against Iran. Also, committing a strategic blunder in 1993 that would eventually get him killed, he apparently plotted to assassinate President George H. W. Bush—after he had left office. In response, President Clinton ordered a missile attack against Saddam's Intelligence Service headquarters, but did not target Saddam himself—leaving him, in some eyes, unpunished for his attempt to assassinate George H. W. Bush.

Saddam undoubtedly breathed a sigh of relief that he had dodged another bullet, literally. What he didn't take into account was the possibility that another George Bush would be elected president of the United States, placing the son of the man he had plotted to kill in command of the world's most powerful military.

With Americans still feeling the pain and fear of 9/11, in 2002 the Bush administration began to build a case for invading Iraq and toppling Saddam Hussein. George W. Bush created a special office in the Pentagon—called the Office of Special Plans—specifically for the purpose of supplying him with intelligence regarding Iraq, a task previously performed by the CIA. He put his friends Secretary of Defense Don Rumsfeld and Paul Wolfowitz in charge of that intelligence reporting, creating a political "interpreting" operation that supplanted expert analysis by the CIA.

Suddenly the reports coming to the president, and leaked to the public, were full of contentions that Saddam possessed an arsenal of chemical and biological weapons, and suggested the possibility of nuclear weapons as well. Those accusations provided the ingredients for a well-orchestrated public relations campaign to lay the groundwork for an invasion with the express purpose of deposing Saddam Hussein. The justification: With WMDs at the ready, Saddam posed a threat to the United States.

After months of preparation and a demand that Saddam leave the country "or else," on March 20, 2003, George W. Bush ordered the invasion of Iraq to begin. U.S. forces rapidly dispatched the Iraqi military and toppled Saddam's government. In December of 2003, Saddam was captured, and three years later, executed.

Mission accomplished, at least for George W. Bush. The man who plotted to kill his father, and committed untold other crimes, is dead. But 12 years later, more than 4,000 American troops have died in Iraq—and $1.7 trillion have already been spent, a number that increases every day. The weapons of mass destruction George W. claimed were there, and used to justify that human and financial cost, were never found.

The people of Iraq? The horror of Saddam has been replaced by the horror of civil war, ISIS, and an entirely uncertain future.

But George W. Bush, Dick Cheney, and Donald Rumsfeld got their man.

Six Trillion Dollar Wars

Whether by plan or accident, President George W. Bush perfected the modern presidential art of hiding the real magnitude and costs of war. If asked today, how many Americans would know that George W. is responsible for two of the three longest wars in U.S. history?

While many veterans who fought prior to the "official" 1964 commencement of the Vietnam War—a war George W. managed to avoid—will deservedly point out that the U.S. was actually engaged in that conflict for almost 20 years, a more formal measurement will identify the War in Afghanistan as America's longest war. And the third longest is the Iraq War.

Any way you choose to measure it, out of 44 presidents spanning 226 years, George W. is responsible for two of the three longest wars, neither of which, by many accounts, accomplished anything or could be considered a "win."

There are teenagers in America today who have not experienced a single day in their lives when American troops have not been fighting somewhere, and it is doubtful that many can offer any clear reason why.

That's what happens when a president starts wars, declares unrealistic objectives, and refuses to quit. In Afghanistan, George W. launched an attack on the Taliban and al Qaeda with the strong support of the American people. Americans mistakenly believed that the plan was to find and hurt the terrorists who attacked their nation on 9/11. They missed the conversation about how the U.S. was going to defy thousands of years of history, create order out of generations of tribal chaos, and somehow reshape Afghanistan into a western democracy—whether its people wanted it or not. The American people's objective was largely achieved in a matter of months, after which our troops could have been brought home or retasked to follow the terrorists who scattered to other nations around the world when the bombs began to fall. George W., though, had something else in mind: somehow using military force to turn warlords into peaceful participants in a governance they neither wanted nor could maintain.

Even if you grant a noble purpose to George W.'s idea, the sacrifice of more than 2,300 American lives, the wounding of more than 20,000, and more than $700 billion in DIRECT costs is an extremely high price to pay for an experiment in westernization that was doomed to fail from the start.

George W.'s Iraq War is even more costly, and arguably more inexcusable. As of 2015, 4,486 U.S. military men and women have died in the Iraq War, far exceeding the toll of 9/11. The cost to taxpayers so far is more than $2 trillion, and hundreds of thousands of Iraqi civilians have died. All for a war that was waged on false pretenses and amounted to a regime change that has achieved nothing but even greater chaos and suffering.

History will not be kind to the George W. Bush foreign policy and war doctrines.

Nor will history be kind when a true accounting of the costs of George W.'s wars is understood—and acknowledged. Having financed the 43rd president's wars on a political installment plan made up of haphazard and "emergency" short-term funding measures that obscure the real price tabs, Americans really have no opportunity to know how much they have actually paid. And even the numbers that are generally reported dramatically understate the costs. Factoring in the long-term costs of veterans' care, disability benefits, and other yet-to-be-incurred expenses, a study by Brown University puts the actual price tag of George W.'s wars at more than $6 trillion:[473] two wars with no good outcomes that will add $6 trillion to the financial burden of a nation already $19 trillion in debt.

For those who keep track of legacies, that will be George W.'s.

CHAPTER 33

SECOND TERM, SECOND RECOUNT

See, in my line of work you got to keep repeating things over and over and over again for the truth to sink in, to kind of catapult the propaganda.

—President Bush, Greece, New York, May 24, 2005[xxv]

W. Steals the Presidency Again

History books will never let Americans forget the paralyzing controversy of the 2000 "Bush v. Gore" election. But what about 2004?

As is often the case, Ohio was a pivotal state on election night. If George W. Bush won Ohio, he would be elected to a second term. If John Kerry prevailed in Ohio, he would be the new president of the United States.

The "official" count in Ohio put Bush on top by almost 119,000 votes. That sounds like a substantial number of votes—until you consider that Ohio is a large state where 5.6 million votes were cast. That margin also shrinks more than a little when you take into account the breadth and scope of voting irregularities and overt efforts by known Bush supporters to suppress likely Kerry voters.

Just one widely reported and never adequately explained case of manipulation accounted for what the *Washington Post* estimated to be 15,000 voters who were effectively prevented from voting due to long lines. Those long lines, primarily in urban precincts in Columbus that would have leaned heavily to Kerry, were created by the Franklin County Board of Elections by shifting voting machines from the urban precincts to largely white, suburban precincts. Those precincts, of course, supported Bush. It is difficult to imagine that the election board didn't know exactly what they were doing. Congressman John Conyers, the dean of the U.S. House of Representatives and a former chairman of the Judiciary Committee, maintains that Franklin County's actions were a violation of the Voting Rights Act—and he has a sound argument.

There were numerous other reported irregularities across Ohio. Some have been explained. Some haven't. However, even cumulatively, those localized episodes are almost negligible when compared to the blatant actions of the Republican secretary of state of Ohio, Ken Blackwell, who served as a cochair of the Bush/Cheney campaign.

Blackwell, Ohio's highest-ranking election official with broad powers to control election procedures, wasn't even subtle in his efforts to help his friend George W. First, prior to the election, he reorganized voting precincts across the state, shifting voters from one precinct to another and resulting in predictable confusion on Election Day. Then, he ordered that "provisional" ballots—those cast when a problem or question arises about a voter's residence or eligibility—would only count if they were cast in the correct precinct. (Traditionally, Ohio has allowed provisional ballots to be counted as long

SECOND TERM, SECOND RECOUNT

as they are cast in the appropriate county.) Blackwell's 2004 changes had the net effect of creating confusion for voters, and then exploiting that confusion to eliminate ballots. Thanks to his clearly effective strategy, almost 50,000 provisional ballots were disregarded.

Blackwell also exercised his authority to remove 133,000 voters from the registration rolls, the bulk of them being Democratic voters. This "cleaning" of the rolls was carried out gradually over a three year period prior to 2004, thus going largely unnoticed. Blackwell acted within the law, but did so in a way that undoubtedly benefited George W. Bush. Another 92,000 ballots were not counted because they were rejected by the voting machines.[474]

When these separate steps are added together, hundreds of thousands of votes were effectively altered by election officials, and the top election official was a high-ranking member of George W. Bush's re-election team. Several media outlets and other observers have examined the totality of the ballots that were excluded in Ohio in 2004, and are left with the uneasy conclusion that the outcome of Ohio's election could have been altered. And whoever carried Ohio would be the president.

Texas Air National Guard: The Real Story

I was accused of planting forged Texas Air National Guard (TANG) documents in a 2004 gambit designed to both clear George W. Bush of accusations of dereliction of duty and destroy the careers of CBS journalists Dan Rather and Mary Mapes. In fact Democratic National Chairman Terry McAuliffe, who made millions in a shady government lease for an office building he owned under Clinton, publicly accused me of executing the plot in a press release.

When former Texas lieutenant governor Ben Barnes piped up claiming Old Man Bush had asked him to wedge W. into the Texas Air National Guard to avoid Vietnam, I had to remind people that Barnes, an LBJ protege, had been driven from public office in the the Sharpestown scandal, a shady real estate deal that rocked Texas politics in the 1970s. LBJ always said Ben was going to be president someday. Instead he narrowly avoided prison.

The way Mapes tells it in her 2005 book *Truth*, the Bush White House forged documents that made out Bush as a slacker as a National Guard pilot, leaked them, then exposed flaws hidden in the documents to prove them forgeries—by all measures, a high-risk tactic to protect their candidate. That's what those of us adept at the political dark arts call a triple bank shot—a dirty trick that demands a steady hand and careful execution.

It sounds complex, but the right person could do it.

As we learned earlier, rumors had always been swirling since his days as governor of Texas that Junior, a notorious party boy, had been derelict in his duties as a young TANG pilot. Through his gubernatorial races and his first campaign for president, nothing much came of the stories. But in the years running up to his 2004 re-election as president, reporters were chasing down nasty tales of Bush being away without leave (AWOL).

It's no secret that, in the run up to the 2004 election, W.'s team was preparing to deflect questions about President Bush's military record. When the Democrats settled on Sen. John Kerry as their candidate, I can attest to hand wringing on the Republican side of the race. "Swift Boat" attacks on the U.S. senator from Massachusetts—where his military record and patriotism were run down in stinging television ads—were a defensive as well as offensive move.

As the DailyKos blog told the story in a series of posts in 2004 and 2005, the Bush White House devised TANG documents with hidden fatal flaws. They called me in to get the documents into the hands of the Kerry campaign, hoping they would run with the accusation. Then, a pre-planned counterattack would expose the flaws; an intense effort to get the "forgery" story into the press would follow. This would embarrass the Kerry team and inoculate Bush from further discussion of his military service.

This would require an adept and experienced dirty trickster.

In 2004, a West Texas rancher named Bill Burkett was feeding hungry reporters a steady diet of information about Bush skipping out of his TANG commitment in the early 1970s and even being AWOL for months—the kind of bombshell that could do real damage to his re-election. He was a yahoo, a conspiracy theorist. But reporters like Mapes and others were in touch with him regularly, hoping he might be telling the truth. (I think he was.)

I stand accused by DailyKos and other progressive bloggers of targeting Burkett in March 2004. Specifically, they say I had my Cuban-American wife, Nydia, call Burkett and offer him a set of White House–forged TANG memos that proved Bush was AWOL. The handoff took place at the annual Houston Livestock and Rodeo, amidst a million cowboys crowded into NRG Stadium. There, the fictitious "Olga Ramirez" (Nydia Stone) allegedly handed off an envelope containing the damning documents.

If Burkett got his hands on a set of incriminating TANG memos, it was a safe bet they would end up in the hands of a journalist—or even the Kerry campaign. Burkett tried for weeks to peddle them directly to the campaign, to no avail. (It was only dumb luck that they ended up in the hands of the sanctimonious Dan Rather. It couldn't have happened to a nicer guy, one of few journalists who was shown the famous Zapruder film right after the JFK assassination.

It took five months, but Rather and Mapes got the documents, didn't properly vet them, and ran a story on *60 Minutes II* on September 8, 2004. Their careers ended not long after; in her book, Mapes blames everyone but herself. In fact, the triple bank shot would only succeed if the documents were handed to a hyper-partisan operative with such a deep hatred for George W. Bush that they would get sloppy. They were meant for the Kerry campaign, but Mapes and Rather were as craven as any Democratic Party staffer.

In this case, the desired result was attained, with a double bonus.

I've always denied forging the TANG memos, and I do to this day. Any number of documents specialists could handle that. But handing final documents off to Burkett, guiding him toward passing them to CBS News, and then advancing the forgery story—that's something very few could do.

Midnight Tours
I've previously commented on "call boys" taking late tours of 41's White House, but White House records indicate that male prostitute Jeff Gannon conceivably spent the night in 43's White House. The Bushes are a clan rife with aberrant behaviors, but the tale of Jeff Gannon is extremely bizarre even by Bush family standards.

Gannon was ostensibly a White House "reporter," but he invariably posed sycophantic, softball questions to White House press secretaries Ari Fleischer and Scott McClellan for nearly two years. Many of the correspondents in the White House press corps thought he was a Bush administration plant. On January 26, 2005, Gannon easily trumped his prior sycophantic queries when he posed the following question to W. at a White House press conference:

"Senate Democratic leaders have painted a very bleak picture of the U.S. economy. Harry Reid was talking about soup lines, and Hillary Clinton was talking about the economy being on the verge of collapse. Yet, in the same breath, they say that Social Security is rock solid, and there's no crisis there. How are you going to work—you said you're going to reach out to these people—how are you going to work with people who seem to have divorced themselves from reality?"[475]

Bush gave a banal response about taking his economic policies to the American people to engender a groundswell of support. But Gannon's question was so partisanly over the top in the milieu of a White House press conference that it ignited the ire of several correspondents who started questioning his authenticity. Shortly thereafter, Gannon was outed as a gay prostitute, and he even had nude pictures of himself posted on Internet escort sites.[476] It was also discovered that the virtual media outlet that employed him as a reporter, Talon News, hired him *after* he started attending White House press conferences. Prior to working for Talon News, Gannon had never been professionally published. So Gannon, a male prostitute, acquired one of journalism's most coveted press passes without ever writing an article for monetary compensation.

The bizarre circumstances surrounding Gannon's two-year stint as a White House press reporter inspired a pair of House Democrats to file Freedom of Information Act requests that inquired about Gannon's access to the White House. The FOIA requests revealed that Gannon made over 200 appearances at the White House during his two-year stint as a "White House reporter," attending 155 of 196 White House press briefings.[477]

Over a period of 22 months, Gannon checked in with the Secret Service, but he failed to check out on 14 days, and on one of those days a press briefing wasn't even held. The fact that Gannon failed to check out on 14 days was indeed perplexing, because that meant that he could've spent some of those nights in the White House.

The Secret Service claimed that there wasn't a "deviation from Secret Service standards and procedures" regarding Gannon's bizarre access to the White House, but Democrats on the House Judiciary Committee proffered a resolution that would have required Bush's attorney general and the secretary of Homeland Security to surrender documents relating to the security investigations and background checks involved in granting Gannon access. However, Republicans on the House Judiciary Committee voted down the resolution, and the individual or individuals in the Bush administration who actually granted Gannon access to the White House remains an enigma.

The Secret Service claimed that it investigated Gannon's background, and found he didn't pose a security risk.[478] I've previously mentioned Henry Vinson's autobiography, *Confessions of a DC Madam: The Politics of Sex, Lies, and Blackmail*, which details his trials and tribulations running the largest gay escort service that's ever been uncovered in DC, and Vinson has some very interesting revelations about Jeff Gannon, sleepovers at the White House, and the Secret Service.

Vinson claims that he met Jeff Gannon in the late 1980s, because Gannon had befriended one of Vinson's employees.[479] When Vinson initially met Gannon, Vinson maintains that Gannon was working as a male prostitute, and he boasted about servicing officials in the upper echelons of the

George H. W. Bush administration and spending nights at the White House.[480] After Vinson was arrested and entered into a plea agreement with the government, government officials debriefed him. According to Vinson, his debriefers had an inordinate interest in his knowledge of Gannon's activities, which perplexed him.[481] If Vinson is being truthful, then the Secret Service was well aware of Gannon's extracurricular activities years before it granted him White House press passes.

Readers of Vinson's *Confession of a DC Madam* are confronted with a quandary concerning Vinson's revelations: should they believe Vinson, a convicted felon, whose statements are partially corroborated by the *Washington Times*? Or should they believe the federal government, which refuses to unseal the documents in his case? Absent any evidence to the contrary, it seems plausible that the government was protecting the darkest side of American politics, and until it decides to unseal all the documentation in Vinson's case, Vinson's word shouldn't be summarily discarded.

Kinky W.

The Midnight Tour male prostitute allegation might seem shocking to many. It should certainly shock the thousands of conservatives and evangelical Christians who turned out to vote for not just W. in 2000 and 2004, but for every Bush who has run for office, and those who might vote for Jeb in the future. But elite deviance is the only consistent code of conduct the Bushes follow. The Bush male prostitution allegation is less shocking when you hear about the dominatrix/lady of the night who says she was hired to take part in male/male/female threesomes with George W. and bisexual men, including fellow Yale Bonesman and later U.S. ambassador to Poland Victor Ashe way back in the 1980s.[482]

Leola McConnell, a retired "muscle dominatrice," and a former liberal Democratic candidate for governor of Nevada, says that Bush and Ashe regularly hired bisexual men for secret sex sessions in the 80s when Bush was a private citizen. She publicized it in her book, *Lustful Utterances: Cohn to Bush 1981–1986.*[483]

McConnell said, "In 1984, I watched George W. Bush enthusiastically and expertly perform a homosexual act on another man, one Victor Ashe. Ashe is the current U.S. ambassador to Poland; and he too should come out, like former New Jersey Gov. James McGreevy, and admit to being a gay American."

"Other homo-erotic acts were also performed by then-private citizen George W. Bush. I know this because I performed one of them on him myself."

I personally knew McConnell and while her profession and lifestyle choices are not everyone's cup of tea, it doesn't matter. I believe her. She had no reason to lie.

McConnell is not alone. Veteran author Kitty Kelley wrote about the Bush-on-Ashe action in her 2004 book *The Family–The Real Story of The Bush Dynasty.*[484] Some sources also claim that George W. also had sex with fellow Yale Bonesman and 2004 presidential opponent John Kerry as part of a bizarre Skull and Bones ritual. Was Kerry a designated loser, willing to go down for his former gay sex partner in 2004?[485]

Months before her book was supposed to be self-published, McConnell issued an open letter to the media.[486] The letter threatened President Bush, saying that either he would admit his homosexual tendencies and acts or she would self-publish her book. A few weeks later, McConnell vanished.

Promotional material about the book online has been taken down. A few months later, "D.C Madam" Deborah Jeane Palfrey was convicted and soon found dead. She supposedly hanged herself.[487] Maybe McConnell disappeared to escape a similar fate.

Aside from bisexual threesomes and S&M fetishes, W. was also rumored to have a fetish for bald heads.[488] Not surprisingly, male gay escort and faux White House journalist Jeff Gannon kept a crew cut.

PART 6

THE BUSH DYNASTY:
NOW AND IN THE FUTURE

CHAPTER 34

NOT SUCH STRANGE BEDFELLOWS

I love Bill Clinton. Maybe not his politics, but I love Bill Clinton . . . My husband, Bill Clinton and I have become friends. And Bill visits us every summer.

—Barbara Bush[xxvi]

Jeb and Hillary's Mutual Admiration Society

Jeb already rendered himself impotent in terms of attacking Hillary Clinton by giving her a medal and gushing compliments toward her. Jeb was the chair of the National Constitution Center and gave her the center's Liberty Medal in 2013, a lifetime achievement award. Jeb and Hillary joked with each other on stage, two of the most pampered elites on earth.

"Hillary and I come from different political parties and we disagree about lots of things. But we do agree on the wisdom of the American people—especially those in Iowa and New Hampshire and South Carolina," Jeb joked, referring to the three states that play a traditionally huge role in presidential primaries. Former presidents Bill Clinton and George W. Bush both also received the same award. Hillary joked at the ceremony that Bill and W. "just had one of their annual play dates up in Kennebunkport," at the Bush family compound in Maine.

She commented, "Jeb and I are not just renewing an American tradition of bipartisanship. We're keeping up a family tradition as well."[489] As we've discussed in this book, the Bushes and the Clintons have a great deal in common and have been allies when it suits them. Hillary's campaign could easily refer to Jeb's flattering comments repeatedly and make him look like either a hypocrite or a buffoon.

Both the Bushes and the Clintons are prime examples of elite deviance, so it shouldn't surprise anyone that they have been allies behind the scenes for many years, keeping the money and power flowing to both families while ballooning the government to Chris Christie proportions at every opportunity. The mutual admiration society between Jeb and Hillary would come as a great surprise to anyone who doesn't know the history of both families. Both dynasties love money and power, and both will do anything to get more of both. People who have gotten in their way have been destroyed, crushed, and even killed.

Jeb Bush and Clintons Share Donors, Soros Connection, and Haiti Ponzi Scheme

Jeb Bush and Hillary Clinton share many of the same Wall Street donors. This is no surprise. During the first Clinton administration, Bill repealed the Glass-Steagall Act in November 1999, seven months after Bill was acquitted in the Senate of impeachment charges. The repeal broke a 65-year ban that limited commercial bank securities activities and affiliations within commercial banks and securities firms.

During W.'s administration, the repeal paid major dividends for Wall Street. Mortgages were given to unqualified home owners and the banks leveraged and insured these risky bets into a financial product called derivative securities. Credit was loose and the regulations were further untied during Bush's presidency. W. turned a blind eye while greedy bankers leveraged the financial security of the world. And when the 2008 crisis hit, W. started the process of bailing out Wall Street, more than doubling the national debt by the end of his administration from $5T+ to over $11T+. Similarly, Jeb more than doubled Florida state debt from $17.8B+ to over $36.4B+. The Bushes sure do enjoy bankrupting future generations!

In the run-up to the 2016 election when the mainstream media was setting the stage for another Bush-Clinton rematch, numerous reports showed that Wall Street was more than content with either option—especially the affiliated Republican-bankers. In 2014, the venerable Maggie Haberman reported that Wall Street was elated that Jeb was going to run for president "and save the GOP's old establishment base from its rising populist wing." However, one of the top Republican-leaning Wall Street lawyers confided, "If it turns out to be Jeb versus Hillary we would love that and either outcome would be fine. We could live with either one."[490]

FEC reports show the Bush and Clinton campaigns share many mega-donors. An analysis by the *Daily Beast* and *Vocativ* have shown that "more than 60 ultra-rich Americans have contributed to both Jeb Bush's and Hillary Clinton's federal campaigns."[491] One donor told the *Washington Post* that "If either of them became president, I'm happy."[492] This exemplifies the reason why we need another Bush about as much as we need another Clinton.

But Jeb has been even more nefarious in his dealings with Clintonistas. George Soros is the largest supporter of left-wing causes and Democrats. In 2004, Soros even stated that defeating W. is the "central focus of my life."[493] He finances Media Matters, the left-wing nonprofit outfit whose sole mission is to repudiate conservative media. During this cycle, Soros is already heavily invested in Hillary having donated millions to her Super PAC Priorities USA Action.[494]

Despite Soros's leftist ideology, he is still a businessman—and is hedged with Jeb. As *Breitbart News* revealed, Bush is the Chairman of BH Logistics, a $24M private equity fund incorporated in April 2014. The firm's major investor is the private Chinese equity firm HNA Group, which has reserve capital of over $58B. The firm was founded by Chen Feng, one of China's wealthiest businessmen who owes his career to George Soros. Soros gave Feng the $25M in startup capital to fund HNA. Not only is Feng Soros's business partner but Soros considers him a protégé—they hold multiple investments together. Therefore, Feng's investment in Jeb is insurance for Soros in the 2016 election.[495]

Jeb and Bill also share a nefarious business connection that deprived victims of the 2010 Haiti earthquake. The connection is InnoVida, a Miami-based company that marketed a composite panel that could be used to assemble temporary housing. Jeb joined the company as $15,000-a-month consultant in late 2007 and then as a board member in 2008. InnoVida's CEO was Miami businessman Claudio Osorio, who was a major donor to Jeb's gubernatorial campaigns as well as the Florida GOP.[496]

Osorio was also a major Clinton backer, having hosted a fundraiser for Hillary Clinton's presidential campaign at his Star Island mansion in Miami Beach in 2007. Osorio had also contributed between $10,000 and $25,000 to the Clinton

Foundation in 2009. His company InnoVida followed up with another $10,000 to $25,000 donation.

While Hillary was secretary of state, Osario obtained a $10M loan from Overseas Private Investment Corporation (OPIC), an independent government agency whose budget is processed through the State Department, to build houses in Haiti. In an internal memo, an OPIC official wrote that "Former president Bill Clinton is personally in contact with the company [InnoVida] to organize its logistical and support needs" and "Secretary of State Hillary Clinton has made available State Department resources to assist with logistical arrangements."[497] While OPIC loans typically take months and even years to approve, InnoVida's loan request was approved in just *two weeks.*

After receiving the $10M loan, InnoVida advertised "Our partnership with OPIC is accelerating our ability to help the earthquake victims. InnoVida's technology will be very helpful to Haiti's long-term recovery plan through the utilization of local labor and rapid deployment of permanent structures that not only provide a better quality of life but also can withstand earthquakes, floods and hurricane-force winds."[498] However these results were never realized.

During Jeb's entire tenure as a board member, Osario, according to Freebeacon.com, was conducting a Ponzi scheme "bilking government and private investors out of a collective $40 million and using their money to fund his lavish lifestyle: making payments on his Miami Beach mansion, buying a Maserati, and maintaining his Colorado ski chalet." $30M was diverted to a foreign bank. The $10M OPIC loan the Clintons expedited was part of Osario's racket.

Osorio was later indicted by federal prosecutors on nearly two dozen fraud and money laundering counts. He is currently serving a 12 1/2-year year federal prison sentence. The Clinton Foundation returned Osario and InnoVida's donations. In 2013, Jeb was ordered by a bankruptcy trustee to repay half of the $470,000 he received from InnoVida. The bankruptcy trustee criticized InnoVida's board members for lack of proper oversight.

Hillary's personal emails add another instructive detail. In a September 2015 release of Hillary's emails she illegally kept on a private server while secretary of state, Judith McHale, the under-secretary of state for public diplomacy and public affairs, wrote to Hillary "We waged a very successful campaign against the negative stories concerning our involvement in Haiti."[499] But only four days earlier Chelsea wrote a memo to both her father and mother that the international relief's "incompetence is mind numbing."

A fraudulent international joint-effort by the Bushes and Clinton? Sounds like the Iraq War!

Teneo, Bush Institute, Clinton & Bush

George W. Bush has taken a cue from the Clintons on profiting from the presidency. In fact, they have colluded together on the speech circuit and their foundations. Bill made a small fortune in speaking and lobbying fees, chiefly through Clinton advisor Douglas Band's Teneo firm. Teneo lobbies in political political issues around the globe, including during Hillary's tenure as Secretary of State. Neither the Clintons nor the Bushes have ever hesitated to mix government and personal finances. But while Hillary Clinton's current bid for the presidency has been greatly damaged by Bill's profiteering off of her tenure as secretary of state, the Bushes have escaped scrutiny of W.'s post-presidency charades.

As early as December 2006, more than two years from the end of his presidency, W. admitted to his biographer Robert

Draper in interviews for *Dead Certain* that he was planning to "give some speeches, just to replenish the ol' coffers." Even with assets at that time as high as $21 million, W. said, "I don't know what my dad gets—it's more than 50–75" thousand dollars a speech, and "Clinton's making a lot of money."[500]

W. did not disappoint, making millions on the speaking circuit including speaking to Get Motivated! Business Seminars starting in 2009.[501] Just as W.'s presidency bankrupted the country, his affiliation with the Get Motivated! Business Seminars was not a success—the company declared bankruptcy in September, 2012. Ironically, Laura Bush was a paid speaker at the distraught company's last event in February 2012.[502] Another association that the Bushes fleeced.

In July 2015, ABC's Brian Ross revealed that W. charged the Texas-based Helping a Hero charity a $100,000 fee to appear at a 2012 fundraiser and asked them to pay a $20,000 private jet bill. The event was being held to raise funds for "U.S. military veterans severely wounded in Iraq and Afghanistan." Laura Bush even charged the same organization $50,000 a year earlier. Meredith Iler, the former chairman of the charity, told Ross: "It was great because (W.) reduced his normal fee of $250,000 down to $100,000." However, Ross cites a *Politico* article which revealed that W. charged fees ranging from $100,000 to $175,000 during that period, meaning there may not even have been any discount given to the charity (at least not a substantial one).[503] And of course the vast majority of veterans were wounded during W.'s presidency.

W. has developed "a brotherly relationship with Bill Clinton" and even calls Slick Willie his "brother from another mother." He must have great affection for Hillary as she is his "sister-in-law."[504] In July 2015, after both Hillary and Jeb declared their candidacies for president, W. and Bill appeared together in Dallas at the George W. Bush Presidential Center "in a bipartisan love fest to promote a joint scholarship program" between the George W. Bush Institute and the Clinton Foundation called the Presidential Leadership Scholars program.[505]

The Presidential Leadership Scholars program was announced in February 2015. The program is prominently featured on the Clinton Foundation's website, and in multiple blog posts by "The Bush Institute."[506] This is proof of the Bush and Clinton libraries commingling funds, which therefore associates W.'s post-presidency with the nefarious donors of the Clinton Foundation. In fact, while the Clinton Foundation has publicly listed all of its donors, the George W. Bush Foundation, which finances his Presidential Center, does not name any of its donors.[507] Having escaped any scrutiny, the Clinton Foundation can be said to be more transparent than W's!

The program also has the support of the Lyndon B. Johnson Presidential Library. That would be the same Lyndon B. Johnson who Jeb called in 2015 "a role model for the sort of president he'd strive to be."[508] Jeb has a long connection with the Johnson family—his first job after graduating the University of Texas was with Texas Commerce Bank. Lady Bird served as the bank's director.

W. and Bill's dealings are also connected to the Clinton email scandal. As of the writing of this book, Hillary is still not under indictment for illegally using a private server during her time as secretary of state. Hillary's close aide Huma Abedin worked during Clinton's tenure at State at both the Clinton Foundation and Teneo Holdings, a "global firm" founded by the former top aide of Bill Clinton. Huma conducted "private business" on her State Department email for Teneo.[509] Teneo is intricately connected to the Clinton-email scandal as Huma's emails contained classified information.

Teneo serves as a "private-enterprise satellite to Clinton Inc."[510] Bill Clinton was both a paid adviser to Teneo and a client. In 2013, Clinton, W., and former prime minister of Great Britain Tony Blair appeared at the Essex House in New York City for a paid event. Doug Band, former Clinton chief of staff, used the event for the launch of Teneo. While introducing the three dignitaries, Band "launched into a long-winded sales pitch. Teneo was the next big thing in executive consulting, he informed the audience. He played a promotional video about the firm. He introduced the heads of Teneo's divisions, describing their résumés and asking each to stand in turn."[511] Afterwards, Clinton, W., and Blair appeared onstage together. W. accepted his speaking fee from Teneo.

W. and Bill have travelled extensively on the paid speech circuit together. Their foundations are currently commingling funds. And W. has even accepted money from Clinton Inc.'s private slush fund enterprise Teneo. These deep connections show an allegiance in corruption. It is the Bush-Clinton way!

CHAPTER 35

THE NEXT CONTENDER FROM THE HOUSE OF BUSH

Immediately after Jeb Bush terminated his bid for the 2016 Republican nomination, there was a flurry of media speculation that this signaled the end of the Bush dynasty. It certainly seemed that Jeb just wasn't up to the level of criminality that his predecessors had reached in their relentless bid for power, yet there was something unfinished in Jeb's abrupt cancellation. As Donald Trump was slamming him for being "timid," "lightweight," and "low energy," Jeb's actions seemed to reveal that Trump's assessment was accurate. He did appear timid and I think it may have been a strategy to remain "presidential" in the face of Trump's attacks. If it was, it didn't work. One has to fight fire with fire. Jeb doesn't have any fire. That makes him a boring and tepid inheritor of the Bush criminal dynasty. Whereas George H. W. and George W. would stand at center stage saying "read my lips" or "if you're not on our side, you're on their side," Jeb takes a different approach. Remember, there are many ways to skin a cat: overt, in-your-face announcements and denials—regardless that the facts confirm otherwise—and Jeb's approach of skulking in the shadows, keeping a low profile, while bringing in millions of dollars through fraud and corrupt business practices. Still, in the long run it made little difference; Jeb was out of the picture.

In the days that followed his resignation, *Meet the Press* host Chuck Todd revealed to his audience, "The Bush dynasty comes to an official end." The *Guardian* boasted, "ding dong the dynasty is dead," while *Vanity Fair* published a piece titled "Requiem for the Bush dynasty." Yet they, in my opinion, are overlooking another Bush cancer, slowly growing, hardly showing, and building its foundation one block at a time. That would be George P. Bush.

Unfortunately, the story of the Bush crime family doesn't end with good ol' Jeb Bush. In fact there seems to be an inheritance of elitism and criminality in the "SON OF JEB." That could be the title of a horror movie, and it would be better if it were. Alas the truth is always darker, especially when digging around the Bush family plot. The "P" stands for Prescott. Gee that's original. All the Bushmen are branded with names linking them to Bushes of prior greatness, as if these brands carried some mystical power. The names Prescott, Herbert Walker, and Walker all come from the legendary Bushes. Prescott is from George H. W.'s father and Walker is from the powerful Scottish Walkers who became banking allies to the Bush clan and later married into the Bushes with the marriage of Dorothy Walker to Prescott Bush. Herbert was George Walker's middle name. Yet Jeb Bush's name is really John Ellis Bush. His name comes not from the powerful and corrupt Prescott or Walker Bushes, but as Barbara Bush wrote in a 2003 memoir, *Reflections: Life After the White House*: "Our son John Ellis Bush, 'Jeb,' the great Governor of Florida, was named after 41's brother Jon and Nan's husband, 'Sandy' Ellis—Alexander Ellis, Jr.—whom we both admired and loved." Yet, there may be something lacking in poor Jeb's middle name: it lacks the crucial linkage to the power elite Bushes.

So what's my point? My point is that George P. Bush, son of Jeb Bush, carries the middle name of the powerful and notorious Prescott Bush. In and of itself, it links George P. to the bad old Bushes of glory and gory days. Could there really be some sort of inherited mystical power in those names? Well, look at George Herbert Walker Bush: powerful, corrupt, clever, and the 41st president of the United States. George Walker Bush: powerful, corrupt, and the 43rd president of the United States. John Ellis "Jeb" Bush: timid, lightweight, corrupt, and zilch. Now comes George Prescott Bush. The name is in the right place for all that is inherent in the Bush Crime Family. Much as the young John F. Kennedy Jr. was seen to be the new king of Camelot, we could be looking at George Prescott to be the new king of the Bush Crime Family, or Bush-a-Nostra.

Born in Houston, Texas, in 1976, George P. attended Gulliver Prep School and earned an undergraduate degree from Rice University. In 1998 he became a public school teacher in Florida and later went to law school in Texas. In 2007 the United States Navy Reserve announced the selection of Bush for training as an intelligence officer. (George H. W. Bush served and was trained in Naval intelligence.) He served for eight months in Operation Enduring Freedom and returned to the United States in 2011. In 2012 he announced his intention to run for state office. He's following a well-established route as set by 41 and 43. By January 2013, Bush filed a campaign finance report stating that he had received $1.3 million in contributions. This was due to his father, former Florida governor and wannabe president, Jeb Bush's massive email campaign. Yes, the Bush privileges keep on rolling. It seems Jeb sent out emails requesting that donors support and donate to young

George P. in his bid for Texas land commissioner. By June 2013, Bush had raised $3.3 million. I guess father Bush's email campaign worked. Who would think of turning down Jeb Bush? Considering that there was no Democrat candidate running against him, and barely a Republican opponent (David Watts), I would say that the $3.3 million was enough to win him the election.

George P. Bush, the Night Stalker

What's missing from the story so far is a little item that happened while George P. was attending Rice University. On December 31, 1994, George P. was investigated for burglary and criminal mischief related to an attempted break-in at the home of his ex-girlfriend, Cristina Cohen. According to Miami-Dade Police Department reports, at 4 a.m. a neighbor saw a half-naked man trying to pry open a window at the Cohen residence. Bush was wearing only black boxer shorts and no shirt. When he arrived at the residence he went to Cristina's window and pulled it open, pushing the screen inward. As Bush was climbing in the window, a neighbor of the Cohens spotted him. An argument ensued and awoke Mr. Cohen. In a mad dash to escape, George P. ran and jumped into his vehicle and fled. Twenty minutes later he returned and drove his car across the Cohen yard damaging about 80 feet of pristine lawn. The police had been called and when they arrived they identified George Prescott Bush as the perpetrator. Young Cristina told police that George P. had been stalking and harassing her since she broke up with him almost two years earlier. Although he should have been arrested immediately, he was not. In a cowardly turn of events, the Cohens would not file charges and even signed a non-prosecution form! Daddy Bush had persuaded the Cohens that it would be in their best interest to let the matter rest. I wouldn't have been surprised if the Cohens packed up and rode outta town.[512]

George Prescott's record as Texas land commissioner has come under well-deserved scrutiny. Texas taxpayers pay George P. a salary of $137,500 a year to run the Texas General Land Office. According to the *Houston Chronicle*, George P. missed nearly half his work days while his father was campaigning for the GOP nomination. In addition, the *Chronicle* revealed that George P. had "dramatically remade the GLO by ousting a majority of its longtime leaders and replacing many of them with people with ties to his campaign and family." Former Land Commissioner Jerry Patterson said that the firings represented "a purge of the best agency in Texas government and a purge of people who have done wonderful things." Although a Bush spokesperson denied the allegations, a list provided by the GLO themselves tells the truth. The list contains the names of at least twenty persons hired with connections to George Prescott's campaign, his law school, or his family. Out of forty jobs that have been filled by George P. Bush during his tenure, only four of them were properly listed through the Workforce Commission. The other ninety percent of his hires were jobs he simply handed out to people without going through the proper channels, and he's paying those people an average of 40 percent higher than the four outside people he hired properly.

According to GLO spokesperson Bryan Preston, "That specific charge reflects a government-first mindset. The *Chronicle*'s story on that is also very misleading and inaccurate. The fact is, all past commissioners have brought a few of their own trusted people in with them including the one who continues lobbying accusations. Leaders want to bring in people who share their vision and ideals so they can be effective in carrying out policies they were elected to carry out. Would people prefer that he hire all strangers and liberals?"[513][514]

In a related article by the *Dallas Morning News*, it was reported that George P. Bush has paid out nearly $1 million in taxpayer dollars to dozens of people his administration fired in exchange for their promise not to sue him or the agency. An analysis of records by the *Houston Chronicle* showed that at least forty people on the payroll received money for as long as five months after termination. State employees are required to work to be paid. There are no severance packages for state jobs. Former state deputy comptroller told the *Chronicle* that "keeping someone on the payroll is just illegal." However, the Bush payoffs are under the heading of "emergency leave." Emergency leave is designed to give state employees a financial cushion in the event of a death in the family, health issues, or other extraordinary events. Clearly Bush feels his payoffs are extraordinary events.

Bush is not alone in the use of post-termination payoffs. The *Chronicle* reported that 20 of the 120 Texas state agencies have at least 133 staffers finish their time on the payroll with an added two weeks or more of "emergency leave." Besides Bush's General Land Office, there is the Attorney General's Office, the Teacher Retirement System, and the Water Development Board. According to the *Chronicle*, Bush has given out nearly 1,850 days of pay to ex-staffers, costing taxpayers at least $655,000 in salaries.

The GLO has admitted to having twenty-six special separation agreements between fired staffers and Bush's GLO. The agreements were intended "to give employees time to seek other employment and to avoid the potential expense to the GLO of any administrative or judicial proceedings related to employment." Translation: GLO agrees to pay you $, if you agree not to bring charges or sue the GLO. (To see a graph of the GLO's top ten Bush payoffs click the following link.[515])

Bush countered reports of wrongdoing by stating that the voters elected him to run the GLO as a business, and in lieu of the lack of severance packages, this is the best way to follow business standards. Others such as Dallas Democrat Senator Royce West say, "It's a misuse, and I hope my colleagues will agree with me."

Getting in trouble with the law is nothing strange to former governor Jeb Bush. In fact all three of his children have broken the law on many occasions. In 2002, Noelle Bush called a Tallahassee Walgreen's pretending to be Doctor "Noelle Scidmore." The twenty-four-year-old daughter of Jeb Bush was eventually led off in handcuffs for attempting to illegally purchase the controlled substance Xanax.[516] Also in 2002, Noelle was found with crack cocaine at a rehab center. This is her second relapse since entering court-ordered drug treatment. Police were called to the Center for Drug Free Living in Orlando by workers who found a white rock-like substance in her shoe. The .2 gram rock tested positive for cocaine. Noelle Bush was not arrested even though possession of any amount of cocaine is a serious felony.[517]

The year 2002 was a banner year for the Bush kids as two security officers at the Tallahassee Mall found Jeb Bush Jr. parked in a blue Jeep Cherokee with an underage female. Both Jeb and the teenage girl were naked from the waist down—and according to the police report, the two were apparently caught in the act. In 2005, Jeb Jr. was arrested by agents of the Texas Alcoholic Beverage Commission and charged with public intoxication and resisting arrest. He was released on $2,500 bond for the resisting arrest charge, and on a personal recognizance bond for the public intoxication charge.[518]

This is all very interesting when you consider then-Governor Bush's stance on drug issues. Besides cutting funding for drug treatment programs for prisoners and probationers, we can thank wife Columba for lecturing the press in late 2001 that it's the duty of parents to teach youths to avoid drugs. This speaks volumes for the hypocrisy of the Bushes as well as their parenting (or lack of) success.

In other recent George P. Bush events, the Texas land commissioner had joined a law suit against the Bureau of Land Management. It seems, according to Bush, that the government is wrongfully claiming that a certain 113-acre tract along the Red River is public land. Bush contends that it is owned by private land owners. The boundaries fluctuate according to the changing courses of the river. Bush stated that "Whether it's the EPA, the BLM, or the Endangered Species Act, they believe bureaucrats know better than landowners. Now they're messing with Texas." In a statement released by Bush he states:

> The Bureau of Land Management needs to stop any plans it has to take over Texas land. This federal bureaucracy is considering claiming ownership of a 116-mile stretch of land along the Red River—land that has been owned by Texans for generations. BLM's land grab is yet another example of the federal government's over regulation and overreach into our lives. These are not the values that America was founded on. It's unjust, unfair and won't be tolerated and as the next Texas Land Commissioner, I will do everything in my power to stop it.

This statement was of course made while Bush was running for Texas land commissioner. I'll bet that got him a few votes.[519] As of March 2016, Bush had joined the lawsuit against the Federal government in hopes of stopping the takeover. The matter has yet to be resolved.

In a complete turnabout from Bush's position as private property rights advocate, this past February, the owners of the popular Galveston County fishing spot known as Rollover Pass in Galveston County are accusing Texas Land Commissioner George P. Bush of hypocrisy for seeking to take their land while casting himself as a champion of private property rights. The Gilchrist Community Association, which is the caretaker of the property owned by the Gulf Coast Rod, Reel and Gun Club, says it has "declared war" on the General Land Office over the contested Rollover Pass. Association president Ted Vega said Bush's actions contradict his December push in support of residents fighting the federal Bureau of Land Management over land along the Red River. "If Mr. Bush has enough time and energy to go fight the battle with the BLM on the land grab that they're doing, and they're not doing anything with us here, then he is initiating the land grab," Vega said. Because the agency does not have the power of eminent domain, it asked Galveston County Commissioners Court to take the land, which it voted to do last month. General Land Office officials said the effort to close Rollover Pass is related to environmental concerns.

In an op-ed article, Andre Gabriel Esparza states that Bush is using bribes and intimidation to steal the much-contested Rollover Pass. The property has been owned by the current citizens since 1940. In 1960 the Army Corp of Engineers asked and was given permission to build a bridge over the pass. Under the premise of natural erosion, the GLO has bribed the county commissioners to use its eminent domain law and seize the land. Esparza cites the 20 million plus dollars coming in from the Texas Department of Transportation. The commissioners are afraid of losing some of that funding if they don't comply with orders from the GLO and George P. Bush. As this situation is unresolved at this time, I can't exactly say what Bush is up to his neck in. However, someone is directing him to turn from private land advocate into pawn of big business.[520]

These are mostly local Texas matters and may or may not come back to haunt George P. On a national scale his endorsement of Donald Trump came as a shock to a great many Republicans. On August 10, 2016, *Politico* ran this; "George P. Bush's Spineless Move to Endorse Trump Is about Power, Not Principle." The scathing piece by Michael Arceneaux offers that Bush, like Paul Ryan, John McCain, and other Republicans, have debased themselves by pledging support to Trump who has publicly slandered them, in a shameful attempt to gain favor should the Republican nominee win the 2016 election. The Bush family was horrified to hear of George P.'s defection. Showing true political spin, Bush explained his support of Trump as a support of the Republican platform and a need to keep Hillary from office. Some say there will be a dividing line within the GOP over the next few years. On one side there were those who stood up to Trump and on the other side, those who caved in and supported Trump. Many political analysts predict that George P. Bush will not be looked upon kindly for breaking with his family and sanity and succumbing to "Trumpism" for the sake of team unity. It's true that Trump bashed George P.'s father relentlessly. Trump bashed George W. and George H. W. and even Barbara Bush. He said things which normally would have called for a life or death duel. Yet George P., for the sake of party unity, endorsed arch rival Trump. Either he has no scruples, or he is truly a man of his party.

George P. has called himself a "mainstream conservative," yet he often quotes rhetoric from Tea Party doctrine. At an event in Pasadena, California, he closed his speech by saying that they "deserve a future that springs from the wells of freedom dug deep under the ground by the founders of our great republic and the heroes of 1863"—a nod to the Texas revolution and war with Mexico. George P. is no ignoramus. He has acquired skills, one of them being: never say too much, always leave room for an about-face. When asked about national issues he would often pull back stating that he's only running for a state office. On national security Bush has said that America should have a "lighter footprint" and "can't be the world's policeman." He adds that the US must show leadership and find creative ways to help allies. His views on climate change: Bush accepts that the earth is warming. He's called for Texas to take action against Gulf Coast erosion and has even spoken of wanting to reduce CO_2 emissions. Fearing blowback from the party base, he adds that "climate change keeps me up at night" meaning that he's still pondering the issue. On this and other sensitive topics, he reverts to saying, "It's not my place as an aspiring public servant because I am by no means a scientist or engineer." He's against same-sex marriage while admitting the inevitability of it. Time and again he avoids direct answers by saying, "it's not a core function of the General Land Office." The PolitiFact scorecard for George P. shows his statements as mostly true (33%), mostly false (33%) and false (33%). This gives him, in my book, 66% towards false statements.

George P. Bush may be smarter than the average Bush, certainly smarter than his father, Jeb. George P. may be the new face of the Republican Party. With an ever-increasing population of Latinos, Bush seems to be poised to tap that huge voting group sometime in the future. He's been described by *Salon* as "salsa-sexy," "a cross between Ricky Martin and John Kennedy Jr. by *USA Today*," "a handsome young political warrior with a *la vida loca* commitment" by the *New York Times*, and "the thinking woman's Ricky Martin" by the *Times* again. As time shows, he's continuing to gather political clout and credibility while keeping a fairly low profile. He's young and has plenty of time to strike. He is firmly aligned with his family while at the same time keeping his individuality at the forefront. He proclaims his Latino ethnicity with pride and this may prove to be his greatest strength. As the old Republican guard crumbles, there will be a need for a new voice to carry the conservative view to the following generations. His time is coming, but watch out. He is after all not just a Bush; he's George *Prescott* Bush.

EPILOGUE

Jeb Bush was supposed to bring the latest restoration of the House of Bush. His campaign was supposed to be "shock and awe." George H. W. has ordered "the Bush dynasty be restored to power," according to *POLITICO*. Even before he declared a formal candidacy, Jeb ginned up the Bush family money machine, with his father's and brothers' networks, raising $30 million for his campaign and an eye-popping $100 million in a Super PAC called Right to Rise.

The $100 million was largely from hedge fund managers, seeking to avoid changes in the tax law that would require them to pay at a tax rate commensurate with everyone else on Wall Street. Imagine how shocked they were when Jeb decided to emulate Donald Trump, calling for a new tax treatment under which his very own benefactors would pay their fair share.

Sitting down with a seasoned political pro who suggested that perhaps Jeb should have taken a different route to the nomination than his forbearers, he said, "It's my campaign, I'll run it." The "Shock and Awe" campaign that was meant to dazzle the GOP faithful quickly fizzled when Jeb seemed utterly incapable of answering simple questions such as how he differed from his father and his brother. Jeb also stumbled badly by insisting the Iraq War was the right thing to do, given present-day proof that strongman Saddam Hussein had no weapons of mass destruction.

After Trump raised the public issue of crimes committed by illegal immigrants becoming an epidemic, Bush tried to score off Trump in a debate by demanding "an apology" to his Hispanic wife. Trump brushed the attempt off and the gambit fell flat with the TV viewers. Jeb looked foolish.

In the end, Jeb did not succeed because, as it turns out, his brother was more likeable. This affability was an asset to Bush in his race against Al Gore, who was a pretentious and odd man. This was back when George W. was telling us he was a "compassionate conservative."

Having worked hard to end the presidential candidacy of Ambassador George H. W. Bush in 1980, and having fought his efforts to get on the ticket for vice president, I am entirely regretful that I went to California to bail Poppy out in 1988, and that I went to Florida to engage in what my friend James Baker would call a street fight for the presidency of the United States. I have done more for the Bushes than they have done for me. The pretenses used to get us into the Iraq War are what compelled me to write this book. The Bushes are not conservatives, just as the Clintons are not liberals. Both are crony capitalists, interested only in money and power.

A friend recounts visiting newly elected President George H. W. Bush in his compound in Kennebunkport, Maine. There was a copy of William F. Buckley's *National Review* on the coffee table. Poppy swept it into the wastepaper basket with the flourish of a hand. "Well, we don't need this crap anymore." Tellingly, he would replace it with the Yale alumni magazine.

Jeb was further rocked when Trump had the gumption to question Jeb's claim that "my brother kept us safe," by pointing out that both Clinton and George W. Bush had explicit reports indicating that an attack on America was coming by flying planes into buildings and did nothing about it, largely because the three intelligence services were not communicating. Prior to the attacks at least some of the 9/11 hijackers were living in plain sight in Florida. Jeb's Department of Motor Vehicles granted them all licenses and the FBI would quickly seal and take away any records or evidence days after the attack on the World Trade Center.

Jeb's campaign was further damaged by courageous former senator Bob Graham working to get 28 pages pertaining to the Saudis that are currently redacted in the 9/11 Commission report released. Attorneys who have seen these documents say they prove that a member of the Saudi family was the principal financier of the 9/11 attacks. The Bush family connections to the Saudis have made the 41st president very wealthy, and the Saudis bailed out the worthless energy company the 43rd president ran into the ground by buying it. Jeb sent a signal that he was still in the pay of the Saudis when his campaign refused to renounce the support of the Saudis' lawyer at court, James A. Baker III, when pro-Israel Republican groups demanded it.

The *New York Times* reported that Poppy was petulant over the Republicans' refusal to simply coronate his anointed son. A source who sat with 41 and was clearly instructed to leak the conversation quoted Bush as saying that he was "irritated." Incredibly, the *Times* would also quote former New Hampshire governor and Bush White House chief of staff, John Sununu: "I have no feeling for the electorate anymore."

Sununu's "feel for the electorate" was no better when he convinced George H. W. Bush to break his Reaganesque, "No new taxes" pledge, or when he engineered the appointment of liberal jurist David Souter to the Supreme Court. Perhaps his "feel for the electorate" was something he contemplated while using government planes and cars to travel to a private rare stamp auction. The Lebanese-American governor is, like FDR, a stamp collector. Sununu would be canned by the Bushes for this indiscretion. It is not incidental that pols in the Granite State have a button with a photo of Sununu in the emblazoned words, "Will Rogers never met this man."

I was trained at political head-hunting by John P. Sears. In this capacity, while I was working for the presidential candidacy of Buffalo Congressman Jack F. Kemp, my friend, Lee Atwater, boasted that Sununu had committed to Bush when we were smoking a joint one night. I made an appointment to see Sununu. I asked Sununu if he was committed to the vice president, and he looked me in the eye and said, "No." He lied.

One could see how Jebbie got off on the wrong foot when he launched his candidacy by saying that he would "take on the pampered elite" in Washington, DC. Jeb, of course, *is* the pampered elite. Can any of us imagine a $4 million personal taxpayer-financed bail-out?

The $100M in dirty Wall Street PAC money is theoretically under the control of Republican political consultant Mike Murphy, a longtime Bush family employee who is both affable and deft with a quote. Given Jeb's reputation as a "control freak," does anyone think Jeb and Murphy don't confer? Funny how Murphy's Super PAC had a briefing for donors in the exact same hotel where Jeb Bush's presidential campaign had summoned Bush backers from across the country. If you believe Jeb and Murphy are not talking, I have a bridge in Brooklyn I'd like to sell you.

After Jeb's branch of the Bush family was summoned to Maine in 2015 for a hand-holding session, they released photographs with the 43rd president as well as First Lady Barbara Bush, who now requires a walker. The session was held to quell deep concerns among the faithful about Jeb's plunge in the polls and a seemingly unorganized campaign. Two sources told me that Barbara, who intimates knew to be haughty, entitled, and vindictive, was "bombed." "She started hitting the vodka and orange juice early," one source told me. "Why should I worry my pretty little head about the body bags coming from Iraq?" she once famously said.

If Donald Trump, who pulled out to a long lead in the polls as the front-runner of the Republican race in the summer of 2015, accomplished nothing else, he destabilized the Jeb Restoration Project. By correctly tagging Bush as "low energy," the billionaire played off the fact that Jeb looked bored, impatient, and robot-like in his pursuit of the presidency. "America needs a cheerleader as well as a leader," Trump told me. "This guy ain't it."

Jeb has suffered greatly from the candidacy of his one-time protégé, Florida senator Marco Rubio. Ironically, the man who would position Rubio for his longshot presidential run is an old Bush hand gone rogue, Republican wiseman Wayne L. Berman, who moves in the rarefied air of the Blackstone Group, Wall Street, the insurance world, and the Capitol. Formerly an executive assistant to New York State Republican Richard Rosenbaum, the well-connected Berman has been working his A-list Rolodex behind the scenes for blue chip clients for years.

Marco's early performances on the stump were truly inspiring, with his carefully honed stump speech being described as "Reaganesque." I was invited to the home of Jose "Pepe" Fanjul in Palm Beach. Working without notes or a podium, the young senator mesmerized a crowd of well-heeled Republicans who jammed the room for a look at the man some were calling "the Republican Jack Kennedy." When Jeb attempted to exploit Rubio's thin attendance record in missed votes in the U.S. Senate, the young Cuban-American senator was ready for him. Pointing out the obvious, Rubio said Jeb was attacking him because they were running for the same position. Jeb's flat-footed performance in the third debate sparked questions as to whether or not he would drop out.

As much as we talk about the Bush Crime Family, it's still important to recognize the individual characteristics of both the progenitors and successors in the House of Bush. While George H. W. Bush is publicly affable, dogged in the pursuit of his goals, and relentless, his goofy manner and verbal idiosyncrasies mask a steely drive and burning ambition as well as duplicitous and secretive nature, as we have seen.

George W. was the family's notorious "black sheep" who generally cared more about drinking and getting laid than succeeding in the oil business, getting elected to Congress, or serving as governor. W. had little patience for the hand-holding and camaraderie of politics at which his father excelled, truly putting in bankers' hours in a White House in which the president's exercise and recreation were sacrosanct. One can see why Vice President Dick Cheney and the band of neo-cons who first came to government under Gerald Ford were able to hijack American foreign policy.

Jeb, however, even by his appearance, is more similar to his mother: haughty, vindictive, and a score-keeper. While Jeb is hardworking and diligent, he is a control freak who serves largely as his own campaign strategist and manager. He believes he is the smartest man in every room and can best be described as entitled, arrogant, and bewildered as to why Republicans did not flock to his banner in the 2016 Republican nomination contest.

When I appeared on Bill Maher's HBO show, *Real Time*, I pointed out that "Bush's greatest liability was his last name," and "we need another Bush like we need another Clinton."

Still, I am astounded by the successful cover-up of the Bush family crimes. That family patriarch Prescott Bush got rich by selling armaments to the Nazis and he held substantial interest in a New York bank while serving as chairman of the U.S. Senate Banking Committee, or that he had an interest in a steel mill which used slave labor from Auschwitz . . . these little tidbits rarely make the standard Bush biographies.

George H. W. Bush's role in evasions surrounding the Kennedy assassination and the fact that he avoided indictment in Iran-Contra simply by refusing to submit to a special prosecutors' questions, and his refusal to turn over pertinent government documents cannot be found in various fawning biographies that constantly stress his "character" and "integrity." *George H. W. Bush: Character at the Core* by Curt Smith and *George H. W. Bush* by Tim Naftali as well as George W. Bush's biography of his father—they all conveniently airbrushed these facts from Poppy's biography. Also missing, of course, is Bush's chairmanship of a task force to traffic millions of dollars of cocaine into the United States in order to sell the coke to raise money to illegally arm the Nicaraguan rebels in Iran-Contra. When I spoke about the drug trafficking operation during a Larry King interview, the seasoned media pro actually laughed at me as if these claims were ridiculous. The definitive account of the government's drug trafficking under Vice President Bush was originally written by Roger Morris and Sally Denton for the *Washington Post* but was spiked under pressure from the CIA and was later in *Penthouse* magazine.

The list of crimes, starting with Samuel Bush and continuing on through Prescott, Poppy, and into George W., is vast and well documented. That these individuals are seen by some as "America's royal family" is a gross misstatement revealing that history is written by the power elite. It also speaks to America's lost authority, the authority to question and bring to justice those who would abuse the powers granted to them by the Constitution of the United States and its citizens. "We the People," means something. It means that *we* are the heart of government. In the swearing in of a U.S. president, he swears to uphold the Constitution. Clearly these Bush criminals have done everything *but* uphold the Constitution.

It is our job, our responsibility, our right, to bring the Bushes to justice, and if we cannot, due to the overwhelming power they maintain, then we must pass the truths to our children, and they to their children and so on. When the word "freedom" means more to us than how many channels we can get, when we realize that our weakness for distraction enables the corruption and perversion of our civil liberties, when we come face to face with the enemy and know that it is us, then we must do what is necessary to bring about change.

George H. W. has ordered "the Bush dynasty be restored to power," according to *POLITICO*. George P. Bush not withstanding, we must never let a Bush take power again.

APPENDIX

THE BUSH COCAINE CONNECTION

–by Roger Stone

The Bush connection to drugs is more than the low-level pot dealing Jeb did at Andover.

Jeb Bush in 1986 was the 33-year-old chairman of the Dade County Republican party and he was up to his eyeballs in the Iran-Contra scandal. Key are Jeb Bush's dealings with operatives such as Al Martin, Oliver North, Richard Secord, Dewey Clarridge, Sam Watson, Fred Ikley and, of course, his father George Herbert Walker Bush. Basically Jeb Bush was in the center of a wasp's nest of dirty-dealing CIA/military operatives engaged in rampant criminality—all in the name of "national security."

On February 19, 1986, Barry Seal, a very prominent CIA drug smuggler and ace pilot, was murdered outside his halfway house in Baton Rouge, Louisiana. Seal, at the time he died, may have been the largest drug smuggler in American history. Over the past 20 years a lot of information about this murder has come out. Based on all this information, from a variety of sources, it is about time for someone to ask Jeb Bush, George Herbert Walker Bush, and Oliver North a simple question. **And that question is: "Did you murder Barry Seal?"**

****

Jeb Bush to intelligence operative Al Martin, who had worked closely with Jeb Bush during the Iran-Contra scandal and was threatening to go public: **"There is no constituency for the truth."**

****

Jeb Bush to intelligence operative **Ross Perot:** "When you look into the [American POW] prisoner cover-up, you find government officials in the drug trade who can't break themselves of the habit."
Ross Perot: "What I have found is a snake pit without a bottom. They will do anything to keep this covered up."

****

Barry Seal was a legendary CIA drug smuggler and ace pilot who had worked for the Agency since he was a teenage pilot prodigy in the late 1950s. By 1986 Seal was having legal problems (criminal and a huge IRS tax liability) that not even his CIA connections could protect him from, and according to Seal's lawyer Lewis Unglesby, Seal was a threat to testify against Vice President George Herbert Walker Bush. In fact, in early 1986 Seal was threatening G. H. W. Bush to get the IRS off his back or he (Seal) was going to blow the whistle on the Contra scheme and CIA drug smuggling.

Two weeks after his argument with Vice President George Herbert Walker Bush, Barry Seal was pumped full of bullets, murdered outside his Baton Rouge halfway house. The three Colombians who were convicted of the crime thought they were working for Lt. Col. Oliver North of the National Security Council. The personal phone number of George Herbert Walker Bush was found in Seal's possessions, even after the "men in black" had swept in to pick the car of the slaughtered CIA drug smuggler clean of evidence. Years later, Texas governor George W. Bush was being flown around in what had been the favorite plane of Barry Seal.

Many folks don't know that on the exact same day (2/19/86) Barry Seal was murdered in Baton Rouge, his mistress "Barbara" was also murdered in Miami; two other men also affiliated with the Medellin drug cartel, Pablo Carrera (Medellin's #2 man) and Pablo Ochill, were also assassinated in Colombia.

Some people think the CIA American drug cartel was switching horses from the Medellin drug cartel to a partnership with the Cali, Colombian drug cartel. The three men convicted of murdering Seal were from Cali, Colombia. The CIA American drug cartel was using the Cali cartel in a killing spree to wipe out the competition and murder anyone who might pose a threat to spill the beans on CIA drug smuggling and the participation of very high U.S. officials.

****

Jeb Bush should be asked about the murders of George Morales and Johnny Molina. This material has been on the public record for 20 years. It really is stunning that Jeb Bush, with such epic Iran-Contra liability, could even be considered for president. It just shows the arrogance of people who think that rules are for everyone else, but not for them. As someone said, "Tyranny is defined as that which is legal for the government but illegal for the citizenry."

Some examples might be gargantuan drug running, money laundering, and murdering people to keep it all covered up. Below there is a lot of material relating to the 1986 murder of CIA drug smuggler Barry Seal as well as CIA/governmental drug smuggling in general. Also please see the lists of sources at the end of this appendix for more information on CIA drug smuggling and the dark side of the Bushes.

****

The Personal Phone Number of VP George Herbert Walker Bush Was Found in CIA Drug Smuggler Barry Seal's Trunk:

The well-respected reporter Daniel Hopsicker, who focuses on the government drug trade, is a must read on the murder of Barry Seal. Read "CIA Linked to Seal's Assassination: George Bush's Personal Phone Number Found in Seals' Trunk" (Daniel Hopsicker, 8/18/97):

Another must-read is the *Real American Desperados* by Daniel Hopsicker (6/4/12).

Hopsicker's book *Barry and 'the Boys': The CIA, the Mob and America's Secret History* (2006) is one of the classics of modern politics. Hopsicker's book has critical information on the murder of Barry Seal and the possible Bush family/Oliver North involvement. Hopsicker concludes that Oliver North murdered Barry Seal and used Colombians to do it.

Texas Governor George W. Bush Later Flown Around in the Favorite Airplane of the Murdered Barry Seal

A fine article is "Why Does George W. Bush Fly in Drug Smuggler Barry Seal's Airplane?" (October 1999) by Daniel Hopsicker and Michael Ruppert. That article is about how after the murder of CIA drug smuggler Barry Seal, his favorite airplane somehow ended up being the exact same plane used to transport George W. Bush.

BARRY SEAL AND HIS ARGUMENT WITH VP GEORGE HERBERT WALKER BUSH IN EARLY 1986

"Lewis Unglesby is today a prominent and very well connected Louisiana lawyer. At the time his name was daily on the front page of the state's newspapers., defending his long-time client and associate, Governor Edwin Edwards.

Unglesby had told us about a confrontation he had with Barry over the fact that Seal was keeping him in the dark about matters Unglesbly considered crucial to defending him . . .

"Barry pushed the phone across the desk to me and said, 'You wanna know what's going on? Here. Dial this number. Tell 'em you're me,' Unglesby related.

"When I did what he requested," he continued, "A female voice answered the phone, sayin' 'Vice President Bush's office, may I help you?'"

CIA Operatives Confirm North's Guilt The assassination of Barry Seal was very likely even not the first attempt on Seal's life by North, we were told by CIA electronics expert Red Hall, on the ground in Nicaragua with Seal on the Sandinista drug sting.

"The only thing I knew was the CIA had a lot to do with it [Barry's murder]. The killers were being directed by Oliver North at the time. It was the same thing Oliver North pulled on us down in Nicaragua."

"Then, I didn't know yet that Oliver North had it for Barry Seal, because he was working with Oliver at that particular point. We was undercover, and we were still down there [Nicaragua], when Oliver blew the whistle on us."

Chip Tatum, another covert operative who had known Seal and shared confidences with him, listened with amusement the first time we breathlessly relayed what we'd discovered: that Oliver North is guilty in the assassination of Barry Seal.

"No shit, Sherlock," he replied, laughing. "It ain't exactly the secret of the century, I can tell you."[512]

AL MARTINS' CONVERSATION WITH JEB BUSH JUST DAYS after the Feb, 1986 Murder of Barry Seal in Baton Rouge. Jeb Bush had been at a meeting in Sept, 1985, where the assassination of Barry Seal had been discussed:

Al Martin: "In this discussion, I had mentioned the recent assassination, only a few days before, of Barry Seal [Feb, 1986, outside his halfway house in New Orleans].

I said to Jeb, "Isn't it convenient that Barry Seal was assassinated when he was? And now suddenly all the information and documents he had are gone missing?"

Jeb had a rather broad smile on his face, and he concurred that it was convenient. He added a little snicker—as he often had a tendency of doing. Also little beads of sweat formed on his forehead, as when he gets nervous. It's something you can notice when he's on television. He still has a tendency to have little beads of sweat around his forehead, when he is either lying about something, or he's nervous about what someone is saying."

My conversations with Jeb at this meeting were overheard by the two Secret Service agents who were always assigned to Jeb when he was in his office at 1390 Brickell Avenue in Miami.

I had intimated that if certain parties in Washington were not prepared to come to my aid pursuant to my grand jury testimony, that it would be entirely possible that certain details of a certain meeting occurring in September of the year [Sept., 1985] before might be leaked out to the press.

Jeb asked me what I was talking about.

I specifically mentioned a September meeting of the Dade County Latin America Chamber of Commerce, which Jeb chaired, and which, of course, was not used as a Chamber of Commerce meeting at all. It was essentially used as a political meeting for covert operational planning pursuant to Iran-Contra.

As I've said before, Oliver North, Richard Secord or Dewey Clarridge or, in a few cases, even Sam Watson and Fred Ikley himself, would show up at these meetings. [note that, to date, Al Martin is the only who has told of these meetings. I guess it's up to you to decide if they really took place.]

Anyway, I had recounted to Jeb, as if he didn't know what the text of that meeting was that he chaired–the conversations he had with Oliver North and Richard Secord and Dewey Clarridge, all of whom attended that meeting.

Dewey seldom attended the meetings, but this time the four of them were discussing the assassination of Barry Seal and how it was to be carried out, since Barry was becoming an increasing liability.

I had told Jeb that I had substantial corroboration of that meeting. And I think Jeb understood what I meant.

It would certainly place him into a conspiracy to assassinate a CIA drug runner for the sake of political expediency.

When I was through speaking, Jeb became quiet and his demeanor became serious and changed. He became flushed, as he often does when he's frightened.

Jeb responded by telling me that it would be most unfortunate if I were to do that, since I might wind up like George Morales or Johnny Molina. Remember: this is what Al Martin wrote, and we have no way of knowing if it's true. But is something rotten in the state of Denmark?[513]

JEB BUSH AND THE MURDERS OF GEORGE MORALES AND JOHNNY MOLINA

What he was referring to, of course, was that, a number of months earlier, George Morales had been set up on a cocaine charge—to distance what Morales was doing from the CIA.

As any serious student of Iran-Contra would know, Morales absolutely screamed "CIA, CIA."

But ultimately he was convicted.

He was bound and gagged in the courtroom before the Republican Judge Hoover, who allowed him to present no CIA defense. He couldn't mention any Bush names, or North, or Secord, or anything.

He got the standard fifteen-year sentence for cocaine trafficking. At the time, in the State of Florida, you had to serve six years nine months mandatory.

Jeb then went on to mention to me about Morales. He said "Of course, Morales will never leave prison alive."

Fast forward to the time when Morales was due to be released from prison in early 1992.

The day before Morales was to be released, he did, in fact, slip on a bar of soap in the prisoner's shower and supposedly died as a result of the fall.

The following day, Morales was due to be picked up at the Miami International Airport by a Congressional charter flight arranged for him by Congressmen Alexander, Rose, Brooks and Gonzalez. He was to be taken to Washington to have a detailed discussion with them and their investigators about his knowledge of Iran-Contra.

At that moment, the threat Jeb was making to me—the sublime threat about not wanting to wind up like Johnny Molina—really didn't mean anything to me because I knew as of the day before that Molina was still alive and well.

I didn't think anything of it until the next day when I got into my office and opened the Miami Herald.

I read that Mr. Molina had in fact "committed suicide" that evening in the parking lot of a restaurant in Pensacola, Florida.

He had "committed suicide" by discharging an entire twenty-round clip of a MAC-10 into his own body.

Of course, by the following day, the body had quickly been cremated—before his family was notified and before an autopsy could be done.

It's the same old story.

It was interesting to note that Jeb had issued that threat at that meeting which was held at about 10:30 a.m.

Molina "committed suicide" at about 9:30 p.m. that evening.

I found the connection rather humorous, but also salient in that Bush knew what was going to happen a number of hours before it actually did.

A second interesting and humorous story I can relate from that September meeting was not only the discussion of Barry

Seal, but the general discussion of narcotics, wherein Jeb was talking to Oliver North.

Dewey Clarridge and Joe Fernandez were there and Jeb was whining about how they were importing so much cocaine for the purposes of maintaining illicit covert revenue streams that, in fact, they were depressing the street value of the price of cocaine.

Revenues were in fact diminishing.

And North chuckled, and said that he had already made arrangements, that he, Dewey, Fred Ikley and Clair George had made arrangements.

What they were referring to by "arrangements" was the opening of the so-called sea routes to substantially increase the amount of cocaine that was being imported.

Jeb Bush said to Oliver North, "All you would manage to do is to further the price of cocaine."

North's attitude was, "Well, we'll simply bring in more and more of the stuff to maintain revenues."

As it has been pointed out in the past, CIA-assisted enterprise narcotics trafficking managed to depress the street price of a value of cocaine from $30,000 in early 1985 to $12,000 by mid-1986.

Later in the conversation, Jeb, wanting to be helpful, threw out a suggestion regarding the separate Guns-For-Drugs Operation being run out of Mena Airport in Arkansas.

He suggested that North start changing the fraction vis-à-vis the Contras.

Instead of one M-16 rifle, 1,000 rounds of ammunition, and the full field kit in exchange for one kilogram of cocaine, Bush suggested that North inform Enrico Bermudez and Eden Pastora that henceforth it was going to be two kilograms of cocaine for the same weapons delivery as it had been in the past.

North rebuffed this suggestion, reminding Bush that the one M-16 rifle, ammunition and field kit cost them a total of a $1,000 net delivered and the value of the kilogram of cocaine was still $17,000 or $18,000.

Al Martin's February 1986 Meeting with Jeb Bush Al Martin: "General Secord had mentioned to Jeb Bush—and I was standing not two feet from him—that some of Jeb's hangers-on (some of the old Cuban Bay of Pigs crowd that were Jeb Bush hangers-on vis-à-vis Jeb wearing his hat as a scamscateer and a money launderer) were beginning to have big mouths.

"And Jeb asked, 'Who?'

" Secord specifically said it was the infamous Manny Perez, who was a very close ally of Jeb's and had been for a long time. Perez used to act as a straw at various fraudulent deals for Jeb. He transported cash. He wired money into accounts he controlled through a variety of other straws. He was also very close with Jeb at Eagle National Bank in Miami.

"Jeb asked General Secord what he, Jeb Bush, was supposed to do about it.

"And Dick Secord said, 'Well, your father controls your show and he's got to clean up his own mess.'

"History records it wasn't long after an article appeared in a certain major newspaper about Manny Perez.

"Evidently Manny's body was found floating in a canal in West Hialeah, and his death was duly declared a 'swimming accident.'

"Perhaps the reader can better understand the phone call I received the day after the November 1998 elections when Jeb Bush won the governorship of the State of Florida.

"On that very same evening, I got a phone call from Neil Lewis in Miami, an attorney who had previously represented both Jeb and me, and who had acted as a conduit for people like me to Jeb and Dick Secord and a variety of others.

"Neil told me that he had a direct message from Jeb stating that if I wished to continue to be a resident of this state and to remain at large and with life that I best not reveal stories such as I have revealed here.

"When Neil relayed the threat to me that evening, I told Neil that when he talked to Jeb the following day (which I knew he would because he wanted to know what my response would be) to tell Jeb that I was aware that my former close colleague, Larry Hamil, prior to the November 1998 elections, had been involved in a political campaign money laundering scheme, wherein Mr. Hamil laundered certain monies of Chinese origin to certain Republicans (not Democrats, but Republican candidates) including the gubernatorial campaign of Jeb Bush.

"Neil laughed and said, 'Are you certain you want me to relay that?'

"I said, 'Yes,' and I didn't talk to Neil after that.

"I can only presume Neil did, in fact, relay that message because the next morning when I got out of bed, I was greeted by a view (outside of my bay windows) of two unmarked cars parked directly in front of my townhouse. They were of the sinister variety I'm used to—dark Chevy Caprices, darkened windows, black-wall tires, four or five aerials coming out of the back of them, Washington D.C. plates.

"There was enough sunlight that I could see two men sitting in each vehicle.

"And that's all they did.

"They simply sat there and looked directly at my unit. They stayed for a few hours in that position and then drove off.

"I had one of my neighbors record the D.C. plates on the car and upon checking them out later in the day, I was informed that no such plates existed.

But nonetheless, the message was sent.[514]

Al Martin continued: "As I am a middle-aged man, I have worked or been involved in illegal covert operation of government all my adult life.

"How many others in my age group can say they have personally known in their adult lifetimes almost 400 people who have died under clouded circumstances?

"The common thread among the deaths of these 400 people was not anything they did—but what they knew.

"I wonder how many others can make the same comment about their lives.

"It's an indication of the type of life I've led.

"Even what I have revealed thus far—it isn't a tenth of what I know. And it is such a task. That's the type of life I've led and what I know. I hope that the flavor of this comes out of what has happened to my friends, those I've known, who became inconvenient to their superiors and who died to maintain the deniability of others.

"The egregious nature of the conspiracy surrounding their death goes to a level that is virtually humorous.

"When Jeb Bush, Oliver North and Dewey Clarridge once spoke about an individual, North laughed and said, "Well, we haven't decided how we will rule his demise yet—whether it will be accident, natural causes, or suicide.""[515]

CIA OPERATIVE CHIP TATUM, WHO WORKED CLOSELY WITH OLIVER NORTH IN THE 1980'S, SAYS OLIVER NORTH SAID GHW BUSH & JEB BUSH WERE GOING TO "ARRANGE SOMETHING OUT OF COLUMBIA" TO TAKE CARE OF BARRY SEAL

Google "Chip Tatum Pegasus" and you will learn a lot about CIA drug smuggling and assassinations.

Mr. North stated the following to the other passengers, "One more year of this and we'll all retire." He then made a remark concerning Barry Seal and Governor Clinton. "If we can keep those Arkansas hicks in line, that is," referring to the loss of monies as determined the week prior during their meeting in Costa Rica. I stood silently by the vat of leaves, listening to the conversation. General Alverez had gone with the Contra leader to discuss logistics. The other three–North, Rodriguez, and Ami Nir–continued through the wooden building, inspecting the cocaine. North continued, ". . . but he (Vice President Bush) is very concerned about those missing monies. I think he's going to have Jeb (Bush) arrange something out of Columbia," he told his comrades, not thinking twice of my presence. What Mr. North was referring to ended up being the assassination of Barry Seal by members of the Medellin Cartel in early 1986.

FORMER DEA AGENT CELE CASTILLO ON GEORGE HERBERT WALKER BUSH AND HIS PARTICIPATION IN CONTRAS DRUG SMUGGLING

In his book *Powerburns: Cocaine, Contras & the Drug War*, Celerino Castillo writes: "The end of my career with the DEA took place in El Salvador. One day, I received a cable from a fellow agent, saying to investigate possible drug smuggling by Nicaraguan Contras operating from the Ilopango Air Force Base.

"I quickly discovered that the Contra pilots were, indeed, smuggling narcotics back into the United States—using the same pilots, planes and hangars that the Central Intelligence Agency and the National Security Council, under the direction of Lt. Col. Oliver North, used to maintain their covert supply operation to the Contras."

Instead of playing along with the criminals inside government profiting from cocaine trafficking, Castillo attempted to seek justice, naming many high-level officials along the way, including North and former president George H.W. Bush.

In fact, after Castillo blew the whistle, Bush made a point to seek out Castillo during one of his south of the border visits, in essence trying to "feel out" Castillo, but at the same time careful not to make any incriminating statement.

"When Bush confronted me and then just walked away after I told him some of the evidence I had, it was obvious he knew what was going on and was involved in the illegal drug trade," said Castillo.

And when Castillo's allegations first went public, he was the first government DEA agent with firsthand knowledge of North's drug dealing sanctioned by Bush and other higher-ups.

CELE CASTILLO FROM HIS BOOK "POWDERBURNS" ON GHW BUSH:

On January 14 [1986], Vice President George Bush visited Guatemala City to put the U.S. stamp of approval on Cerezo's inauguration. I met Bush at the obligatory cocktail party at the ambassador's residence. Embassy personnel and Guatemalan dignitaries elbowed through the crowd, jockeying for floor space near the Vice President. I was standing alone, watching the steel-faced secret service agents watching everyone else, when Bush approached. He read the tag on my lapel identifying me as a member of the U.S. embassy, and asked what I did. As he shook my hand, someone snapped a photo. I told him I was a DEA agent assigned to Guatemala. He said, "Well, what do you do?" I knew it wasn't wise to bring up the Contras—this man was part of the Administration, and Reagan had even declared himself to be a Contra.

I just blurted it out. "There's some funny things going on with the Contras in El Salvador."

Bush didn't reply. He simply smiled and walked away, seeking another hand to shake. After that exchange, I knew that he knew."[516]

FBI Undercover Agent Darlene Novinger and the Cocaine Connection

From Rodney Stich's book *Drugging America: A Trojan Horse:* After testifying in Harrisburg, Darlene returned to her Florida assignment with the South Florida Drug Task Force. Because of her earlier associations with the Smatt brothers, who by now were reportedly major drug smugglers, the FBI suggested that Darlene renew her contacts with them. In December 1982 she called Raymond Smatt in Jamaica, who invited Darlene to his mansion, where she stayed for several weeks. Raymond then suggested that Darlene stay with another brother William, who had a mansion in Miami, where she stayed for several days before going back to Jamaica.

Claiming Vice President Involved in Drugs

During one of many conversations with William Smatt at his Jamaica mansion, William started talking about the corrupt nature of the American judicial system and the White House. In one instance he said, "Let's take, for instance, the vice president and his son, referring to George Bush and his son, Jeb Bush."

Darlene asked, "What about them, you mean George Bush and his son; which son?" Smatt responds, "Jeb."

Darlene responded, "You mean, Jeb with the Miami Republican party?" "Yes," he replied. Darlene started explaining what occurred:

"I was in one of the drug lords mansions which I was trained to encounter and infiltrate. I was sitting on a couch and a conversation turned up that would lead to something that would change the rest of my life. I was sitting and talking about justice in the judicial system. Well, these people were not American citizens, but they had strong opinions about the American judicial system, and how it worked, and they wanted to express it to me. I'll never forget this day. What came out was the following.

They proceeded to tell me how money is the way to justice. Without it, there is no chance. You're living in a Disney World to believe otherwise. This is what I was told by them. They proceeded to tell me how they had to pay the Republican Party in Miami. At that time, Jeb Bush was the chairman of the Republican Party in Florida [editor's note: Jeb was Dade County GOP chairman in the early 1980s].

They told me about the visits Vice President George Bush made to their mansion. The story that unfolded was incredible that I thought I had heard everything until this gentleman was done showing me correspondence. His office phone was ringing at this time. Lo and behold, it was the Miami Republican Party calling. He was screaming at them because he said, "I just gave you a couple hundred-thousand dollars and I want this done!"

Darlene explained how Smatt told her about providing pharmaceutical-grade drugs to aircraft arriving from Washington, DC, which were then flown back to Washington and delivered by courier to the Bush White House. Smatt told Darlene of the money that he provided to the head of the Republican Party in Florida, and the relationship he had with Florida politicians. He was complaining that they kept asking him for more money. Darlene explained:

"I asked him why he continued to do business with them if he didn't like them. He said it was very simple. His contributions were going to the vice president and his sons' interests because he was going to be appointed roving ambassador in the Caribbean. Meaning something called the Caribbean Basin initiative, which was to their benefit to get passed because they would make a lot of money, on top of everything else.

"He proceeded to tell me how he and his family, particularly he, furnished prostitutes to Jeb Bush and George Bush when they were in Miami, Florida, and of the use of cocaine by these individuals and George Bush's staff in Washington, D.C. He proceeded to also tell me about flying pharmaceutical grade cocaine, and how the currier delivered it to the vice president's office in Washington, D.C." Darlene continued to explain what was said:

"At that point I was sitting there with absolutely nothing to say other than, I could not believe it. I then sort of regrouped and said, 'How do I know that what you're saying is true? That just seems so incredible.'

Darlene explained William Smatt opening his desk drawer and "showing me personal correspondence from the vice-president, his son, photographs, and checks. I had no reason to believe that this man who I had known for years made this up."

At another time, while staying at Raymond Smatt's Miami mansion, Raymond said that Vice President George Bush and Jeb Bush had used cocaine at his Miami home.

Darlene Novinger and Her 1982 Report to the FBI Office in Harrisburg:

Darlene said that after she submitted her report in December 1982, an investigation was commenced. Darlene said that in January 1983, newspapers reported that Vice President George Bush's entire staff on the South Florida Drug Task Force was replaced. She assumed this was due to her report. She also remembered a

Washington Post article in January 1983 that stated many members of the South Florida Task Force were using drugs . . .[518]

Darlene Novinger was Set Up to be Murdered by Drug Traffickers by Justice Department personnel who intentionally blew her cover, revealing she was an informant. Someone in government wanted Darlene dead. She survived.

Darlene returned to her assignment in Florida and found herself being set up by someone in the Miami U.S. attorney's office to be killed. She explained that while staying at the Raymond Smatt mansion in Jamaica, and while talking to Raymond, the phone rings. It was a call from his brother, William Smatt in Miami, who stated that his contact in the Miami U.S. attorney's office found out that Darlene was an FBI informant. Darlene explained:

"That particular office, the Miami U.S. attorney's office, almost cost me my life. I was at the mansion of a major drug lord in Jamaica, and a phone call was made when I was in the living room of their house. I could hear part of the conversation and they were talking about me. I could hear Raymond acting, 'The FBI in Miami said who was working for them?' They were talking about me!

"I felt trapped. There I was in his home, on an island, trapped, and I'm hearing this man get this call, and I thought, 'I'm going to die.' I really did. I thought, whew, it was a close one, I'll tell you. And he kept looking at me and he was a little grumpy. I said, 'The next thing you know, they'll have me working for the CIA.'

"Eventually he lightened up, and I talked my way out of that one. Later, I found out that that gentleman was very heavily involved and he was not playing on the up and up . . . ."

Apparently, whoever told William Smatt that Darlene was an FBI undercover agent knew that Darlene was staying in Jamaica at the Raymond Smatt residence, and wanted Darlene killed. That would solve the problem with the report on Vice President George Bush and his son, Jeb.[519]

BO GRITZ LETTER TO VP G. H. W. BUSH IN 1988 REGARDING U.S. GOVERNMENT HEROIN SMUGGLING[520]

Bo Gritz Letter to George Bush
1 February 1988, Sandy Valley, NV
Honorable George Bush, Vice President, United States of America, Washington, D.C.

Sir:

Why does it seem that you are saying "YES" to illegal narcotics in America?

I turned over video tapes to your NSC staff assistant, Tom Harvey, January 1987, wherein General KHUN SA, overlord of Asia's "Golden Triangle", offered to stop 900 tons of heroin/opium from entering the free world in 1987. Harvey told me, ". . . there is no interest here in doing that." General Khun Sa also offered to identify U.S. Government officials who, he says, have been trafficking in heroin for more than 20 years.

November 1986, Scott Weekly and I went into Burma in coordination and cooperation with The White House. Tom Harvey told me you received a letter from Arthur Suchesk, Orange County, CA, dated 29 August 1986. Dr. Suchesk said that Gen Khun Sa had access to U.S. POWs. Harvey said the letter had received "highest attention". He gave me a copy along with other case documents. I was asked if it was possible to verify the information. According to Harvey, the CIA said Khun Sa had been assassinated some months before. Harvey supplied Scott and myself with language under White House and NSC letterhead that would help us gain access to Khun Sa. It worked. Unfortunately, Khun Sa knew nothing about US

POWs. He did, however, offer to trade his nation's poppy dependence for a legitimate economy.

Instead of receiving an "Atta Boy" for bringing back video tape showing Khun Sa`s offer to stop 900 tons of illegal narcotics and expose dirty USG officials, Scott was jailed and I was threatened. I was told that if I didn't "erase and forget" all that we had discovered, I would, "hurt the government". Further, I was promised a prison sentence of "15 years".

I returned to Burma with two other American witnesses, Lance Trimmer, a private detective from San Francisco, and Barry Flynn from Boston. Gen Khun Sa identified some of those in government service he says were dealing in heroin and arms sales. We videotaped this second interview and I turned copies over in June 1987, to the Chairman of the Select Committee on Intelligence; Chairman of the House on Foreign Affairs Task Force on Narcotics Control; Co-Chairman, Senate Narcotics Committee; Senator Harry Reid, NV; Representative James Bilbray, NV; and other Congressional members. Mister Richard Armitage, Assistant Secretary of Defense for International Security Affairs, is one of those USG officials implicated by Khun Sa. Nothing was done with this evidence that indicated that anyone of authority, including yourself, had intended to do anything more than protect Mr. Armitage. I was charged with "Misuse of Passport". Seems that it is alright for Oliver North and Robert MacFarlane to go into Iran on Irish Passports to negotiate an illegal arms deal that neither you nor anyone else admits condoning, but I can't use a passport that brings back drug information against your friends.

Lance Trimmer and I submitted a "Citizen Complaint of Wrongdoing by Federal Officers" to Attorney General Edwin Meese, III on 17 September 1987. Continuous private and Legislative inquiries to date indicate that the Attorney General's Office has "lost" the document. Congressional requests to the Government Accounting Office have resulted in additional government snares and stalls.

January 20, 1988, I talked before your Breakfast Club in Houston, Texas. A distinguished group of approximately 125 associates of yours, including the Chief Justice of the Texas Supreme Court, expressed assurance that you are a righteous man. Almost all of them raised their hand when I asked how many of them know you personally. If you are a man with good intent, I pray you will do more than respond to this letter. I ask that you seriously look into the possibility that political appointees close to you are guilty of by passing our Constitutional process, and for purposes of promoting illegal covert operations, conspired in the trafficking of narcotics and arms.

Please answer why a respected American Citizen like Mister H. Ross Perot can bring you a pile of evidence of wrongdoing by Armitage and others, and you, according to TIME magazine (May 4, page 18), not only offer him no support, but have your Secretary of Defense, Frank Carlucci tell Mr. Perot to "stop pursuing Mr. Armitage". Why Sir, will you not look into affidavits gathered by The Christic Institute (Washington, D.C.), which testify that Armitage not only trafficked in heroin, but did so under the guise of an officer charged with bringing home our POWs. If the charges are true, Armitage, who is still responsible for POW recovery as your Assistant Secretary of Defense ISA, has every reason not to want these heros returned to us alive. Clearly, follow on investigations would illuminate the collective crimes of Armitage and others.

Several years ago a secretary working for Armitage asked me "Why would he have us expunge his official record of all reference to past POW/MIA assignments and activities?" Not knowing, I ventured a guess that maybe he was considering running for public office and didn't feel the POW -Vietnam association would be a plus in his resume. It was about the same time a CIA agent named by Khun Sa turned up dead in Bangkok under "mysterious circumstances". Also about this time, as an agent of NSC's Intelligence Support Activity, I was told by ISA Chief Jerry King, ". . . there are still too many bureaucrats in Washington who don't want to see POWs returned alive". I failed to realize the fullness of his meaning, or these other events, until in May 1987, Gen Khun Sa, in his jungle headquarters, named Richard Armitage as a key connection in a ring of heroin trafficking mobsters and USG officials. A U.S. agent I have known for many years stopped by my home last month enroute to his next overseas assignment. He remarked that he had worked for those CIA chiefs named by Khun Sa, and that by his own personal knowledge, he knew what Khun Sa said was true. He was surprised it had taken so long to surface.

I am a registered Republican. I voted for you twice. I will not do so again. If you have any love or loyalty in your heart for this nation; if you have not completely sold out, then do something positive to determine the truth of these most serious allegations. You were Director of the CIA in 1975, during a time Khun Sa says Armitage and CIA officials were trafficking in heroin. As Director of Intelligence you were responsible to the American people for the activities of your assistant–even as you should know what some of these same people are doing who are close to you now as our Vice President because I feel these "parallel government" types will only be promoted by you, giving them more reason to bury our POWs.

I am enclosing some documentation that supports the charges made. Chief is a letter from Khun Sa to the U.S. Justice Department dated 28 June 1987, wherein Richard Armitage is named along with Theodore Shackley (your former Deputy Director CIA from Covert Operations) and others. Please also note William Stevenson's article, "Bank of Intrigue-Circles of Power". You, Armitage, and General Richard Secord are prominently mentioned. Stevenson, you might remember, authored A MAN CALLED INTREPID. Also Tom Fitzpatrick's article, "From Burma to Bush, a Heroin Highway", should interest you. Both of these men are prize winning journalists. The book, CRIMES of PATRIOTS, "A True Tale of Dope, Dirty Money, and the CIA", by Jonathan Kwitny, reporter for the Wall Street Journal, details for you the bank connections that Khun Sa mentions. Finally, the basic primer that spells out exactly how this dope for covert operations gambit began, is Alfred McCoy's THE POLITICS OF HEROIN IN SOUTHEAST ASIA. All of these should be required reading for the man appointed chief cop by our President to safeguard America from illegal narcotics. These are just a sampling of many works now available that chronical disgraceful conduct by those sworn to protect and defend our Constitution.

Parting shot Mr. Vice President: On 28 January 1988, General Khun Sa tendered an offer to turn over to me one metric ton (2,200 pounds) of heroin. He says this is a good faith gesture to the American people that he is serious about stopping all drugs coming from the infamous Golden Triangle. I, you and Nancy Reagan are really serious about saying "NO" to drugs, why not test Gen Khun Sa? I challenge you to allow me in the company of agents of your choice to arrange to receive this token offer worth over $4 billion on the streets of New York City. It will represent the largest "legal" seizure of heroin on record. You can personally torch it, dump it in the ocean, or turn it into legal medication; as I understand there is a great shortage of legal opiates available to our doctors.

I think Gen Khun Sa's offer is most interesting. If you say "YES" then the ever increasing flow of heroin from Southeast Asia (600—tons—'86, 900 tons—'87, 1200—tons'88) may dry up—not good for business in the parallel government and super CIA circles Oliver North mentioned. If you say "NO" to Khun Sa, you are showing colors not fit for a man who would be President.

What is your decision? I challenge you to demonstrate exactly where you stand with respect to big-business-drugs, parallel government, misuse of U.S. tax-payer dollars in foreign drug suppression programs that don't work, no interest in dialogue that will stem the flow of illegal narcotics, return of POWs while they are still alive? I for one am not for a "USA, Inc." with you or anyone else as Chairman of the Board.

Respecting Your Office,

James "Bo" Gritz,

Concerned American,

Box 472 HCR-31Sandy Valley, NV 89019

Books on Governmental/CIA Drug Smuggling and Related Criminal Activities

1) *Powderburns*: Cocaine, Contras & the Drug War by former DEA agent Celerino Castillo III (2010)
2) *Dark Alliance* by Gary Webb (1999)
3) *Barry and the Boys*: the CIA, the Mob and America's Secret History by Daniel Hopsicker (2006, written in 2001, lawsuits delayed it for 5 years. Extremely important book.)
4) *Whiteout* by Alexander Cockburn (1999)

5) *Cocaine Politics*: Drugs, Armies and the CIA in Central America by Peter Dale Scott and Jonathon Marshall (1998)

6) *Lost History*: Contras, Cocaine, the Press & 'Project Truth' by Robert Parry (1999)

7) *The Conspirators*: Secrets of an Iran-Contra Insider by Al Martin (2000)

8) *The Big White Lie*: The Deep Cover Operation That Exposed the CIA Sabotage of the Drug War: An Undercover Odyssey by Michael Levine and Laura Kavanau-Levine (2012)

9) *The Politics of Heroin*: CIA Complicity in the Global Drug Trade by Alfred W. McCoy (1972 and republished 2003)

10) *Out of Control*: The Story of the Reagan Administration's Secret War in Nicaragua, the Illegal Arms Pipeline, and the Contra Drug Connection by Leslie Cockburn (1987)

11) *Blue Thunder*: How the Mafia Owned and Finally Murdered Cigarette Boat King Donald Aronov by Thomas Burdick and Charlene Mitchell (1990)

12) *The Mafia, CIA, & George Bush* by Pete Brewton (1992)

13) *Called to Serve* by James "Bo" Gritz (1991)

14) *Crossfire*: Witness in the Clinton Investigation by L. D. Brown (1997)

15) *The Secret Life of Bill Clinton*: The Unreported Stories by Ambrose Evans Pritchard

16) *American Desperado*: My Life—From Mafia Soldier to Cocaine Cowboy to Secret Government Asset by Jon Roberts & Evan Wright (2012)

17) *Cocaine, Death Squads, and the War on Terror*: U.S. Imperialism and Class Struggle in Colombia by Oliver Villar and Drew Cottle (2011)

18) *The Crimes of Patriots*: A True Tale of Dope, Dirty Money, and the CIA by Jonathan Kwitney (1987)

19) *The Politics of Cocaine*: How U.S. Foreign Policy Has Created a Thriving Drug Industry in Central and South America by William L. Marcy (2010)

20) *How to Get Away with Murder in America*: Drug Lords, Dirty Pols, Obsessed Cops, and the Quiet Man Who Became the CIA's Master Killer by Evan Wright (2012)

21) *Defrauding America*: Encyclopedia of Secret Operations by the CIA, DEA, and other Covert Agencies (third edition) by Rodney Stich (1998)

22) *Drugging America*: A Trojan Horse (second edition) by Rodney Stich (2005)

23) *The New Clinton Chronicles (YouTube)*: http://www.youtube.com/

24) *Conspiracy—The Secret History*: The Secret Heartbeat of America, the CIA and Drugs by Daniel Hopsicker (2004)

25) *Kill the Messenger*: How the CIA's Crack-Cocaine Controversy Destroyed Journalist Gary Webb by Nick Schou (2006)

26) *Dope, Inc*: The Book That Drove Henry Kissinger Crazy by Executive Intelligence Review (1992)

27) *Disavow*: A CIA Saga of Betrayal by Rodney Stich

28) *Welcome to Terrorland*: Mohamed Atta & the 9–11 Cover-Up in Florida by Daniel Hopsicker (2005)

29) *Opium, Empire and the Global Political Economy*: A Study of the Asian Opium Trade 1750–1950 by Carl Trocki (1999)

30) *The Boys on the Tracks*: Death, Denial, and a Mother's Crusade to Bring Her Son's Killers to Justice by Mara Leveritt (1999)

31) *The Strength of the Wolf*: The Secret History of America's War on Drugs by Douglas Valentine (2004)

32) *The Strength of the Pack*: The Personalities, Politics and Espionage Intrigues That Shaped the DEA by Douglas Valentine (2009)

Books about the Darker Side of the Bushes

1) *Family of Secrets*: The Bush Dynasty, the Powerful Forces That Put It in the White House, and What Their Influence Means for America by Russ Baker (2008)
2) *The Immaculate Deception*: Bush Crime Family Exposed by Russell S. Bowen (1991)
3) *George Bush*: The Unauthorized Biography by Webster Griffin Tarpley (2004)
4) *Fortunate Son*: George W. Bush and the Making of an American President by J. H. Hatfield (2002)
5) *Bushwhacked*: Inside Stories of True Conspiracy by Uri Dowbenko (2003)
6) *The Two Faces of George Bush* by Anthony C. Sutton (1988)
7) *American Dynasty*: Aristocracy, Fortune, and the Politics of Deceit in the House of Bush by Kevin Phillips
8) *The Family*: The Real Story of the Bush Dynasty by Kitty Kelley (2004)
9) *The Bush Junta*: A Field Guide to Corruption in Government by Mack White & Gary Groth (2005)
10) *October Surprise* by Barbara Honegger (1989)
11) *October Surprise* by Gary Sick (1992)
12) *Trick or Treason*: The October Surprise by Robert Parry (1993)
13) *The Complete and Extraordinary History of the October Surprise* by Brian Joseph (2009)
14) *The October Surprise X-Files*: The Hidden Origins of the Reagan-Bush Era by Robert Parry

15) *Bush's Brain*: How Karl Rove Made George W. Bush Presidential by James Moore and Wayne Slater (2004)

16) *Jeb*: America's Next Bush by S. V. Date

Books by Iran-Contra Figures (some who were running gargantuan amounts of drugs into the U.S., committing financial crimes, and murdering people—somehow they forgot to put that in their books).

1) *Under Fire*: An American Story by Oliver L. North with William Novak (1992)

2) *Honored and Betrayed*: Irangate, Covert Affairs, and the Secret War in Laos by Richard Secord (1992)

3) *Shadow Warrior*: The CIA Hero of Hundred Unknown Battles by Felix I. Rodriguez (1989)

4) *Spymaster*: My Life in the CIA by Ted Shackley (2006)

5) *A Spy for All Seasons*: My Life in the CIA by Duane R. Clarridge

6) *Hazardous Duty*: An American Soldier in the Twentieth Century by John Singlaub (1992)

Question: If you truly have character, do you really have to have books written by and about you pertaining to "character" and "integrity?"

1) *George Bush*: Man of Integrity by Doug Wead (1988)

2) *Profiles in Character* by Jeb Bush and Brian Yablonski (1996)

ENDNOTES

1. David Simon, *Elite Deviance*.
2. "George P. Bush's Political Future: How Far Can He Go?" *The Week*. March 13, 2013.
3. "Jeb Bush: I Would Govern Like Lyndon Johnson as President." *Breitbart News*. February 15, 2013.
4. "Jeb Bush: The U.S. Chamber of Commerce's Waterboy." *Townhall.com*. December 17, 2014.
5. "The Bushes, as Distinct and Alike as Brothers Can Be." *New York Times*. January 17, 2015.
6. S. V. Date, *Jeb—America's Next Bush*.
7. "Jeb the Wheeler and Dealer: Roger Stone's Astounding Allegations Against Jeb Bush." ora.tv. September 25, 2015.
8. Ibid.
9. "Barbara Bush On Jeb Running for President: 'We've Had Enough Bushes'." *Huffington Post*. April 25, 2013.
10. "Jeb Wins the All-Important Barbara Bush Primary." *Time*. February 14, 2015.
11. "Early Voting for Jeb Bush as Wall Street Bucks Flow to GOP Contender." CNBC.com. June 15, 2015.
12. "Jeb Bush Exploits Non-Candidate Status to Rewrite Campaign Finance Playbook." *Miami Herald*. March 1, 2015.
13. Ibid.
14. Ibid.
15. " Jeb Bush Jr. Endorses Huntsman." *Real Clear Politics*. August 10, 2011.
16. "Jeb Bush, Ana Navarro and the Question That May Have Been Misheard." *New York Times*. May 12, 2015.
17. "I'm a Republican, and I Want Joe Biden to Run." CNN.com. September 28, 2015.
18. "GOP Operative Ana Navarro a Warrior for the Cause." *Tampa Bay Times*. February 1, 2013.
19. "The Future of the Republican Party is by the Pool at the Biltmore." *BuzzFeed News*. February 12, 2013.

20. "With Joy in My Heart: Jeb Refutes Trump's 'Low Energy' Taunt." *Breitbart News*. August 29, 2015.

21. "Jeb's Growing List of Unfortunate Comments." Politico.com. October 2, 2015.

22. "Jesse Ventura: Jeb Bush Sent Me a Box of Cuban Cigars." ora.tv. August 13, 2015.

23. Geoff Earle and Marisa Schultz, "Jeb Had a Great Recession." *New York Post*, July 1, 2015.

24. Geoff Earle, "Jeb Bush Talk Not Cheap Either—Got $10m." *New York Post*. July 2, 2015.

25. Ibid.

26. "Jeb the Wheeler and Dealer: Roger Stone's Astounding Allegations Against Jeb Bush." ora.tv. September 25, 2015.

27. "The Jeb Bush Illegal Drug and Liquor Distributorship at Andover." capital-hilloutsider.com. January 29, 2013.

28. "Revisiting Jeb Bush's Bad Behavior at Andover." *Vanity Fair*. January 2015.

29. "Jeb Bush Shaped by Troubled Phillips Academy Years." *Boston Globe*. February 1, 2015.

30. Daniel Hopsicker, *Barry and The Boys, The CIA, The Mob and American's Secret History*. p. 311.

31. D.G. "Chip" Tatum, *The Tatum Chronicles*.

32. Terry Reed, *Compromised: Clinton, Bush and the CIA*. pp. 211–213.

33. "Jeb the Wheeler and Dealer: Roger Stone's Astounding Allegations Against Jeb Bush." ora.tv. September 25, 2015.

34. "Term 'Anchor Baby' Not Derogatory." C-SPAN.com. August 24, 2015.

35. "Jeb Can't Win: His 'Anchor Babies' Remark Draws Fire From Hillary—and Trump." Slate.com. August 21, 2015.

36. "The Words Jeb Bush May Come to Regret." Politico.com. February 26, 2015.

37. "Jeb Bush in '94: 'Sodomy' Shouldn't Be Given Same Protections as Race, Religion." Buzzfeed.com. January 5, 2015.

38. "Jeb Bush, While Florida Governor, Invested $1.3 Million in State Pension Fund Money in Pornography: Report." *New York Daily News*. May 7, 2015.

39. "Bush Calls His 'Bilingual, Bicultural' Background a Campaign Asset." Politico.com. February 9, 2015.

40. "Transcript: Read Full Text of Former Gov. Jeb Bush's Campaign Launch." *Time*. June 15, 2015.

41. "Jeb Bush Says He Speaks 'More Spanish Than English At Home'." abcnews.go.com. June 18, 2015.

42. "Term 'Anchor Baby' Not Derogatory." C-SPAN.com. August 24, 2015.

43. "Jeb Bush On Illegal Immigrants Crossing the Border: 'An Act of Love'." *Real Clear Politics*. April 6, 2014.

44. "Jeb Bush's Father-In-Law Hopes to Reconcile with Daughter." Jacksonville.com. February 14, 2001.

45. "The Year That Changed Jeb Bush Forever. How a Radical Class—Part Lord of the Flies, Part Peace Corps—Introduced a Preppy Teenager to Mexico and the Love of His Life." Politico.com. May 21, 2015.

46. "The Mysterious Columba Bush." *The Atlantic*. June, 2015.

47. "Is Jeb Bush a Republican Obama?" *The Atlantic*. February 4, 2015.

48. "Columba Bush's Painful, Unlikely Road From Mexico Toward the White House." *Washington Post*. March 21, 2015.

49. "Honoring the Family Name: Culture: 'I'm Not Interested in Politics,' Says Columba Bush, the President's Daughter-In-Law. Still She Knows How to Campaign for a Cause: Her Native Mexico." *L.A. Times*. July 31, 1991.

50. "Michelle Obama Takes Heat for Saying She's Proud of My Country; for the First Time." Foxnews.com. February 19, 2008.

51. "Honoring the Family Name: Culture: 'I'm Not Interested in Politics,' Says Columba Bush, the President's Daughter-In-Law. Still She Knows How to Campaign for a Cause: Her Native Mexico." *L.A. Times*. July 31, 1991.

52. "The Mysterious Columba Bush." *The Atlantic*. June, 2015.

53. "Bush Spouse Backs Jeb, But Is Wary of Family Business." *New York Times*. February 21, 2015.

54. "Bush: Wife Meant to Hide Shopping Spree From Me." *St. Petersburg Times*. June 22, 1999.

55. "Bush's Wife is Caught Smuggling Clothes." *Independent*. October 22, 2011.

56. "Gov. Jeb Bush Denies Rumor of Affair with Appointee." *St. Augustine Record*. May 15, 2001.

57. "Fla. Gov. Bush Denies Affair." abcnews.go.com. May 14, 2001.

58. "Ex-Official Accuses Husband of Threat." *Tampa Bay Times*. July 30, 2004.

59. http://www.waynemadsenreport.com/articles/20150408.

60. Ibid.

61. Ibid.

62. Ibid.

63. Ibid.

64. Ibid.

65. Ibid.

66. Ibid.

67. "Embarrassing Bush Divorce Papers." cbsnews.com. January 26, 2004.

68. "F.D.I.C. Sues Neil Bush and Others at Silverado." *New York Times*. September 22, 1990.

69. "A Savings and Loan Bailout, and Bush's Son Jeb." *New York Times*. October 14, 1990.

70. "Jeb Bush Dogged by Decades of Questions About Business Deals." *Washington Post*. June 28, 2015.

71. "Jeb Bush's Tie to Fugitive Goes Against Business-Savvy Image He Promotes." *Washington Post*. March 18, 2015.

72. Ibid.
73. "When Dad Was VP, Jeb Bush Lobbied the Administration for a Medicare Fraudster." *Huffington Post*. February 20, 2015.
74. Ibid.
75. Al Martin, *The Conspirators, Secrets of an Iran-Contra Insider*, p. 88.
76. "Fugitive Accuses Bush." *Sun Sentinel*. April 21, 1995.
77. "Jeb Bush's Rush to Make Money May Be a Hurdle." *New York Times*. April 20, 2014.
78. "How Jeb Bush's Firm Made Him Rich—and Created a Nest Egg for His Family." *Washington Post*. July 2, 2015.
79. "Jeb Bush's Administration Steered Florida Pension Money to George W. Bush's Fundraisers." *International Business Times*. April 14, 2015.
80. "Election 2016: Jeb Bush Got $1.3M Job at Lehman After Florida Shifted Pension Cash to Bank." *International Business Times*. August 19, 2015.
81. "Florida Got Lehman Help Before Run on School's Finds (Update 1)." *Bloomberg*. December 18, 2007.
82. "Florida Stands to Lose $1 Billion Because of Lehman Brothers' Bankruptcy." *Tampa Bay Times*. June 4, 2009.
83. "As Florida Governor, Jeb Bush Bought Land from Timber Company That Later Paid Him $1 Million." *International Business Times*. June 19, 2015.
84. "Testing Time—Jeb Bush's Educational Experiment." *New Yorker*. January 26, 2015.
85. "By the Numbers: Jeb Bush's Tax Returns." *Tamps Bay Times*. June 30, 2015.
86. "FIU Turns to Partnership Firm for International Online Degrees." *Miami Herald*. February 13, 2013.
87. "Election 2016: Jeb Bush Leveraged Political Connections for Clients and Allies After Leaving Florida Governorship, Emails Show." *International Business Times*. August 13, 2015.
88. "Higher-Ed Hustle: For-Profit Colleges Cast Shadow Over Presidential Race." *Miami Herald*. August 15, 2015.
89. "Election 2016: Jeb Bush Leveraged Political Connections for Clients and Allies After Leaving Florida Governorship, Emails Show." *International Business Times*. August 13, 2015.
90. "GOP Contenders Line Up to Blast Im." *The Hill*. February 28, 2015.
91. "Dear Sirs, I Am the Son of George H.W. Bush and I Have a Business Proposition for You." *Mother Jones*. June 11, 2015.
92. "Old Lawsuit with Ties to Jeb Bush Resurfaces." *Tampa Bay Times*. July 11, 2013.
93. "Election 2016: Jeb Bush Got $1.3M Job at Lehman After Florida Shifted Pension Cash to Bank." *International Business Times*. August 19, 2015.
94. "How Jeb Bush Spent His Years on Wall Street." *Wall Street Journal*. August 4, 2015.
95. "Election 2016: Jeb Bush Got $1.3M Job at Lehman After Florida Shifted Pension Cash to Bank." *International Business Times*. August 19, 2015.

96. "Exclusive: Why Doesn't Jeb Want to Talk About Lehman Bros?" *Fox Business.* July 10, 2015.

97. "The Lucrative Obamacare Connections That Jeb Bush Is Trying to Cut." *Washington Post.* December 26, 2014.

98. "Jeb Bush and Tenet Healthcare Corp." *American Thinker.* December 20, 2014.

99. "The Words Jeb Bush May Come to Regret." *Politico.* February 26, 2015.

100. "Jeb Bush Discloses Donors to His Education Nonprofit." *USA Today.* July 1, 2015.

101. http://www.geni.com/people/Samuel-Bush/304802783420002961.

102. "Shaping Columbus: Samuel Prescott Bush, Columbus Steel Tycoon." *Columbus Business First.* August 24, 2012.

103. "Illinois Central Historical Society: The Edward Harriman Story and The Historical Guide to North American Railroads," compiled by George H. Drury, Librarian, *Trains Magazine,* Kalmbach Publications.

104. "The Bushes of America." *The East African.* August 17, 2009. Kevin Phillips, *American Dynasty: Aristocracy, Fortune, and the Politics of Deceit in the House of Bush,* p. 22.

105. *Legacy of Leadership,* http://www.knowitall.org/

106. Kevin Phillips, *American Dynasty: Aristocracy, Fortune, and the Politics of Deceit in the House of Bush,* p. 22.

107. Schuyler Ebbets, *Dynasty of Death, A Historical Perspective of the Bush Family,* Part 1.

108. Webster G. Tarpley and Anton Chaitkin, *George Bush, The Unauthorized Biography,* p. 14.

109. Ibid.

110. Ibid.

111. Richard F. Bensel, *Yankee Leviathan: The Origins of Central State Authority in America.*

112. Kevin Phillips, *American Dynasty: Aristocracy, Fortune, and the Politics of Deceit in the House of Bush.*

113. "3 High Military Honors"(*Columbus*) *Ohio State Journal,* August 8, 1918. Kris Millegan, et al. *Fleshing Out Skull and Bones, Investigations into America's Most Powerful Secret Society,* p. 257.

114. Columbus, *Ohio State Journal,* September 6, 1918.

115. Webster G. Tarpley and Anton Chaitkin, *George Bush, The Unauthorized Biography,* p. 18.

116. Kevin Phillips, *American Dynasty: Aristocracy, Fortune, and the Politics of Deceit in the House of Bush,* p. 23.

117. Webster G. Tarpley and Anton Chaitkin, *George Bush, The Unauthorized Biography,* p. 19.

118. Interview with Prescott Bush, *Oral History Research Project.*

119. "A Hoover Vignette," Phillip R. Shriver, *Ohio History Journal,* Ohio History Connection, publications.ohiohistory.org.

120. Public statement of Averell Harriman, *New York Times,* October 6, 1920, p. 1.

121. Webster G. Tarpley and Anton Chaitkin, *George Bush, The Unauthorized Biography*, p. 22.
122. Kevin Phillips, *American Dynasty: Aristocracy, Fortune, and the Politics of Deceit in the House of Bush*, p. 37.
123. Ibid.
124. Russ Baker, *Family of Secrets, The Bush Dynasty, America's Invisible Government, and the History of the Last Fifty Years*, p. 29.
125. Webster G. Tarpley and Anton Chaitkin, *George Bush, The Unauthorized Biography*, p. 23.
126. "New Bank Building on Hanover Street," *New York Times*, September 3, 1916.
127. *Time*, December 22, 1930.
128. Skull and Bones Membership list 1833–1985.
129. Webster G. Tarpley and Anton Chaitkin, *George Bush, The Unauthorized Biography*, p. 31.
130. John A. Kouwenhoven, *Partners in Banking: An Historical Portrait of a Great Private Bank, Brown Brothers Harriman & Co.1818–1968*.
131. Arthur M. Schlesinger, Jr., and Roger Bruns, eds. *Congress Investigates: A Documented History, 1792–1974*.
132. Kris Millegan, *Fleshing Out Skull and Bones, Investigations into America's Most Powerful Secret Society*, p. 2.
133. "I Paid Hitler" by Fritz Thyssen, 1941, reprinted by Kennikat Press, Port Washington, New York, 1972.
134. Webster G. Tarpley and Anton Chaitkin, *George Bush, The Unauthorized Biography*, pp. 28–29.
135. Robert Sobel, *The Life and Times of Dillon Read*.
136. James P. Warburg sworn affidavit, New York City, New York, 8/15/1949.
137. Toby Rogers, "Prescott Bush, $1,500,000 and Auschwitz," *How the Bush Family Wealth Is Linked to the Jewish Holocaust*, p. 43.
138. Ibid.
139. *Pravda*, September 21, 1922.
140. Anthony C. Sutton, *America's Secret Establishment : An Introduction to the Order of Skull and Bones*.
141. *The Order of Skull and Bones and Illegal Financing* by Jedediah McClure in *Fleshing Out Skull and Bones*, p. 362.
142. *State Department Policy as Stated in Revolutionary Cyclone*, http://history.sandiego.edu/gen/20th/1910's/cyclone.html.
143. *The Order of Skull and Bones and Illegal Financing* by Jedediah McClure in *Fleshing Out Skull and Bones*, p. 364.
144. Ibid.
145. Elimination of German Resources for War; Hearings Before a Subcommittee of the Committee on Military Affairs, United States Senate, Seventy-Ninth Congress, July 2, 1945.

146. *Nazi Conspiracy and Aggression Supplement B, by the Office of United States Chief of Counsel for the Prosecution of Nazis Criminality,* United States Government Printing Office, 1948.

147. Webster G. Tarpley and Anton Chaitkin, *George Bush, The Unauthorized Biography,* p. 22.

148. 1928 New York City Directory of Directors.

149. Ibid.

150. *U.S. Senate Nye Committee Hearings,* September 14, 1934, pp. 1197–98.

151. Webster G. Tarpley and Anton Chaitkin, *George Bush, The Unauthorized Biography,* pp. 37–38.

152. Toby Rogers, *"Prescott Bush, $1,500,000 and Auschwitz,"* How the Bush Family Wealth Is Linked to the Jewish Holocaust, p. 45.

153. Adolph Hitler, *Mein Kampf.*

154. Phyllis Tilson Piotrow, *World Population Crisis: The United States Response.*

155. Glen Yeadon, *The Nazi Hydra in America, Suppressed History of a Century.*

156. Webster Tarpley and Anton Chaitkin, *The Bush Family Ties to Eugenics and Race Hygiene.*

157. Edwin Black, *War Against the Weak: Eugenics and America's Campaign to Create a Master Race,* and http://historynewsnetwork.org/article/1796.

158. Adolf Hitler, *Mein Kampf.*

159. William Ray Van Essendelft, *History of the Sterilization League of America 1935–1964,* thesis submitted to the faculty of the graduate school of the University of Minnesota March, 1979, available on microfilm, Library of Congress.

160. Webster G. Tarpley and Anton Chaitkin, *George Bush, The Unauthorized Biography,* p. 74.

161. Kitty Kelley, *The Family, The Real Story of the Bush Dynasty.*

162. Archives & Special Collections at the Thomas J. Dodd Research Center, Prescott S. Bush Papers, MSS19910001.

163. "The Bush Tragedy." *New York Times,* February 1, 2008.

164. Phyllis Tilson Piotrow, *World Population Crisis: The United States Response.*

165. Kitty Kelley, *The Family, The Real Story of the Bush Dynasty.*

166. Ibid.

167. "National Affairs: A Splendid Job." *Time.* December 13, 1954.

168. Webster G. Tarpley and Anton Chaitkin, *George Bush, The Unauthorized Biography,* p. 76.

169. Roger Stone and Mike Colapietro, *Nixon's Secrets,* p. 495.

170. *The Path to Power: The Years of Lyndon Johnson,* Knopf, 1982.

171. *"Cronies: Oil, the Bushes, and the Rise of Texas, America's Super State"* New York, Public Affairs, 2004.

172. www.senate.gov.

173. Kitty Kelley, *The Family, The Real Story of the Bush Dynasty,* p. 245.

174. Ibid. p. 246.
175. Donnie Radcliffe, *Simply Barbara Bush*, p.132.
176. Kitty Kelley, *The Family, The Real Story of the Bush Dynasty*, p. 75.
177. Ibid. p. 100.
178. Ibid. p. 101.
179. Ibid. p. 102.
180. Joe Hyams, *Flight of the Avenger: George Bush at War*, p. 14.
181. Kitty Kelley, *The Family, The Real Story of the Bush Dynasty*, p. 99.
182. Fitzhugh Green, *George Bush, an Intimate Portrait*, p. 16.
183. Webster G. Tarpley and Anton Chaitkin, *George Bush, The Unauthorized Biography*, p. 105.
184. Nicholas King, *George Bush: A Biography*, pp. 30–31.
185. "The Day Bush Bailed Out." *New York Post*, August 12, 1988.
186. George Bush and Victor Gold, *Looking Forward*, p. 36.
187. George Bush and Doug Wead, *George Bush: Man of Integrity*, pp. 4–5.
188. Interview of George Bush by Doug Wead, private collection of Doug Wead.
189. Allen Wolper and Al Ellenburg, *The Day Bush Bailed Out*, p. 1ff.
190. Ibid.
191. Harcourt, Brace, Jovanovich, *Flight of the Avenger: George Bush at War*.
192. Kitty Kelley, *The Family, The Real Story of the Bush Dynasty*, pp. 140–141.
193. Ibid. p. 141.
194. Quoted in Ned Anderson to Anton Chaitkin, December 2, 1991, in possession of the authors.
195. Kitty Kelley, *The Family, The Real Story of the Bush Dynasty*, p. 155.
196. Ibid. p. 96.
197. Kevin Phillips, *American Dynasty, Aristocracy, Fortune, and the Politics of Deceit in the House of Bush*, p. 200.
198. Andrew Kreig, *Presidential Puppetry*, p. 100.
199. Darwin Payne, *Initiative in Energy: Dresser Industries, Inc. 1880–1978*, Simon and Schuster, p. 232ff.
200. Russ Baker, *Family of Secrets*, p. 25.
201. Prescott Bush, interview for the Columbia University Oral History Research Project, 1966.
202. Webster G. Tarpley and Anton Chaitkin, *George Bush, The Unauthorized Biography*, p. 142.
203. Kitty Kelley, *The Family, The Real Story of the Bush Dynasty*, p. 162.
204. Darwin Payne, *Initiative in Energy: Dresser Industries, Inc. 1880–1978*, pp. 176–177.
205. Joseph J. Trento, *Prelude to Terror: Edwin P. Wilson and the Legacy of America's Private Intelligence Network*, Carroll & Graf, pp. 13–14.
206. Webster G. Tarpley and Anton Chaitkin, *George Bush, The Unauthorized Biography*, p. 143.

207. "How He Got Here." *Esquire,* June 1991.
208. Webster G. Tarpley and Anton Chaitkin, *George Bush, The Unauthorized Biography,* p. 145.
209. Ibid. p. 147.
210. *Wikipedia,* https://en.wikipedia.org/wiki/Seven_Sisters_(oil_companies).
211. "MEMORANDUM: MESSRS. GEORGE BUSH AND THOMAS J. DEVINE," p. 3.
212. "Letter from Neil Mallon to Allen Dulles," April 10, 1953. Allen Dulles Papers, 1845–1971. Seely G. Mudd Manuscript Library, Princeton University. Discovered by independent researcher Bruce Adamson.
213. "The Man Who Wasn't There." *The Nation,* August 13–20, 1988.
214. Ibid.
215. Carl Jensen and Project Censored, "Twenty Years of Censored News," Seven Stories Press, 1997.
216. Joseph J. Trento, *Prelude to Terror: Edwin P. Wilson and the Legacy of America's Private Intelligence Network,* Carroll & Graf, p. 16.
217. Ibid. p. 17.
218. Webster G. Tarpley and Anton Chaitkin, *George Bush, The Unauthorized Biography,* pp. 152–153.
219. E. Howard Hunt, *Give Us This Day,* p. 215.
220. Prescott Bush to Allen Dulles, 1969. Allen Dulles Papers, 1845–1971. Seeley G. Mudd Manuscript Library, Princeton University, box 10, folder 11.
221. Herbert S. Parmet, *George Bush: The Life of a Lone Star Yankee,* p. 94.
222. Russ Baker, *Family of Secrets,* p. 48.
223. Russ Baker, *Family of Secrets,* p. 49.
224. The Mary Ferrell Foundation, Warren Commission document 14, www.maryferrell org.
225. Russ Baker, *Family of Secrets,* pp. 52–63.
226. Letter from de Mohrenschildt to Bush, available through the Mary Ferrell Foundation, www.maryferrell.org.
227. Warren Commission testimony, p. 267.
228. "Oil Drilling Deal Set." *New York Times,* November 30, 1956.
229. Edward Jay Epstein, diary entry 29th March, 1977.
230. Ibid.
231. Russ Baker, *Family of Secrets,* pp. 117–118.
232. Fitzhugh Green, *George Bush: An Intimate Portrait,* p. 113.
233. Russ Baker, *Family of Secrets,* p. 174.
234. Robert Dallek, *Nixon and Kissinger: Partners in Power.*
235. George Bush and Victor Gold, *Looking Forward,* pp. 120–121.
236. Kitty Kelley, *The Family, The Real Story of the Bush Dynasty,* pp. 338, 440, 444.
237. Ibid.
238. Ibid. p. 344.

239. Webster G. Tarpley and Anton Chaitkin, *George Bush, The Unauthorized Biography*, p. 189.
240. Bush, George Herbert Walker, Scholastic Library Publishing Inc., 2008.
241. "George Bush, Plucky Lad." *Texas Monthly*, June 1983.
242. "President Bush: The Challenge Ahead." *Congressional Quarterly*, Washington, 1989, p. 94.
243. "Bush Backed Nazi Race Science." *Executive Intelligence Review*, May 3, 1991, and *New Federalist*, Volume 5, No. 16, April 29, 1991.
244. Webster G. Tarpley and Anton Chaitkin, *George Bush, The Unauthorized Biography*, p. 206.
245. *New York Times*, July 22, 1969.
246. Webster G. Tarpley and Anton Chaitkin, *George Bush, The Unauthorized Biography*, p. 207.
247. Ibid. p. 208.
248. Hassan Ahmed and Joseph Brewda, *Kissinger, Scowcroft, Bush Plotted Third World Genocide*, pp. 26–30.
249. George Bush and Victor Gold, *Looking Forward*, p. 121.
250. "George Bush, Plucky Lad." *Texas Monthly*, June 1983.
251. *Washington Post*, December 12, 1972.
252. *Washington Post*, January 22, 1973.
253. Thomas Patzinger, *Oil and Honor*, pp. 64–65.
254. Bob Woodward and Carl Bernstein, *All the President's Men*.
255. Webster G. Tarpley and Anton Chaitkin, *George Bush, The Unauthorized Biography*, p. 248.
256. Maurice Stans, *The Terrors of Justice: The Untold Side of Watergate*.
257. Webster G. Tarpley and Anton Chaitkin, *George Bush, The Unauthorized Biography*, p. 263.
258. Russ Baker, *Family of Secrets*, p. 236.
259. Kitty Kelley, *The Family, The Real Story of the Bush Dynasty*, pp. 338, 440, 499.
260. Nicholas King, *George Bush: A Biography*. Dodd.
261. Webster G. Tarpley and Anton Chaitkin, *George Bush, The Unauthorized Biography*, p. 273.
262. Kitty Kelley, *The Family, The Real Story of the Bush Dynasty*, pp. 514–519.
263. George Bush and Victor Gold, *Looking Forward*, p. 130.
264. Webster G. Tarpley and Anton Chaitkin, *George Bush, The Unauthorized Biography*, p. 291.
265. Loch K Johnson, *A Season of Inquiry: The Senate Intelligence Investigation*, pp. 108–109.
266. Collins to Ford, November 12, 1975, Ford Library, John O. Marsh Files, Box 1.
267. Nedzi to Ford, November 12, 1975, Ford Library, John O. Marsh Files, Box 1.

268. Letter from Richard Nixon to George Bush, November 12, 1975, Richard Nixon Presidential Library, Yorba Linda, California.

269. Letter from George Bush to Richard Nixon, December 4, 1975, Richard Nixon Presidential Library, Yorba Linda, California.

270. Webster G. Tarpley and Anton Chaitkin, *George Bush, The Unauthorized Biography*, pp. 209–304.

271. Ibid. p. 311.

272. Untitled article, *New York Times*, February 18, 1976.

273. Russ Baker, *Family of Secrets*, p. 295.

274. Jonathan Beaty and S. C. Gwynne, *The Outlaw Bank: A Wild Ride into the Secret Heart of BCCI*, p. 274.

275. "The Same Old Dirty Tricks." *The Nation*, August 23, 1988.

276. "Dead, Beat and Blood." *The Guardian*, July 16, 2006.

277. Kitty Kelley, *The Family, The Real Story of the Bush Dynasty*, p. 548.

278. Ibid. p. 547.

279. Ibid.

280. Ibid. p. 548.

281. Ibid. p. 549.

282. Warren Hinckle and William Turner, *Deadly Secrets: The CIA and Mafia War Against Castro and the Assassination of JFK*.

283. Donald Freed, *Death in Washington*.

284. Webster G. Tarpley and Anton Chaitkin, *George Bush, The Unauthorized Biography*, p. 320.

285. *The Guardian*, November 20, 1997.

286. Kitty Kelley, *The Family, The Real Story of the Bush Dynasty*, p. 556.

287. Webster G. Tarpley and Anton Chaitkin, *George Bush, The Unauthorized Biography*, pp. 327–329.

288. Ibid. pp. 323–333.

289. Jeff Greenfield, *The Real Campaign*, pp. 36–37.

290. Kitty Kelley, *The Family, The Real Story of the Bush Dynasty*, p. 580.

291. Ibid. p. 585.

292. James A. Bill, *The Eagle and the Lion: The Tragedy of American-Iranian Relations*, p. 331.

293. EIR Special Report: "Treason in Washington: New Evidence on the October Surprise" March 1992.

294. Joseph J. Trento, *Prelude to Terror: Edwin P. Wilson and the Legacy of America's Private Intelligence Network*, Carroll and Graf, pp. 202–203.

295. Ibid. p. 209.

296. Ibid. p. 205.

297. Ibid. pp. 205–207.

298. "Tehran Militants Said to Hand Over Custody of Captives; Government Takes Control." *New York Times*, November 28, 1980.

299. "By the Numbers: Jeb Bush's Tax Return." *Tampa Bay Times*, June 30, 2015.
300. "Where's Bill Casey." Consortiumnews.com.
301. Lee H. Hamilton and Henry J. Hyde, *Joint report of the Task Force to Investigate Certain Allegations Concerning the Holding of American Hostages by Iran in 1980.* U.S. Government Printing Office 1993, pp. 167–168.
302. "Taking a Bush Secret to the Grave." consortiumnews.com, September 27, 2011.
303. "Tested Under Fire." *Dallas Morning News*, May 13, 2015.
304. *"Bush's Son Was to Dine With Suspects Brother." Houston Post*, March 31, *1981.*
305. *Nathaniel Blumberg, The Afternoon of March 30*
306. *"Bush's Son Was to Dine With Suspects Brother." Houston Post*, March 31, *1981.*
307. Ibid.
308. Article on Neil Bush press conference, *Rocky Mountain News*, April 1, 1981.
309. Ibid.
310. "Vice President Confirms His Son was to Have Hosted Hinckley Brother." *Houston Post*, April 1, 1981.
311. Felix Rodriguez and John Weisman, *Shadow Warrior,* pp. 213–214.
312. *Washington Post*, June 10, 1990.
313. Excerpt from *Section 8066 of Public Law 98–473, The Continuing Appropriations Act for Fiscal Year 1985:* Iran-Contra Report, November 13, 1987, p. 3981.
314. *The Tower Commission Report: The Full Text of the President's Special Review Board,* p. 217.
315. Deposition of Michael Tolliver, Iran-Contra Report, May 1987, Vol. 9.
316. Affidavit of Eugene Hasenfus, #03575 in the Iran-Contra Collection, October 12, 1986, pp. 2–3.
317. *Laredo* (Texas) *Morning Times,* May 15, 1989.
318. North notebook entry, January 9, 1986.
319. *Tower Commission Report,* pp. 67–68, 78.
320. *Washington Post*, October 11, 1986.
321. *New York Times*, March 2, 1989.
322. "Covert Action." No. 33, Winter 1990, p. 15.
323. Stenographic transcripts of Hearings Before the U.S. Senate Committee on Foreign Relations, Nomination Hearing for Donald Gregg to be Ambassador to the Republic of Korea. Washington D.C., May 12, and June 15, 1989.
324. "FBI Reportedly Probes Contras on Drug Charges." Associated Press, April 10, 1986.
325. *"Who had the means and motives to kill Kennedy in 1963?"* May 22, 2005.
326. From author St. John Hunt's conversations with E. Howard Hunt.
327. Fabian Escalante, *CIA Covert Operations 1959–1962: The Cuba Project,* pp. 42–43.
328. "Mad Cow Morning News." Daniel Hopsicker, 2004.

329. Daniel Sheehan, affidavit, December 12, 1986.

330. http://spartacus-educational.com/JFKseal.htm.

331. Ibid.

332. *CBS Evening News,* July 28, 1988.

333. Terry Reed and John Cummings, *Compromised: Clinton, Bush, and the CIA,* p. 217.

334. Ibid. p. 212.

335. Daniel Hopsicker, *Barry and the Boys: The CIA, The Mob and America's Secret History,* pp. 375–376.

336. "Inside the Octopus: The Barry Seal Story." *High Times,* June 5, 2002.

337. Daniel Hopsicker, *Barry and the Boys: The CIA, The Mob and America's Secret History,* pp. 375–376.

338. Al Martin, *The Conspirators: Secrets of an Iran-Contra Insider,* pp. 194–195.

339. Ibid.

340. Ibid.

341. "Gave Contras $4 Million, Drug Smuggler Testifies." *Los Angeles Times,* April 8, 1988.

342. Al Martin, *The Conspirators: Secrets of an Iran-Contra Insider,* pp. 195–198.

343. Ibid. p. 196.

344. The Chip Tatum Chronicles: Testimony of Government Drug Running and *http://whatreallyhappened.com/RANCHO/POLITICS/MENA/ TATUM/tatum.html.*

345. Al Martin, *The Conspirators: Secrets of an Iran-Contra Insider,* p. 197.

346. "Speech about Iran-Contra" PBS, March 4, 1987.

347. http://www.rense.com/general31/scont.htm.

348. Kitty Kelley, *The Family, The Real Story of the Bush Dynasty,* pp. 782–783.

349. Ibid. p. 787.

350. Frederick Kempe, *Divorcing the Dictator,* pp. 26–30.

351. "Exploring State Criminality: The Invasion of Panama." *Journal of Criminal Justice and Popular Culture,* 1994.

352. "EXCLUSIVE: Screenwriter mysteriously killed in 1997 after finishing script that revealed the 'real reason' for US invasion of Panama had been working for the CIA. . . and both his hands were missing." *Daily Mail UK,* January 17, 2015.

353. "U.S. Denounced by Nations Touchy About Intervention." *New York Times,* December 21, 1989.

354. United Nations Security Counsel Draft Resolution S/21048.

355. "El Chorrillo Two Years After the U.S. Invaded Panama, Those Displaced by the War Have New Homes." *Christian Science Monitor,* December 20, 1991.

356. Webster G. Tarpley, *Executive Intelligence Review,* March 31, 1989.

357. Patrick Brogan, *World Conflicts: A Comprehensive Guide to World Strife Since 1945.*

358. John Bulloch, Harvey Morris, *The Gulf War: Its Origins, History and Consequences* (1st published ed.).

359. Terry Bryant, *History's Greatest War.*
360. Webster Tarpley and Anton Chaitkin, George Bush: *The Unauthorized Biography,* p. 562.
361. Ibid. p. 563.
362. Kitty Kelley, *The Family, The Real Story of the Bush Dynasty,* p. 787.
363. Ibid. p. 788.
364. Testimony of Nayirah, Congressional Human Rights Caucus, October 10, 1990.
365. "How George Bush Sr. Sold the 1991 Bombing of Iraq to America." *Counter Punch,* December 28, 2002.
366. "Lingering Gulf War Mystery: How Many Iraqis Really Died?" *Washington Post,* June 30, 1991.
367. *Observer Review,* July 22, 1997.
368. *Lobster 33,* Summer 1997.
369. Paul Rodriguez and George Archibald, "Homosexual Prostitution Inquiry Ensnares VIPs with Reagan, Bush: 'Call Boys' Took Midnight Tour of White House," *Washington Times,* June 29, 1989, p. A1.
370. "Nebraska Joins Probers of GOP High-Roller King." *Washington Times,* December 15, 1998, p. A4.
371. "GOP Confirms King's Affiliation." *Washington Times,* November 24, 1998, p. A6.
372. "Purpose of King Group Questioned." *Omaha World-Herald,* January 8, 1998, p. 1.
373. Nick Bryant, *The Franklin Scandal: A Story of Powerbrokers, Child Abuse, & Betrayal,* pp. 279–305.
374. "Power Broker Served Drugs, Sex at Parties Bugged for Blackmail." *Washington Times,* June 30, 1989, A1.
375. "In Death, Spence Stayed True to Form." *Washington Times,* November 13, 1989, p. A1.
376. Bryant, *The Franklin Scandal: A Story of Powerbrokers, Child Abuse, & Betrayal,* p.287.
377. "Spence Arrested in N.Y., Released; Once-Host to Powerful Reduced to Begging, Sleeping in Park." *Washington Times,* August 9, 1989, p. A1.
378. Bryant, *The Franklin Scandal: A Story of Powerbrokers, Child Abuse, & Betrayal,* pp. 181–215.
379. Ibid. pp. 45–59.
380. Ibid.
381. Ibid.
382. Ibid.
383. Ibid. p. 55.
384. Ibid. p. 58
385. John DeCamp, *The Franklin Cover-Up,* p. 12.
386. Bryant, *The Franklin Scandal: A Story of Powerbrokers, Child Abuse, & Betrayal,* p. 57.
387. Ibid. pp. 66–69.

388. Ibid. p. 70.

389. Ibid. p. 76.

390. Ibid. p. 73.

391. John DeCamp, *The Franklin Cover-Up*, p. 53.

392. Bryant, *The Franklin Scandal: A Story of Powerbrokers, Child Abuse, & Betrayal*, p. 79.

393. "A Lurid, Mysterious Scandal Begins Taking Shape in Omaha." *New York Times*, December 18, 1988, section 1, p. 30.

394. "Sen. Schmit Told of Pressure to Halt Probe." *Omaha World-Herald*, June 17, 1989, p. 1.

395. John DeCamp, *The Franklin Cover-Up*, p. 175.

396. Ibid. p. 176.

397. Bryant, *The Franklin Scandal: A Story of Powerbrokers, Child Abuse, & Betrayal*, p. 106.

398. Ibid. p. 108.

399. Ibid. p. 130.

400. "Purpose of King Group Questioned." *Omaha World-Herald*, January 8, 1998, p. 1.

401. Bryant, *The Franklin Scandal: A Story of Powerbrokers, Child Abuse, & Betrayal*, p. 134.

402. "Judge Orders King to Hospital, Finds Him Unable to Stand Trial." *Omaha World-Herald*, April 5, 1990.

403. Bryant, *The Franklin Scandal: A Story of Powerbrokers, Child Abuse, & Betrayal*, p. 165.

404. Ibid. p. 166.

405. Ibid. p.170.

406. Ibid.

407. Ibid.

408. Ibid.

409. Ibid.

410. "Caradori Faced Criticism of Probe Utah Firm." *Omaha World-Herald*, July 12, 1990.

411. "Spence as Much an Enigma in Death as He Was in Life." *Washington Times*, November 13, 1989.

412. Rodriguez and Archibald, "Homosexual Prostitution Inquiry Ensnares VIPs with Reagan, Bush: 'Call Boys' Took Midnight Tour of White House."

413. Seper and Hedges, "Power Broker Served Drugs, Sex at Parties Bugged for Blackmail."

414. Henry Vinson and Nick Bryant, *Confessions of a DC Madam: The Politics of Sex, Lies, and Blackmail*, pp. 103–104.

415. Ibid. p. 105.

416. "New Top State Judge: Abolish Grand Juries & Let Us Decide," *New York Daily News*, January 31, 1985.

417. "Grand Jury Says Abuse Stories Were a 'Carefully Crafted Hoax,'" *Omaha World-Herald*, July 25, 1990.

418. "Franklin Committee a Disgrace to Nebraska," *Omaha World-Herald*, July 31, 1990.

419. Bryant, *The Franklin Scandal: A Story of Powerbrokers, Child Abuse, & Betrayal*, p.438.

420. Ibid.

421. Ibid.

422. Seper and Hedges, *Spence as Much an Enigma in Death as He Was in Life*.

423. Ibid.

424. Vinson and Bryant, *Confessions of a DC Madam: The Politics of Sex, Lies, and Blackmail*, p. 196.

425. "The Bombshell That Didn't Explode; Behind the Times's ' Scoop' and Press Coverage of the Call-Boy Ring," *Washington Post*, August 1, 1989.

426. Deborah Davis, *Katharine the Great*, p. 140.

427. "George W., Knight of Eulogia." *The Atlantic*. May 2000.

428. Ibid.

429. Ibid.

430. "At the Height of Vietnam, Bush Picks Guard." *Washington Post*. July 28, 1999.

431. "New Questions on Bush Guard Duty." *60 Minutes*. September 8, 2004.

432. Ibid.

433. "Learning How to Run: A West Texas Stumble." *New York Times*, July 27, 2000.

434. "Slick W." *Mother Jones*, March-April, 2000.

435. "The Bush–bin Laden Connection." *Texas Observer*, November 9, 2001.

436. Peter Truell, Larry Gurwin, *False Profits: The Inside Story of BCCI*, 1992.

437. "A Mysterious Mover of Money and Planes." *Time*, June 4, 2001.

438. "Slick W." *Mother Jones*, March-April, 2000.

439. *Washington Post*, July 30, 1999.

440. Russ Baker, *Family of Secrets, The Bush Dynasty, America's Invisible Government, and the History of the Last Fifty Years*, p. 341.

441. *Wall Street Journal*, October 9, 2002.

442. Russ Baker, *Family of Secrets, The Bush Dynasty, America's Invisible Government, and the History of the Last Fifty Years*, p. 341.

443. *Wall Street Journal*, October 9, 2002.

444. *Boston Globe*, July 18, 2002.

445. *Counter punch*, July 12, 2002.

446. *LA Times*, July 14, 2002.

447. Russ Baker, *Family of Secrets, The Bush Dynasty, America's Invisible Government, and the History of the Last Fifty Years*, p. 355.

448. *Guardian*, October 9, 2002.

449. "Ann Richards, Plain-Spoken Texas Governor Who Aided Minorities, Dies at 73." *New York Times*, September 14, 2006.

450. "George W. Bush and the New Political Landscape." *Texas Monthly*, December 1994.

451. "Katrina Funds Earmarked to Pay for Neil Bush's Software Program." *Houston Chronicle*, March 23, 2006.

452. Associated Press, Tallahassee, October 28, 2002.
453. http://whatreallyhappened.com/WRHARTICLES/911security.html
454. Ibid.
455. Ibid.
456. Ibid.
457. Ibid.
458. http://whatreallyhappened.com/WRHARTICLES/bush_newyork_9–11. html.
459. http://web.archive.org/web/20030429031414/http:/anderson.ath. cx:8000/911/hj05.html
460. Ibid.
461. Ibid.
462. Ibid.
463. Ibid.
464. Craig Unger, *House of Bush, House of Saud* pp. 9–10.
465. Ibid.
466. Ibid. p. 14.
467. Ibid. p. 7.
468. Ibid. p. 297.
469. Ibid.
470. Ibid. p. 296.
471. Ibid.
472. "Iraq war Costs U.S. More than $2 trillion." *Reuters*, March 14, 2013.
473. "Recounting Ohio." *Mother Jones*, November 2005.
474. "Wrong Man, Wrong Place." *Vanity Fair*, June 2005.
475. "Online Nude Photos Are Latest Chapter in Jeff Gannon Saga." *Washington Post*, February 16, 2005.
476. "The Comings and Goings of Jeff Gannon." *Counterpunch*, May 22, 2005.
477. "Wrong Man, Wrong Place." *Vanity Fair*, June 2005.
478. Henry Vinson and Nick Bryant, *Confessions of a DC Madam: The Politics of Sex, Lies, and Blackmail*, pp. 150–151.
479. Ibid.
480. Ibid.
481. *Prison Planet*, September 24, 2007.
482. "Is Bush's Penchant for Torture Tied to a Secret Sado-Masochistic Past?" *Pensito Review*, October 26, 2007.
483. http://www.rense.com/general57/newbook.htm.
484. Ibid.
485. http://theconspiracyzone.podcastpeople.com/posts/26837.
486. http://thelede.blogs.nytimes.com/2008/05/02/skepticism-and-sadness-after-death-of-dc-madam/#more-1442.
487. http://www.abovetopsecret.com/forum/thread129164/pg1.

488. "Likely Presidential Rivals Jeb Bush and Hillary Clinton Share a Stage as She Is Awarded a Lifetime Achievement Medal." *Daily Mail UK*, September 11, 2013.

489. "Wall St. Republican's Dark Secret." *Politico*, April 28, 2014.

490. "Hillary Clinton's Mega-Donors Are Also Funding Jeb Bush." *Daily Beast*, August 4, 2015.

491. "Finance Records Reveal Donor Class Happy With Rubio, Bush or Clinton Presidency." *Breitbart News*, July 17, 2015.

492. "Top 10 Reasons George Soros is Dangerous." *Human Events*, April 2, 2011.

493. http://www.al.com/news/index.ssf/2015/07/biggest_donors_to_hillary_clin.html.

494. "Jeb Bush Funded by George Soros's Chinese Business Partner." *Breitbart News*, September 29, 2015.

495. "Documents Show Jeb Bush's Involvement with Troubled Company." *Washington Post*, January 19, 2015.

496. "Clinton's Facilitated Donor's Haiti Project That Defrauded U.S. Out of Millions." *Free Beacon*, July 17, 2015.

497. "Jeb Bush's Big InnoVida Headache." *National Review*, January 22, 2015.

498. http://www.politico.com/magazine/story/2015/09/hillary-clinton-email-213110.

499. "In Book, Bush Peeks Ahead to His Legacy." *New York Times*, September 2, 2007.

500. "President Bush Endorsed Clinton Speaking Fees." *Daily KOS*, June 27, 2014.

501. "Get Motivated Seminars Close Lawsuits—Complain of Unpaid Bills." *Seattle Times*, September 1, 2012.

502. "To Help Veterans Charity, George W. Bush Charged $100,000." abcnews.com, July 8, 2015.

503. "George Bush Picks Jeb Over 'Sister-In-Law' Hillary in 2016." CNN, December 7, 2014.

504. "A Bush and a Clinton Side by Side on Stage, and Not a Political Zinger Between Them." *New York Times*, July 9, 2015.

505. https://www.clintonfoundation.org/blog/2015/05/17/mark-updegrove-role-patience-passion-and-public-opinion-effective-leadership and https://www.clintonfoundation.org/blog/2015/02/25/scott-snook-developing-successful-leaders.

506. "Are the Clintons More Transparent Than the Bushes?" *Mother Jones*, April 30, 2015.

507. http://www.miamiherald.com/news/politicsgovernment/article1947288.html#storylink=cpy.

508. "Exclusive: Top Hillary Clinton Adviser Did Private Clinton Business on State Department Email." *Breitbart News*, September 23, 2015.

509. "Teneo & the Clinton Machine." *Judicial Watch*, April 30, 2015.

510. "Scandal at Clinton Inc." *New Republic*.

511. Ibid.

512. http://www.thesmokinggun.com/buster/george-p-bush/
george-p-bush-stalking-758409

513. http://www.dailynewsbin.com/news/like-father-like-son-george-p-bush-
embroiled-in-texas-corruption-scandal/22519/

514. http://www.breitbart.com/texas/2015/09/24/
tempest-around-george-p-bush-whats-real-story/

515. http://www.dallasnews.com/news/politics/2016/05/22/george-p-bush-
paid-fired-employees-1-million-to-keep-them-from-suing-report-says

516. http://usatoday30.usatoday.com/news/nation/2002/01/29/noelle-bush.
htm

517. http://www.cbsnews.com/news/more-drug-problems-for-noelle-bush/

518. http://www.nbcnews.com/id/9373195/ns/us_news-crime_and_courts/t/
florida-gov-jeb-bushs-son-arrested/#.VLHydMYkQ

519. http://www.georgepfortexas.org/statement-by-george-p-bush-on-the-red-
river-land-dispute-and-potential-federal-seizure-of-texas-land/

520. http://www.dontcomply.com/
breaking-texas-land-boss-george-p-bush-steals-private-property-bribes/

521. Daniel Hopsicker, *Barry & the Boys: The CIA, The Mob and America's Secret
History*, pp. 375–376.

522. Al Martin, *The Conspirators: Secrets of an Iran-Contra Insider*, pp. 194–195.

523. Ibid. pp. 195–198.

524. Ibid. p. 201.

525. Celerino Castillo & Dave Harmon, *Powderburns: Cocaine, Contras & the Drug
War*, p. 132.

Chapter Epigrams

i   Igor Bobic, "Jeb Bush Addresses 2016 and His Family Name." *Huffington Post*.
February 5, 2015

ii   Michael Kranish,"Jeb Bush Shaped By Troubled Phillips Academy Years."
Boston Globe. February 1, 2015

iii   Pam Key, "Jeb Bush: We Need to Control Borders by Politely Asking Illegals
to Leave." *Breitbart*. January 25, 2015

iv   Kitty Kelley, *The Family* pp. 354–355

v   Wayne Madsen, "Exclusive: Jeb Bush Linked to Cartel Money Laundering
While Serving CIA." *Prison Planet*. August 13, 2015

vi   Jeff Gerth, "A Savings and Loan Bailout, and Bush's Son Jeb." *New York Times*.
October 14, 1990

vii   Tom Hamburger and Robert O'Harrow Jr., "Jeb Bush's Tie to Fugitive Miguel
Recarey Goes Against Business Savvy Image He Promotes." *Washington Post*.
March 18, 2015

viii Michael Barbaro, "Jeb Bush's Rush to Make Money May Be His Hurdle." *New York Times*. April 20, 2014.

ix "Jeb Bush on Obamacare: 'We've created a monstrosity '". *Reuters News*.

x Jacob Weisberg, "The Bush Tragedy." *New York Times*. February 1, 2008.

xi Ben Aris and Duncan Campbell, "How Bush's Grandfather Helped Hitler's Rise to Power." *The Guardian*. September 25, 2004

xii http://www.bbc.co.uk/radio4/history/document/document_20070723. shtml.

xiii Daniel Bates, "'If you need me I'll be there': George HW Bush moved to tears as he reads out poem for his family to granddaughter Jenna (who also can't help crying)" Dailymail.com. June 12, 2012.

xiv Russ Baker, "An Enduring Mystery About Bush 41's WWII Escape from Death." LewRockwell.com. September 4, 2014.

xv Joseph J. Trento, "Prelude to Terror: Edwin P. Wilson and the Legacy of America's Private Intelligence Network." *Carroll & Graf*. 2005, p. 17.

xvi Robert Dallek, "Nixon and Kissinger: Partners in Power. Harper Collins, 2007.

xvii Jacob Weisberg, "The Bush Tragedy." *New York Times*. February 1, 2008.

xviii Russ Baker, "Bush and the JFK Hit, Part 5: The Mysterious Mr. de Mohrenschildt." *Who.What.Why*. October 14, 2013.

xix http://www.realclearpolitics.com/video/2015/11/01/bush_i_love_my_ dad_id_kill_for_him_id_go_to_prison_for_him.html

xx George H. W. Bush speech at the 1988 Republican National Convention (August 18, 1988).

xxi Beccah G. Watson, "Where Wings Take Dream." *Harvard Crimson*. November 14, 2003

xxii Robert Trigaux, "Bush Built Success on Harken Sale." St. Pete Times. July 21, 2002

xxiii https://www.youtube.com/watch?v=-ej7ZEnjSeA.

xxiv http://www.dailykos.com/story/2015/07/09/1400788/-He-s-not-stupid-he-s-my-brother#.

xxv Dan Froomkin, "White House Watch." The Washington Post. May 25, 2005

xxvi "Barbara Bush: I love Bill Clinton," http://www.politico.com/story/2014/01/ barbara-bush-bill-clinton-102418.html.

BIBLIOGRAPHY

BOOKS

Baker, Russell. *Family of Secrets*, New York: Bloomsbury, 2009.

Bill, James A. *The Eagle and the Lion*. New Haven: Yale University Press, 1988.

Black, Edwin. *War Against the Weak*. Dialog Press, 2012.

Brewton, Pete. *The Mafia, CIA and George Bush*. S.P.I. Books Trade, 1992.

Brogan, Patrick, *World Conflicts: A Comprehensive Guide to World Strife Since 1945*. London: Bloomsbury, 1989.

Bulloch, John, and Harvey Morris. *The Gulf War: Its Origins, History and Consequences* (1st published ed.). London: Methuen, 1989.

Bush, George W. *41: A Portrait of My Father*. New York: Penguin Random House, 2014.

Bush, George, and Victor Gold. *Looking Forward*. New York: Doubleday, 1987

Bush, George, and Douglas Wead. *George Bush: Man of Integrity*. Harvest House, 1988.

Caro, Robert. *The Path to Power*. New York: Alfred A Knopf, 1982.

Dallek, Robert. *Nixon and Kissinger: Partners in Power*. Harper Collins, 2007.

Green, Fitzhugh. *George Bush an Intimate Portrait*. Hippocrene Books, 1989.

Hatfield, J. H. and Nick Mamatas. *Fortunate Son: George W. Bush And The Making of an American President*. Soft Skull, 2000.

Hinckle, Warren, and William Turner. *Deadly Secrets*. Thundermouth Press, 1982.

Hitler, Adolf. *Mein Kampf,* reprint. Boston: Houghton Mifflin Co., 1971.

Hopsicker, Daniel. *Barry and the Boys*. Mad Cow Press, 2001.

Hunt, E. Howard. *Give Us This Day*. Arlington House, 1971.

Hyams, Joe. *Flight of the Avenger*. New York: Harcourt, Brace, Jovanovich, 1991.

Kelley, Kitty. *The Family*. New York: Random House (large print in association with Doubleday, New York), 2004.

Kempe, Frederick. *Divorcing the Dictator*. New York: Putnam, 1990.

King, Nicholas. *George Bush: A Biography*. Dodd, Meade and Company, 1980.

Kouwenhoven, John A. *Partners in Banking*. New York: Doubleday & Co., 1983.

Kreig, Andrew. *Presidential Puppetry*. Eagle View Books, 2013.

Martin, Al. *The Conspirators*. Montana: National Liberty Press, 2001, 2002.

Millegan, Kris. *Fleshing Out Skull and Bones*. Oregon: TrineDay, 2003, 2008.

Patzinger, Thomas. *Oil and Honor*. New York: Putnam, 1987.

Payne, Darwin. *Initiative in Energy: Dresser Industries, Inc. 1880–1978*. New York: Simon and Schuster, 1979.

Phillips, Kevin. *American Dynasty*. New York: The Penguin Group, 2004

Piotrow, Phyllis Tilson. *World Population Crisis*. New York: Praeger Publishers, 1973

Radcliffe, Donnie. *Simply Barbara Bush*. New York: Warner Books, 1989.

Reed, Terry, and John Cummings. *Compromised*. New York: S.P.I. Books, 1994.

Rodriguez, Felix, and John Weisman. *Shadow Warrior*. New York: Simon and Schuster, 1998.

Sanger, Margaret. *Woman and the New Race*. CreateSpace Independent Publishing Platform, 2013.

Schlesinger, Arthur M., Jr., and Roger Bruns, eds. *Congress Investigates: A Documented History, 1792–1974*. New York: Chelsea House Publishers, 1975.

Scott, Hugh E. *G.H.W. Bush & First Son Dub-ya: The Phony Fighter Pilots: Exposed for the 2016 Election*. Amazon Kindle Edition, 2015.

Sobel, Robert. *The Life and Times of Dillon Read.* New York: Dutton-Penguin, 1991.

Stone, Roger and Mike Colapietro. *Nixon's Secrets.* New York: Skyhorse, 2014.

Stone, Roger, with Mike Colapietro. *The Man Who Killed Kennedy.* New York: Skyhorse, 2013.

Tarpley, Webster G. and Anton Chaitkin. *George Bush The Unauthorized Biography.* Washington, DC: Executive Intelligence Review, 1992 (reprinted by Imprint of Tree of Life Books 2004).

Thyssen, Fritz. *I Paid Hitler,* reprint. New York: Kennikat Press, 1972.

The Tower Commission Report: The Full Text of the President's Special Review Board. Bantam Books, 1987.

Trento, Joseph J. *Prelude to Terror.* Carroll & Graf, 2005.

Unger, Craig. *House of Bush, House of Saud: The Secret Relationship Between the World's Two Most Powerful Dynasties.* Scribner, 2004.

Yeadon, Glen. *The Nazi Hydra in America:* Progressive Press, 1991–2008.

INTERNET

http://www.geni.com/people/Samuel-Bush/304802783420002961 (Legacy of Leadership, http://www.knowitall.org/)

http;//history.sandiego.edu/gen/20th/1910's/cyclone.html

http://coat.ncf.ca/our_magazine/links/53/Plot1.html

https://en.wikipedia.org/wiki/Seven_Sisters_(oil_companies)

The Mary Ferrell Foundation, Warren Commission document 14, www.maryferell.org)

http://www.ratical.org/ratville/JFK/JohnJudge/112600.html

http://spartacus-educational.com/JFKhopsicker.htm

http://spartacus-educational.com/JFKseal.htm

http://whatreallyhappened.com/RANCHO/POLITICS/MENA/TATUM/tatum.html

http://www.rense.com/general31/scont.htm

http://www.dailymail.co.uk/news/article-2905392/Holly

NEWSPAPER AND MAGAZINE

Archives & Special Collections at the Thomas J. Dodd Research Center, Prescott S. Bush Papers, MSS19910001.

Bargar, Brian, and Robert Parry, *"FBI Reportedly Probes Contras on Drug Charges,"* Associated Press, April 10, 1986.

Bensel, Richard F., "Yankee Leviathan: The Origins of Central State Authority in America 1859–1877," *Cambridge University Press,* 1990.

Brooke, James, *"U.S. Denounced by Nations Touchy About Intervention,"* New York Times, December 21, 1989.

Bryant, Terry, *"History's Greatest War,"* Global Media, 2007.

Bush, George Herbert Walker, Scholastic Library Publishing Inc., 2008.

Cohen, Mitchel, *"How George Bush Sr. Sold the 1991 Bombing of Iraq to America,"* Counter Punch, December 28, 2002.

Covert Action No. 33, Winter 1990.

Ebbets, Schuyler, "Dynasty of Death, A Historical Perspective on the Bush Family," *Global Research,* October 22, 2006, part 1.

"EIR Special Report: *Treason in Washington: New Evidence on the October Surprise,"* Executive Intelligence Review, March 1992.

"El Chorrillo Two Years After the U.S. Invaded Panama, Those Displaced by the War Have New Homes," Christian Science Monitor, December 20, 1991.

"Elimination of German Resources for War," Hearings Before a Subcommittee of the Committee on Military Affairs, United States Senate, Seventy-Ninth Congress, July 2, 1945.

Goldsmith, Paul "The Bushes of America," *East African,* August 17, 2009.

Hamilton, Lee H., and Henry J. Hyde, *1993 Joint Report of the Task Force to Investigate Certain Allegations Concerning the Holding of American Hostages by Iran in 1980,* U.S. Government Printing Office.

Harry Hurt III, *"George Bush, Plucky Lad,"* Texas Monthly, June 1983. *"President Bush: The Challenge Ahead,"* Congressional Quarterly, Washington, 1989.

"Illinois Central Historical Society: The Edward Harriman Story and The Historical Guide to North American Railroads," compiled by George H. Drury, Librarian, *Trains Magazine*, Kalmbach Publications.

International War Crimes Tribunal, *Initial Complaint of the Commission of Inquiry*, dated May 6, 1991.

Jensen, Carl, and Project Censored, *"Twenty Years of Censored News,"* Seven Stories Press, 1997.

Johns, Christina Jacquelina, and P. Ward Johnson, *"Exploring State Criminality: The Invasion of Panama,"* Journal of Criminal Justice and Popular Culture, 43–52, State Crime, The Media, and the Invasion of Panama, Praeger, 1994.

Kathleen Klenetsky, *"Bush Backed Nazi Race Science,"* Executive Intelligence Review, May 3, 1991 and New Federalist, Volume 5, No. 16, April 29, 1991.

Kramer, Richard Ben, *"How He Got Here,"* Esquire Magazine, June 1991.

"Letter from Neil Mallon to Allen Dulles," April 10, 1953, Allen Dulles Papers, 1845–1971, Seely G. Mudd Manuscript Library, Princeton University. Discovered by independent researcher Bruce Adamson.

Lovelace, Craig, "Shaping Columbus: Samuel Prescott Bush, Columbus Steel Tycoon," *Columbus Business First*, August 24, 2012.

McBride, Joseph, *"The Man Who Wasn't There,"* The Nation, August 13–20, 1988.

Murphy, Caryle, *"Lingering Gulf War Mystery: How Many Iraqis Really Died?"* Washington Post, June 30, 1991.

National Affairs: "A Splendid Job," Time Magazine, December 13, 1954.

Nazi Conspiracy and Aggression, Supplement B, by the Office of United States Chief of Counsel for the Prosecution of Nazis Criminality, United States Government Printing Office, 1948.

"New Bank Building on Hanover Street" New York Times, September 3, 1916.

1928 New York City Directory of Directors, U.S. Senate Nye Committee Hearings, September 14, 1934.

"Oil Drilling Deal Set," New York Times, November 30, 1956.

Parmet, Herbert S., *"George Bush: The Life of a Lone Star Yankee,"* New Brunswick reprint, 2000.

Parry, Robert, *"Taking a Bush Secret to the Grave,"* consortiumnews.com, September 27, 2011.

Peet, Preston, *"Inside the Octopus: The Barry Seal Story,"* High Times, June 5, 2002.

Peppard, Alan, *"Tested Under Fire,"* Dallas Morning News, May 13, 2015.

Rogers, Toby, *"Prescott Bush, $1,500,000 and Auschwitz, How the Bush Family Wealth Is Linked to the Jewish Holocaust* Clamor Magazine, May/June 2002.

Roos, Charles, Rocky Mountain News, article on Neil Bush press conference, April 1, 1981.

Section 8066 of Public Law 98–473, *The Continuing Appropriations Act for Fiscal Year 1985: Iran/Contra Report,* November 13, 1987.

Shriver, Phillip R., *"A Hoover Vignette,"* Ohio History Journal, Ohio History Connection.

Sick, Gary, *"The Election Story of the Decade". "Creating a Task Force to Investigate Certain Allegations Concerning the Holding of Americans as Hostages by Iran in 1980,* House of Representatives, New York Times, op–ed, April 15, 1991.

Speech, Sproul Hall, University of California, Berkeley, December 2, 1964.

"*Tehran Militants Said to Hand Over Custody of Captives; Government Takes Control,*" New York Times, November 28, 1980.

Testimony of Nayirah, Congressional Human Rights Caucus, October 10, 1990.

"*3 High Military Honors*"(Columbus) Ohio State Journal, August 8, 1918 Interview with Prescott Bush in the Oral History Research Project conducted by Columbia University in 1966.

United Nations Security Council Draft Resolution S/21048

Van Essendelft, William Ray, *History of the Sterilization League of America 1935–1964,*" thesis submitted to the faculty of the graduate school of the University of Minnesota, March 1979, available on microfilm micro film, Library of Congress.

Weisberg, Jacob, "*The Bush Tragedy,*" New York Times, February 1, 2008.

Wolper, Allen, and Al Ellenburg, "*The Day Bush Bailed Out,*" New York Post, August 12, 1988.

Wiese, Arthur, "*Vice President Confirms His Son Was to Have Hosted Hinckley Brother,*" Houston Post, April 1, 1981.

Wiese, Arthur, and Margaret Downing, "*Bush's Son Was to Dine With Suspects Brother,*" Houston Post, March 31, 1981.

INDEX